Building Strong Brands and Engaging Customers With Sound

Minna-Maarit Jaskari
School of Marketing and Communication, University of Vaasa, Finland

A volume in the Advances in Marketing, Customer Relationship Management, and E-Services (AMCRMES) Book Series

Published in the United States of America by
    IGI Global
    Business Science Reference (an imprint of IGI Global)
    701 E. Chocolate Avenue
    Hershey PA, USA 17033
    Tel: 717-533-8845
    Fax: 717-533-8661
    E-mail: cust@igi-global.com
    Web site: http://www.igi-global.com

Library of Congress Cataloging-in-Publication Data

Names: Jaskari, Minna-Maarit, 1971- editor.
Title: Building strong brands and engaging customers with sound / edited by
  Minna-Maarit Jaskari.
Description: Hershey, PA : Business Science Reference, [2024] | Includes
  bibliographical references and index. | Summary: "Sound research is
  fragmented into many disciplines and this book impacts the research
  community by offering a more holistic perspective to wide variety of
  sounds in branding"-- Provided by publisher.
Identifiers: LCCN 2023054106 (print) | LCCN 2023054107 (ebook) | ISBN
  9798369307786 (hardcover) | ISBN 9798369307793 (ebook)
Subjects: LCSH: Branding (Marketing) | Sound--Psychological aspects. |
  Music in advertising. | Acoustical engineering.
Classification: LCC HF5415.1255 .B845 2024 (print) | LCC HF5415.1255
  (ebook) | DDC 658.8/27--dc23/eng/20240124
LC record available at https://lccn.loc.gov/2023054106
LC ebook record available at https://lccn.loc.gov/2023054107

This book is published in the IGI Global book series Advances in Marketing, Customer Relationship Management, and E-Services (AMCRMES) (ISSN: 2327-5502; eISSN: 2327-5529)

British Cataloguing in Publication Data
A Cataloguing in Publication record for this book is available from the British Library.

All work contributed to this book is new, previously-unpublished material.
The views expressed in this book are those of the authors, but not necessarily of the publisher.

For electronic access to this publication, please contact: eresources@igi-global.com.

Advances in Marketing, Customer Relationship Management, and E-Services (AMCRMES) Book Series

ISSN:2327-5502
EISSN:2327-5529

Editor-in-Chief: Eldon Y. Li, National Chengchi University, Taiwan & California Polytechnic State University, USA

MISSION

Business processes, services, and communications are important factors in the management of good customer relationship, which is the foundation of any well organized business. Technology continues to play a vital role in the organization and automation of business processes for marketing, sales, and customer service. These features aid in the attraction of new clients and maintaining existing relationships.

The **Advances in Marketing, Customer Relationship Management, and E-Services (AMCRMES) Book Series**

addresses success factors for customer relationship management, marketing, and electronic services and its performance outcomes. This collection of reference source covers aspects of consumer behavior and marketing business strategies aiming towards researchers, scholars, and practitioners in the fields of marketing management.

COVERAGE

- Cases on Electronic Services
- B2B marketing
- Cases on CRM Implementation
- Online Community Management and Behavior
- CRM and customer trust
- Customer Retention
- Social Networking and Marketing
- Database marketing
- Customer Relationship Management
- Data mining and marketing

IGI Global is currently accepting manuscripts for publication within this series. To submit a proposal for a volume in this series, please contact our Acquisition Editors at Acquisitions@igi-global.com or visit: http://www.igi-global.com/publish/.

Titles in this Series

For a list of additional titles in this series, please visit:
http://www.igi-global.com/book-series/advances-marketing-customer-relationship-manage-
ment/37150

Globalized Consumer Insights in the Digital Era
Fatih Sahin (Bandirma Onyedi Eylul University, Turkey) and Cevat Soylemez (Kutahya Dumlupinar University, Turkey)
Business Science Reference • © 2024 • 296pp • H/C (ISBN: 9798369338117) • US $325.00

AI Impacts in Digital Consumer Behavior
Thomas Heinrich Musiolik (Woxsen University, India & University of Europe for Applied Sciences, Germany) Raul Villamarin Rodriguez (Woxsen University, India) and Hemachandran Kannan (Woxsen University, India)
Business Science Reference • © 2024 • 372pp • H/C (ISBN: 9798369319185) • US $325.00

Contemporary Trends in Innovative Marketing Strategies
Belem Barbosa (University of Porto, Portugal)
Business Science Reference • © 2024 • 394pp • H/C (ISBN: 9798369312315) • US $275.00

Navigating the Shifting Landscape of Consumer Behavior
Fatih Sahin (Bandirma Onyedi Eylul University, Turkey) and Cevat Soylemez (Kutahya Dumlupinar University, Turkey)
Business Science Reference • © 2024 • 341pp • H/C (ISBN: 9798369315941) • US $275.00

Smart and Sustainable Interactive Marketing
Hamid Reza Irani (University of Tehran, Iran) and Hamed Nozari (Department of Management, Azad University of the Emirates, Dubai, UAE)
Business Science Reference • © 2024 • 320pp • H/C (ISBN: 9798369313398) • US $265.00

Connecting With Consumers Through Effective Personalization and Programmatic Advertising
Jorge Remondes (Instituto Superior de Entre Douro e Vouga, Portugal & ISCAP, Instituto Politecnico do Porto, Portugal) Paulo Madeira (Instituto Superior de Entre Douro e Vouga, Portugal) and Carlos Alves (Instituto Superior de Entre Douro e Vouga, Portugal)
Business Science Reference • © 2024 • 308pp • H/C (ISBN: 9781668491461) • US $250.00

For an entire list of titles in this series, please visit:
http://www.igi-global.com/book-series/advances-marketing-customer-relationship-manage-
ment/37150

701 East Chocolate Avenue, Hershey, PA 17033, USA
Tel: 717-533-8845 x100 • Fax: 717-533-8661
E-Mail: cust@igi-global.com • www.igi-global.com

Table of Contents

Detailed Table of Contents

Giuseppe Ciaburro, Università Degli Studi Della Campania, Italy
Elif Hasret Kumcu, Aksaray University, Turkey

This study examines the implementation of soundscape in shopping centers for amplifying the branding experience, generating a distinctive and immersive atmosphere dubbed Brandscape. Visual aesthetics historically influenced commercial venue layout and branding, but recent discussions emphasize sound's impact on consumer attitudes and buying behaviors. Integrating soundscape elements into shopping centers provides a distinctive approach to creating a memorable brand identity. By purposefully crafting the acoustic atmosphere, vendors can evoke emotions, reinforce brand ideals, and cultivate a deeper connection with their target customers. Our study delves into the key principles of effective Brandscape design through the integration of soundscape in shopping centers. The study examines the psychological effect of sound on consumer behavior and investigates how different auditory stimuli can impact mood, arousal, and attention. Furthermore, it emphasizes the significance of preserving coherence between the brand's visual identity and the chosen soundscape, resulting in a unified and all-encompassing sensory encounter for consumers.

Chapter 2

Minna-Maarit Jaskari, University of Vaasa, Finland
Hannele Kauppinen-Räisänen, University of Helsinki, Finland
Marie-Nathalie Jauffret, International University of Monaco, Monaco

This chapter focuses on the impact of music on customers' shopping experiences, both in physical and online luxury retail service settings. It highlights the strategic importance of music in enhancing luxury brand experiences, underscoring the need for congruity between music and brand to avoid unfavourable outcomes. It builds on earlier research on the impact of background music in service settings. Two exploratory studies show how consumers understand the power of music to enhance brand image. The discussion emphasises the strategic role of music in luxury brand experiences, contributing valuable insights for luxury brand management.

Chapter 3

Clara Gustafsson, Lund University, Sweden

How do nondescript spaces of transfer (Warped Space), as such, relate to the widespread headphone culture in those spaces? To address this question, the chapter presents a reading of Vidler (1999) on Warped space, Simmel (the Stranger) and Bull (2012) on Toxic Audiotopia. The chapter concludes that Warped spaces or spaces of transfer call for people not to connect, and it was also found that this is supported by the emphasis on looking rather than hearing, and the 'othering' of all others that can be seen happening amongst travelers if analyzed as all Strangers. So because the space of transfer is not conducive to connecting with others – rather the opposite – and because travelers see each other in an object-like way in that space, it has been a particularly suitable space for headphone listening. For marketers, I suggest that marketing efforts can favorably be about creating appealing images and sounds reminiscent of other places that people long for, and also about creating art or ads for Warped space, that convey meaning and are imaginative and reassuring at the same time.

In this chapter, a conceptual approach is proposed for how sonic elements of advertising can be utilized to create a connection with a particular target segment based on their homogeneous political viewpoints. After a literature review of pertinent topics, theoretical development of the proposed approach is presented, followed by sections related to how Integrated Marketing Communications strategy can employ sonic elements in a way that appeals to some target markets while minimizing potential backlash from others. Audience fragmentation, where technology is changing how consumers view entertainment, is identified as an opportunity for how advertising is morphing in contemporary society. A formative model is presented that can potentially be used as a starting point for further research, which is briefly discussed along with limitations.

Chapter 5

This chapter presents the production perspective of the sound branding and music branding agencies, the core mission being to investigate the notions of those who produce the sound and musical identity of brands, what is thought about the public, their reactions, and how this influences the development of projects. Given the scarcity of contributions on the perception of professionals and scholars regarding sound and music in branding, an exploratory qualitative approach was implemented. Six individualized semi-structured interviews were conducted with professionals from agencies specializing in the development of sound and music products for brands, three Brazilians and three Portuguese, and one interview with a neuroscientist and neuromarketing specialist. Therefore, about consistent with practical implications, producers of branded sound and music experiences and brand audiences can benefit from the results of this research.

Natasha Saqib, University of Kashmir, India
Hardik Dhull, Matu Ram Institute of Engineering and Management,
India
Sanskriti Agrawal, Lakhmi Chand University, India

The purpose of this study is to explore the strategic utilization of sound and music in brand communication, known as sonic branding, with a particular emphasis on the telecom sector. This research aims to investigate the profound impact of Airtel's jingle on the development of brand identity and its influence on consumer engagement within the telecom industry. This research employs an exploratory case study approach. The jingle was found to evoke both emotional and cognitive associations with the brand, contributing significantly to consumer engagement. The findings emphasize the critical role of sonic branding in the telecom sector and its potential to create a distinctive sonic identity. This study contributes to the growing body of knowledge on the significance of sonic branding in contemporary marketing. It adds value by specifically examining the telecom sector and Airtel's jingle as a case study, offering insights that can be valuable to both academics and practitioners in the field.

Anu Norrgrann, University of Vaasa, Finland

This chapter examines how service providers use music in assembling experiencescapes in the context of contemporary and street dance classes and group exercise services. Taking a socio-material approach, the role of music is explored in the interplay of practices, meaning making and entanglements between material/digital and social entities making up the service brand experience. The chapter discusses ways in which music is utilized, and draws attention to elements and interactions, and symbolic complementarities and tensions involved with its integration into the dance / exericise experiencescape. The rich empirical account draws on multiple forms of qualitative, ethnographic data, including in-depth interviews with dance and exercise class instructors.

This chapter analyses the pivotal role of sound in shaping the customer journey and elevating brand experiences. We explain the profound influence of auditory elements, in particular sound, music, silence, or noise, on consumer perception and behavior. By demystifying sonic branding and its implications for brand experiences, we highlight the often-overlooked potency of sound in creating memorable customer experiences. Finally, we draw on a real-world case study of Intel to illustrate sound strategies that have been successful for businesses.

Preface

Have you ever caught yourself humming a jingle long after you have turned off the radio? Do you still remember some of those from your youth? That's the magic of sounds in branding – it sticks with us. When I first embarked on editing "Building Strong Brands and Engaging Customers with Sound," I was fascinated by how tunes and tones could forge such strong connections between us and brands. Born from a mixture of curiosity and a bit of nostalgia for those catchy jingles of my youth, this book aims to shine a light on the often-underappreciated world of sound in marketing.

In this book, we dive into the often-overlooked world of sound in branding, breaking new ground beyond the visual-heavy dialogue that dominates the field. My goal, alongside a talented pool of scholars and practitioners from around the globe, is to shine a spotlight on how sound not only complements but can significantly enhance brand identity and consumer engagement.

We cover a wide variety of topics ranging from advertising jingles and the ambiance of retail environments to the intricacies of luxury shopping experiences and the personal bubbles created by headphones in public spaces. Each chapter, contributed by experts passionate about the intersection of sound, music, and branding, brings unique perspectives and rich insights.

This book is intended for anyone intrigued by the subtle, yet powerful role of sound in our daily brand interactions. Whether you're an academic looking to expand your research, a marketing professional seeking to leverage sound in your campaigns, or simply a curious reader, this exploration into the soundtrack of consumer culture is for you.

This book unites academic researchers and practitioners from different countries, each contributing their distinctive insights on sonic branding. From examining consumer behavior in retail settings to the philosophical considerations of headphone culture, our authors investigate the complex relationship between sound and brand identity through a variety of disciplinary lenses.

By integrating these varied perspectives, this book does more than just cover new ground; it seeks to bridge the gap between theoretical research and practical application. The insights provided here are not only academically rigorous but also immediately relevant to professionals seeking to innovate within the realm of brand management and consumer engagement. Moreover, this collective work serves as a steppingstone for future inquiries into sonic branding. It encourages an ongoing dialogue among academics, industry professionals, and students, continuing to push the boundaries of what we know about sound and its power to shape brand perceptions.

Our journey through the sonic landscape of branding would not have been possible without the dedication and passion of each contributor. Their willingness to explore, question, and share has not only enriched this book but also set the stage for continued exploration in the field of sonic branding. Join us on this enriching journey to explore the world of sounds and music in branding and consumer engagement. Here is a glimpse into the chapters and the unique perspectives they offer:

Chapter 1: Using Soundscape to Design Branded Environment

In the opening chapter, Giuseppe Ciaburro and Elif Hasret Kumcu delve into the innovative concept of brandscape by examining the integration of soundscape in shopping centers. Focusing on the psychological impact of sound on consumer behavior, the authors explore how carefully curated acoustic atmospheres can shape brand identity and foster deeper connections with customers. This chapter offers an exploration of effective brandscape design principles and the diverse ways in which auditory stimuli can influence mood, arousal, and attention within commercial venues.

Chapter 2: Luxury Shoppers' Experiences with Background Music: Implications for Luxury Brand Management

Minna-Maarit Jaskari, Hannele Kauppinen-Räisänen, and Marie-Nathalie Jauffret shift the focus towards luxury retail, investigating the impact of background music on luxury shoppers' experiences. This chapter underscores the strategic importance of congruity between music and brand in the luxury sector. Through exploratory studies, the authors shed light on consumers' perception of music in enhancing brand image, offering valuable insights for luxury brand management practitioners aiming to optimize the role of music in creating a luxurious shopping environment.

Chapter 3: Headphone Culture in Public Spaces of Transfer: Linking Ubiquitous Private Listening to Warped Space

Clara Gustafsson explores the intersection of private listening habits and nondescript spaces of transfer, introducing the concept of Warped Space. Drawing on theoretical frameworks from Vidler, Simmel, and Bull, the chapter unveils how headphone culture thrives in spaces that discourage social connections. For marketers, Gustafsson suggests strategies that leverage appealing visuals and sounds to create imaginative and reassuring environments in these spaces, providing insights into the dynamics of headphone listening and its implications for branding in transit environments.

Chapter 4: Political Affiliation of Musical Artists Contributing to Sonic Elements of Advertising

Paul Barretta's chapter delves into the intersection of music, advertising, and political affiliation. Exploring the potential of using musical artists with similar political views to appeal to specific market segments, the chapter offers insights into how sonic elements can strengthen messaging while aligning with consumers' political perspectives. The chapter also discusses the evolving landscape of audience viewing and opportunities for advertisers to use sonic elements to appeal to politically segmented markets, presenting a "streaming first" perspective.

Chapter 5: An Investigation into Sound and Music in Branding: Premises and Practices of Production

Cristiana Martins de Matos provides a unique production perspective on sound and music branding by conducting interviews with professionals in the field. This chapter explores the thoughts and considerations of those shaping the sound and musical identity of brands. The qualitative approach offers insights into the perspectives of professionals and scholars, contributing to a more nuanced understanding of the relationship between sound production and brand identity.

Chapter 6: Sonic Branding in the Telecom Sector: A Case Study of Airtel's Jingle

Natasha Saqib, Hardik Dhull and Sanskriti Agrawal provide a focused exploration of sonic branding in the telecom sector, using Airtel's jingle as a case study. The research investigates the jingle's impact on brand identity and consumer engagement within the telecom industry. The study reveals emotional and cognitive associations with the brand, highlighting the critical role of sonic branding in creating a distinctive identity. This chapter contributes valuable insights to the growing body of knowledge on the significance of sonic branding in contemporary marketing.

Chapter 7: Using Music to Assemble Dance and Exercise Class Experiencescapes

Anu Norrgrann examines the role of music in shaping experiencescapes in the context of contemporary dance and exercise classes. Taking a socio-material approach, the chapter explores the interplay between music, practices, and symbolic elements in creating the overall service brand experience. Through qualitative ethnographic data, Norrgrann illuminates the ways in which music is utilized and the complexities involved in its integration into the dance and exercise experiencescape.

Chapter 8: Harmonizing Brand Experience: The Role of Sound in Shaping the Customer Brand Experience Journey

In the concluding chapter, Mohamed del Abdelrazek, Marwa Tourky, and William S. Harvey focus on the pivotal role of sound in shaping the customer journey and enhancing brand experiences. This chapter demystifies the influence of auditory elements, including sound, music, silence, or noise, on consumer perception and behavior. Through a real-world case study of Intel, the authors illustrate successful sound strategies, emphasizing the often-overlooked potency of sound in creating memorable customer experiences.

As you navigate through these chapters, you will discover the profound and multifaceted role of sound in branding and consumer engagement. This book is designed not just to inform but to inspire—encouraging you to listen more intently to the world around you and consider how sound influences your own experiences with brands.

I am struck by the richness of the dialogue this book represents. It is more than just a snapshot of where we stand today in our understanding; it is an open invitation for all of us to delve deeper, question further, and explore the uncharted territories of sound in branding together. My heartfelt thanks go to every author and reviewer whose contributions have made this exploration not only possible but profoundly impactful. Your diverse viewpoints and insights have woven a narrative that extends far beyond the pages of this book, touching the hearts and minds of those in academia and industry alike.

As this book takes its place in your collection, whether on a physical shelf or a digital library, it carries with it the hope for an ongoing conversation. A conversation that continues to push the boundaries, challenge our perceptions, and enrich our engagements with the world of brands through the power of sound and music.

Thank you for joining us on this inspiring path. Your curiosity, engagement, and passion for learning are what truly drive this field forward. Here's to continue this remarkable journey together, exploring the sounds that shape our experiences and the music that moves us.

Editor:

Minna-Maarit Jaskari
School of Marketing and Communication, University of Vaasa, Finland

Chapter 1
Using Soundscape to Design Branded Environments

Giuseppe Ciaburro

iD https://orcid.org/0000-0002-2972-0701

Università Degli Studi Della Campania, Italy

Elif Hasret Kumcu

Aksaray University, Turkey

ABSTRACT

This study examines the implementation of soundscape in shopping centers for amplifying the branding experience, generating a distinctive and immersive atmosphere dubbed Brandscape. Visual aesthetics historically influenced commercial venue layout and branding, but recent discussions emphasize sound's impact on consumer attitudes and buying behaviors. Integrating soundscape elements into shopping centers provides a distinctive approach to creating a memorable brand identity. By purposefully crafting the acoustic atmosphere, vendors can evoke emotions, reinforce brand ideals, and cultivate a deeper connection with their target customers. Our study delves into the key principles of effective Brandscape design through the integration of soundscape in shopping centers. The study examines the psychological effect of sound on consumer behavior and investigates how different auditory stimuli can impact mood, arousal, and attention. Furthermore, it emphasizes the significance of preserving coherence between the brand's visual identity and the chosen soundscape, resulting in a unified and all-encompassing sensory encounter for consumers.

DOI: 10.4018/979-8-3693-0778-6.ch001

INTRODUCTION

The soundscape identifies the acoustic environment or the combination of sounds present in a particular place or space that characterize sound perception (Puyana-Romero et al., 2019). It includes natural sounds produced by the environment, such as wind, water, birdsong, or rustling leaves, as well as human-generated sounds, such as traffic, voices, or music. The concept of soundscape suggests an assessment of the quality and character of the sounds that surround us (Brown, 2012). It underscores the idea that sound is not just background noise but plays a crucial role in our perception and experience of a place. In urban planning, soundscape analysis is used to evaluate and improve the acoustic environment of public spaces to improve the overall quality of life (Puyana-Romero et al., 2016). With the advancement of technology, virtual and augmented reality platforms have also explored the creation of realistic and interactive soundscapes to further enhance user immersion and experience (Ciaburro et al., 2021). Overall, soundscape is a term used to describe the aural characteristics and atmosphere of a particular location or the intentional design and manipulation of sound in various applications (Axelsson et al., 2010).

The concept of Brandscape refers to the collection of brands present in a specific market or market segment, and it is widely acknowledged as a cultural phenomenon. In the realm of consumer research literature, this term is frequently employed to depict the way consumers derive personal significance from brands (Klingmann, 2010). Beyond the physical attributes of a brand, the notion of Brandscape encompasses its broader socio-cultural impact. This perspective is further elaborated upon through the term Brandscape, which pertains to the transfer and transformation of brand and brand identity as perceived by consumers (Gilstrap et al., 2021). This transformation, in turn, exerts an influence on individual and societal perspectives, making it a focal point of this concept. A Brandscape can be interpreted as a cultural network of service environments, interlinked, and structured by discursive, symbolic, and competitive relationships with a dominant, market-leading experiential brand. This Brandscape not only organizes a market within the experience economy but also serves as a space that can be interpreted and experienced in various ways that shape identity (Thompson et al., 2004).

The sensory experience in a store is crucial for the sale of a product, as it can arouse emotions and emotional connections in customers. A welcoming, stimulating, or relaxing environment can generate a sense of well-being and make customers more likely to stay in the store, explore the products and shop. A unique and distinctive atmosphere can help the store stand out from the competition (Strang, 2005). Creating a unique experience can grab customers' attention and make them more likely to choose that store over others. The atmosphere of a store is a powerful tool for communicating a brand's personality and values. An environment consistent with your brand identity can create a deeper emotional connection with customers and positively influence their perception of your brand (Korsmeyer et al., 2011). A warm and inviting atmosphere can make customers feel comfortable in the store. Courteous and helpful staff, pleasant background music and a warm and comfortable atmosphere can increase customer confidence and positively influence their propensity to purchase. The store atmosphere can influence the buying behavior of customers. For example, relaxing music can encourage a longer dwell time, while a well-crafted product presentation can encourage impulsive buying. A unique and immersive atmosphere can create a memorable customer experience. Positive and memorable experiences motivate customers to return to your store in the future and recommend it to friends and family, thus generating a positive effect on long-term sales (Wörfel et al., 2022).

The emotional experience of the customer can therefore be adequately stimulated through an adequate design of the soundscape of the shop. To do this you need to understand the purpose and context of the space or project where the soundscape will be implemented, considering the type of environment, the intended atmosphere, and the target audience (Yu et al., 2016). It is therefore necessary to identify the prominent or characteristic sounds that are present or desired in the environment, considering the spatial distribution and the interaction of different sound sources (Puyana-Romero et al., 2016). The result must be a balanced mix of sounds to ensure that no single element dominates, and that the overall soundscape is coherent and harmonious. Particular attention must be paid to the dynamics and variation in the soundscape to avoid monotony. This requires the incorporation of different sonic intensities, patterns, or temporal changes to mimic the natural ebb and flow of a given environment using spatial audio techniques to create a sense of depth and realism in the soundscape (Hellström et al., 2011).

This chapter delves into the application of soundscape in shopping malls to enhance the branding experience, creating a distinct and immersive environment referred to as the Brandscape. While visual aesthetics have historically dominated the design and branding strategies in retail spaces, recent research indicates that sound profoundly influences consumer perceptions and purchasing behaviors. Incorporating soundscape elements into shopping malls provides an innovative approach to establishing a unique and memorable brand identity. By carefully selecting and designing the auditory environment, retailers can strategically evoke emotions, reinforce brand values, and establish a deeper connection with their target audience.

This research examines the essential considerations in designing an effective Brandscape through the implementation of soundscape in shopping malls. It investigates the psychological impact of sound on consumer behavior, exploring how different auditory stimuli can affect mood, arousal, and attention. Furthermore, the study emphasizes the importance of maintaining consistency between the brand's visual identity and the chosen soundscape, ensuring a cohesive and comprehensive sensory experience for customers.

Additionally, the chapter explores various techniques for implementing soundscape in shopping malls, including curated playlists, customized compositions, and interactive installations. It delves into the role of sound elements in different areas of the mall, such as entrances, storefronts, aisles, and communal spaces, with the aim of creating a harmonious and engaging environment throughout the entire shopping journey. Moreover, the chapter addresses potential challenges and ethical considerations related to soundscape implementation, such as noise pollution and individual preferences. It stresses the need for flexibility and adaptability in designing soundscapes that cater to diverse consumer demographics and cultural contexts.

In conclusion, the incorporation of soundscape in shopping malls presents a novel and potent tool for creating compelling Brandscape. By leveraging the auditory dimension, retailers can enhance brand perception, engage customers on a deeper level, and ultimately drive sales. However, successful implementation necessitates careful planning, consideration of consumer psychology, and a seamless integration with the brand's visual identity. With the right approach, soundscape has the potential to revolutionize the retail landscape, offering a multi-sensory experience that leaves a lasting impression on consumers.

BRANDED ENVIRONMENT

Atmosphere is a factor that surrounds the environment and includes many variables, because it includes everything that can be noticed through sensory perception. The role that the atmosphere plays on consumer behavior is very important. In this context, according to Kumar and Kim (2014:690), store atmosphere, it affects store and product evaluations and approach-avoidance behavior. Marques, Trindade and Santos (2016: 25) show in their study that atmospheric variables are of great importance for both hypermarkets and supermarkets. Garaus (2017:270) found that atmospheric harmony can increase store satisfaction and revisit intention. The atmosphere of a shopping center plays an important role in creating the corporate image of consumers about that shopping center. This atmosphere can be effective in attracting consumer attention, conveying messages, and generating emotional reactions. In this context, sensory elements such as the interior and exterior design of the shopping center and the symbolic signs used play a critical role in shaping the environmental image. These environmental stimuli can not only form consumers' perceptions, but also trigger purchasing behavior. For example, reactions to sensory stimuli in the design of a shopping mall can create a combination of imaginary, emotional and valued-liked consumption experiences in consumers. This can be used to describe motivated consumer behavior through emotional dimensions such as satisfaction, entertainment, interest and pleasure (Kent, 2003, 134). As a result, the atmosphere of the shopping center stands out as an important factor affecting consumers' perceptions, emotional reactions and purchasing behavior. Therefore, retailers need to focus on encouraging consumers to have a positive consumption experience by carefully designing the shopping mall atmosphere. These studies highlight the importance of store atmosphere on the retail experience. The role of atmosphere in the retail experience is complex and involves many variables. Atmosphere is a multidimensional phenomenon that greatly affects the consumer experience and is perceived holistically by consumers. In Figure 1 is shown a representation of a pyramid diagram illustrating the layers of brand identity, from core values and mission at the base to visual elements.

Figure 1. Representation of a pyramid diagram illustrating the layers of brand identity, from core values and mission at the base to visual elements.

This pyramid represents the hierarchical structure of brand design, with the foundation built on core values and mission, supporting the subsequent layers that define the brand's personality, expression, experience, and associations. The pinnacle of the pyramid represents the tangible visual elements that encapsulate the brand's identity. Feel free to customize the content and design to suit your specific needs.

It is critical to consider all variables during the shopping experience. Shopping malls aim to increase customer satisfaction and make customers stay in shopping malls longer. Existing studies indicate that the combination of color and lighting is positively received and can directly increase customer satisfaction. Therefore, shopping malls are taking steps to increase customer satisfaction by offering this combination with applications such as dim walls and decorative lighting of spaces or 3D light shows on special occasions. Additionally, factors such as appropriate color schemes, pleasant smell and comfortable temperature increase customers' desire to spend longer time in shopping malls, which in turn increases the likelihood of spending in stores. Considering the impact of emotional states, there is potential for mall management to offer various ways to improve their customers' shopping experience. This can increase the success of shopping malls by triggering customers' desire to spend more time in shopping malls. As a result, managers can use color schemes and music to increase or decrease the time different consumer segments spend in shopping malls. For example, when targeting older consumers, they can reduce the density of shopping malls by using music that may not be suitable for younger age groups. (Elmashhara & Soares 2020:452).

Today's brand design is a process that does not limit brand identity only to the visual image and reaches a wide range of dimensions, involving the interaction of both visible and invisible elements. This process plays a role in creating the brand experience and as an important component of the brand strategy. The brand experience occurs through a "space" that represents a three-dimensional complexity where various elements and services come together. This venue offers the brand experience to consumers as a whole. Brandscape is a reflection of this spatial branding, as the brand experience of a particular company is extended through physical spaces, indoors or outdoors. Brandscape plays an important role in enabling consumers to interact more deeply with the brand. The design of physical spaces is used to convey brand values and enrich the brand experience. By providing consumers with a tactile experience, brands can establish emotional connections and create loyal customers. Brand design no longer includes only the visual image but also the brand experience experienced through spaces. This helps brands build deeper and more sustainable relationships and becomes a key component of their brand strategy (Lee & Ahn, 2014:144-145).

It is necessary to emphasize the importance of the unique experiences that the Brandscape will offer and a comprehensive understanding of consumer perceptions. To establish a more effective connection with consumers and ensure perceived authenticity, the brand can incorporate the co-creation experience into its brandscape design by encouraging consumer participation. One of the key attributes of Brandscape is the authenticity of the experiences offered to the consumer. However, this authenticity must be carefully designed and communicated so that it can be reflected in the consumer's perceptions. In particular, since consumer perceptions have a complex structure, all aspects of these perceptions should be taken into account in brandscape design. Brands should make consumers a part of the experience to direct and influence consumer perceptions. This means that consumers must act not just as passive observers, but as participants who actively shape the experience. This involvement can strengthen the connection between consumer and brand and increase perceived authenticity. As a result, as suggested by Lee (2019), brands' integration of co-creation experience in brandscape design allows authentic experiences to be more effectively communicated to consumer perceptions and to establish a stronger bond with consumers. This can help brands be more successful in the competitive market (Lee, 2019:10).

It follows that an effective brand environment requires a multi-sensory design in which not only the visual features are essential, but all the possible ways in which the customer interacts with the brand are crucial. Among these, sound is a vehicle for conveying the fundamental message, which is an added value that the designer must consider.

THE ROLE OF SOUNDSCAPE IN ENHANCING BRANDING

The term shopping mall is used as a term to describe organized shopping centers with a central management team (Merrilees et al., 2016:262). Shopping malls are considered indoor spaces that replace traditional shopping districts and host modern retail experiences. These areas have become preferred venues for eating and drinking, entertainment, and social interaction as well as shopping activities (Alnuman & Altaweel, 1170). Malls are generally considered a planned collection of several retail stores. This approach contrasts with the model of a high street, which is often dominated by multiple owners. For this reason, there may be inconsistencies between the scope and visual features of the stores. Shopping malls have their origins in spaces such as markets, arcades that house a variety of retailers or vendors, often creating exciting shopping experiences. Department stores have enriched the retail experience with a strong focus on areas such as store design, visual displays, in-store promotions, wide range of products as well as the provision of services such as banking, travel services, reading rooms, restrooms, cafeterias, and restaurants. Department stores have a structure like a coherent collection of stores offering different product categories under one roof (Merrilees et al., 2016:264).

Shopping malls are considered places that significantly affect consumers' lifestyles (Kesari and Atulkar, 2016). This is because shopping malls are considered not only as areas for commercial activities, but also as centers of social and social interaction (Ng, 2003). In shopping malls, visitors form an emotional relationship with the shopping center because of the social, leisure, financial, familial, cultural and environmental experiences they have (El Hedhli et al., 2013). In this context, visitors' emotional impressions of the shopping center leave a trace in mental memory as a part of their shopping experience (Lee et al., 2002), and these impressions shape the identity of the shopping center (Ali et al., 2021:1180). Mall identity tends to make shopping experiences more enjoyable and functional, which has the potential to make shoppers feel good in the end. Therefore, shopping center management should strive to develop interior and exterior designs to reflect the intended personality.

Shopping center managers should emphasize hedonic value. This can be achieved through factors such as entertainment options, service packages, aesthetic and comfortable spaces, relaxing lighting, attractive color schemes, empathetic store employees, social events and can increase visitors' perceptions of hedonic value. Mall managers must provide an exciting shopping experience that will help shoppers escape the stress and anxiety of daily life. Shopping malls should create a suitable environment to attract such visitors, but also support compulsive shopping tendencies (Ali et al., 2021:1190). Various specialized or non-specialized shopping malls, including large and small stores, movie theaters, amusement parks, fast food restaurants, social venues, coffee houses and similar elements, represent many aspects of people's lifestyles (Shafiee and Es-Haghi, 2017:1114). Understanding how shopping malls shape consumers' lifestyles and the role of these venues in society represents an important area of research in consumer behavior and retail management. Shopping malls should be considered as complex spaces that shape and represent people's daily lives.

Consumer mall branding is based on two key components: mall atmosphere and mall products. These two factors contribute to the construction of a shopping mall brand in consumer perception. A satisfying mall brand experience reinforces the meaning of the mall brand by acting as a bridge between mall products and the mall atmosphere. Consumer shopping center brand meaning comprehensively addresses the brand meaning attributed to a shopping center. It is thought that the music played throughout the mall may be a high component of the perceived mall image but may be of minimal importance to consumers in terms of consumer mall brand meaning. Experiential branding is crucial to consumer mall brand experiences. It is also concluded that customer mall satisfaction is a critical driver of customer mall brand attitudes, and that satisfaction is also an indicator of the mall experience. Shopping mall atmosphere (ambiance) has a significant impact on customer mall satisfaction, which is an important factor in shaping customer mall brand attitudes (Merrilees et al., 2016:270).

Consumers tend to visit multi-purpose malls from time to time because these centers provide access to a wide collection of brands under one roof. Customers' revisiting behavior of these stores can be affected by various factors. These factors are customers' satisfaction with the store, word of mouth. It can have significant impacts on consent marketing effectiveness and repeat visit requests and behavior. Indoor conditions and perceived purchasing value of shopping malls play an important role in determining consumer behavior. However, it is observed that other environmental factors such as music and color also have significant effects on consumers' emotional reactions, satisfaction, and loyalty towards shopping malls (Sadeghian et al., 2019:205).

Cultural dimensions, especially local culture, are a salient factor that significantly influences consumer behavior. Although because functionality may be a universal value independent of cultural context, these cultural differences can affect the basic segmentation criteria in business strategies. The concept of value can be universally accepted, regardless of cultural context. Regarding the hedonic dimension, the absence of a similar universality highlights how important it is to consider cultural diversity when examining the phenomenon of global shopping malls (Lucas et. al. 2021:12).

A shopping center represents a sound environment characterized by specific sources that can be shaped in the sense of conveying specific messages and creating engaging and hospitable atmospheres. That is, it involves designing a soundscape that is consistent with the customer's expectations and that makes them feel like they are in the right place to be able to enjoy their shopping experience in the best possible way (Ozcevik et al., 2008). The concept of soundscape is based on the human perception of sound and refers to the acoustic environment perceived by one or more people in a certain context. The acoustic environment includes all sounds coming from sound sources modified by the environment. Sound sources can be natural or generated by human activity (Ciaburro et al., 2021). According to the ISO definition (ISO 12913-1: 2014), the soundscape approach considers the acoustic environment not as something to be eliminated, but as a resource to be enhanced. Countries' acoustic policies tend to reduce noise in all possible ways without considering the possibilities of designing the acoustic environment in a way that contributes to people's well-being and the assessment of the quality of a given city (Ciaburro et al., 2021). The soundscape approach aims to investigate how people perceive an acoustic environment. It does not simply reduce noise levels as a response to acoustic discomfort but seeks to identify the conditions and sound sources that cause such discomfort (Iannace et al., 2021). Furthermore, it tries to identify the factors and sound sources that can improve the evaluation of the quality of an acoustic environment without necessarily reducing its sound level (Iannace et al., 2015).

The soundscape is a concept that refers to the totality of sounds present in a specific environment or space. It is one of the fundamental components of human sensory experience and has a significant impact on our perception and interaction with the world around us (Schafer, 1993). The soundscape can be understood as a sort of "auditory landscape", in which different sound sources mix, overlap and create a unique sound environment. This environment can be natural, such as the forest, the sea, or the countryside, or it can be artificial, such as a busy road, a shopping center, or a train station. The soundscape may include sounds of the natural acoustic environment, made up of natural sounds (including, for example, animal vocalizations and the sounds of natural elements); Artificial environmental sounds encompass various elements, including musical compositions, sound design, commonplace activities like conversation and work, and the mechanical sounds arising from industrial technology usage.

The soundscape concept was developed in the 1970s by Canadian artist R. Murray Schafer in his 1977 book "The Tuning of the World" (Schafer, 1977), which highlighted the importance of paying attention to the quality and complexity of the sounds around us. Schafer argued that the soundscape of a place can reveal a lot about its environmental, social, and cultural characteristics. Today, as technology advances and cities expand, soundscapes have become increasingly complex and sometimes chaotic. In many urban areas, the constant noise of traffic, sirens, advertisements, and human conversations has become the norm, significantly affecting our quality of life and mental health. However, the importance of preserving and restoring natural soundscapes and creating quieter and more pleasant urban environments is increasingly clear. Listening carefully and consciously to the soundscape can lead to greater awareness and appreciation of the sounds around us and the creation of spaces and places that promote well-being and communication. This because the soundscape is a key element of our sensory experience and our relationship with the surrounding environment. Understanding and preserving it helps us create more sustainable, healthy, and harmonious environments (Dumyahn, 2011).

Soundscapes are an increasingly relevant element in branding and marketing, helping to create an engaging and memorable sensory experience for consumers. Sound is a powerful emotional stimulus and can influence how people perceive a brand or company. A well-designed soundscape can convey a brand's values, identity and vibe subtly but effectively. An example of a soundscape in branding is the jingle, a short melody or distinctive sound that is associated with a brand. Jingles are often used in radio and television advertisements to create brand recognition and memorability. An iconic example is the McDonald's jingle "I'm lovin' it". In addition to jingles, the soundscape can also include ambient sounds, such as background music in a store or hotel, sound effects in a promotional video, or the distinctive voices and sounds of a call center (Thompson, 2002).

Some companies use original soundtracks or popular music tracks to accompany their advertisements or promotional videos. This can help create an emotional association with the brand and convey a certain message. Just as some brands use sound effects or iconic sounds to distinguish themselves from competitors and create a recognizable immediacy. Still, some companies invest in developing a unique sound design for their products or services. This can help create a better user experience and distinguish the brand from others. Through a carefully curated soundscape, a brand can create a positive association with its audience and evoke specific emotions. For example, a coffee shop chain might use a soundscape that includes the sound of coffee being ground, the sound of cups being filled, and the barista preparing drinks. This soundscape could create a welcoming and inviting atmosphere, which results in a positive experience for customers and keeps them coming back (Octaviani et al., 2021).

Figure 2. Key Elements of a Soundscape

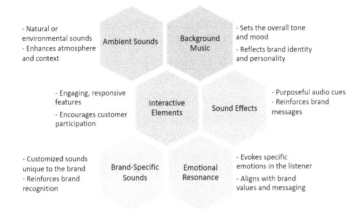

Additionally, soundscape can also be used to differentiate a brand from the competition. For example, an airline could create a unique soundscape composed of relaxing and comfortable sounds to distinguish it from other airlines and create a premium atmosphere. Using soundscape in branding is an effective way to engage and influence consumers through a unique sensory experience. A well-designed soundscape can enhance brand perception and create an emotional connection with the target audience. This is because sound can add a distinctive and memorable element to a company's branding strategy. Sound can evoke emotion, create associations, and communicate brand values and personality (Figure 2). It is important that the sound is consistent with the brand and attracts the attention of the target audience, to help strengthen the brand identity and create a memorable experience for consumers (Spence, 2011).

In the intricate world of mall soundscapes, a pivotal consideration is the delicate balance between prioritizing local culture and catering to the diverse musical tastes of customers. This prompts a reflection on the mall's role as a cultural hub and its approach to shaping a sensory environment that resonates with its surroundings. One perspective involves investigating whether the mall consciously aligns its soundscape with the rich tapestry of local culture. Does it seek to become an extension of the community, weaving the sounds of the locale into its auditory fabric? This alignment could manifest in the incorporation of region-specific music genres, traditional tunes, or even ambient sounds reflective of the local environment. Such an approach not only contributes to the preservation and celebration of local culture but also enhances the sense of place for both residents and visitors.

On the other hand, the mall may opt to prioritize the diverse musical tastes of its customers, transforming itself into a dynamic and inclusive space that caters to a broad spectrum of preferences. In this scenario, the soundscape becomes a curated playlist of genres and styles, mirroring the heterogeneity of the mall's clientele. From contemporary hits to niche genres, the musical selection aims to create an atmosphere that is both familiar and appealing to a wide audience. This reflection invites exploration into the motivations and considerations behind these choices. Does the mall see itself as a cultural curator, fostering a connection with the local community through shared sonic experiences? Or is its primary goal to create a universally enjoyable atmosphere that transcends cultural boundaries? In essence, the interplay between prioritizing local culture and catering to the musical tastes of customers is a nuanced dance. The soundscape becomes a reflection of the mall's identity—whether it seeks to be a cultural beacon deeply embedded in its surroundings or a versatile space that dynamically adapts to the eclectic tastes of its diverse patrons. Understanding this dynamic can provide insights into the mall's overarching vision and its commitment to creating a unique and resonant environment for everyone who steps through its doors.

SENSORY PERCEPTIONS AND SOUND BASED STRATEGIES

According to a perspective expressed by Hultén (2010), sensory perceptions, especially sensory experiences such as smell, sound, sight, taste, and touch, can have significant effects on individuals. These effects may contribute to individuals forming a particular perception of value. In particular, these sensory experiences have the potential to make a positive contribution to brand identity and image. Sensory perceptions such as smell, sound, visuality, taste, and touch can serve as a means of enriching consumer experiences. This experiential enrichment can increase the consumer's feeling of being a part of the brand, which can provide the consumer with the opportunity to form a deep connection with a particular brand. As Hultén (2010) notes, these sensory experiences can help strengthen brand perception in a positive way. Through these sensory experiences, consumers can better understand the value of the brand and establish a stronger emotional bond with the brand. This can represent an important way to build brand loyalty and shape consumer behavior. In conclusion, based on Hultén's (2010) observation, it should be acknowledged that sensory experiences play a key role in strengthening brand identity. Therefore, if brands carefully manage these sensory perceptions and effectively use these sensory elements to enrich the consumer experience, it has the potential to positively impact brand image (Hultén, 2010:269).

Differentiation and positioning of a brand in the human mind is an indispensable element of the multi-sensory brand experience. The brand must seize the opportunity to engage people's five senses in order to create and maintain a unique and memorable image among consumers. This is accomplished through the use of sensory strategies expressed through the human senses. These strategies contribute to people having a richer experience in emotional, cognitive, behavioral, symbolic or sensory dimensions, and these experiences increase the value of a brand. In this context, sensory perceptions such as smell, sound, sight, taste or touch are handled with an empirical logic and add a certain value to the consumer. In particular, these sensory experiences can strengthen a brand's image by triggering positive emotional responses. Brands get the opportunity to offer consumers a unique and special experience by using these sensory elements. As expressed by Hultén (2010), multi-sensory brand experience offers the consumer a more in-depth and multi-layered experience. These experiences encourage the consumer to form a stronger bond with the brand and increase the value of the brand. Therefore, it is extremely important for brands to enrich the consumer experience by using sensory strategies in creating and maintaining brand identity and image. As Hultén (2010) emphasizes, multi-sensory brand experience allows the brand to establish a deeper interaction with consumers and be perceived positively by the consumer. This allows brands to gain a competitive advantage in the market.

It can help them build a loyal customer base (Hultén, 2010: 268-269). Sensory sound strategies, used to strengthen brand identity and image, are a form of sensory expression that adds meaning to human experience and can be a source of inspiration by brands using sound and especially music. These strategies are often used to stimulate memories through music by recalling music from people's youth. Brands such as Abercrombie & Fitch stand out with their unique audio strategies. The voice of such brands is expressed through famous songs that are carefully selected and mixed to create the right atmosphere in the brand's service environment. In particular, each song has a heavy bass element and the music played creates a loud and nightclub atmosphere. This creates an atmosphere where songs are constantly played to create the perception for customers that this is an expected experience. While this constant flow of music increases customers' interaction with the brand, employees dancing in harmony with the music provides customers with a relaxed party atmosphere and reinforces the feeling of "reviving". Sensory experiences such as jingles and sounds add to the sonic experience of the brand. For example, Swedish fashion retailer Lindex uses jingles and TV commercials to strengthen its brand image. These jingles are adjusted to fit seasonal themes and emotional expressions, for example, when the

"Fashion Report Paris" theme comes up in a period, an accordion sound is added to the jingle to reflect the Paris theme. Because this sound is subtly placed, customers need to focus carefully. But music is used consistently beyond seasonal changes. The sensory sound strategy emphasizes the importance of shaping the sound experience using sensory expressions such as atmosphere, theme, and attention. Additionally, the brand's sound can be legally protected and adopted as a sound trademark, used as a signature sound with a distinctive character. As highlighted in Hultén's (2010) study, sensory voice strategies serve as an effective tool for strengthening brand identity and image, allowing brands to sensory enrich the consumer experience (Hultén, 2010: 266-267). Intensive use of shopping malls, high visitor traffic and various events are among the factors that increase sound levels. Therefore, this sound pollution may negatively affect acoustic comfort and have negative consequences, especially on personnel working in shopping malls (Alnuman & Altaweel, 1170).

Music provides an important means of expressing, implying, and depicting emotional events and processes as an essential part of the human experience. This can be explained by the temporal nature of music as well as the close relationship of composers, performers, and listeners to the behavioral morphology of emotional states. Music appears to be full of musical devices that can evoke a variety of responses that are not overtly emotional or do not appear emotional on the surface. The capacity of music to produce emotional effects is evident even through the type of music known as "absolute music", which does not only contain words. Absolute music can cause spurious emotional, physiological and motor responses. This reflects the fact that basic emotions can be triggered by the impact of music, although usually at low intensity. Among the effects of music while listening, distinct physiological reactions such as a lump in the throat, tears or excitement are frequently observed. Such situations represent the most impressive, memorable and deeply subjective effects of music on people. However, such responses are rare and require a special listening environment for music to lead to a sublime aesthetic experience. In conclusion, music is an expressive tool that enriches people's emotional expression and experiences. The emotional impact of music on people is the result of a complex interaction between the structural properties of the music and the personal experiences of the listener. The power of music, combined with its capacity to express emotional depth, can transport people to unique and unforgettable experiences (Konecni, 2008:126-127). When the emotional responses and reactions of music on people are considered in the context of experience development, these processes are complex and based on the interaction of many factors. Additionally, emphasis is placed on identifying themes associated with tourists' decision-making processes at different consumption stages. In this context, stimuli created by the influence of music occur through different auditory elements. These elements vary, including those that are controllable (such as sounds or language) and those that cannot be controlled (such as the physical environment). While controllable stimuli carry emotional messages expressed through music, uncontrollable elements, such as external factors such as the physical environment, have the potential to contribute to emotional reactions. The effect of music depends on how individuals process and internalize these stimuli. This process refers to the mental imagery process described by MacInnis and Price (1987). This process involves individuals' ability to perceive, interpret, and internally experience music. Importantly, these processes lead to emotional responses that the brain and psychophysiological activity can measure. The emotional impact of music on people is closely related to individuals' perceptions, thoughts, and inner experiences, as well as to the music itself (Moreno-Lobato et al. 2023:8).

CREATING A UNIQUE ATMOSPHERE: MUSIC SELECTION AND SOUND EFFECTS

Creating a unique atmosphere in a shopping center requires special care in music selection and sound effects. To do this effectively it is essential to understand the shopping center's target customers. For example, if the shopping center mainly targets a young audience, the music selection will need to be contemporary and modern. If, however, the shopping center has a more mature audience, the music must be suitable for this target. Music must therefore be carefully chosen to pique customer interest and keep them engaged. You can create a playlist that includes a variety of music genres, alternating more energetic songs with more relaxing ones, to fit the shopping mall environment. Furthermore, it is advisable to consider the different time slots, for example by offering more lively music during lunch hours or on weekends.

In addition to the music selection, sound effects can be incorporated to create a unique atmosphere. For example, you might consider adding nature sounds (such as birds chirping or the sound of waves) to create a relaxing atmosphere in an atrium area. Or you can insert sounds of a busy market near a food sales area to stimulate customers' appetites. A quality audio system is essential to ensure clear and crisp reproduction of music and sound effects. Investing in a good sound system and quality speakers can make a difference in the sound experience of visitors. Real-time monitoring of customer feedback can return useful information: Customer feedback can be used to evaluate the quality of the shopping mall's sound atmosphere. You can organize surveys or track comments that customers leave on social media. This will help understand whether the music selection and sound effects meet audience expectations and, if necessary, adjust improve the overall sound experience.

In the literature there are several contributions that have studied how to use sound for a conscious design of environments intended for customer hospitality. Wargnier et al. (2010) analyzed the role of sound, in particular music, on consumer attitudes and their purchasing behavior in shopping centers. The study conducted by Wargnier and Dubois in 2010 and published in the "International Journal of Management Reviews" is a review of the literature on the effect of music on consumer behavior. The authors review a range of previous research on the topic to draw conclusions about how music can influence various aspects of purchasing behavior. These aspects include the length of time customers spend in stores, spending, perception of the store environment and customer satisfaction. The main finding of their study is that music can have a significant impact on consumer behavior in retail environments, but the effects can vary based on several factors, including music genre, volume, and congruence with the store brand. The article provides a broad overview of existing research in this field and offers a clear view of the trends and challenges in understanding the role of music in consumer experiences. Lindstrom (1999) addressed the importance of the senses, including sound, in marketing and creating consumer experiences both in physical stores and online. The book "Brand Sense: Sensory Secrets Behind the Stuff We Buy" by Martin Lindstrom, published in 1999 by Simon & Schuster, explores the role of the senses in brand building and consumer behavior. The author addresses the idea that branding should not just be limited to the visual aspect, but involve all the senses, including hearing, smell, touch, and taste. Lindstrom analyzes how multisensory experiences influence brand perception, consumer loyalty and purchasing decisions. The book draws on research and real-life examples to demonstrate how companies can leverage the use of all the senses to create more effective and engaging brands. Lindstrom argues that sensory experience is critical to a brand's success and offers entrepreneurs and marketers guidance on harnessing the full potential of the senses in brand building. North et al. (1999) examined the influence of background music on product choice in shopping malls. The study conducted by North, Hargreaves and McKendrick in 1999, published in "Nature", examines the effect of in-store music on consumers' product choices. The authors conducted an experiment in which participants shopped in a supermarket while music played in the background. They found that the type of music influenced consumers' product choices. For example, when classical music was played, consumers tended to select high-class products, while with pop music they oriented towards more popular products. This study helped demonstrate how background music can influence consumer purchasing preferences in a retail environment. The findings suggest that carefully choosing background music can be an important marketing strategy to positively influence consumer decisions in stores.

Yalch et al. (1990) discussed the impact of ambient music on consumer attitudes and purchasing decisions when shopping in malls. The study conducted by Yalch and Spangenberg in 1990 and published in the "Journal of Consumer Marketing" examines the effects of music in the store on customer purchasing behavior. The authors conducted an experiment in which participants shopped at a retail store while background music played. They found that the presence of music positively influenced customers' stay in the store and increased sales. Music seemed to foster a more pleasant and welcoming atmosphere, encouraging customers to stay longer and make larger purchases. This study helps to highlight the importance of the use of music in the retail environment and underlines how the careful choice of music can positively influence consumer behavior, encouraging greater stay and spending in stores. Puccinelli et al. (2009) addressed the importance of sensory experience, including sound experience, within shopping centers and how this influences the consumer purchasing process. The study conducted by Puccinelli and colleagues in 2009, published in the "Journal of Retailing, focuses on customer experience management in the retail industry, with a particular focus on the consumer purchasing process. The authors examine the entire shopping process, from the initial interaction with the store through to the purchase decision and completion of the transaction. They address several aspects that influence the customer experience, including the store environment, staff assistance, product presentation and overall customer satisfaction. The article suggests that effective customer experience management is crucial to success in the retail industry. This involves creating an environment where customers feel comfortable and well supported, thus facilitating the purchasing process, and increasing the likelihood of customer loyalty. The paper provides a clear view of the key factors influencing consumer purchasing behavior in retail stores. Southworth (2011) explores the relationship between the sound environment of a city and people's spatial behavior. It focuses on how sound affects the perception of urban spaces. Southworth examines how the acoustic design of spaces, such as shopping centers, can shape visitor behavior and experiences. This contribution provides a theoretical basis for understanding the importance of sound in the shopping center environment and can be useful for the design of such spaces.

Seo et al. (2016) examines the impact of ambient music on the purchasing behavior of adult consumers. The authors collected and analyzed a series of previous research to evaluate how the presence of background music influences various aspects of shopping behavior, such as the duration of shopping, the amount spent and the overall experience of consumers in commercial contexts. The overall findings of this meta-analysis provide valuable insights into the role of music in optimizing the shopping mall environment to improve customer experience and positively influence adult purchasing decisions. Guéguen et al. (2004) conducted an experiment conducted in a beer drinking environment to examine the effect of ambient music sound level on beer drinking behavior. The authors examined whether the volume of music influences the rate of consumption of alcoholic beverages. The experiment revealed that the sound level of ambient music can have a significant impact on drinking behavior, as participants tended to drink faster when the music was played at a louder volume. This study provides an interesting contribution to understanding how the sound environment, such as the volume of music, can influence consumer behavior in specific contexts, such as bars or pubs. Dubois et al. (2011) investigated the effects of background music on consumer behavior in a supermarket through a field experiment. In the experiment, the researchers examined how the presence of ambient music influences various aspects of customer behavior, including time in the store, purchases made and overall customer satisfaction. The results revealed that ambient music has a positive impact on customers' dwell time in the supermarket and their overall level of satisfaction. However, the effect on purchase volume was found to be moderate. This study offers an interesting perspective on the use of music in commercial contexts, highlighting how it can influence the consumer experience and suggesting that the choice of background music can be an important element in designing marketing strategies for supermarkets and similar.

Smith et al. (1966) examined the effects of background music on worker concentration. The authors conducted an experiment in which participants had to perform work tasks while ambient music was played. The results indicated that background music had a negative effect on workers' concentration, reducing their productivity. This study suggested that the presence of music in work environments could negatively affect employees' cognitive abilities and performance. The article contributes to the understanding of how the sound environment can influence worker behavior and performance and has important implications for the design of workspaces and company policies regarding the use of background music. The effects of songs with pro-social lyrics on consumer purchasing behavior was examined in this other study (Laitala et al. 2016).. The authors conducted an experiment in which participants listened to music with lyrics that promoted positive social values while shopping in a retail environment. The results indicated that songs with pro-social lyrics had a positive impact on consumers' purchasing behavior. Participants tended to be more inclined to make sustainable purchases and make choices that promote the environment. This study provides interesting evidence on the use of music with pro-social messages as a lever to positively influence consumer behavior in commercial contexts, suggesting that music can be a tool to promote more responsible purchasing behavior. Alvarsson et al. (2010) studied the effect of natural sound and environmental noise on recovery from stress. The authors examined how exposure to nature sounds, such as bird chirps or water sounds, affects an individual's ability to recover from stress compared to exposure to common environmental noises. The results showed that natural sounds promote greater recovery from stress compared to environmental noises. Exposure to natural sounds led to a decrease in perceived stress levels and the restoration of physiological function. This study suggests that the sound environment, particularly the use of nature sounds, can play an important role in promoting well-being and stress management in urban or indoor environments, with significant implications for spatial design and policies. of public health.

Dall'Ara et al. (2018) analyzed the literature on the effect of music on consumer purchasing behavior. This study was published as part of the book "Transformative Consumer Research for Personal and Collective Well-being" at Springer. The authors reviewed a wide range of previous research investigating how music influences consumers in commercial contexts. They explored the effects of music on length of store visits, overall spending, consumer preferences, and perception of the store environment. The main finding of this study is that background music can significantly influence consumers' purchasing behavior, but the effect varies based on several factors, including music genre, volume, and brand congruence of the shop. The authors also propose several topics for further future research in this field, paving the way for a deeper understanding of the interaction between music and consumer behavior in commercial contexts. Kellaris et al. (1993) observed the effects of background music on the perception and processing of advertisements. The authors propose a hypothesis based on the concept of contingency, suggesting that the effect of background music on the perception of ads depends on how the music interacts with the ad itself. They suggest that music can enhance or interfere with ad perception based on various factors, including the congruence between the music and the advertising message. The results of the study indicate that the effect of music on the perception of ads is influenced by the congruence between the music and the content of the ad. When music is congruent with the advertising message, it can improve ad processing. Conversely, when there is inconsistency, music can interfere with the perception of the ad. This study provides an interesting perspective on the complex relationship between music and advertising, suggesting that the choice of background music in advertisements should be carefully considered based on the message it is intended to convey.

From the analysis of these excellent contributions, sound represents an essential contribution in the design of shopping environments. From these studies it is possible to obtain useful suggestions on the approach to adopt to create pleasant and comfortable environments (Trotta, 2020).

DESIGNING SUCCESSFUL SOUNDSCAPE BRANDING IN SHOPPING MALLS

Creating successful soundscape branding in shopping malls involves careful planning and consideration of various elements to enhance the overall shopping experience. In the following there are several advices to incorporate in our design the essential elements to create a perfect soundscape to get the best environments for an effective marketing strategies. To create an effective soundscape branding strategy, we need to understand your shopping center's brand identity, target audience and unique selling points. The soundscape should align with these elements to create a cohesive and memorable experience. It is therefore necessary to identify the core values, mission, and personality of the shopping center (brand values and personality). Priorities need to be set: Should the brand be exclusive, family-friendly, trendy, or themed? This path will lead us to define the type of soundscape that will complete the identity of the environment. To do this, we need to know the primary and secondary target audiences: we can consider the demographics, preferences, and lifestyles of potential customers. The soundscape should match the tastes and expectations of the buyers: It is good practice to analyze competitors and their approach to soundscape branding. To differentiate the shopping center being designed from others, we can select the sounds that differentiate it in the market by identifying what makes the shopping center unique: It could be the architectural design, the mix of shops or a special service. The soundscape should highlight these aspects. Gathering feedback from current shoppers or conducting surveys will help understand their perception of the brand: This can reveal which aspects of the shopping experience need to be improved through sound. Create a narrative that embodies your brand (brand storytelling): This narrative can help you select the right music and sound elements to tell your story effectively. Considering how visual brand elements, such as logos and color schemes, can be translated into sound or audio cues is critical to building brand recognition. Develop clear guidelines on how your brand should sound (brand guidelines): These guidelines can specify the genres, tempo, and mood of the music, as well as the use of sound effects or voiceovers. Once we fully understand the brand identity, we can make informed choices about the music, sounds and audio elements that will create a cohesive and engaging soundscape for your shopping center.

Figure 3. Brand's Sound Identity Key Elements

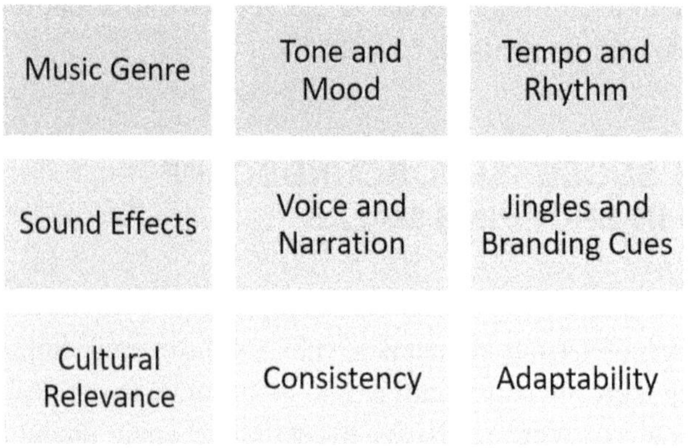

Music Genre	Tone and Mood	Tempo and Rhythm
Sound Effects	Voice and Narration	Jingles and Branding Cues
Cultural Relevance	Consistency	Adaptability

After that we must define the Brand's Sound Identity: Develop a clear and consistent sound identity that reflects your brand. This includes selecting music genres, soundscapes, and audio elements that match your brand's personality and message. Defining your brand's sound identity involves creating a distinct and consistent audio profile that represents your brand. We must consider the following aspect when defining our brand's sound identity (Figure 3):

- Music Genre: Choose the music genres that best align with your brand. For example, classical music may convey elegance and sophistication, while pop music might suggest a more vibrant and youthful atmosphere.
- Tone and Mood: Determine the tone and mood you want to convey. Is your brand playful, soothing, energetic, or inspirational? The choice of music and soundscapes should reflect this.
- Tempo and Rhythm: Decide on the tempo and rhythm that suit your brand. Faster tempos can create a sense of urgency and excitement, while slower rhythms may promote relaxation.
- Sound Effects: Incorporate sound effects or audio cues that are consistent with your brand's identity. These can be subtle cues like the sound of nature for an eco-friendly brand or cheerful bells for a festive ambiance.
- Voice and Narration: If you use voiceovers in your soundscape, consider the tone and style of the narration. Should it be professional, friendly, or authoritative? The voice should resonate with your brand's personality.
- Jingles and Branding Cues: Create jingles or short audio cues that are unique to your brand. These can be used as auditory signatures and enhance brand recognition.
- Cultural Relevance: If your shopping mall serves a specific cultural or regional audience, ensure that the soundscape respects and resonates with that culture. This can include using culturally relevant music and sound elements.
- Consistency: Maintain consistency in your sound identity across all touchpoints, from in-store music to digital promotions. This consistency hclps reinforce your brand's audio identity.
- Adaptability: Your sound identity should be adaptable to different seasons, events, or zones within the shopping mall while remaining coherent with the overall brand.

Defining the brand's sound identity is a critical step in creating a compelling and memorable soundscape branding strategy for your shopping mall. It helps in crafting a unique and consistent audio experience that reinforces your brand's values and connects with your target audience.

To enhance the customer experience, you need to curate playlists with a mix of music and sound effects. We consider the preferences of the target audience and ensure that the playlists are regularly updated to stay current. This allows us to create playlists that can be adapted for different seasons and special events. For example, we create playlists specifically for holidays, sales events, or cultural celebrations to enhance the shopping experience. We customize playlists for different zones within the mall: music and sounds in the food court, fashion and entertainment areas should be in line with the specific environment and customer expectations of each zone. We regularly update and rotate playlists to keep the soundscape fresh and engaging: Stale or repetitive music can put shoppers off. Let's make sure that the songs and soundscapes we choose are consistent with the brand identity we're proposing: They should reinforce the brand's values and personality. Then let's look at the volume levels and acoustics in the different areas of the mall: It is important to ensure that the music and sounds are not too loud or intrusive and that they provide a pleasant background atmosphere. For this reason, it may be necessary to implement sound insulation techniques to prevent the spread of sound between different areas of the shopping center. This ensures that the soundscape of each zone remains distinct and does not interfere with adjacent areas. By using acoustic materials and design elements that help absorb excess sound, we can reduce echo and create a more pleasant listening environment. Investing in audio systems with dynamic volume control allows us to adjust sound levels according to factors such as time of day or customer density. Regularly test and monitor sound levels and acoustics to ensure they meet desired standards. Feedback from shoppers can be invaluable. Balancing customized playlists with adequate volume and acoustics is crucial to creating a pleasant and engaging soundscape in your mall: Enhance the overall shopping experience by strengthening your brand identity.

Incorporating interactive and engaging elements, along with seasonal and event-based themes, into your soundscape branding strategy for shopping malls can significantly enhance the overall shopping experience. One way to achieve this is by hosting live music performances, such as acoustic sets, bands, or solo artists, in common areas. This not only captivates shoppers but also creates a unique atmosphere. Moreover, integrating interactive installations or art pieces that respond to sound or movement provides an immersive and engaging experience for visitors. To serve specific purposes, consider using soundscapes like guided meditation sessions for relaxation, trivia games with sound cues, or sound art that complements the mall's theme. Encouraging shopper participation in creating soundscapes adds another layer to the experience. This can be facilitated through interactive kiosks allowing visitors to choose songs or sound effects, or even contribute to a communal playlist. Audio tours guiding shoppers through the mall, sharing interesting facts, store highlights, or historical information through headphones or smartphone apps, are also effective.

Tailoring the soundscape to match various holidays and seasons further enhances the strategy. For example, incorporating holiday music, sound effects, and themed announcements during Christmas, Halloween, or Valentine's Day. Adjusting the soundscape to suit different seasons, such as upbeat and lively music for summer or cozy and comforting tunes for winter, contributes to a dynamic environment. Creating special soundscape themes for sales events, like Black Friday or back-to-school promotions, involves using high-energy music and sound effects to build excitement. Recognizing and celebrating cultural events and festivals relevant to your target audience, and incorporating associated music and sounds, is another impactful approach. Additionally, using sound to highlight new store openings, special discounts, or exclusive offers during events is effective. Designing specific areas with unique soundscape themes that align with the event or season, such as a beach-themed area during summer or a winter wonderland during the holiday season, further enriches the shopping experience. By integrating interactive elements and seasonal/event-based themes into your soundscape branding strategy, you create a more dynamic and engaging shopping environment. These elements not only increase foot traffic but also encourage longer dwell times, making the shopping mall experience memorable for visitors.

Furthermore, testing and gathering feedback, as well as providing training and raising staff awareness, are crucial aspects of maintaining a successful soundscape branding strategy in shopping malls. Regularly conduct surveys and questionnaires among shoppers to assess their perceptions of the soundscape. Ask about the music, volume levels, and the overall ambiance. Organize focus groups to obtain in-depth insights from shoppers. Their feedback can help you understand how the soundscape impacts their shopping experience, utilizing data analytics to track shopper behavior and engagement. Monitor metrics like dwell time, foot traffic, and sales during different soundscapes and events. Monitor social media and online reviews to gauge public opinion about your soundscape branding. Respond to comments and reviews to show that you value shopper feedback. Employ mystery shoppers who can provide anonymous feedback on the shopping experience, including their impressions of the soundscape. Experiment with different soundscapes in controlled A/B tests to determine which ones resonate best with your target audience. Regularly audit the sound systems and acoustics to ensure that they meet the desired quality and standards.

Train your staff to understand the importance of the soundscape in enhancing the shopping experience. They should be able to assist in maintaining the desired atmosphere. Provide training to your staff, including store employees and mall management, on the importance of the soundscape in enhancing the shopping experience. They should be aware of the soundscape branding strategy and its impact. Train staff to respond to shopper inquiries or concerns related to the soundscape. They should be equipped to handle questions about music choices and sound volume. Ensure that staff members understand the importance of maintaining brand consistency in their interactions and the soundscapes throughout the mall. Train staff on emergency protocols related to the soundscape, such as how to handle technical issues or volume adjustments in case of customer complaints. Foster clear communication channels with staff, so they can report issues related to the soundscape promptly. Encourage them to share customer feedback. Educate staff on the sensory aspects of the shopping experience, emphasizing that the soundscape is just as important as visual elements. Staff members can actively participate in events and activations related to the soundscape, helping to engage shoppers and create a memorable experience. By continuously testing, gathering feedback, and providing training and awareness to your staff, you can fine-tune your soundscape branding strategy, adapt to changing customer preferences, and ensure that the soundscape remains an asset to the overall shopping experience in your mall.

By following these steps and creating a unique and engaging soundscape, you can strengthen your shopping mall's brand identity and provide an enjoyable and memorable experience for shoppers.

CONCLUSION

In today's ever-evolving world of marketing and consumer engagement, the use of soundscapes to design branded environments has emerged as a powerful and innovative strategy. The integration of auditory elements to shape the atmosphere and character of physical spaces, such as retail stores, shopping malls, and hospitality venues, has proved to be a game-changer in creating memorable and immersive customer experiences. Sound, as an essential component of our sensory perception, possesses a unique ability to evoke emotions, trigger memories, and establish a strong connection between brands and consumers. The strategic use of soundscapes enables businesses to tell their stories, communicate their values, and differentiate themselves from competitors. It transforms the ordinary into the extraordinary, turning a mundane shopping trip into a journey through a carefully curated world of sensory delights.

One of the most remarkable aspects of soundscape branding is its adaptability. A well-designed soundscape can be tailored to meet the specific goals and objectives of a brand, making it versatile and suitable for a wide range of applications. Whether it's the serenity of a spa, the high-energy excitement of a sports event, or the cozy ambiance of a coffee shop, soundscapes have the power to transport customers into a realm that aligns seamlessly with the brand's identity and messaging. Crucially, soundscape branding is not limited to playing music but extends to encompass a broader spectrum of auditory elements, including ambient sounds, sound effects, voiceovers, and interactive features. This multidimensional approach enables brands to craft a comprehensive and holistic experience that resonates with their audience. It is a world where the sound of footsteps, birdsong, or a barista's steaming milk can be as significant as the music playlist.

Beyond creating an immersive environment, soundscapes have the potential to significantly impact consumer behavior. From influencing dwell time in retail stores to enhancing the perception of a brand's quality and value, the strategic use of sound adds another layer to the overall customer journey. This impact is evident in studies revealing how specific music tempos can influence shopping speed, or how a well-crafted playlist can lead to increased sales in a retail setting. Furthermore, soundscape branding offers a unique opportunity to adapt to changing seasons, holidays, and special events. By incorporating seasonal and event-based themes into the soundscape, brands can connect with customers on a deeper level, creating a sense of anticipation and excitement that brings them back for more.

In conclusion, the evolution of soundscape branding signifies a dynamic shift in the way businesses approach customer engagement. It underscores the significance of sensory experiences in our modern world, where consumers seek meaningful and memorable interactions with brands. By thoughtfully crafting soundscapes that align with their brand identity, values, and goals, businesses can transform physical spaces into emotionally resonant environments, leaving an indelible mark in the hearts and minds of their customers. As technology continues to advance and consumer expectations evolve, it is evident that soundscape branding will remain a valuable and relevant strategy for businesses seeking to create authentic and compelling branded environments. It is, without a doubt, a harmonious symphony of innovation and emotion that sets the stage for the brands of the future.

REFERENCES

Ali, S., Mishra, M., & Javed, H. M. U. (2021). The impact of mall personality and shopping value on shoppers' well-being: Moderating role of compulsive shopping. *International Journal of Retail & Distribution Management*, *49*(8), 1178–1197. doi:10.1108/IJRDM-07-2020-0272

Alnuman, N., & Altaweel, M. Z. (2020). Investigation of the Acoustical Environment in A Shopping Mall and Its Correlation to the Acoustic Comfort of the Workers. *Applied Sciences (Basel, Switzerland)*, *10*(3), 1170. doi:10.3390/app10031170

Alvarsson, J. J., Wiens, S., & Nilsson, M. E. (2010). Stress recovery during exposure to nature sound and environmental noise. *International Journal of Environmental Research and Public Health*, *7*(3), 1036–1046. doi:10.3390/ijerph7031036 PMID:20617017

Axelsson, Ö., Nilsson, M. E., & Berglund, B. (2010). A principal components model of soundscape perception. *The Journal of the Acoustical Society of America*, *128*(5), 2836–2846. doi:10.1121/1.3493436 PMID:21110579

Brown, A. L. (2012). A review of progress in soundscapes and an approach to soundscape planning. *International Journal of Acoustics and Vibration*, *17*(2), 73–81. doi:10.20855/ijav.2012.17.2302

Ciaburro, G. (2021, July). Recycled materials for sound absorbing applications. []. Trans Tech Publications Ltd.]. *Materials Science Forum*, *1034*, 169–175. doi:10.4028/www.scientific.net/MSF.1034.169

Ciaburro, G. (2021). Deep Learning Methods for Audio Events Detection. Machine Learning for Intelligent Multimedia Analytics: Techniques and Applications, 147-166.

Ciaburro, G., & Iannace, G. (2021). Acoustic characterization of rooms using reverberation time estimation based on supervised learning algorithm. *Applied Sciences (Basel, Switzerland)*, *11*(4), 1661. doi:10.3390/app11041661

Dall'Ara, E., Dubois, D., & Fortin, D. (2018). The Effects of Music on Shopping Behavior: A Literature Review and Agenda for Future Research. In *Transformative Consumer Research for Personal and Collective Well-being* (pp. 101–115). Springer.

Dubois, D., & Gallet, P. (2011). The effects of background music on consumer behavior: A field experiment in a supermarket. *International Journal of Management and Marketing Research*, *4*(1), 61–72.

Dumyahn, S. L., & Pijanowski, B. C. (2011). Soundscape conservation. *Landscape Ecology*, *26*(9), 1327–1344. doi:10.1007/s10980-011-9635-x

El Hedhli, K., Chebat, J. C., & Sirgy, M. J. (2013). Shopping well-being at the mall: Construct, antecedents, and consequences. *Journal of Business Research*, *66*(7), 856–863. doi:10.1016/j.jbusres.2011.06.011

Elmashhara, M. G., & Soares, A. M. (2020). The influence of atmospherics general interior variables on shoppers' emotions and behavior. *International Review of Retail, Distribution and Consumer Research*, *30*(4), 437–459. doi:10.1080/09593969.2020.1724556

Garaus, M. (2017). Atmospheric harmony in the retail environment: Its influence on store satisfaction and re-patronage intention. *Journal of Consumer Behaviour*, *16*(3), 265–278. doi:10.1002/cb.1626

Gilstrap, C., Teggart, A., Cabodi, K., Hills, J., & Price, S. (2021). Social music festival brandscapes: A lexical analysis of music festival social conversations. *Journal of Destination Marketing & Management*, *20*, 100567. doi:10.1016/j.jdmm.2021.100567

Guéguen, N., Jacob, C., & Le Guellec, H. (2004). Sound level of environmental music and drinking behavior: A field experiment with beer drinkers. *Alcohol, Clinical and Experimental Research*, *28*(3), 349–351.

Hellström, B., Sjösten, P., Hultqvist, A., Dyrssen, C., & Mossenmark, S. (2011). Modelling the shopping soundscape. *Journal of Sonic Studies*, *1*(1).

Hultén, B. (2011). Sensory marketing: The multi-sensory brand-experience concept. *European Business Review*, *23*(3), 256–273. doi:10.1108/09555341111130245

Iannace, G., & Ciaburro, G. (2021). Modelling sound absorption properties for recycled polyethylene terephthalate-based material using Gaussian regression. *Building Acoustics*, *28*(2), 185–196. doi:10.1177/1351010X20933132

Iannace, G., Ianniello, C., & Ianniello, E. (2015). Music in an Atrium of a Shopping Center. *Acoustics Australia*, *43*(2), 191–198. doi:10.1007/s40857-015-0017-4

International Organization for Standardization. (2014). *ISO 12913-1: 2014 acoustics—Soundscape—part 1: definition and conceptual framework*. ISO.

Kellaris, J. J., Cox, A. D., & Cox, D. (1993). The effect of background music on ad processing: A contingency explanation. *Journal of Marketing*, *57*(4), 114–125. doi:10.1177/002224299305700409

Kent, T. (2003). 2D23D: Management and design perspectives on retail branding. *International Journal of Retail & Distribution Management*, *31*(3), 131–142. doi:10.1108/09590550310465503

Kesari, B., & Atulkar, S. (2016). Satisfaction of mall shoppers: A study on perceived utilitarian and hedonic shopping values. *Journal of Retailing and Consumer Services*, *31*(4), 22–31. doi:10.1016/j.jretconser.2016.03.005

Klingmann, A. (2010). *Brandscapes: Architecture in the experience economy*. Mit Press.

Konecni, V. J. (2008). Does music induce emotion? A theoretical and methodological analysis. *Psychology of Aesthetics, Creativity, and the Arts, 2*(2), 115–129. doi:10.1037/1931-3896.2.2.115

Korsmeyer, C., & Sutton, D. (2011). The sensory experience of food. *Food, Culture, & Society, 14*(4), 461–475. doi:10.2752/175174411X13046092851316

Kumar, A., & Kim, Y. K. (2014). The store-as-a-brand strategy: The effect of store environment on customer responses. *Journal of Retailing and Consumer Services, 21*(5), 685–695. doi:10.1016/j.jretconser.2014.04.008

Laitala, K., & Klepp, I. G. (2016). Musical shopping lists: Effects of songs with prosocial lyrics on shopping behavior. *Journal of Environmental Psychology, 46,* 24–30.

Lee, C. (2019). *Co-creating the brand modelling the perceived authenticity in a branded environment through co-creation* (Order No. 27737542). Available from ProQuest Dissertations & Theses Global. (2382062162). Retrieved from https://www.proquest.com/dissertations-theses/co-creating-brand-modelling-perceived/docview/2382062162/se-2

Lee, D. J., Sirgy, M. J., Larsen, V., & Wright, N. D. (2002). Developing a subjective measure of consumer well-being. *Journal of Macromarketing, 22*(2), 158–169. doi:10.1177/0276146702238219

Lee, H.-K., & Ahn, S. (2014, February 28). A Study on the Characteristics of Branded Environments in Hotel Spaces. Korean Institute of Interior Design Journal. Korean Institute of Interior Design. . doi:10.14774/JKIID.2014.23.1.143

Lindstrom, M. (1999). *Brand Sense: Sensory Secrets Behind the Stuff We Buy.* Simon & Schuster.

Lucas, M. R., Ayres, S., Santos, N., & Dionisio, A. (2021). Consumer experiences and values in Brazilian Northeast shopping centers. *Innovative Marketing, 17*(3), 1–16. doi:10.21511/im.17(3).2021.01

MacInnis, D. J., & Price, L. L. (1987). The role of imagery in information processing: Review and extensions. *The Journal of Consumer Research, 13*(4), 473–491. doi:10.1086/209082

Marques, S. H., Trindade, G., & Santos, M. (2016). The importance of atmospherics in the choice of hypermarkets and supermarkets. *International Review of Retail, Distribution and Consumer Research, 26*(1), 17–34. doi:10.1080/09593969.2015.1042495

Merrilees, B., Miller, D., & Shao, W. (2016). Mall brand meaning: An experiential branding perspective. *Journal of Product and Brand Management*, *25*(3), 262–273. doi:10.1108/JPBM-05-2015-0889

Mohammad Shafiee, M., & Es-Haghi, S. M. S. (2017). Mall image, shopping well-being and mall loyalty. *International Journal of Retail & Distribution Management*, *45*(10), 1114–1134. doi:10.1108/IJRDM-10-2016-0193

Moreno-Lobato, A., Di-Clemente, E., Hernández-Mogollón, J. M., & Campón-Cerro, A. M. (2023). How emotions sound. A literature review of music as an emotional tool in tourism marketing. *Tourism Management Perspectives*, *48*, 101154. doi:10.1016/j.tmp.2023.101154

Ng, C. F. (2003). Satisfying shoppers' psychological needs: From public market to cyber-mall. *Journal of Environmental Psychology*, *23*(4), 439–455. doi:10.1016/S0272-4944(02)00102-0

North, A. C., Hargreaves, D. J., & McKendrick, J. (1999). Instore music affects product choice. *Nature*, *400*(6740), 269.

Octaviani, R., Rizkiyani, D., Sudarsono, A. S., & Sarwono, S. J. (2021, August). Soundscape evaluation to identify audio visual aspects in café for student's activities. In *INTER-NOISE and NOISE-CON Congress and Conference Proceedings* (Vol. 263, No. 3, pp. 3845-3853). Institute of Noise Control Engineering. 10.3397/IN-2021-2539

Ozcevik, A., & Yuksel Can, Z. (2008). A study on the adaptation of soundscape to covered spaces: Part 2. *The Journal of the Acoustical Society of America*, *123*(5), 3812. doi:10.1121/1.2935537

Puccinelli, N. M., Goodstein, R. C., Grewal, D., Price, R., Raghubir, P., & Stewart, D. (2009). Customer experience management in retailing: Understanding the buying process. *Journal of Retailing*, *85*(1), 15–30. doi:10.1016/j.jretai.2008.11.003

Puyana-Romero, V., Ciaburro, G., Brambilla, G., Garzón, C., & Maffei, L. (2019). Representation of the soundscape quality in urban areas through colours. *Noise Mapping*, *6*(1), 8–21. doi:10.1515/noise-2019-0002

Puyana Romero, V., Maffei, L., Brambilla, G., & Ciaburro, G. (2016). Acoustic, visual and spatial indicators for the description of the soundscape of waterfront areas with and without road traffic flow. *International Journal of Environmental Research and Public Health*, *13*(9), 934. doi:10.3390/ijerph13090934 PMID:27657105

Puyana-Romero, V. P., Maffei, L., Brambilla, G., & Ciaburro, G. (2016). Modelling the soundscape quality of urban waterfronts by artificial neural networks. *Applied Acoustics*, *111*, 121–128. doi:10.1016/j.apacoust.2016.04.019

Sadeghian, M., Hanzaee, K. H., Mansourian, Y., & Khonsiavash, M. (2020). Investigation the effective factors on malls patronage: A qualitative research approach. *Revista Conrado*, *16*(72), 204–209.

Schafer, R. Murray (1977). The soundscape: our sonic environment and the tuning of the world. [United States]: Distributed to the book trade in the United States by American International Distribution.

Schafer, R. M. (1993). *The soundscape: Our sonic environment and the tuning of the world*. Simon and Schuster.

Seo, Y., & Maffioli, F. (2016). The impact of background music on adult consumers' shopping behavior: A meta-analysis. *Service Industries Journal*, *36*(1-2), 65–87.

Smith, P. J., & Curnow, R. (1966). Effects of background music on concentration of workers. *The Journal of Applied Psychology*, *50*(6), 493–496. PMID:5978043

Southworth, M. (2011). Sonic environment and spatial behavior. In *The Sonic Environment of Cities* (pp. 147–158). Routledge.

Spence, C. (2011, April). Sound design: Using brain science to enhance auditory & multisensory product & brand development. In (((ABA))) [Nomos Verlagsgesellschaft mbH & Co. KG.]. *Audio Branding Academy Yearbook*, *2010/2011*, 33–51.

Strang, V. (2005). Common senses: Water, sensory experience and the generation of meaning. *Journal of Material Culture*, *10*(1), 92–120. doi:10.1177/1359183505050096

Thompson, C. J., & Arsel, Z. (2004). The Starbucks brandscape and consumers' (anticorporate) experiences of glocalization. *The Journal of Consumer Research*, *31*(3), 631–642. doi:10.1086/425098

Thompson, E. (2002). The soundscape of modernity. Architectural acoustics and the culture of.

Trotta, F. (2020). *Annoying music in everyday life*. Bloomsbury Publishing USA. doi:10.5040/9781501360664

Wargnier, P., & Dubois, D. (2010). The impact of music on consumer behaviour: A literature review and preliminary findings. *International Journal of Management Reviews*, *12*(2), 207–230.

Wörfel, P., Frentz, F., & Tautu, C. (2022). Marketing comes to its senses: A bibliometric review and integrated framework of sensory experience in marketing. *European Journal of Marketing*, *56*(3), 704–737. doi:10.1108/EJM-07-2020-0510

Yalch, R. F., & Spangenberg, E. R. (1990). Effects of store music on shopping behavior. *Journal of Consumer Marketing*, *7*(2), 55–63. doi:10.1108/EUM0000000002577

Yu, B., Kang, J., & Ma, H. (2016). Development of indicators for the soundscape in urban shopping streets. *Acta Acustica united with Acustica*, *102*(3), 462–473. doi:10.3813/AAA.918965

Chapter 2
Luxury Shoppers' Experiences With Background Music:
Implications for Luxury Brand Management

Minna-Maarit Jaskari
https://orcid.org/0000-0002-5412-7176
University of Vaasa, Finland

Hannele Kauppinen-Räisänen
https://orcid.org/0000-0001-5341-2533
University of Helsinki, Finland

Marie-Nathalie Jauffret
https://orcid.org/0000-0002-6774-0244
International University of Monaco, Monaco

ABSTRACT

This chapter focuses on the impact of music on customers' shopping experiences, both in physical and online luxury retail service settings. It highlights the strategic importance of music in enhancing luxury brand experiences, underscoring the need for congruity between music and brand to avoid unfavourable outcomes. It builds on earlier research on the impact of background music in service settings. Two exploratory studies show how consumers understand the power of music to enhance brand image. The discussion emphasises the strategic role of music in luxury brand experiences, contributing valuable insights for luxury brand management.

DOI: 10.4018/979-8-3693-0778-6.ch002

INTRODUCTION

The influence of the retail environment on consumer behavior and brand experience has long been a topic of interest for both brand managers and academic researchers (Kotler, 1973; Turley & Milliman, 2000; Gustafsson, 2015; Joy et al., 2023). One particularly notable example that has garnered academic interest is the retail environment created by Hollister Co. (Stevens et al., 2019). Hollister Co. is a teen fashion company, and its retail environment builds on Southern Californian surfing culture. With the nightclub-like atmosphere, complete with loud music that muffles speech, strong fragrances, minimal, almost dark lighting, and visually appealing, minimally clothed staff, the company has aimed at attracting popular and cool kids and inviting an intense response from them (Stevens et al., 2019; Brown et al., 2018). Indeed, Hollister Co. presents a polarizing example that has sparked debate, simultaneously serving as an intriguing example of how retail environment and its atmospherics can be used to draw consumers' attention, convey brand image, influence consumer behavior, and stand out from competition (Joy et al., 2023; Lindstrom, 2005).

The existing body of research on retail atmospherics has identified multiple elements that have an impact on the overall experience, such as store layout, product representation, material features, and odors (Bitner, 1992; Turley & Milliman, 2000; Joy et al., 2023). An additional element is background music, which has received extensive scholarly attention over the decades (e.g., Chebat et al., 2001; Garlin & Owen, 2006; Morin et al., 2007; Hynes & Manson, 2016; Jain & Bagdare, 2011; Kellaris, 2008; Milliman, 1986). It has been studied in various retail contexts such as in supermarkets (North et al., 1999), restaurants (North et al., 2015), bars (Jacob, 2006), home electronics retail (Andersson et al., 2012), florists (Jacob et al., 2009), and banks (North et al., 2000), just to mention a few. Several studies' findings indicate that background music, or certain aspects of it, can influence consumers emotionally, cognitively, or behaviorally (e.g., Anderson et al., 2012; Beverland et al., 2006; North et al., 2015; Vida et al., 2007; Yalch & Spangenberg, 1990). Although research indicates that background music affects consumers, the findings are inconsistent, highlighting the need for further investigation into this topic (Garlin & Owen, 2006; Joy et al., 2023; Michel et al., 2017).

Music unquestionably plays an important role in shaping consumer experiences. It is implied to be a powerful tool for brand managers given its fairly immediate influence on consumer behavior (Bruner, 1990; Gustafsson, 2015; Jain et al., 2011; Oakes, 2000). Brand managers and academic research, have both recognized the importance of utilizing not only music strategically, but also sounds to effectively convey the brand. This is often referred to as sound or sonic branding (e.g., Gustafsson, 2019; Gustafsson, 2015; Jackson, 2003). To illustrate, the Finnish airline company

Finnair has built their soundscape on the brand's Nordic heritage, and explicitly apply sonic branding to convey a holistic brand experience. The touchpoints where consumers' experience soundscapes are for example onboard, in lounges, as hold music in phone calls, in marketing communication content, and in marketing campaigns (Finnair, 2023).

This chapter focuses on the impact of music on shopping experiences both in physical and online luxury retail environments. The study aims to address two identified shortcomings. First, despite extensive research on background music in various contexts, it is surprising that relatively little research has been conducted specifically within luxury retail environments. Still, the shopping experience in physical store is vital for the success of luxury brands (Kauppinen-Räisänen et al., 2020). Not surprisingly, engaging customers through memorable and delightful experiences has become a cornerstone of luxury management. As physical touchpoints for luxury brands, retail environments play a crucial role in shaping the consumer experience, offering unique opportunities to cultivate, strengthen, and celebrate brand relationships and engagement (Akaka et al., 2015; Dion & Borraz, 2017). Second, most studies investigating the effect of music on consumer behavior have focused on physical retail environment, whereby the online retail environment remains rather uncovered. Despite the fact, that luxury goods are increasingly purchased online, surprisingly, only a few studies have considered the impact of background music in online service settings (e.g., Hwang & Oh, 2020; Liu et al., 2013; Zhang et al., 2023).

This chapter contributes by showing how music ought to be considered strategically to ensure that the used music enhances the luxury brand experience in a holistic manner. For example, some earlier research has demonstrated that specific genres of music are better suited for particular types of stores, and any incongruity between brand and music can lead to unfavorable outcomes. Hence, the study findings support that music—in physical and online retail environments—ought to be considered from a branding point of view to ensure music-brand fit or congruity (Beverland et al., 2006; North et al., 2015).

The chapter proceeds as follows: First, the earlier literature on the impact of background music in service settings is briefly discussed, and the need for additional research in the luxury context is elaborated. Then, taking a qualitative approach, the two studies explore consumers' experiences of music in luxury retail environments. As a result, the chapter provides a holistic, yet nuanced understanding of customers' experiences and interpretations of background music in luxury retail environments. The discussion focuses on the outcomes from the standpoint of brand management. It emphasizes the significance of using music strategically in the co-creation of luxury brand experiences.

THE IMPACT OF BACKGROUND MUSIC ON CONSUMERS IN LUXURY SERVICE SETTING

In 1973, Kotler emphasized the importance of the physical retail environment in stimulating emotions, influencing cognitive processes, and impacting consumer behavior through various sensory elements. Kotler referred to this as atmospherics or the "quality of the surrounding space" (1973, p. 50). Booms and Bitner (1982) expanded Kotler's idea by defining the physical retail environment as a space where services are delivered and customers interact, including tangible items that facilitate the service process. Then Bitner (1992) introduced the concept of servicescape, which focuses on the physical surroundings of a service encounter and how it influences customers. Mossberg (2007), drawing inspiration from the experience era (Pine & Gilmore, 1999), coined the term "experiencescapes" to describe these environments. Rosenbaum and Massiah (2011) contributed with an expanded servicescape framework comprising physical, social, social-symbolic and natural dimensions. Not surprisingly, several research identify background music as an important part of the physical retail environment or servicescape (e.g. Line & Hanks, 2020).

Consumer Responses to Background Music in Service Settings

As pointed out above, background music is one of the major elements in physical atmospherics (Bitner, 1992; Kotler, 1973; Line & Hanks, 2020; Milliman & Fugate, 1993; Rosenbaum & Massiah, 2011). Research on the impact of music on consumers in retail and other service settings is extensive, and music is considered to be "the most commonly studied general interior cue" (Turley & Milliman, 2000, 195). Garlin and Owen's (2006) meta-analysis on background music in service settings found five types of dependent variables used in earlier studies. These were affective variables (such as arousal or pleasure), financial returns (such as value of sales or items purchased), attitude and perception (such as liking or brand loyalty), temporal effects (such as perceived versus actual waiting time), and behavioral variables (such as store choice or impulse behavior). Several researchers have tried to grasp this complex and often unconscious process, that is impacted by musical elements, the consumer, and the service setting in general (Joy et al., 2023; Michel et al., 2017).

There are varied perceptions regarding what constitutes the elements of music, with typical elements including tempo, harmony, tone, loudness, melody, and form. In this chapter, we review earlier studies in retail and service settings, focusing on tempo, harmony, tone and timbre, as well as loudness that are the elements typically studied background music settings. Moreover, we review studies focusing on the genre of music and explore the impact of both musical elements and diverse individual factors—such as demographics, personality, music preferences, and knowledge—on mediating consumer response. Through this, the review aims to highlight the complex role of music in influencing consumer behavior within retail settings.

Tempo: Feel the Beat?

Musical tempo is a component of rhythm and refers to the speed or rate at which a musical passage progresses (Oakes, 2000). While tempo is typically considered as part of rhythm with meter and beat (Schwartz & Krantz, 2017, p. 377), it is the most studied element of music in service setting. Milliman is frequently cited as one of the pioneering researchers who delved into the effects of background music on in-store shopping behavior (1982). His study specifically investigates the impact of background music tempo in in-store shopping behavior. Milliman (1982) developed an experimental design to look at how three different treatments affected the way people shopped in a supermarket: (1) no music, (2) slow music (less than 73 bpm), and (3) fast music (over 94 bpm). The results demonstrate how the tempo of background music in stores significantly affects both the movement pace of supermarket customers and the daily gross sales volume they purchase. The effect of musical tempo on customers in service settings is extensively studied, maybe because comparative, quantifiable measurement is straightforward, requiring the only use of a metronome to track or vary the number of beats per minute (Oakes, 2000). In their meta-analysis, Turley and Milliman conclude that the effect of tempo is highest for arousal while it is not always pleasurable (2000).

Several researchers criticize the oversimplification of tempo-related studies arguing that other musical elements such as harmony, timbre, or individuals' preference for music may impact the results (Herrington & Capella, 1996; Oakes, 2000). To illustrate, Kellaris and Kent (1991) examined how tempo interacts with other musical elements and concluded that tempo and harmony influenced consumer evaluations of the music's attractiveness interactively.

Harmony: The Dance Between Consonance and Dissonance

Musical harmony refers to the combination of musical notes to sound pleasing together. Pleasant harmony is produced through consonance, while dissonance refers to unpleasant disharmony (Schwartz & Krantz, 2017, p. 377). In practice, harmony pertains to the arrangement of chords and their progressions including one or several instruments and human voice. In Western music, harmony typically revolves around major and minor scales, with intentional deviations commonly found for example in jazz.

While harmony is much more than just major or minor key (mode), earlier research has typically focused on major and minor scales. For example, in their study, Kellaris and Kent (1991) discovered that the major mode was perceived as more aesthetically pleasing compared to both the minor mode and the dissonant wholetone scale.

In a subsequent study by Kellaris and Kent (1992), they identified a significant correlation between modality and perceived duration. Quite interestingly, when music was played in a major key, the duration was perceived to last the longest, followed by a minor key resulting shorter perceptions of time, and atonal music with shortest estimations of duration.

Although various researchers have explored modality, Oakes (2000) highlights that only the study by Kellaris and Kent (1992) recognized the potential interactive effects of other musical elements. In their study, they digitally modified the harmony of a composition while keeping other variables unchanged. This is an important notion and reminds of difficulty in studying only one musical element at a time. Indeed, in musical composition, harmony is constructed from a multitude of distinct elements. Each of these elements offers a plethora of variations. Consequently, there exists a vast array of possibilities when crafting a single harmonic structure. Given this complexity, investigating the influence of harmony on consumer behavior presents notable challenges.

Oakes (2000) posits that delving deeper into the impact of musical harmony on consumer responses is needed. He also suggests employing distinct musical techniques in advertising, such as transitioning from dissonance to consonance to symbolize the resolution of an issue, might influence consumer responses in manners that remain insufficiently explored in scholarly marketing research.

Tone and Timbre: You Can't Play Sad Songs with Banjo

The tone of sound refers to the fact that same note can sound different depending on where the sound comes from. It is closely related to harmony, scales, and chords. In composition, specific notes, chords, and chord progressions are used to evoke emotions (Bakker & Martin, 2015). To illustrate, specific chord progressions can be used to evoke for example melancholy, sadness, uplifting, happiness, and inspiration, typically combined with specific chord types, instruments, melodies, and rhythms.

Broemekier et al. (2008) studied whether two emotional tones of background music (happy or sad) or preference (liked or disliked) impacted consumers shopping intentions in a woman's clothing store context. In their mixed-method study combining survey and interviews, 126 female participants watched a 5-minute video of a typical store visit. After viewing the video, the respondents were asked questions about regarding the music and their intentions to shop in the store. The authors conclude that intentions to shop were higher if the participant perceived the music to be happy and if they liked the music.

Tone is closely related to timbre that refers to the identity of a particular musical instrument. Composers choose particular instruments in order to convey certain emotions since different instruments are more or less capable of representing different emotional tones (Hailstone et al., 2009). To illustrate, Hailstone et al. (2009), investigated how perception of emotions is influenced by altering the musical instrument on which the music is played. They recorded 40 novel melodies each representing one of four emotions (happiness, sadness, fear, or anger) on four different instruments (an electronic synthesizer, a piano, a violin, and a trumpet), controlling for melody, tempo, and loudness between instruments. 47 participants were asked to select which emotion they thought each musical stimulus represented and a significant interaction between instrument and emotion judgement was found with a similar pattern in young and older adults. In a second study, the interaction between timbre (instrument identity) and perceived emotion was replicated showing that timbre independently affected the perception of emotions.

To conclude, tone and timbre can be used to evoke certain emotions, yet surprisingly few studies have focused on the influence on tone and timbre in luxury retail environments.

Loudness of Music: Pump Up the Volume?

Loudness in music encompasses two distinct but related aspects: dynamics and volume. Dynamics refer to relative loudness and how loudness changes within musical composition (Schwartz & Krantz, 2017, p. 377) Also, when the music is presented live, the orchestra uses dynamics to express the message of the music. Volume, on the other hand, refers to actual auditory level at which music is played. In most service settings, volume can be readily adjusted by managers or staff, and in extreme cases, it can even be muted entirely.

According to Michel et al. (2017), musical volume has mixed impact of customers, potentially due to service settings. For example, Morrison et al. (2011) report positive effects on consumer satisfaction in clothing store whereas North et al. (2020) reported that loud music impacted service setting evaluation negatively. Moreover, Herrington and Cappella (1996) concluded that customers were not impacted by the volume of the background music in a supermarket. Smith and Curnow (1966) studied the impact of soft and loud music on the shopping duration in supermarkets, and their results indicated that the use of loud music resulted in shorter shopping times among consumers. To conclude, the earlier research has inconclusive results on how loudness impacts customers (Michel et al., 2017; Oakes, 2000). It can be suggested that loudness is a situational and contextual variable, and its perception is dependent on other variables, such as store type.

Genre: Should We Jazz It Up?

Moving on from distinct music elements to combination of those, musical genre is probably the most used way to categorize music (Aucouturier & Pachet, 2003). However, musical genre itself is not well-defined and there are several ways to define musical genres, ranging from a few global genres to hundreds of sub-genres (Pachet & Cazaly, 2000). While some pieces of music are easy to categorize as representing one genre, much of contemporary music does not obey these rules. It is obvious that musical genre itself is not a clear-cut categorization, and the boundaries between different music genres are blurred, unclear and partly overlapping. For example, classical music pieces are not only played in classical music genre, but other genres as well, ranging from jazz to metal. Thus, musical genres should be considered more as guiding principles. Still, genres are a good way to think about music-brand fit and understand, what kind of music would foster the brand message.

Despite this challenge in defining musical genres, consumers perceive musical genre enhancing certain aspects of the brand or service experience (Beverland et al., 2006). Thus, it is not surprising that several researchers have studied how different genres of music impact consumers in service settings (Oakes, 2000). For example, North et al. (2000) studied the effect of background music on customers' perception of the atmosphere in two contexts: a banking hall and a city bar. Their focus was on the genre of the music. In the first study, classical music, easy-listening music, and no music were played over the course of 3 weeks. 331 participants were asked to rate the characteristics of the banking hall in which it was played as well as the music in terms of 20 adjectives using an 11-point scale. Customers' responses indicated a positive correlation between ratings of the banking hall and the music on each of the scales. In the second study, contemporary British pop, classical music, or no-music was played over the course of nine days. Similarly, to the previous study, customers (328) rated both the atmosphere and the music played there in terms of 11 adjectives using an 11-point scale. There was a positive correlation between ratings of the atmosphere and ratings of the music. The authors conclude that based on their findings, music can have a direct influence on the major dimensions along which customers perceive the atmosphere of a commercial environment.

North et al. (1999) studied also how stereotypical French or German music influenced supermarket customers' choices of French and German wines in the United Kingdom. French and German folk music were played in the study setting, with the acoustic dominating the French music and the Bierkeller band dominating the German music. Over a two-week period, the music was played on alternate days from an in-store display of French and German wines. 82 people took part in the study and completed a survey after selecting their wine. The findings suggest that music influences customers' product choices, as French music increased sales of French wines, and German music increased sales of German wines.

Musical genres that are studied in background music research are not many, and include mostly generic genres, such as classical music (Areni & Kim, 1993; North et al., 1999; Grewal et al., 2003, North et al., 2015), pop music (Jacob et al., 2009; Sweeney & Wyber, 2002; North et al., 2000), Top 40/Pop (Areni & Kim, 1993; Jacob et al., 2006), easy listening (North et al., 2000), instrumental (North & Hargreaves, 1996; Yalch & Spangenberg, 1993), stereotypical (North et al., 1999; Jacob, 2006; Jacob et al., 2009), New Age (North & Hargreaves, 1996; Yalch & Spangenberg, 1993), jazz (Wilson, 2003, North et al., 2000), and absence of music (e.g., Jacob et al., 2009; Grewal et al., 2003; North & Hargreaves, 1996).

In their literature review Michel et al. (2017) conclude that musical genre often has mixed effects on customer's affective states but seem to have positive effects on customer's behavior. More specifically, they argue that classical music and top 40 music often have a beneficial impact on the customer's responses compared to easy listening or jazz music.

However, the earlier research on the effect of musical genre on consumers is inconclusive. The lack of consensus in findings might stem from several factors, including the intricate nature of musical genres or individual tastes. For instance, Rentfrow and Gosling (2003) discovered that factors like personality, self-perception, and cognitive abilities play a role in shaping musical preferences across fourteen distinct genres. Lately, Greenberg et al. (2023) coined personality traits and musical styles, for example "extraversion" was correlated with contemporary musical styles whereas "openness" was correlated with sophisticated musical styles.

Individual Factors Moderating the Impact of Music

Indeed, while music has an impact on consumers, it is typically moderated by individual factors such as demographic variables (Yalch & Spangenberg, 1993), personality traits (Greenberg et al., 2003), knowledge of music, familiarity of music (North et al., 1997) and preference for music (Greenberg et al., 2003; Rentfrow & Gosling, 2003). It is also suggested that gender may be a moderating factor on music volume, but results are contradictory and suggestive (Kellaris & Altsech, 1992; Kellaris & Rice, 1993).

As the studies described above illustrate consumers' reactions to background music are researched from various perspectives. However, it is evident that music is multidimensional and complex that presents difficulties when it comes to understanding how it influences consumer behavior. One of the main challenges is that music rarely impacts in isolation but rather in conjunction with other senses. Indeed, multi-modal integration pertains to how sensory systems operate in conjunction, forming a holistic experience through several senses, all stimuli assessed together (Bitner, 1992; Gustafsson, 2015; Joy et al., 2023).

The cross-modal associations between music and taste have received a great deal of scholarly attention. Just to illustrate some, North (2012) studied the effect of background music on the taste of wine. In his study, 250 subjects received either a glass of red wine or a glass of white wine. The subjects were asked to drink the wine within five minutes in one of five rooms. In each of the five rooms, different background music was playing: (a) Carmina Burana - Orff (powerful and heavy), (b) Waltz of the Flowers - Tchaikovsky (subtle and refined), (c) Just Can not Get Enough - Nouvelle Vague (zingy and refreshing), (d) Slow Breakdown - Michael Brook (soft and mellow), e) and a room with no music. After wine tasting, the subjects were asked to judge the taste of the wine on the scales of (a) powerful and heavy, (b) subtle and refined, (c) zingy and refreshing, and (d) soft and mellow. Based on their results, the evaluation of the taste of the wine corresponded to the nature of the music, exemplifying the multi-modal integration of taste and sound. In a similar vein, Kontukoski et al. (2015) studied cross-modal associations between music and taste and found that exposure to "sweet" or "sour" musical pieces impacted participants food-relating thinking processes and behaviours.

From Physical Stores to Online Settings

Most of the studies on background music in service settings have predominantly focused on physical retail environments. However, there are some notable exceptions in the digital realm. For instance, Ding and Lin (2012) found that the tempo of background music positively influences consumer arousal in online commerce. A more recent study by Zhang et al. (2023) delved into the effects of background music placement in live-streaming commerce, specifically within the fashion sector. Their findings indicated that background music enhances both consumer arousal and purchase intentions. Interestingly, continuous music playback throughout the live stream heightened arousal, whereas playing music specifically during the purchasing phase was linked to elevated purchase intentions.

As the review above illustrates, there is extensive research on the impact of background music on consumers affect, cognition, and behavior, even if the results are not conclusive. The main limits of these studies lies in the assumption that consumer reactions are uniform or that certain elements can be detached from the holistic consumer experience (e.g., Joy et al., 2023). One way to understand the experience more fully is to give the consumer a voice through qualitative research. Indeed, since most of the earlier studies used a quantitative approach, consumers' reception, interpretation, and meaning making are, to a great extent, lacking from the earlier research (Gustafsson, 2019).

From the brand management perspective, previous studies provide consistent evidence of the importance of musical fit to service setting and brand experience (Michel et al., 2017; Yeoh & North, 2010; Broekemier et al., 2008; Beverland et al., 2006; North & Hargreaves, 1998). One of the special service settings is luxury. While the shopping experience is often at the heart of luxury, and there are several studies conducted on luxury shopping experience (Shahid et al., 2022; Kauppinen-Räisänen et al., 2020; Kauppinen-Räisänen et al., 2019; Dion & Borraz, 2017), no studies on the role of music in the luxury shopping experience has been undertaken to the best of the authors' knowledge.

Luxury Shopping Experience

Factors driving positive shopping experiences are diverse, encompassing aspects like product range, security, and overall atmosphere (Singh & Prashar, 2014; Terblanche, 2018; Wu et al., 2014). However, it is important to note that these experiences are not uniform across different consumption settings. For instance, experiences in restaurants, hotels, and various retail types can vary considerably (Singh & Prashar, 2014; Terblanche, 2018; Wu et al., 2014). Furthermore, these experiences are closely linked to eliciting customer delight. Such delightful experiences are not confined to a specific stage but can emerge throughout the consumption process, whether it is during shopping or while visiting establishments, including luxury stores (Voorhees et al., 2017).

Essentially, both physical and online stores hold crucial role in shaping the consumer experiences with luxury brands. Indeed, store environments present unique opportunities to craft delightful encounters for consumers (Shahid et al., 2022; Akaka et al., 2015). Evidently, it is not sufficient anymore to merely meet customer expectations, as today's consumers increasingly crave positive, standout experiences (Zomerdijk & Voss, 2010). Moreover, it is well acknowledged that luxury consumption extends beyond simply owning branded goods (Cristini et al., 2017; Gummerus et al., 2023; Kauppinen-Räisänen et al., 2019). Hence, creating captivating and positive experiences that attract and emotionally engage customers have become a crucial aspect of luxury stores and a key aspect of luxury management (Dion & Borraz, 2017).

Kauppinen-Räisänen et al. (2020) focused on the drivers of positive shopping experiences in physical luxury stores, and detected those customers felt that such experiences where made of extraordinary service excellence, unique multi-sensory emotional stimulation conforming to the brand, and a feeling of personal importance and assurance. That study stressed the importance of acknowledging that the experience is made of various elements and understanding these enables the luxury brand owner to create an environment that allows the customer to be immersed into the brand universe and live a delightful experience.

Recently, Shahid et al. (2022) investigated the causal effect of sensory marketing cues and brand experience on emotional attachment and subsequent brand loyalty in a luxury service setting. Based on the results they conclude that sensory cues positively enhance retail brand experience, leading to increasing emotional attachment and brand loyalty. Music was one variable within acoustics in sensory marketing scale adapted from (Wiedmann et al., 2018) including items such as music being nice to listen, soundscape being pleasant, sound being wonderful and having appealing tones. However, their study doesn't have an explicit focus on music keeping the sensory clues on aggregate level. Indeed, similarly to earlier studies, this study emphasizes how consumers perceive the service setting holistically. For example, Wiedmann et al. (2018) studied the multisensory marketing in the context of luxury hotels concluding that multisensory marketing is an important way to influence brand experience and sensory cues (visual, acoustic, haptic, olfactory, and gustatory) need to used together and in relation to each other in order to enhance a holistic experience.

While we agree with the holistic formation of consumer experience, we underline that music is one of the sensory elements contributing to customers' luxury experience serving as a symbol, and a cue for luxury (Kauppinen-Räisänen et al. 2020; Wiedmann et al., 2018).

When it comes to music genres specifically, classical music is frequently associated with luxury, affluence, and class (Yeoh & North, 2010) not only in retail environments but also in advertisements and in product design. For example, Yeoh et al. (2022), studied the influence of classical music, pop music, sound effects and silence on consumers' perception of a high-end luxury sports car. Participants perceived the car's power, driving excitement and engine technology to be highest when the ad was paired with sound effects. They also perceived the car to be most elegant and indicated the highest price for the car when the ad was paired with classical music. In the context of product sound research, Lageat et al. (2003) studied the perception of luxury sounds, where participants rated eight different lighters on the luxury attribute. Interestingly, in their study, two different customer segments were identified in the context of lighters: for the first segment, luxury was associated with the sound of matte, even, and low in pitch, while the other segment perceived luxury sound as clear, resonant, and clicking. Although the results suggest that individuals associate specific sounds with luxury, they also emphasize the subjective nature of evaluating both sound and luxury.

While earlier studies frequently associated classical music with luxury, interestingly the relationship between luxury clothing brands and hip-hop culture has evolved over time. To illustrate, brands like Balenciaga and Louis Vuitton working with Kanye West, Saint Laurent's and Dior's collaboration with Travis Scott, Prad and Franck Ocean have tapped into hip-hop culture to appeal to youthful audiences, while in November 2018, the collaboration of Chanel and Pharell Williams under the supervision of Karl Lagerfleld, drew inspiration from hip-hop aesthetics, showcasing its influence in high-end and luxury fashion brands. This luxury-hip-hop coexistence manifests in various ways: luxury brands becoming staples in hip-hop culture, the integration of brand names into song lyrics, and collaborations between luxury brands and hip-hop celebrities (Polfuß, 2022).

In conclusion the existing literature offers substantial insights into the role of background music in service settings, although the findings are not always conclusive (Oakes, 2000). Many studies have primarily focused on using a quantitative approach to examine the impact of certain musical components on consumer behavior, whereby past studies tend to overlook the subjective opinions and experiences of consumers when it comes to background music in a servicescape. Recognizing that consumers experience the servicescape holistically, it is crucial to delve deeper into their subjective interpretations.

Moreover, the customer experience in luxury retail is undeniably vital for the success of luxury brands (Kauppinen-Räisänen et al., 2020). However, there is a noticeable gap in research concerning the role of background music within the context of luxury retail environments. Additionally, much of the research on background music is centered around physical retail environments. Yet, with the evolving digital age, many customer interactions, if not all, are shifting to or incorporating online channels. This includes the purchase of luxury items (Liu et al., 2013). Therefore, to understand consumers' evaluation of background music in luxury servicescape, online service setting cannot be overlooked.

METHOD

To comprehend how consumers perceive and interpret the significance of music within luxury retail environments, two separate explorative studies were conducted. The first study concentrated on revealing consumer experiences of the integration of music into luxury shopping in a physical store. The second study delved into the experiences for music in luxury online store and its congruence with luxury brand image. The ensuing sections provide a detailed description of each study.

Study 1: Consumer Experiences of Music in Luxury Shopping Experiences

The first explorative study utilized a qualitative approach to delve into consumers' experiences of sonic experiences in a physical luxury retail environment. Data was collected through face-to-face semi-structured interviews complemented by a photo elicitation technique. To prompt imaginative thinking and discussions about luxury, interviewees were shown collages of photographs depicting luxury stores. An interview guide, which included open-ended questions about the luxury shopping experience, was developed to sought insights into elements of the store that shape experiential experiences. Notably, terms such as sound, music, or sonic were purposefully omitted to assess participants' innate awareness of the sound environment.

The study was based on 97 interviews with purposefully selected respondents who could offer in-depth insights into the subject. The target was luxury consumers who, at a minimum, occasionally consumed and engaged with luxury brands. Data collection took place in the Principality of Monaco, an apt a suitable location for the research. The interviews lasted 30 minutes on average and were recorded and transcribed.

The analysis of the data began with a close reading of the interviews and extracting parts where sounds were discussed. Further, the analysis focused on analyzing what was mentioned about the sound and how it was discussed.

Study 2: Consumers' Experiences and Evaluations of Music in the Online Luxury Shopping Experience

The second exploratory study was inspired by the findings of the initial study. For the second study, we simulated an online shopping scenario. International respondents were informed that they had secured a gift card valued at 500 euros for a French luxury online store. Their task was to allocate this hypothetical sum on their desired purchases. To gather data on their shopping experience and, specifically, their perceptions of background music, we employed a self-report methodology. Respondents made the task on their own time. They were guided through the process with a comprehensive script, and their feedback was captured using a semi-structured interview guide.

We recruited respondents and divided them into three distinct groups. The first group shopped without any predefined background music; however, they were prompted to indicate if any music played during their shopping experience. The second group were asked to play a song "Don't be so shy - so shy" by the French singer Imamy in the background at a slow pace (80 bpm). Further, the third group listened to the same track but at a faster tempo (120 bpm). We selected this particular song not only because it is sung in English, but also due to its representation of the contemporary French chanson style, making it a fitting choice for the ambiance of a French luxury brand. The music was delivered to the participants through online link.

Following the online shopping simulation, respondents were encouraged to provide open-ended feedback about their experience. To aid in illustrating their navigation patterns, they were advised to capture and include screenshots as they browsed through web pages. In the end, they were prompted to specifically comment on the presence or absence of background music. The written reports were sent online to the researcher after completing the report.

In terms of demographics, our sample comprised 30 respondents: 9 in a non-music context, 10 exposed to slow music, and 11 to fast-paced music. Gender distribution revealed 25 females and 5 males. The participants' ages varied between 20 and 49, with an average age of 34,5.

Unlike in the first study, background music was explicitly presented to those groups instructed to listen to music. This discrepancy does not undermine our study's objectives, as we aim not to directly analyze the influence of background music on participants' behavior, but rather to understand the significance of music more comprehensively in their overall experience. Also, participants were unaware that the music varied between groups. Thus, data is well-suited for the study.

As with the first data, the analysis began with a close reading of the reports. Further, the analysis aimed to discern similarities and differences in how the participants described their shopping experiences, considering the three distinct musical settings.

FINDINGS

Study 1

The significance of music, both broadly and specifically within a luxurious servicescape, was affirmed by our findings. Notably, nearly 15% of our international respondents (14 out of 97) referenced music or related sonic elements when discussing factors that enhance the luxury in-store experience. This observation becomes even more remarkable considering that participants were never directly prompted to comment on music.

The primary discovery was that music emerged as a pivotal element shaping the experiential experiences of both the luxury retail environments and the overall shopping experience. The analysis revealed—above all—aspects related to the antecedents, influences and consequences of music as a means of such experiences.

Music manifested as a nuanced expression of quality, characterized by tone (e.g., soft music, calm music), genre (e.g., old music), volume (e.g., quiet music), and subjective interpretations (e.g., good music). The analysis showed that these quality expressions function as antecedents as they have emotional influences. These expressions evoked pleasure, but—above all—caused an emotional state characterized by the absence of arousal "[…] brings comfort and relaxing atmosphere […]", "[…] I always feel relaxed, comfortable, and safe […]" and "[…] I feel relaxed because of the music […]".

Interestingly, while the absence of stress was mentioned, some participants specifically mentioned their desire to spend more time in such a musical environment. This suggests behavioral consequences, particularly in terms of duration of stay. Indeed, consistent with this observation, previous research has highlighted how background music affects the time consumers spend in retail environments (e.g., Milliman 1982; 1986). Moreover, past research also suggests that time has an impact on shopping expenditure (Caldwell & Hibbert 1999; Jain & Bagdare, 2011; Vida et al., 2007). While background music can influence consumer experience regardless of whether it is consciously noticed or not, our findings indicate that some consumers are intentionally drawn to retail environments with intriguing soundscapes.

While many of the responses were positive, there were also some negative reactions. Predominantly, these negative comments revolved around the volume of the music, often described as "noise" or "noisy music." Such loud or intrusive music was perceived as unpleasant, prompting comments like "don't want to continue shopping…". These findings are aligned with Michel et al. (2017) who concluded that musical volume may have mixed impact on customers.

Study 2

The findings of the second study—luxury online store—reinforce the significance of brand-music fit - aligning music with a brand's identity and the varied ways in which music can shape the shopping experience.

Some respondents expressed a favorable sentiment towards the inclusion of music in online shopping experiences. One of the participants commented, "it was pleasant, it gave me a good feeling and made me dream, I felt more focused". These respondents felt that the right choice of music brought added depth, evoking feelings reminiscent of brick-and-mortar shopping and enhancing their online browsing atmosphere. As one participant shared, "I liked the particular music, and it instantly brought a good feeling; the music led me to daydream," highlighting the potential for music to create a positive, immersive shopping ambiance. Also, background music was able to bring the real store closer to the customer as illustrated by one respondent, "The background music brought a new aspect to online shopping and made me feel that I was in a real store or otherwise closer to the brand."

While some respondents were positive, others expressed reservations with the idea of music in online stores. For some, the concern was primarily about the potential for poorly chosen tracks to disrupt and even hinder their shopping experience. For example, one of the respondents commented, "The melancholic music conflicted with colourful and individualistic products" as well as other responded shared, "At first, the music didn't evoke any images, but then it started to annoy, and I acted quickly to get out of the store." Some find music in general disturbing in retail stores: "Music is disturbing, both in online and clothing stores; it is okay in a grocery store." This suggests that while music can be an enhancement, it also carries the risk of becoming a deterrent if not implemented thoughtfully, as mentioned by a respondent, "this was first good but was it too melancholic after a while."

Finally, some respondents had a more neutral or conditional stance on the matter. They were neither strictly for nor against the idea of music in online stores but expressed that its value depended on factors like personal taste and the ability to control the audio. The sentiment of wanting to have control over the music was prevalent, with comments such as "Should be able to choose myself," or "I doubt that musical tastes are so different, it is hard to find suitable music", indicate that while some are open to the idea, they would prefer to have agency over their auditory experience.

Respondents often linked luxury brands with sophisticated musical genres such as classical and instrumental pieces, particularly those featuring the piano. Timeless compositions like Chopin's Spring Waltz and Nocturne Op. 9 emerged as favorites, complementing the refined aura of high-end brands. Jazz, especially styles evoking Parisian vibes, was also popular, enhancing feelings of exclusivity. While opera added a touch of grandeur, it is worth noting that the perfect musical fit might vary from brand to brand, reflecting their unique identities. To illustrate, one respondent commented, "The music should be more calm and prestigious - now the music is confusing, it does not fit Hermes."

The tempo played a significant role in shaping the respondent's experience and perception of the brand, with both slow and fast tempos evoking distinct reactions. For some, slower tempos evoked feelings of calm and concentration, yet for others, it intensified irritations, especially when juxtaposed with high prices or the brand's image. Conversely, fast-paced music was met with varied reactions; while certain respondents appreciated its energizing nature, others felt it rushed their shopping experience or misaligned with their perception of luxury. Moreover, for those exposed to faster tempos, there was a perceived alignment between the music and the online store's vibrant visual aesthetics, termed as music-visual appearance congruency.

DISCUSSION

Based on the results from the two exploratory studies, it is evident that music and sounds have an impact on consumers' experiences. In general, background music and sounds can be purposefully curated to be atmospheric, or they can be unintentional like street noise (Hynes & Manson, 2016). Due to this influence, brand management must treat soundscapes as strategic tools, not just as an afterthought. It is not just about choosing a playlist; it is about aligning auditory details with the brand's identity to create a harmonious and memorable brand experience throughout the customer journey.

Our findings are aligned with prior research which emphasizes the significance of music as a vital sensory cue in physical retail environments. However, the online landscape presents more challenges. In contrast to a retail environment where consumers enter a pre-defined soundscape, the online realm intrudes into the consumer's personal space, often contending with an existing soundscape—for instance, the online shopper might already be playing their own music, have tv running on the background. Also, it may be that consumers don't have the sound on while browsing the online store. While our data suggests that music can have an impact on consumer experience in online service settings, managing this impact becomes inherently more complex due to these overlapping soundscapes.

Both studies illustrate how consumers highlight specific genres, they deem fitting for the brand. This suggests that consumers inherently understand the power of music to reinforce a brand's image. Particularly for luxury brands, respondents frequently associate them with genres such as mainstream jazz, French classical tunes, and instrumental tracks, with classical music standing out prominently. Previous research supports these associations, indicating that both luxury and genres like classical music are linked with attributes such as excellency, class, and affluence.

The findings stress the role of music-brand congruity and the multitudinous impact of music on the shopping experience. While there are clear, potentially stereotypical, associations between brand types, like luxury, and musical genres, such as classical music, these serve merely as a starting point for crafting a retail soundscape. More importantly, the chosen music should enhance the brand's identity. Indeed, deviating from these conventional associations can be an important strategic choice, aiming to offer a distinctive and unforgettable luxury brand experience.

Our research aligns with prior studies that highlight the influence of music tempo on customers' duration of stay and consumption habits (e.g. Oakes, 2000; Turley & Milliman, 2000). However, our findings delve deeper, uncovering nuanced interactions between music tempo and various sensory cues affecting customer experience. For example, respondents noted that faster-paced music complemented the visual aesthetics of an online store but simultaneously felt it rushed their shopping experience. Conversely, slower music was found to foster a more relaxed and focused retail environment, allowing customers to browse at a leisurely pace and affecting their perception of product pricing. These insights underscore the holistic nature of customers' subjective evaluations, emphasizing the interplay of multiple servicescape elements in shaping their overall shopping experience. For effective brand management, a comprehensive strategy that thoughtfully integrates all facets of the servicescape is essential.

CONCLUSION

This chapter has focused on background music in both physical and online luxury service settings and investigated its role in consumer experiences. Through two explorative studies, we shed light on the underlying experiences that consumers have concerning music in luxury experience. These experiences are intertwined with several factors: the overarching brand identity, the mood the brand wishes to evoke, the price points of the products, and even the visual aesthetics of the store or website. This highlights the critical role of musical congruence within the luxury servicescape.

Our research highlights the pivotal role of music and sounds in shaping brand perception and crafting a distinctive identity. Music isn't merely an afterthought or a peripheral component—it is a powerful tool that, when used strategically, can encapsulate, and elevate the essence of luxury. The findings accentuate the necessity for high-end and luxury brands to prioritize music in their strategy, ensuring it harmoniously blends with other brand elements to offer a complete, immersive luxury experience for the consumer.

Our primary conclusion is that music plays an important role in shaping consumer experiences both in physical and online shopping environments. Online retailers, in particular, should recognize the significance of music in enhancing the consumer shopping experience. It is crucial to understand and utilize the alignment between music and brand identity, as it offers tangible benefits in shaping consumer perceptions and enriching their interactions with the brand. This becomes even more important with luxury brands where the shopping experience has utmost significance to overall brand experience.

Studies in marketing have shed light on music's impact on consumers in service settings. While we have uncovered numerous insights, we must acknowledge the vast unknown. Insights from various fields reveal music's capacity to ameliorate Alzheimer's symptoms, the cognitive amplification of the "Mozart effect"', and the curative properties of music therapy. Our current understanding, rich as it is, might just be scratching the surface of the profound ways that music touches the human soul and body. Thus, future research should integrate findings from other sound fields.

REFERENCES

Akaka, M. A., Vargo, S. L., & Schau, H. J. (2015). The context of experience. *Journal of Service Management, 26*(2), 206–223. doi:10.1108/JOSM-10-2014-0270

Andersson, P. K., Kristensson, P., Wästlund, E., & Gustafsson, A. (2012). Let the music play or not: The influence of background music on consumer behavior. *Journal of Retailing and Consumer Services, 19*(6), 553–560. doi:10.1016/j.jretconser.2012.06.010

Areni, C. S., & Kim, D. (1993). The influence of background music on shopping behaviour: Classical versus top-forty music in a wine store. *Advances in Consumer Research. Association for Consumer Research (U. S.), 20*, 336–340.

Aucouturier, J. J., & Pachet, F. (2003). Representing musical genre: A state of the art. *Journal of New Music Research, 32*(1), 83–93. doi:10.1076/jnmr.32.1.83.16801

Bakker, D. R., & Martin, F. H. (2015). Musical chords and emotion: Major and minor triads are processed for emotion. *Cognitive, Affective & Behavioral Neuroscience, 15*(1), 15–31. doi:10.3758/s13415-014-0309-4 PMID:24957406

Beverland, M., Lim, E. A., Morrison, M., & Terziovski, M. (2006). In-store music and consumer-brand relationships: Relational transformation following experiences of (mis)fit. *Journal of Business Research, 59*(9), 982–989. doi:10.1016/j.jbusres.2006.07.001

Bitner, M. J. (1992). Servicescapes: The impact of physical surroundings on customers and employers. *Journal of Marketing, 56*(2), 57–71. doi:10.1177/002224299205600205

Booms, B. H., & Bitner, M. J. (1982). Marketing services by managing the environment. *The Cornell Hotel and Restaurant Administration Quarterly, 23*(1), 35–40. doi:10.1177/001088048202300107

Broekemier, G., Marquardt, R., & Gentry, J. W. (2008). An exploration of happy/sad and liked/disliked music effects on shopping intentions in a women's clothing store service setting. *Journal of Services Marketing, 22*(1), 59–67. doi:10.1108/08876040810851969

Brown, S., Stevens, L., & Maclaran, P. (2018). Epic aspects of retail encounters: The Iliad of Hollister. *Journal of Retailing, 94*(1), 58–72. doi:10.1016/j.jretai.2017.09.006

Bruner, G. C. II. (1990). Music, Mood, and Marketing. *Journal of Marketing*, *54*(4), 94–104. doi:10.1177/002224299005400408

Chebat, J.-C., Chebat, C. G., & Vaillant, D. (2001). Environmental background music and in-store selling. *Journal of Business Research*, *54*(2), 115–123. doi:10.1016/S0148-2963(99)00089-2

Cristini, H., Kauppinen-Räisänen, H., Barthod-Prothade, M., & Woodside, A. (2017). Toward a general theory of luxury: Advancing from workbench definitions and theoretical transformations. *Journal of Business Research*, *70*, 101–107. doi:10.1016/j.jbusres.2016.07.001

Ding, C. G., & Lind, C.-H. (2012). How does background music tempo work for online shopping? *Electronic Commerce Research and Applications*, *11*(3), 299–307. doi:10.1016/j.elerap.2011.10.002

Dion, D., & Borraz, S. (2017). Managing status: How luxury brands shape class subjectivities in the service encounter. *Journal of Marketing*, *81*(5), 67–85. doi:10.1509/jm.15.0291

Finnair (2023, October 30). Finnair Brand Book. https://brand.finnair.com/en

Garlin, F. V., & Owen, K. (2007). Setting the tone with the tune: A meta-analytic review of the effects of background music in retail setting. *Journal of Business Research*, *59*(6), 755–764. doi:10.1016/j.jbusres.2006.01.013

Greenberg, D. M., Wride, S. J., Snowden, D. A., Spathis, D., Potter, J., & Rentfrow, P. J. (2022). Universals and variations in musical preferences: A study of preferential reactions to Western music in 53 countries. *Journal of Personality and Social Psychology*, *122*(2), 286–309. doi:10.1037/pspp0000397 PMID:35130023

Grewal, D., Baker, J., Levy, M., & Voss, G. B. (2003). The effects of wait expectations and store atmosphere evaluations on patronage intentions in service-intensive retail stores. *Journal of Retailing*, *79*(4), 259–268. doi:10.1016/j.jretai.2003.09.006

Gummerus, J., Von Koskull, C., Kauppinen-Räisänen, H., & Medberg, G. (2023). Who creates luxury? Unveiling the essence of luxury creation through three perspectives: A scoping review. *Qualitative Market Research*. 10.1108/QMR-02-2023-0025

Gustafsson, C. (2015). Sonic branding: A consumer-oriented literature review. *Journal of Brand Management*, *22*(1), 20–37. doi:10.1057/bm.2015.5

Gustafsson, C. (2019). Sonic Branding. The Oxford Handbook of Sound and Imagination, 1, 359.

Hailstone, J. C., Omar, R., Henley, S. M., Frost, C., Kenward, M. G., & Warren, J. D. (2009). It's not what you play, it's how you play it: Timbre affects perception of emotion in music. *Quarterly Journal of Experimental Psychology, 62*(11), 2141–2155. doi:10.1080/17470210902765957 PMID:19391047

Herrington, J. D., & Capella, L. M. (1996). Effects of music in service environments: A field study. *Journal of Services Marketing, 10*(2), 26–41. doi:10.1108/08876049610114249

Hwang, A. H. C., & Oh, J. (2020). Interacting with background music engages E-Customers more: The impact of interactive music on consumer perception and behavioral intention. *Journal of Retailing and Consumer Services, 54*, 101928. doi:10.1016/j.jretconser.2019.101928

Hynes, N., & Manson, S. (2016). The Sound of Silence: Why music in supermarkets is just a distraction. *Journal of Retailing and Consumer Services, 28*(1), 171–178. doi:10.1016/j.jretconser.2015.10.001

Jackson, D. M. (2003). *Sonic Branding: An Introduction*. Palgrave Macmillan. doi:10.1057/9780230503267

Jacob, C. (2006). Styles of background music and consumption in a bar: An empirical evaluation. *International Journal of Hospitality Management, 25*(4), 716–720. doi:10.1016/j.ijhm.2006.01.002

Jacob, C., Guéguen, N., Boulbry, G., & Sami, S. (2009). 'Love is in the air': Congruence between background music and goods in a florist. *International Review of Retail, Distribution and Consumer Research, 19*(1), 75–79. doi:10.1080/09593960902781334

Jain, R., & Bagdare, S. (2011). Music and consumption experience: A review. *International Journal of Retail & Distribution Management, 39*(4), 289–302. doi:10.1108/09590551111117554

Joy, A., Wang, J. J., Orazi, D. C., Yoon, S., LaTour, K., & Peña, C. (2023). Co-creating affective atmospheres in retail experience. *Journal of Retailing, 99*(2), 297–317. doi:10.1016/j.jretai.2023.05.002

Kauppinen-Räisänen, H., Koskull, C., Gummerus, J., & Cristini, H. (2019). The new wave of luxury: The meaning and value of luxury to the contemporary consumer. *Qualitative Market Research, 22*(3), 229–249. doi:10.1108/QMR-03-2016-0025

Kauppinen-Räisänen, H., Mühlbacher, H., & Taishoff, M. (2020). Exploring the luxurious shopping experiences. *Journal of Retailing and Consumer Services, 57*. 10.1016/j.jretconser.2020.102251

Kellaris, J. J. (2008). Music and consumers. Handbook of Consumer Psychology, 828-847.

Kellaris, J. J., & Altsech, M. B. (1992). The experience of time as a function of musical loudness and gender of listener. *Advances in Consumer Research. Association for Consumer Research (U. S.), 19*, 725–729.

Kellaris, J. J., & Kent, R. J. (1991). Exploring tempo and modality effects on consumer responses to music. *Advances in Consumer Research. Association for Consumer Research (U. S.), 18*, 243–248.

Kellaris, J. J., & Kent, R. J. (1992). The influence of music on consumers' temporal perceptions: Does time fly when you're having fun. *Journal of Consumer Psychology, 1*(4), 365–376. doi:10.1016/S1057-7408(08)80060-5

Kellaris, J. J., & Rice, R. C. (1993). The influence of tempo, loudness, and gender of listener on responses to music. *Psychology and Marketing, 10*(1), 15–29. doi:10.1002/mar.4220100103

Kontukoski, M., Luomala, H., Mesz, B., Sigman, M., Trevisan, M., Rotola-Pukkila, M., & Hopia, A. I. (2015). Sweet and sour: Music and taste associations. *Nutrition & Food Science, 45*(3), 357–376. doi:10.1108/NFS-01-2015-0005

Kotler, P. (1973). Atmospherics as a marketing tool. *Journal of Retailing, 49*(4), 48–64.

Lageat, T., Czellar, S., & Laurent, G. (2003). Engineering hedonic attributes to generate perceptions of luxury: Consumer perception of an everyday sound. *Marketing Letters, 14*(2), 97–109. doi:10.1023/A:1025462901401

Lindstrom, M. (2005). Broad sensory branding. *Journal of Product and Brand Management, 14*(2), 84–87. doi:10.1108/10610420510592554

Line, N. D., & Hanks, L. (2020). A holistic model of the servicescape in fast casual dining. *International Journal of Contemporary Hospitality Management, 32*(1), 288–306. doi:10.1108/IJCHM-04-2019-0360

Liu, X., Burns, A. C., & Hou, Y. (2013). Comparing online and in-store shopping behavior towards luxury goods. *International Journal of Retail & Distribution Management, 41*(11/12), 885–900. doi:10.1108/IJRDM-01-2013-0018

Michel, A., Baumann, C., & Gayer, L. (2017). Thank you for the music–or not? The effects of in-store music in service settings. *Journal of Retailing and Consumer Services, 36*, 21–32. doi:10.1016/j.jretconser.2016.12.008

Milliman, R. E. (1982). Using background music to affect the behavior of supermarket shoppers. *Journal of Marketing*, *46*(3), 86–91. doi:10.1177/002224298204600313

Milliman, R. E. (1986). The influence of background music on the behavior of restaurant patrons. *The Journal of Consumer Research*, *13*(2), 286–289. doi:10.1086/209068

Milliman, R. E., & Fugate, D. L. (1993). Atmospherics as an emerging influence in the design of exchange environments. *Journal of Marketing Management*, *3*(1), 66–74.

Morin, S., Dubé, L., & Chebat, J. C. (2007). The role of pleasant music in servicescapes: A test of the dual model of environmental perception. *Journal of Retailing*, *83*(1), 115–130. doi:10.1016/j.jretai.2006.10.006

North, A. C. (2012). The effect of background music on the taste of wine. *British Journal of Psychology*, *103*(3), 293–301. doi:10.1111/j.2044-8295.2011.02072.x PMID:22804697

North, A. C., & Hargreaves, D. J. (1996). Situational influences on reported musical preference. *Psychomusicology: Music, Mind, and Brain*, *15*(1-2), 30–45. doi:10.1037/h0094081

North, A. C., & Hargreaves, D. J. (1998). The effect of music on atmosphere and purchase intentions in a cafeteria 1. *Journal of Applied Social Psychology*, *28*(24), 2254–2273. doi:10.1111/j.1559-1816.1998.tb01370.x

North, A. C., Hargreaves, D. J., & McKendrick, J. (1999). The influence of in-store music on wine selections. *The Journal of Applied Psychology*, *84*(2), 271–276. doi:10.1037/0021-9010.84.2.271

North, A. C., Hargreaves, D. J., & McKendrick, J. (2000). The Effects of Music on Atmosphere in a Bank and a Bar 1. *Journal of Applied Social Psychology*, *30*(7), 1504–1522. doi:10.1111/j.1559-1816.2000.tb02533.x

North, A. C., Sherdian, L. P., & Areni, C. S. (2016). Music congruity effects on product memory, perc and choice. *Journal of Retailing*, *92*(1), 83–95. doi:10.1016/j.jretai.2015.06.001

Oakes, S. (2000). The influence of the musicscape within service environments. *Journal of Services Marketing*, *14*(7), 539–556. doi:10.1108/08876040010352673

Pachet, F., & Cazaly, D. (2000, April). A taxonomy of musical genres. In RIAO (pp. 1238-1245).

Pine, J., & Gilmore, J. (1999). *The Experience Economy*. Harvard Business School Press.

Polfuß, J. (2022). Hip-hop: A marketplace icon. *Consumption Markets & Culture*, *25*(3), 272–286. doi:10.1080/10253866.2021.1990050

Rentfrow, P. J., & Gosling, S. D. (2003). The do re mi's of everyday life: The structure and personality correlates of music preferences. *Journal of Personality and Social Psychology*, *84*(6), 12–36. doi:10.1037/0022-3514.84.6.1236 PMID:12793587

Rosenbaum, M. S., & Massiah, C. (2011). An expanded servicescape perspective. *Journal of Service Management*, *22*(4), 471–490. doi:10.1108/09564231111155088

Schwartz, B. L., & Krantz, J. H. (2017). *Sensation and perception*. Sage Publications.

Shahid, S., Paul, J., Gilal, F. G., & Ansari, S. (2022). The role of sensory marketing and brand experience in building emotional attachment and brand loyalty in luxury retail stores. *Psychology and Marketing*, *39*(7), 1398–1412. doi:10.1002/mar.21661

Singh, H., & Prashar, S. (2014). Anatomy of shopping experience for malls in Mumbai: A confirmatory factor analysis approach. *Journal of Retailing and Consumer Services*, *21*(2), 220–228. doi:10.1016/j.jretconser.2013.08.002

Smith, P. C., & Curnow, R. (1966). Arousal hypothesis and the effects of music on purchasing behavior. *The Journal of Applied Psychology*, *50*(3), 255–256. doi:10.1037/h0023326 PMID:5936035

Stevens, L., Maclaran, P., & Brown, S. (2019). An embodied approach to consumer experiences: The Hollister brandscape. *European Journal of Marketing*, *53*(4), 806–828. doi:10.1108/EJM-09-2017-0558

Sweeney, J. C., & Wyber, F. (2002). The role of cognitions and emotions in the music-approach-avoidance behavior relationship. *Journal of Services Marketing*, *16*(1), 51–69. doi:10.1108/08876040210419415

Terblanche, N. S. (2018). Revisiting the supermarket in-store customer shopping experience. *Journal of Retailing and Consumer Services*, *40*(Jan), 48–59. doi:10.1016/j.jretconser.2017.09.004

Turley, L. W., & Milliman, R. E. (2000). Atmospheric Effects on Shopping Behavior: A Review of the Experimental Evidence. *Journal of Business Research*, *49*(2), 193–211. doi:10.1016/S0148-2963(99)00010-7

Vida, L., Obadia, C., & Kuntz, M. (2007). The effects of background music on consumer responses in a high-end supermarket. *International Review of Retail, Distribution and Consumer Research, 17*(5), 469–482. doi:10.1080/09593960701631532

Voorhees, C. M., Fombelle, P. W., Gregoire, Y., Bone, St., Gustafsson, A., Sousa, R., & Walkowiak, T. (2017). Service encounters, experiences and the customer journey: Defining the field and a call to expand our lens. *Journal of Business Research, 79*, 269–280. doi:10.1016/j.jbusres.2017.04.014

Wiedmann, K. P., Labenz, F., Haase, J., & Hennigs, N. (2018). The power of experiential marketing: Exploring the causal relationships among multisensory marketing, brand experience, customer perceived value and brand strength. *Journal of Brand Management, 25*(2), 101–118. doi:10.1057/s41262-017-0061-5

Wilson, S. (2003). The effect of music on perceived atmosphere and purchase intentions in a restaurant. *Psychology of Music, 31*(1), 93–112. doi:10.1177/0305735603031001327

Wu, M.-Y., Wall, G., & Pearce, P. L. (2014). Shopping experiences: International tourists in Beijing's Silk Market. *Tourism Management, 41*, 96–106. doi:10.1016/j.tourman.2013.09.010

Yalch, R., & Spangenberg, E. (1990). Effects of store music on shopping behavior. *Journal of Consumer Marketing, 7*(2), 55–63. doi:10.1108/EUM0000000002577

Yalch, R., & Spangenberg, E. (1993). Using store music for retail zoning: A field experiment. *Advances in Consumer Research. Association for Consumer Research (U. S.), 20*, 632–636.

Yeoh, J. P., & North, A. C. (2010). The effect of musical fit on consumers' memory. *Psychology of Music, 38*(3), 368–378. doi:10.1177/0305735609360262

Yeoh, J. P. S., Han, M. G., & Spence, C. (2022). The impact of musical fit and sound design on consumers' perception of a luxury car ad. *Luxury, 9*(2-3), 165–184. doi:10.1080/20511817.2022.2224496

Zhang, S., Guo, D., & Li, X. (2023). The rhythm of shopping: How background music placement in live streaming commerce affects consumer purchase intention. *Journal of Retailing and Consumer Services, 75*, 103487. Advance online publication. doi:10.1016/j.jretconser.2023.103487

Zomerdijk, L. G., & Voss, C. A. (2010). Service design for experience-centric services. *Journal of Service Research, 13*(1), 67–82. doi:10.1177/1094670509351960

Chapter 3

Headphone Culture in Public Spaces of Transfer:
Linking Ubiquitous Private Listening to Warped Space

Clara Gustafsson
Lund University, Sweden

ABSTRACT

How do nondescript spaces of transfer (Warped Space), as such, relate to the widespread headphone culture in those spaces? To address this question, the chapter presents a reading of Vidler (1999) on Warped space, Simmel (the Stranger) and Bull (2012) on Toxic Audiotopia. The chapter concludes that Warped spaces or spaces of transfer call for people not to connect, and it was also found that this is supported by the emphasis on looking rather than hearing, and the 'othering' of all others that can be seen happening amongst travelers if analyzed as all Strangers. So because the space of transfer is not conducive to connecting with others – rather the opposite – and because travelers see each other in an object-like way in that space, it has been a particularly suitable space for headphone listening. For marketers, I suggest that marketing efforts can favorably be about creating appealing images and sounds reminiscent of other places that people long for, and also about creating art or ads for Warped space, that convey meaning and are imaginative and reassuring at the same time.

DOI: 10.4018/979-8-3693-0778-6.ch003

USING THE NOTION OF WARPED SPACE TO DISCUSS HOW SPACES OF TRANSFER CONTINUALLY PROMOTE HEADPHONE CULTURE

Headphone culture and commuting are linked – even though the first Walkman users had to endure resistance from fellow travelers (e.g. Du Gay et al., 1997). Today it seems self-evident that many, or most, bring their headphones and listen to music/ sound during traveling or a commute. However, there is little deeper discussion of why the headphones are ubiquitous in these spaces. In this chapter, my mission is to make visible the interplay between the public spaces in question and the widespread culture of headphone listening there. In order to shed some new light on this interplay, I will apply an archeological and artistic work in the form of the concept of Warped Space (Vidler, 1999), to conceptualizations of private listening and headphone use from sonic research. In this case, the bridging concept – between architecture and sonic research – is that of The Stranger (Simmel, 1972).

Warped space is, in my interpretation of Vidler: a space which has a distinct public character, mostly with an uninspired standard design – a space that is so large, impersonal, and void of meaning that it inspires anxiety in many. I believe it is often a space of transfer, taking people from A to B – although Vidler only hints at it in his chapter "Terminal Transfer" where he discusses warped spaces of air transfer as spaces that are not places (p.180). Notably, on the cover of the book "Warped Space" there is a large picture of an escalator hall in a nondescript place, empty of people – a choice of illustration which gives support to my interpretation of a Warped space as a space of transfer. *Non-spaces* (Augé 1992) is another term that is used to refer to airports, large malls, etc. However, I will use Vidler's concept of warped space for a similar analysis, because it offers a richer perspective. Similarly, *soundscapes* is a central term in Sound Studies. It was coined by Schafer (1993), meaning the sonic scapes we are all living in – mainly consisting of the noise of our everyday lives. I agree that the term soundscape is generally useful tool for the analysis of everyday life sounds. However, I believe that the present chapter investigates at the *intersection* between silence and sound, public and private, in a way that requires *space* to be the overarching concept and area under scrutiny here. Consequently, I will use the terms *space* and *warped space* for the purposes of the present paper.

The contribution of this chapter is an understanding of headphone use in contemporary society – more specifically – in warped space. This can help understand the musical world of commuters in relation to the silent reality of the warped space itself (as these spaces are usually made to absorb sound), and include insights on the impact of marketing and advertising in warped space. These insights contribute to the book's notion of engaging customers with brands, in the sense that customers are available for certain advertising messages more than others during this commute or transit. This includes both what they are more likely to be drawn to in their private listening, and for instance QR-codes on bill boards in the space, leading to content to listen to. The main insights of this chapter can also be applied to building brands in related industries (flights, trains, subway, waiting halls, etc.) using sounds – something that may be an interesting way to expand on these ideas in the future.

The aim of this chapter is to introduce warped space into the discussion of headphone culture and make problematic the choices available to people in these spaces. In order to trace Vidler's line of thought and compare it to my own reading of Simmel's Stranger, I will briefly go back to some of Simmel's work in the chapter. Other trajectories I will take is into Bull's (2000) work on the idea of a space (a car) as a *music machine*, his idea of *Toxic Audiotopia* (Bull, 2012) and Du Gay et al.'s well-rounded early take on headphone culture and headphone use. In other words, the present chapter uses the concepts of 1) warped space, 2) the stranger, and 3) audiotopia to analyze headphone culture in public spaces of transfer in a new way.

Concerns: To Better Understand why Headphone use is Ubiquitous in Spaces of Transfer

I will take the familiar public space of the commute and make it complex by studying the notion of people as *strangers* and in a warped space. Transitional public spaces – the part of warped spaces that I am analyzing here – are perhaps more of a generalized twilight zone than people even think of in their daily lives. I will try to understand these public spaces as warped spaces, in order to better understand the way that travelers en masse chose to use music/headphones. I do not think the link is between this particular public space and the choice of sound as an escape (see Bull 2012 and 2000) is arbitrary, neither do I think that the only reason why people would need an escape there is because they need to pass time. In this chapter, I will discuss possible connections between a certain type of public space and headphone/ music use, and in so doing, I suggest a parallel and more macro level explanation to that of people seeking an *escape* through private listening there (ibid).

Bull (2000) depicts the car as a "music machine". His work inspires me to examine music listening in public spaces as multifunctional and complex, rather than just a miraculous match of technology development and a need that people have to create their own "*music bubbles*" where they go (see Bull 2000). I believe this is a behavior that has at least a few more reasons behind it. Much like the car has certain design properties that lends it to be a "music machine" to those few people traveling in it, the design or architectural properties of the public warped space will provide some particular reasons why it lends itself to headphone listening. I think that the macro level implications of these reasons are important enough to warrant some meaning to the kind of analysis that I will make here. Although it is a subjective account on many levels, my discussion in the present essay departs from previous research that is at the core of several fields, notably sociology and sound studies.

Background: How can Simmel's Stranger help Explain the link Between Warped Space and Ubiquitous Private Listening?

For the purpose of this chapter, I will define Warped Space, and then show my perspective of it as I am using a small piece of the original conceptualization. I am tweaking it more toward the *traditional* transitional space instead of the artful transitional space. The urban habitat of the stranger overlaps with warped space in many, important, instances. In the overlap (lobbies, subway trains, stations, etc.) both are warped spaces. I hope to provide more clarity about this from starting out with transitional space as the warped space which is examined here, and then moving on to talking about the theory of the stranger.

Simmel's theory of the Stranger is widely used by researchers in subjects that are aiming to understand the dynamics of various groups – subjects such as Marketing, Management, Sociology and Architecture. He put forth his theory in several different publications, and the one from 1972 is the most often cited version. There, he clearly states that the stranger is someone who were not in the place from the beginning, but stays in place and does not move on, and so becomes the stranger in that place compared to others who were there from the beginning. So the stranger is not a vagrant, and this is also something that Simmel is clear about. He also originally wrote about various *types*, not originally focusing in on *the stranger*. Later on, he also wrote about the metropolis, and the metropolitan stranger, which he thought was extra interesting because the qualities of the city lend themselves very well to discussions on exclusion and inclusion. Importantly, Simmel believed that there were a couple of special advantages to being a stranger, and I will go through these, below. As I will argue, understanding both the limits and the reach of the Stranger's very specific type of role in a group will be key to understanding the link between Warped space and ubiquitous private listening.

The Central Concepts of Space, Warped Space, and Audiotopia

Space is different from place, and at the same time space can involve place (see e.g., Parkes and Thrift, 1980). Simply put, place is both particular and culturally embedded. In other words, it is marked out by a specific spot on the map and persons have their lives, memories and thoughts linked up to a place. Space is more overarching and potentially fluctuating than place (see e.g., Parkes and Thrift, 1980; Lefebvre, 1991). Some similarities are that both spur an architectural interest, and a mental notion of a site, and last but not least – a close connection with time (see e.g. Parkes and Thrift, 1980). In this chapter, I am not trying to make space complex as such. Rather, I am interested in Warped space mainly because I believe it has little, or no, potential for personalization compared to place. I believe that this very quality of space makes it able to take on a different role for travelers and commuters and other people in transfer than place can do. In particular, I will suggest how spaces of transfer are linked to ubiquitous private listening in headphones, and that link is via some of the qualities of Vidler's (1999) Warped space (i.e., spaces of transfer).

One of the main philosophers on space, Lefebvre (1991) is mainly interested in what he calls "social space". His key idea is that space is *produced*, and that its history cannot be ignored. Social space is produced through communication and relationships. This then leads to the argument that there is "dominated," and "appropriated" space (Lefebvre, 1991:165). "Dominated" space is transformed by technology, and "invariably the realization of a master's project." (p.165). Lefebvre argues that most spaces are becoming dominated. He argues that "Dominated space is usually closed, sterilized, emptied out." (ibid). Appropriated space is the opposite, he says. I suggest that the dominated space has similarities with Warped space. As we will see, below, the notion of Warped space does not presuppose an absence of appropriation, but it does not invite it either. I believe Lefebvre's definition is more intentional in politicizing the power struggles that space can be utilized to shine a light on, whereas Vidler is more concerned with the space itself, as it relates to matters of architecture and art. Lefebvre himself writes that attempts to redirect the purpose of a dominated space which was purposefully built as a dominant space, into an a appropriated space, seldom are successful because it does not fulfill "the needs of [the residents'] would-be communal life." (p.168). It can be argued that Lefebvre shows the same division as Vidler of a space that is communal, and a space that is not. While Lefebvre stresses the importance of the communal aspects (what he calls appropriated space), Vidler stresses the anxiety provoked by the non-communally arranged space – i.e., dominated space in Lefebvre's' terms, and Warped space in Vidler's. This is interesting here because from a cultural viewpoint, perhaps Lefebvre's theory makes more sense initially, but I believe that Vidler's theory brings in a new perspective – one where the space itself is centered on, and then compared to human actions in it. Again, I suggest that Warped space is much less susceptible to personalization – or appropriation if you will – than place. Perhaps what Lefebvre calls *appropriated space* is what most of us would just call '*place*'. At least this makes sense when looking at Parkes and Thrift (1980:24), who are using *the home* as an example of a *place*. I believe the home must be the most appropriated space of all, for the largest number of people.

Vidler describes two types of *warped spaces – psychological* and *artistic*. In this chapter, I will focus on the psychological, and touch briefly on the artistic. The labelling and division into psychological and artistic warped space that Vidler makes seem to stem from the literature he uses to discuss them. For the psychological part he uses a completely different literature, prominently Walter Benjamin and Georg Simmel. For the artistic perspective, he also uses existing architectural experiments as his examples to talk about how digital techniques have transformed the architectural perspectives. In Vidler's definition, Warped space in the psychological sense is *both* a city space that is not empty but filled with deliberate architecture, *and* a space with a particular ability to cause anxiety in people's minds. Artistic warping is what happens when new forms of depicting the psychological warped space are shown, and thus breaking with tradition. I read the definition of Warped space as intentionally vague and thus open to various interpretations. Consequently, I choose to interpret it as a theory of public or semi-public space that does not invite people to interact with each other but tend to keep people separated – and often even feeling small, insignificant, meaningless – to promote the effectiveness of the transfer, commute, travel, or the like. My interpretation comes from a place of trying to understand the social actions of the people in the space, and so I focus on the connection aspect. Perhaps Vidler was originally more interested in the power/lack of power built into the warped space itself. For instance, because the spaces are large and public and have a very robust quality to them, they may seem permanent. But Vidler points out that because they are often meaningless, they may also become obsolete. He gives the example of airport corridors and waiting halls, and speculates that maybe they will not be needed at all in the future.

Vidler (1999) goes into some detail about *the hotel lobby* as a warped space, inspired by the writings of one of Simmel's students, Siegfried Kracauer. From Simmel (1972), Vidler (1999) also gets an idea of warped space as about *seeing* others, not *hearing* them (p.68). Vidler (1999) stresses that the warped spaces he investigates are in a bodily sense *beyond the control* of the humans going into them, he calls some of them "terminal transfer" (p.184) and those go on seemingly endlessly without an ending to be seen. Importantly, I see warped spaces as public transfer spaces that offer no built-in opportunity for connection, and even is designed to prevent connection.

My interpretation may very well be partly incorrect, and not what Vidler intended, but either way, it gives us a particular, and also very large, Warped space to examine – so we can think even beyond the hotel lobby and the airport. I suggest that the Warped space of public transitional space involves waiting halls, elevators, escalator halls, train carriages, the inside of an aircraft, air terminals and other public or semi-public spaces that involve travel or commute and are designed in a manner that makes us think we could be just about anywhere – a design that is very uninteresting and is the same from place to place around the world. Curiously, these are also prime spaces for headphone listening. What is it about these two phenomena that brings them together, and what is the importance of understanding Warped space when trying to understand headphone culture? I will discuss this further in the chapter, and provide insights, and implications for marketers.

Sound Studies researcher Michael Bull (2012) has also examined what he calls *private listening* in public, with a focus on problems that this can cause for the individual, and for human interaction in these spaces. Although unusual in its stance, building up a conceptualization of private listening, i.e., listening in headphones, around what he calls "Audiotopia", his perspective centers only on the culture pertaining *private* listening. In the present chapter a focus on the private, or culture, perspective is juxtaposed to a focus on the *space* in which private listening and headphone culture happen. Although I assume that private listening often presupposes a public space for it to exist or happen as something that needs to be pointed out distinctly as *private*, those spaces concerned are just briefly mentioned by Bull as a backdrop for the individual stories of the studied headphone users going about their commute. Bull builds up audiotopia as the landscape of listening that the listeners are creating for themselves with individualized playlists and the like. He does not at all go into the idea behind the spaces from an architectural viewpoint, even though he makes some inferences about what happens to the space that is the backdrop for all this private listening. In his view of audiotopia, Bull describes how listeners create a sound overlay of perceived silence for themselves, consisting of the music that they are used to listening to. In the present chapter, I focus more on everything *around* Audiotopia, which gives a different perspective where the most interesting form of silence is that of the Warped space itself. In the chapter, I choose to see Audiotopia and private listening firstly from the viewpoint of the warped space. In other words, my primary concern is how warped space is populated by ubiquitous listeners passing through it, and not firstly at how the listeners perceive of their journey.

The Stranger

Simmel's Stranger is often used in analyses of city life – as Simmel brilliantly points out, it is not a city if you can immediately pinpoint who is a Stranger there. The way Vidler uses Simmel's notion is more tied to the idea of a stranger in a space – his idea is more along the lines of: what kind of space hosts, or holds, strangers? The answer he gives is: warped spaces. The interesting question regarding Simmel here is: Why does Simmel's theory lend itself so well to Vidler's purposes? I believe one reason is because Simmel himself talked about the Stranger in the metropolitan space, and so had the Stranger situated in a certain sort of space, much like Vidler is interested in a certain space, and not just any kind of space.

The way that Simmel (1972) defines the stranger is that it is not a temporary wanderer – the stranger is always a stranger, it is not something temporary. The stranger belongs to the group but is still always a non-member of the group in the way of not having belonged there since the start. This means that the stranger is not completely estranged in the way it sounds at first, and yet also that there is no chance for the stranger to change status in the group. According to Simmel, there are advantages to being the stranger – for example, being a stranger lends itself to trading, and to objectivity. Being a stranger is a function of Metropolitan life, according to Simmel, and Metropolitan life is something that he explored in many of his writings. Vidler takes note of this, and hones in on the particular aspects of space that lurk behind Simmel's conceptualizations. Vidler (1999:68) interprets Simmel as talking about the "distance" of Metropolitan designs as at the core of why people feel alienated in cities. The main ideas then become that public spaces alienate, and that the stranger is the ultimate alienated city dweller (ibid:69). From this, together with some other literature studies, Vidler extrapolates the notion of Warped space.

In my interpretation of Warped space, I like to go back to Simmel and the city dweller that is the stranger, and the vast spaces that alienate, and peel some layers off of Vidler's Warped space to make it only about transitional space. In the transitional space, commuters become a group – a group of commuters – and they are all strangers in that group (excluding those who travel together with someone they know). In addition, this is generally a permanent state during the entire journey, as long as they remain convinced that the space is only transitional. According to Simmel (1972) the stranger is not seen as an individual by the group, but instead as and instance of the Other. This is important here because it enables there to be a group of strangers who are all de-individualized to one another – all just nameless fellow 'travelers' – others, on their way to somewhere else. When *everyone* is a stranger – are the rules of the game different from those of Simmel's writings? After all, he does not describe such a situation himself. In some sense, the rules could very well be the same, but then apply to the mass of travelers, rather than to a few strangers in a group. The alienation that public space offers is making them all appear in a constant state of stranger-ness. Nobody was born on the subway, and nobody can claim to *belong* to the tram (except maybe the driver and the conductor). They are all transitional and they are all strangers – because the Warped space makes them so.

Vidler (1999:69) stresses the way that Simmel's metropolitans 'see' – and 'other' – each other in urban space, rather than listen to each other and 'hear' each other. Vidler is not completely clear on what the consequences of seeing and othering are for warped space, except for calling the entire section on Simmel "Estrangement: Georg Simmel" (p.67), which clearly shows the intention toward describing the estrangement of warped space. I would like to take this opportunity to make clear connections between Simmel's theories of estrangement and Vidler's warped space. I believe that the othering, where the other is not seen as an individual and where listening is not important (only seeing) which Simmel describes concerning metropolitans in urban spaces are also valid for strangers in warped space. That observation is the foundation of my next argument which is about today's ubiquitous headphone use in warped spaces. Now – why do the Strangers tend to put on headphones in Warped space? I believe that the notion of Toxic Audiotopia (Bull, 2012) can help shed some light on this question.

The Strangers' Use of Toxic Audiotopia in Warped Space

Interestingly, Bulls notion of *Toxic Audiotopia* suggests that commuters do not *want* to be in a *shared space*, which implies that they perceive that shared spaces have some adverse effect on them. For instance, he refers to how they create their own sound overlays that they themselves think of as 'silence' . They do this to find *an escape* from the commute, according to Bull. The concept of Audiotiopa has been described, at length, in an earlier section. If compared with my idea (above) of commuters as *all* strangers and *all* transitional, where I was leaning heavily on Vidler's perspective, I detect interesting differences concerning this in Simmel, and Bull's perspectives. According to both Vidler and myself, Warped or transitional spaces are so set and so impermeable that they overshadow the person/s in it with its own logic, whereas Bull seems to be operating more along the lines that *individual persons happen to spaces* and can infer their own logic in that space. I believe that this is an interesting and unexplored intersection of ideas, where theories of headphone culture do not yet completely meet with theories of space and alienation. Following Vidler, I am thinking of the architecture of transfer (i.e., warped space) as setting the very premise for anything else that takes place in the space. Simmel is situated somewhere in between Vidler's and Bull's perspectives, with a focus on the possible status of the person in the space from the point of the relations of people in the space. I believe this is why Simmel's writings are especially useful in order to make these theories meet; Simmel simply states that the Stranger is particularly interesting in a metropolitan setting – while not stating anything else about the setting as necessary to his analysis. This stance enables an analysis of all spaces that are metropolitan in their design, considering the concept of the Stranger.

Going back to Toxic Auditotopia – Audiotopia means that the listener creates their own world of sound to bring with them. The toxic part is about losing some of their hearing ability over time from having that constant sound overlay play directly into their ears for too long, during their commutes. If you will, Bull (2012) provides knowledge of the commuters, and their sonic habits. As I have explained, above, commuters can be seen as all Strangers, and warped space is not a space of human connection, but rather of anxiety. I suggest that the notion that the commuters on board a train are all Strangers is strengthened by their ubiquitous headphone use, separating them off from each other by means of their hearing. In terms of Warped space, is this behavior somehow imposed on them by the stranger-ness of themselves and others in transitional space? Or is warped space in itself so anxiety-provoking and alienating to them that they feel the need to try to escape the space and enter their Audiotopia? On the one hand, some people carry their headphones into other spaces as well, notably to the food store. When paying, they cannot really have a full interaction with the person at the till – and they are inevitably considered rude with their headphones and music on. On the other hand, using headphones in a warped space is considered normal, and people work around it if they must talk for some reason. This is in line with Simmel's analysis of the hearing vs seeing in metropolitan space. With Vidler's addition of the warped space, I believe it is possible to divide the metropolitan spaces of Simmel into at least two categories based on what is expected there in terms of seeing vs hearing: Normal space (i.e., relational space of connection) and warped space. While the seeing is expected everywhere, the warped spaces promote only *the seeing*, and the normal spaces promote both *the hearing and seeing*. The manned till at a store is a *normal* space where connection, by seeing and hearing, is expected. The escalators in the subway are in a *warped* space where no connection is expected, and *seeing* that there are other passengers is enough – no talking or listening is expected there.

Warped Spaces call for Seeing and a Lack of Connection: Making way for Ubiquitous Headphone Use

Warped spaces are not friendly, cozy places – they are impersonal and designed to look more or less meaningless, except for providing the function they are there to provide. The function is not to have people connect, but to have people move, be still, and transfer as expected. Is the quiet activity of headphone listening rebelling against the warped space? No, because connecting and speaking and disrupting the flow of the warped design would be rebellious. Creating a private world for one, of audiotopia, seems to cement the Stranger status of the warped space traveler, as well as create more separation and quiet *surrendering to the space*, between the fellow travelers. The point is that ubiquitous headphone listening makes travelers act even *more* like strangers, and so it enforces the grip of the warped space on each individual in the space. Of course, the individual may feel like the music is a better solution than just sitting there on the train, listening to the train's movements (see Bull 2012, 2020). At the aggregate level it is a train full of strangers cut off from one another by not listening, and not hearing, one another. In principal, the implications of this analysis are on a more aggregate level – it shows how the listeners' actions of *individual* listening create another type of space *for them all*. We cannot understand that Warped spaces can have this isolating and disconnecting effect on people, unless we understand that Warped spaces are either empty, or populated by Strangers in transit. In addition, we need to take into consideration that they are largely meaningless to people and that this is included in their design – as they are transitional, and just *pointing the way to another place*. This means that another place is in general where the actual meaning of traveling/commuting lies for the individual in transit, and the Warped space has little or no intrinsic value for the individuals in it. If we think of it this way, we can see that it would take much more for people to try to connect and act as social beings in warped space, than to isolate. *The warped spaces call for them to refrain from connecting*, and the characteristics of warped space created their status as Strangers there.

With the Stranger status as a starting point, the technology of the smart phone is a welcome contribution in creating a sense that the isolation of the warped space brings something that the individual *wants* – their individual audiotopia, bringing a sense of managing one's time – because one is *not* completely in charge of one's own time schedule, or even one's own immediate space, within the warped space. In other words, while Bull (2012:527) argues that "…today any space whatsoever can potentially be transformed into a private auditory space of listening…", I believe it is important to make a difference between the many possibilities for private listening today, and the possibilities to change a space into an "auditory space". Although spaces of transfer offer possibilities for private listening, there is very little to nothing that a stranger in that space can do to make a personal change to the actual space. In fact, even all the strangers in that space together do not tend to make the space itself change in any lasting way. Warped spaces form the way that people behave in them, not the other way around. Simply put, they are built so that people will want to get through them and out on the other side, not stay in them. Still, we often must stay in them for some period of time, to get through to our destination. If private listening in headphones helps individuals move through these spaces without feeling completely trapped and anxious, people will use private listening – importantly – while being socially accepted in their headphone use because as I have argued here: *the hearing is not socially important in the warped space*. But saying that private listening frees them of the space they are in, or changes the space itself, is not accurate.

I believe we need to distinguish between headspace and other kinds of space. Warped spaces are spaces for Strangers to get from A to B. They are not magical musical places – except that they might seem so, very temporarily, for some lucky traveler/listener/stranger at some point. I think it is more useful to think of warped spaces as the powerful public structures that they are, than to try to find ways to express them as joyous musical vehicles like the private car. However, I think the mistake is easily made because of the ubiquitous use of headphones in these spaces. I believe that the ubiquitous use of headphones signals the oppressing power of those structures, and that the warped space itself is a prominent reason for the ubiquitous private listening in those spaces. Seeking an escape or the like, is perhaps the logical or normal next step for many people stepping into a warped space, but there is no real escape within the warped space. A real escape would be, for example, going by car instead of in warped space and personalizing that car so that it becomes a private space (cf. Bull 2020). Headphones may offer a perceived escape via creating a certain headspace, such as by creating an audiotopia, but the Warped space itself does not budge – and so it offers no escape. My point is that the escape through Audiotopia which Bull writes about is perfectly in line with what the warped space and the accompanying metropolitan estrangement invite people to do and not to do. This means that engaging in private listening is a socially normal way to act within that space. Then, as I have argued, the script of the warped space is for travelers to *all* act as Strangers. Because they follow this script by closing their hearing off to the space and to the people around them, I believe that for most people private listening in warped spaces signals an *adaptation* or even a *surrendering* to the space, to a larger degree that it offers an *escape*.

CONCLUSION: WHY HAS UBIQUITOUS PRIVATE LISTENING TAKEN OVER IN SPACES OF TRANSFER, AND HOW CAN MARKETERS BEST ADDRESS THIS GROUP OF STRANGERS?

I have made the case that connecting and speaking and disrupting the flow of the warped space would be rebellious, whereas listening to headphones is in line with what the warped space calls for, and so cannot mean rebelling against the warped space. The interesting notion of Audiotopia (Bull, 2012) – fleeing into one's own world of sounds and music via headphones – comes from a place of looking for refuge from the aspects of the warped space, although warped space itself cannot be escaped from by listening to headphones in it. However, from a marketing perspective, I believe that it is useful to think of audiotopia as creating *a different headspace* – although the warped space, importantly, stays the same and very little personalization can take place there. It makes sense in several ways that headphone sound has become a *mode of personalization* in a space which virtually cannot be personalized. The use of sound in headphones goes in line with the qualities of warped space. The seeing is important here in the urban milieu, but the listening is not socially prioritized (see Simmel, 1972). As I will describe in this final part of the chapter, Marketers and branders will do well in choosing to dial into the headspace that is personalized via headphones among consumers in these warped transfer spaces, and not try to change or go against these dynamics that I have described in the present chapter.

Warped spaces are calling for a lack of connection, and seeing rather than hearing, and I have argued that they also promote the notion that all the people in the space are *Strangers*. My reading of Vidler (1999) on Warped space, Simmel (the Stranger) and Bull (2012) on Toxic Audiotopia had the goal of saying something new about ubiquitous headphone wearing in spaces of transfer (Warped spaces). I conclude that Warped spaces or spaces of transfer call for people *not* to connect, and in my analysis, I also found that this is supported by the emphasis on seeing rather than hearing, and the 'othering' of all others that can be seen happening amongst travelers if we analyze them as all Strangers (as defined by Simmel, 1972). In other words, because the space of transfer is not conducive to connecting with others – rather the opposite – and because travelers see each other in an object-like way in that space, it is clear to see why headphone listening has become ubiquitous there. From a social perspective, it is a perfect milieu for going inside oneself and cutting others off in terms of hearing – because important social and architectural cues for accepting that behavior in warped spaces were already in place before the advent of the headphones.

For marketers, I suggest that marketing efforts can favorably be about creating an appealing image of *other places*. Whereas travel agencies and airlines will do well to advertise in subways, train carriages, and escalator halls, it is not advisable to remind consumers in transit spaces of where they are at this moment, because they tend to want to think of being elsewhere and doing other things when in transit spaces (cf. Bull 2012). I would suggest that advertisements cater to the consumers' idea that they have a full life *elsewhere*, and how to make the most out of their dreams for that life. Nostalgia and utopia are useful guiding principles for the content. When it comes to reminding them of chores – of having to take out a home insurance, or about buying tampons – this is not the right place. This is because consumers are already under pressure here, they are already in a space that creates anxiety (cf. Simmel and Vidler). In spaces of transfer it could be a good idea to have QR-codes displayed, leading to interesting sound solutions that amuse, because consumers are already wearing their headphones and they are not connecting with other people, so they are more likely to be free to engage with the ad. Another interesting solution could be an advertisement that runs as a series, where the ad continues with a new instalment next week – because those who are commuters might be amused, as they will be seeing the continuation, and it breaks the monotony of the warped space in a subtle and suitable manner.

There is a lot that can be done in terms of marketing to consumers in warped space – I would suggest that the most important part is to not advertise to consumer travelers in a way that makes them feel trapped and bothered, because that could extremely easily happen in this space. They are in a space that turns them into Strangers. As I have argued in the present chapter, the space itself urges for expedience and non-connection, while people are hardwired to connect – meaning that when entering Warped spaces, people are stripped of an important layer of their usual social instincts. This means that it is very important to carefully consider themes and color choices and keep it slightly on the bright side, as well as understand that many mundane product categories and some complex services, while needed in highly stressful situations (e.g. funeral services), are not at all suitable to be advertised in the anxiety provoking warped space.

Consumers are under constant "surveillance" by marketers' trying to define target groups and the like – and consumers are aware of it (Pridmore and Lyon, 2011:115). I believe it is important not to convey any sense of surveillance when marketing to consumers in the environment of the warped space – because there, consumers can feel more vulnerable and trapped than out in the street or when reading a magazine at home. Podcasts will have many listeners in transit, and companies will gain from advertising accordingly. Another way for a company to go would be to sponsor a temporary or permanent exhibition in a warped space. This is something Vidler (1999) devotes special attention to, because a warped space can be easily changed into a less cold or less meaningless environment with a simple projection on the wall – yet this is seldom done. In other words, there is room for improvement in how warped spaces are altered or accessorized – importantly by advertisements and art. As a Marketer, I believe it is important to realize how much extra value you can provide for consumers within a warped space if you chose to create something at once meaningful, imaginative, and reassuring. Private listening is there to stay, and so that needs to be taken into account in any marketing effort in a warped space, regardless of whether the marketing material is to be mainly visual or sonic. For any brand, this means figuring out whether these spaces are for them; Do you sell dreams – go ahead! Do you sell mundane products – your brand is better off choosing other outlets. As most brands do sell dreams, in some shape or form, these spaces will be available for a wide array of brands. The next thing to consider is then to make the message light and dreamy, and to understand that consumers are already in a state of disconnection that causes discomfort and anxiety when in a warped space. They are ready to listen inside their headphones, but not necessarily listening outside of them. This means that brands will benefit from understanding that they are trying to access a privatized headspace with their message, if they reach out for the consumer in the warped space. This means that any commercials in podcasts should preferably cater to the needs of the person in transit, in these ways discussed here, because the warped space is a frequent space for podcast listening.

Challenges for future research on this topic include how to change warped space (see e.g., Vidler 1999 on artistic warped space); and imagining what warped space will be in the future; as well as how the *time* aspect of warped space relates to ubiquitous listening. Already in 1997, duGay et. al pointed out that "the Walkman broke with the established classifications of public and private space…" (p.120), and this is still true of all private listening in public space – although the headphones are more accepted, they do not have a set place in public life. In other words, headphones are still entirely private. DuGay et. al also pointed out that as headphones were getting smaller, more voices were raised "concerning its role in inducing anti-social behavior." (1997, p.120). While this chapter in part addresses these same issues, yet using a different vocabulary, there are also some problems that come with the *public* space as such, and this still requires more attention, especially a contemporary approach that caters more directly to sonic aspects of everyday life in public spaces is welcome (cf. Bull 200, and DeNora 2000). I hope the reader of this chapter can now also better understand, or at least infer, why ubiquitous listening has *not* resulted in headphone use becoming a publicly sanctioned practice overall. Another interesting way to move beyond what has already been written might be to consider the Audiotopia as a *headspace*, and compare it to other spaces. In a research chapter called "The Music That's Not There" the music in the actual headspace is studied – this, for instance, includes the bass sound in headphone-listening (Knakkergaard 2014). A bass sound cannot be accurately reproduced in the space between our ears, which means that all such sounds are artificially reproduced for headphone-listening. This in turn, means that the bass sound that we think we hear in our headphones is actually never really there (ibid). This is an important starting point for research on headspace as a space, and can be taken in several different directions. The notion of a sound that is not there has long been of interest to mankind. The notion of the sonic limits of headspace is also something that is not entirely a new phenomenon, although Knakkergaard's approach is intensely virtual and thorough, mapping out sounds that have to be reproduced specifically for headphone use and providing both the philosophy and pragmatics behind the practice. The connection to Marketing also needs to be made – how will consumers react to the knowledge that the sound they are listening to is a fabrication for their ears only, which cannot be replayed with the same sound in another space than their own headspace? Does it matter to them?

As we are now getting further down the rabbit whole – I would like to finally address entirely new ways in which *the public space* would gain from more attention, and how it relates to *the individual's listening*. Public space, the way I have interrogated it here, is a cold and unfriendly, largely meaningless and nondescript space – when you are there, you feel like you could be, in a sense, anywhere. A particularly good example of this is the airport with its long, even seemingly never-ending, transport escalator halls; the "Terminal Transfer," as Vidler (1999, p.184) calls it. When we picture them in our minds, do we consider them as silent or full of sound, or something else? What color do they have? Any smells? In general, we might conjure up a drab picture, not much sound, no smells. We have a sense of these spaces, as both meaningless and overbearing, and this is one of Vidler's main points with Warped space. If we combine this with Bull's notion of the imaginary world of the Audiotopia, or just the lure of a playlist full of color on the screen and a private selection of music to pick and choose from – the contrast between the public space; grey, necessary and dull, and the private space of color on the screen of the smartphone and voluntary sounds between our ears – the difference is stark. Marketers have not yet made the most of this condition of the private (appropriated, with Lefebvre's words) and the public (warped, with Vidler's words). Perhaps a new key to exploring it is to see headspace as an actual space, virtually and in reality? Maybe the sounds that are *not* there (Knakkergaard, 2014) are the most important sounds of the future – both concerning public space and individual listening? There is a connection with power that I have not addressed fully – Warped space is overbearing, connection is not called for, and what does that do to people if they surrender by closing their ears to each other? Are spaces that are not there (cf. Knakkergaard, 2014, Bull 2012) replacing something that used to be there, or is the new technology creating new non-existing spaces and sounds? The lure for researchers of both the headspace and the warped space is that we have not solved the puzzle yet, and that it has long been right in front of us when we study the metropolitan consumer/traveler/commuter. For Marketers, the question will be how to best reach into these spaces, but also to map them out. As we have understood, public space is shaping people, while marketers might have thought this was *their* role. To succeed in warped space today, Marketers need to understand that the space sets the rules. Market *researchers* can have a go at bending the rules of warped space, perhaps in the light of its relation to headphone culture and headspace. The notion that many of these spaces and sounds might not even really exist should be sufficiently tantalizing to spur more research on what we actually can say about them, and how they interact with marketing, architecture, art, and sociology as well as the everyday lives of people.

REFERENCES

Augé, M. (1995). *Non-Places: An Introduction to Anthropology of Supermodernity* (J. Howe, Trans.). Verso. (Original work published 1992)

Bull, M. (2000). *Sound Moves: iPod culture and urban experience*. Taylor and Francis.

Bull, M. (2012). IPod Culture: The Toxic Pleasures of Audiotopia. In T. Pinch & K. Bijsterveld (Eds.), *The Oxford Handbook of Sound Studies* (pp. 526–543).

DeNora, T. (2000). *Music in Everyday Life*. Cambridge University Press. doi:10.1017/CBO9780511489433

Du Gay, P., S. Hall, L. Janes, H. Mackay, and K. Negus (1997). *Doing cultural studies: the story of the Sony Walkman*. Sage in association with the Open University.

Knakkergaard, M. (2014). The Music That's Not There. In *M. Grimshaw-Aagaard, The Oxford Handbook of Virtuality* (pp. 392–404). Oxford University Press.

Lefebvre, H. (1991). The production of space. D. Nicholson-Smith, Trans. Blackwell.

Parkes, D. N., & Thrift, N. J. (1980). *Time, Spaces, and Places: A Chronographic Perspective*. John Wiley & Sons.

Pridmore and Lyon. (2011). Marketing as Surveillance: Assembling Consumers as Brands. In *Zwick and J. Cayla, Inside Marketing: Practices, ideologies, devices* (500th ed., pp. 115–136). Oxford University Press.

Schafer, M. (1993). *The soundscape: our sonic environment and the tuning of the world*. Destiny Books.

Simmel, G. (1972). *On individuality and social forms*. University of Chicago Press.

Vidler, A. (1999). *Warped Space: Art, Architechture, and Anxiety in Modern Culture*. The MIT Press.

Chapter 4
Political Affiliation of Musical Artists Contributing to Sonic Elements of Advertising

Paul G. Barretta

ⓘ https://orcid.org/0000-0002-6940-587X
Wagner College, USA

ABSTRACT

In this chapter, a conceptual approach is proposed for how sonic elements of advertising can be utilized to create a connection with a particular target segment based on their homogeneous political viewpoints. After a literature review of pertinent topics, theoretical development of the proposed approach is presented, followed by sections related to how Integrated Marketing Communications strategy can employ sonic elements in a way that appeals to some target markets while minimizing potential backlash from others. Audience fragmentation, where technology is changing how consumers view entertainment, is identified as an opportunity for how advertising is morphing in contemporary society. A formative model is presented that can potentially be used as a starting point for further research, which is briefly discussed along with limitations.

INTRODUCTION

The use of music from an artist known to have a particular set of political views can be the source of connection with an important target market for some advertisers. Carefully constructed advertisements using sonic elements may lower the risk of backlash from consumers with opposing political views. In this chapter, underlying

DOI: 10.4018/979-8-3693-0778-6.ch004

theory and practical examples are presented to assert that advertisers can utilize music as a secondary element of advertisements as a way of creating that connection, and therefore strong appeal. The balancing act of appealing to a target group without offending consumers outside of that target group is an important issue for advertisers. Political views are often an emotional hot button for some viewers, so using political viewpoints as an appeal for non-political products can be risky. Therefore, the use of a secondary element is presented as a way of creating the connection while minimizing the risk of backlash.

LITERATURE REVIEW

Politics and Music

The United States is currently divided from a political perspective (A. H.-Y. Lee, 2022; Schmitt et al., 2022), and has been dramatically so for about the past 8 to 10 years; it is a global phenomenon, not just a national one (Ramswell, 2018). Music has long been a tool to reflect, and contribute to politics (Dunaway, 1987). Similar to ways in which politically based content can be used as a segmentation tool for magazines (Mangrum, 2021) and newspapers (Kaplan, 2013), the politics that a musician associates themselves with can be used to manage perception of brands and products through sonic elements of advertising to particular market segments.

Two North American artists who famously avoided giving permission for their music to be used in advertising brands or products are Neil Young and Bruce Springsteen. Young even wrote a song, "This Note's For You," to emphasize his stance (Allan, 2010). In early 2021, Springsteen made an exception by appearing in a Super Bowl commercial for Jeep, along with his music. Most notable about the commercial is that the content of the voiceover and the music chosen are focused on mending political division throughout the United States (Steinberg, 2021). The content is far from subtle, and the association of music and politics is clear. It is this association as opportunity that we are exploring in this chapter at a deeper level.

Although the present chapter focuses on the use of music from an artist with recognizable political views, it is important to note that a tangential relationship exists in the literature, particularly that of how advertising is used by politicians and political parties. For example, Schenck-Hamlin et al. (2000) found that ads related to a specific candidate were more likely to be perceived as cynical (and prompt calls for accountability) than advertisements related to issues. Not surprisingly, more contemporary research has focused on digital advertising and politics. For example, Brodnax & Sapiezynski (2022) found that digital targeting of ads to states during the 2020 U.S. Presidential election played an important factor during primary elections.

Wilkins & Christians (2001) have asserted that a political advertisement can be considered ethical when it presents needed information, and when it "provides a logical and/or emotional reason to vote for a particular candidate providing that appeal allows for counterargument and reflection" (Wilkins & Christians, 2001, p. 112).

A strong part of why politics and music are so deeply intertwined is sociological in nature. For example, many researchers have found that rap music and hip hop culture are political expression of the black experience in the United States (Rose, 1991), and similarly the development of what was known as "hillbilly music" developed into country music, mostly reflective of rural, white American experience (Barretta, 2017; Peterson, 1997). At a deeper level, music has also been researched in relation to political activism, both by producer and consumer. For example, Anyiwo et al. (2022) found a positive relationship between how youth perceive rap music and how they developed in a sociopolitical manner; also that consumption of rap music as well as levels of engagement with artists on social media affected their likelihood to engage in social activism. Similarly, Belcher & Haridakis (2011) found a link between genre of music consumption by members of college student political group membership and political activism.

Producers have also used music and politics together. For example, Hill (2022) asserts that musicians use political activism as a way of managing not only their image or brand, but also to enact social change. A recent example of musicians interacting with politics was when the Boston, Massachusetts based band Dropkick Murphys used social media to distance themselves from, and criticize, a U.S. politician who had been using their music publicly. What followed was a rally of support for the politician, and negative attention for the band (Wilcox, 2022).

Advertising and Controversy

Addressing viewer response to advertising of political parties, de Run & Ting (2014) find that although audiences recognize such advertising is providing information, there is a level of skepticism and therefore it must be presented in a way that avoids negative responses. In any arena, an advertiser generally does not concern themselves with consumers outside of their target audience, as long as that content does not offend those outside the target, for fear the ad might backfire. Such backfiring was seen in April 2023 when Bud Light used social media to support the LGBTQ+ community by publicizing the gift of a Bud Light can with the likeness of transgender influencer Dylan Mulvaney (Lim et al., 2023). The result was a negative response from conservatives, many of whom were Bud Light consumers who publicly lambasted the company for their support of the LGBTQ+ community.

There have been a number of researchers who explored the importance of considering the audience, both intended and unintended. For example, McCleskey

(2021) provided an excellent theory-based analysis of how sex appeal has been used in advertising. Particular attention was paid to negative effects related to exposure of that advertising to children – an unintended audience – and how marketers can best manage the concern and remain ethical. Gender is another area where previous literature highlights a point of concern. Wolin (2003) provided an analysis of gender related advertising research that spanned three decades and found during that time period, gender stereotypes were diminishing; furthermore, males and females respond differently to different advertising strategies, and an effective practice is to create separate appeals for females and males. Of course in the twenty-plus years since then it has become apparent that gender identity has become more fluid (Flores, 2021); however, it is still an effective strategy. Even more importantly, perhaps even more so because of the fluidity of gender among viewers, gender is an area where potential backlash should be considered.

Part of the balancing act that advertisers must play has to do with getting attention on one hand, but not going so far as to create negative responses. For example, advertising with a humor appeal by a regional consumer bank, FirstBank, resulted in increased awareness, but at the same time a flurry of complaints from viewers ("FirstBank," 2015). Reflecting an important notion in IMC strategy that the advertiser, more so than the agency responsible for creating advertisements, is primarily responsible for advertising strategy and content, Kashmiri et al. (2019) found that firms with CEOs who are focused more on promotion than on regulatory issues are more likely to produce controversial advertising, and therefore more at risk of backlash.

When a firm encounters backlash from controversial advertising, it is clear that response matters. First and foremost, timely response is important, as seen in the case of South African pharmacy chain Clicks Group, Ltd. who quickly removed a hair care product advertisement that was found to be racist (Kew & Bowker, 2020). The content of the response is also important, as seen in a comparison of two different outdoor advertising companies' handling of backlash in response to the same advertisement promoting gay sex. Faced with negative attention from activists, one firm actively managed the situation and supported the advertiser, taking a stance for tolerance and acceptance. Contrarily, the other took a laid back approach, failing to take much of a stance and as a result received negative attention (Jaques, 2013).

Perceptual Threshold

Taking these two themes together, the relationship between politics and music, and the risk of negative consequences experienced when an advertiser risks backlash from an unintended audience, is further informed by an understanding of perceptual threshold. Perceptual threshold is related to what began almost a half century ago as the just-noticeable-difference in product design and quality (Kamen, 1977). More contemporarily, perceptual threshold – the point at which the human brain is expected to perceive a difference - has been used in a number of ways important to marketing communications. For example, Huh et al. (2013) found there is a perceptual threshold for ad frequency above which consumers will avoid, or even be irritated by an ad. In terms of message retention, Wedel & Pieters (2000) used eye tracking software to determine perceptual thresholds related to how long viewers focus on elements of a print ad, and whether or not the message being communicated is saved in long-term memory.

This chapter is proposing that using music from politically charged musicians can serve as a positive advertising element for a target audience with similar political leanings, with a low risk of backlash from consumers who do not have the same political leanings – perhaps even those with opposing views. An interestingly equivalent phenomenon was advanced by Ramsøy & Skov (2014) when they researched conscious processing of visually perceived stimuli and found "the threshold for conscious processing of a stimulus is affected by the individual level of preference for the stimulus being briefly displayed." In the case of sonic stimulus in an advertisement, the stimulus is the song, and the viewing and listening audience is consciously processing the political viewpoints.

THEORETICAL DEVELOPMENT

The main assertion of this chapter is that the use of sonic elements of advertising can be a subtle way of appealing to a specific target audience with a homogeneous political view, but without offending consumers outside that audience in a way that risks backfiring. In other words, musical elements of an advertisement can be used to appeal to a particular group because of similar political affiliations that group may have with the artist of a chosen song. The appeal of political like-mindedness with an artist is strong enough to be effective, yet subtle enough to minimize the risk of backfiring.

Because prior attitudes affect how ads are perceived by an audience (Stammerjohan et al., 2005), advertisers can use well-known political views of music artists to subtly establish a connection to the political preferences associated with a target consumer segment. Some uses are obvious and direct, for example the use of Democrat leaning Demi Lovato's song "Commander in Chief" in a video presented and paid for by The Lincoln Project, a Political Action Committee throughout the 2020 U.S. Presidential election. Others are more subtle, for example the use of a song by Lovato in a TJ Maxx commercial (*TJ Maxx Ad*, n.d.), appealing to a young adult audience, and using long-time Democratic leaning artist Cher in a commercial for Mac cosmetics (*Cher MAC Commercial*, n.d.).

Although not yet widely used, or obvious, there are other examples which are constructed in a somewhat subtle manner - intentional enough to appeal to a particular target segment, but subtle enough not to offend those outside the segment. For example, the music of rap/rock artist Kid Rock, who has been a strong supporter of the Republican Party since 2015 or earlier, was used in a Chevrolet commercial that appeals to rural Americans advertising pick-up trucks (*Chevy Silverado Kid Rock*, n.d.). Similarly, and less subtly, was the use of Toby Keith, a country artist singing about being a "Ford Truck Man" in a variety of television commercials (Halliday, 2002) and related video content featuring the musician and his music. The political affiliation that each of these artists has with the Republican party of the United States will appeal to the rural, conservative members of the target markets for pickup trucks. On the other hand, the use is not so strong that it is intended to not catch the attention of others from outside this demographic in an offensive manner.

IMC Strategy

According to the strategic theory behind Integrated Marketing Communications, an overall message is best communicated using multiple elements that complement each other using a variety of channels, based on the strengths and weaknesses of those channels. There have been debates over whether or not the favorability or unfavorability of music can affect consumer perceptions of a product through classical conditioning (Gorn, 1982; Kellaris & Cox, 1989), though Stewart et al. (1990) found over thirty years ago that musical elements complement and provide greater benefit than verbal cues, particularly for emotionally rich ads.

Since then, other researchers have pointed out that music in advertising can be more than a background element, and instead it can hold meaning for its audience (Scott, 1990), work in conjunction with visual elements of a commercial (Hung, 2001), and that sonic elements of marketing communications help a brand tell its story (Khamis & Keogh, 2021). Furthermore, with the increasing digitization of advertising content, reach and effectiveness are growing far beyond only the television screen (Mulhern, 2009), providing greater opportunities for content and reach.

Unlike segmentation of marketing a political candidate (Baines et al., 2003), the use of sonic elements in advertising can be a way of appealing to market segments for non-political products. This is because it is part of an overall strategy to reach a specific target market with a specific homogeneous set of political views through a mix of marketing channels.

Perception in Advertising

This chapter is not debating the pairing of one type of musical element or another, but instead it is shining a light on the intentional use of music chosen because of the political views of an artist well-known among members of a target market segment who have homogeneous political views consistent with that artist. Similar to color congruency in a print ad as a secondary element that may affect attitude toward an advertisement (J. Lee & Kim, 2022), music in a television or Internet advertisement is a secondary element that may affect a viewer's attitude toward the advertisement. A viewer's attitude toward a brand has been shown to be influenced directly by their attitude toward an advertisement, and also indirectly, mediated by their cognitions of the brand (MacKenzie et al., 1986). Also of note is that subject matter related to political affiliation is emotionally charged, indicating it might be more likely to induce affective responses, which are more powerful than cognitive responses in viewers (Batra & Ray, 1986)

Lantos & Craton (2012) assert that when viewers process information in a television commercial using the peripheral route, where there is low involvement of information processing, music can significantly impact reactions to the message being communicated. Furthermore, Allan (2008) used content analysis of primetime television commercials to contend that popular music used in advertisements played the role of advancing the narrative of the commercial, more so than focusing on the product or brand. This supports the contention of this chapter that music related to a specific artist is a way of creating connection with a particular audience, as viewers of a commercial will process narratives based on their existing belief systems (Chang, 2009). Further support is found in evidence that music works in conjunction with other elements of an advertisement to frame a cultural context (Hung, 2000; Murray & Murray, 1996), such as political views.

The composition of the advertisement will likely be important if the political affiliation of the musical artist is to have an effect, as this connection is referential. According to Zhu & Meyers-Levy (2005), using background music in an advertisement requiring the viewer to engage in intensive processing while viewing an advertisement without a heavy dramatic message will leave viewers with more cognitive resources to process the music as a secondary element and will likely perceive referential meaning. Therefore, the political affiliation of the artist who is performing that music, if known to the viewer, will signal a connection.

Politics and Perception

There is a great deal of research into advertising political candidates (Gordon et al., 2023; Granato & Wong, 2004; N. Kaplan et al., 2006), and some studies have examined the relationship between political beliefs and consumption (Goenka & van Osselaer, 2023) or satisfaction of products (Fernandes et al., 2022). However, there is a dearth of research relating to how homogeneous political views can be used as an advertising element for non-political products, be they goods or services. At a more direct level, political affiliation has been shown to be an important tool in segmenting a market, and even developing a consumer-brand relationship (Flight & Coker, 2022), promoting brand attachment through socio-political activism. Will this technique of segmentation through political affiliation be effective at a more subtle level? The answer likely lies in the strength of a person's political beliefs, and how meaningful they are to their cognitive perception. Conceptually, support for the effectiveness of this technique is presented throughout this chapter.

There are growing ideological differences between conservatives and liberals, much of it rooted in personality traits and leading to behavioral differences (Carney et al., 2008; Lisjak & Ordabayeva, 2023). Political beliefs have the potential for dictating strong opinions or behavior. For example, a study of behavioral responses to COVID-19 related health protections in Argentina found that political orientation had a statistically significant influence on behavior (Torrente et al., 2022). Lending further credence to the idea that advertisers can employ politically affiliated content to affect consumer perceptions, Villagra et al. (2021) point out that politically associated corporate activism has been on the rise, and there is a difference in how consumers perceive that activism based on their beliefs. In particular, conservatives generally have a negative reaction to such activism, while liberals are overall more receptive.

MUSIC, POLITICS, AND IMC STRATEGY

Bringing together the three pillars of theoretical development presented above, it is not surprising that the examples cited in the introduction have graced the advertising airwaves. What is surprising is that there have not been more examples of reliance on political affiliation as a secondary element in advertising. Perhaps there is a fear of backlash; according to Blair & Shimp (1992), the possibility exists that a person who has had a prior negative experience with a song will carry that negative emotion forward and associate it with the product or brand being advertised. In such a case, a company could risk offending a viewer, either within or especially outside of the target market. Consider what was described in the previous section with Bud Light, Dylan Mulvaney, and the large segment of its conservative rural consumers (Lim et al., 2023). Further explaining the hesitancy is that advertising has gone through a long period of risk aversion, believed to negatively affect creativity of content (Bilby et al., 2023). However, using a song from an artist with a strong, well-known political affiliation would be more of an internal reference perception and not strong enough to evoke backlash.

At the other end of the spectrum, there is also the possibility that the effect of political affiliation from the musical artist, particularly because background music is a secondary element, is too subtle. This is likely not a significant concern for two main reasons. First, as noted earlier in the *Perception in Advertising* section, if the advertisement is developed properly, viewers should be affected by the song with referential meaning. Consumers for whom the artist's political views are meaningful enough to serve as referentially important are those viewers with the same political views, and therefore they will make the connection, particularly at the subconscious level.

Similarly, the second reason there is only low risk of subtlety being a barrier is the strength of subliminal perception. While we have known for decades that subliminal advertising was a myth, and it does not immediately drive behavior on its own (Rogers, 1992), there is something to the perception capabilities of the human brain, and its use in IMC strategy. This chapter is not suggesting the type of auditory subliminal perception where subjects are affected by disguised content from self-report after listening to audio recordings (Harris et al., 1996; Merikle, 1988). Instead, it is relying on the understanding that "(p)sychologists generally agree that it is possible to perceive things without being consciously aware of them" (Belch & Belch, 2021, p. 122). Therefore, while watching a commercial constructed according to the findings presented by Zhu & Meyers-Levy (2005), a viewer who shares the same political beliefs as the musical artist may likely recognize the song, and make a positive connection.

A strong theoretical foundation for the assertion of this chapter lies in recent findings about the self-congruity of music, particularly in terms of social identity theory (Tekman & Hortaçsu, 2002) and personality fit (Greenberg et al., 2021). When we consider political affiliation to be a social group (Smaldino, 2019), it brings important meaning to the finding that

group ideology, attitudes, values, and belief systems and, therefore, listening to artists with similar personalities serves to reinforce individual and group identity and gives the listener a sense of pride and belonging to a social world. The self-congruity effect is hence a way for people to define and reinforce in-group and out-group boundaries (Greenberg et al., 2021, p. 147).

Furthermore, use of the music of a particular artist because of their like-minded political affiliation is a form of covert signaling to those associating with that (political) social identity group. Through this frame, an advertiser can convey a marketing communication message conveying a favorable reference to a particular market segment without prompting a negative reaction, or even alienating people from outside the social identity group (Smaldino et al., 2018). In other words, they can use music as a secondary element to reach a particular consumer segment with a homogeneous set of political beliefs while avoiding backlash from others who may not be of the same political notions.

SONIC ELEMENTS, POLITICAL APPEAL

Some examples of using music from artists who have a particular political affiliation that will likely appeal to a particular segment were provided in an earlier section of this chapter. Whether or not this was the intended purpose of the songs' inclusion can only be ascertained by asking the producers of the commercials; however, the amount of effort and planning that goes into producing a national commercial would indicate that such intention is a safe assumption to make. Even more valuable would be an assessment of how effective the commercials were in achieving the communications objectives set by the companies and agencies who created the ads. This information is not publicly available; however, for the purposes of this chapter these points are explored at a conceptual level.

Let's take an example of what Witzling & Shaw (2019) investigated about lifestyle segmentation of food consumers and political affiliation. In particular, their focus was motivations to purchase locally sourced food products. Their findings showed that in general, liberals are motivated by considering food sources that support local food producers and are willing to pay more for eating at environmentally sustainable restaurants. They found that more conservative food consumers also have an interest in local ingredients, but for different reasons, such as the importance and appeal of respecting tradition in how meals are prepared. How would the conceptual approach written about in this chapter be applied in this situation?

Using this context as an example, an organization marketing a product related to food-related lifestyle (FRL) would structure their campaign to reach two related but distinct target segments - call them *liberals* and *conservatives*. Like many two-pronged campaigns, each of these segments have some things in common, and some ways in which they are differentiated. What they have in common is that the concept of buying local is an attractive option for a food source. Where they differ is their reasons for why it is attractive (support local businesses for *liberals* / honoring tradition for *conservatives*). The primary elements of advertisements would highlight these differences through techniques such as visuals of a farmers market for local businesses and cooking with fresh ingredients for tradition, respectively, and possibly appropriate text and voiceover content. A media planning group would identify the appropriate vehicles to reach each target segment, and advertising time would be purchased to best reach the consumers in each market segment.

This approach allows the advertiser to tie content of each song with the message communicated by the advertisement. To strengthen the messaging of each of these example advertisements, the commercial for the *liberals* segment could use a song such as "Food Around the Corner," by the band Green Day, a band known in the United States to be aligned with the Democratic political party more so than the Republican party. The advertisement for the *conservatives* segment could use a song such as "You Get What You Pay For" by Sammy Hagar, known in the United States for his affiliation with the Republican political party. The Green Day song is more of a quirky ditty than a full song, with one of the band members singing, "There will be food around the corner for me" and not much else. The sentiment of this song is consistent with the idea of a local farmers market where consumers can purchase food from a local source. For the use of the Sammy Hagar song, the music and lyrics are upbeat and positive:

"C'mon, make me a deal / Where everybody wins (everybody wins) / I'm good for my word / But if you want more, remember / You get what you pay for / You get what you pay for."

The sentiment of these lyrics are consistent with the theme of using fresh, locally sourced ingredients to honor the tradition of a recipe. "I'm good for my word" connotes loyalty and patriotism, both important to conservative ideals (Broadwater, 2023), and "You get what you pay for" conveys the quality of the locally sourced food products.

FRAGMENTING AUDIENCE

Paying attention to the opportunity for using sonic elements of television advertising to segment and target a market based on political views comes at a very important time, with the increasingly fragmented state of television program viewing. With a significant shift from broadcast and cable viewership to streaming, advertisers are experiencing opportunities for robust reach and scale by thinking "stream first" (Levin, 2021) the way web based content switched to "mobile first" approaches as mobile device browsing began to overtake computer based web browsing (Gibbs, 2016). Attention paid to how media buying is changing seems like a natural evolution from over a decade ago when successful media buying began to account for a shift from broadcast to Internet Protocol Television (Brooks, 2007). From a content perspective, the time is ripe for exploring ways to create content that can serve a fragmenting viewing market.

The FRL example provided above was a basic approach to highlight how sonic elements of advertising can be used to address a political affiliation based segmentation strategy. To broaden this point from a practical perspective, recent advances in technology allow marketers to reach audiences using different methods, and with a much more targeted reach. Consumers have become less *mass media* and more reachable through identifiable segments based not only on interest, but also on viewing device. As fragmentation of television viewing continues, most notably through streaming services, advertisers can have a more focused target audience for their content.

Like paid search engine ads, advertisers on streaming television services can gain access to narrower fields of interest than purchasing broadcast or cable air time based on Gross Ratings Point (GRP) metrics. With technology merging the Internet and television from the perspective of how content is provided to where audiences view that content on a variety of devices (da Silva Klehm et al., 2022), advertising practices will continue to change. Those best able to navigate those changes will likely be the most successful. Two other important differences are crucial to the idea of using sonic elements as a way of appealing to political viewpoints: length of commercial time, and access to more precise data.

K. Stewart et al. (2019) compared traditional television advertising effectiveness measures (attitude towards ad, attitude towards brand, intention to purchase, intentions to seek more product info and opt-in to receive more product info) for Digital Video Advertising (DVA) which did not include streaming services. They found

DVA for hedonic products resulted in stronger attitudes toward the ad and brand and intentions to purchase … (while) DVA for low-involvement products resulted in stronger purchase intentions and likelihood to opt-in for more information. Moreover, there was an interaction between product category and involvement across all five measures of DVA effectiveness. (K. Stewart et al., 2019, p. 2469)

Also included in their findings is that there were differences in measured levels based on device. With the tremendous rate of speed with which television viewership is fragmenting, for the purposes of this chapter advertising on streaming television is more akin to DVA now than it was in 2019, and there are opportunities for advertisers to begin creating content with a "streaming first" approach (Levin, 2021). Part of this opportunity includes the use of sonic elements, and in particular the use of political affiliation as a targetable segment.

One of those tools can be length of time. Even though songs have been treated as a secondary element of a commercial, it does not mean we should ignore which, or how long the portion of the song used should be. Especially when a song with lyrics is used, the commercial's producer can choose the most impactful lyrics to be heard during the advertisement. Having flexibility of time, most commonly in 15 second increments up to a full minute, means that producers can be specific about two important facets of the sonic element - congruency with the political leanings of the target market, and complementarity with the visual elements of the commercial's content.

The second important opportunity brought to advertisers courtesy of technology and fragmenting viewership related to streaming is the future of precision in measurement. Potentially, it could be commonplace for advertisers on a streaming service to measure conversions similar to what we now have in digital advertising. Looking ahead, advertisers will have at their disposal opportunities to measure reach far more precisely than traditional, linear television. Instead of looking at viewer demographics based on a Nielsen rating provided by the networks, advertisers will potentially also have access to psychographic data that can be analyzed in conjunction with political affiliation. Looking even further into the future - which is likely not very far in the future - will be the types of analytics consistent with those currently provided by paid search engine and social media advertising.

We are in the realm of potential opportunities; now is the time to consider innovative strategic planning. Envisioning the technological advances discussed above working in conjunction with the assertion that music from politically charged artists can be an important sonic element in advertising brings the opportunity of risk management the likes of which are impossible in linear advertising. Similar to how digital paid ads increased the effectiveness of A/B testing methods originally developed for magazine advertising, the feasibility of greater precision in responses to, and effectiveness of streaming television advertisements will allow advertisers to perform A/B testing on their content. It is perfectly reasonable to believe that two versions of a television commercial could be created, each with a different audio track to measure a particular conversion. Therefore, the potential barrier of backlash could be reduced in near real time - or possibly real time. This makes the potential for using sonic elements of advertising combined with a political affiliation appeal more effective and feasible than ever.

FORMATIVE MODEL

This being a conceptual chapter, presenting a visual understanding of the proposed approach serves as a formative model. It is a summary of the content presented, and potentially a launching pad for operationalizing a study to test some or all of the concepts presented. Perceptual threshold presented in the literature review section is an ideal starting point for a formative model. The proposed use of sonic elements related to political affiliations of a music artist inherently involves paying close attention to the balancing act of appealing to one group based on similar political affiliations while avoiding backlash from an audience with opposing views. If music serves as a referential connection as described by Zhu & Meyers-Levy (2005), then members of the audience with a like-minded and known political affiliation will have a positive reaction; however, members of opposing political leanings will not develop a negative perception. Another group of people would be those without strong political views, and/or those who do not have knowledge of an active political affiliation of the artist.

Figure 1. Model of Political Sonic Perception

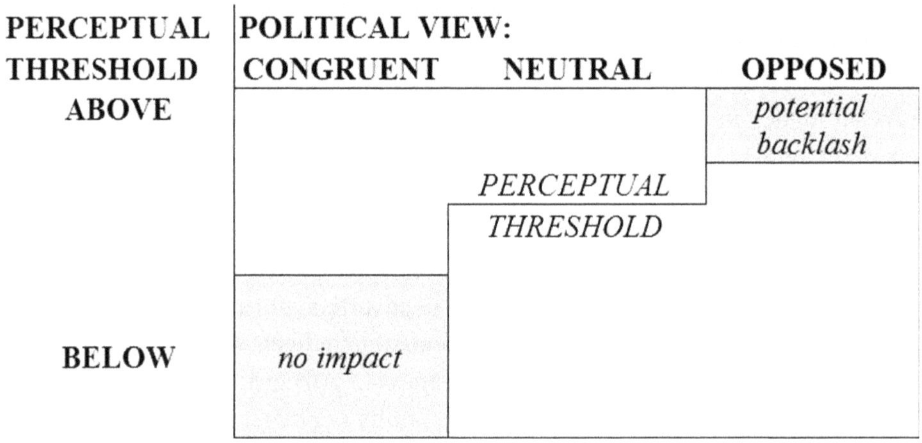

The model of political sonic perception displays that there are audience perceptions either above or below the perceptual threshold based on whether the audience has the same, opposing, or neutral political views compared to the artist who is performing the sonic element. Those in the neutral category consist of people who either are not aware of the artist or their political affiliations, or who themselves are not emotionally committed to the politics of the artist, even if they are aware of them. The shaded areas represent those areas with a likelihood that the political affiliation will be noticed. In the case of consumers with the same political affiliation, there is a greater likelihood that the congruent political affiliation will be recognized. This is a positive outcome, because it creates a sense of connection with the consumer. Below the perceptual threshold in this case causes no harm. It means that consumers with the same political views did not recognize the connection.

For the audience with political views opposed to those of the artists, it is important to note that most of the audience falls into the area below the perceptual threshold. Because they are hearing a song from an artist as a secondary element of the commercial, the artist will likely not attract their attention. This is where the challenge is. This perceptual threshold will be based on a combination of an individual's level of political concern, the degree of political activism of the artist, and quite possibly the particular song being used. Consumers opposed to the political viewpoint of the artist who fall above the perceptual threshold become potential baklashers.

An excellent example of this challenge presented itself during the lead up to the 2024 U.S. Presidential race, related to worldwide pop star Taylor Swift. Although Swift has long been outspoken about issues important to democratic leaning audiences such as LGBTQ+ rights, she spent many years avoiding publicly stating any political party views until 2018, and then again in the 2020 election, in all cases supporting democratic candidates (Voght & Parker, 2024). Leading up to the 2024 Presidential election, Swift became the subject of conspiracy theories propagated by conservative republicans whereby Swift is part of a covert Government effort to re-elect sitting President Joe Biden. According to a Monmouth University poll, while the majority of Americans (73%) rejected the theories, 32% of republicans polled believed the conspiracy theory to be true. Furthermore, considering only republicans who reported they heard of the theory, the percent was even higher, at 44% (Blake, 2024). With this in mind, suppose a brand had previously chosen to use Swift's music as part of an advertisement for their product as a way of appealing to a democratic leaning target segment. With such a strong belief in a conspiracy theory related to Taylor Swift, the brand would have run the risk of backlash from an unintended audience once the theories began to emerge and spread. Clearly, there is no way to know exactly where the line of perceptual theory may lie.

LIMITATIONS AND FUTURE RESEARCH

The idea that an advertisement can use a recognizable song from a recognizable artist with a particular political affiliation is presented as a strategy that will carry low risk of backfiring. The limitation of this chapter is that one cannot know whether or not that risk is low enough to take. Whether or not an advertiser can identify the perceptual threshold that will create connection without risking backlash. As seen with Bud Light and Dylan Mulvaney (Lim et al., 2023), the ramifications of backfiring can have serious negative consequences. Therefore, this is potentially a problematic approach. Pragmatically, knowing the risk of backfiring is contextual. It behooves a marketer to consider their audience – both those who would be reached in a positive manner, and those who could risk being reached in a negative manner

– and simultaneously the degree of politicization of the artist and possibly even the song. Are they a lightning rod for backlash, or mildly politicized in the eyes of the general public?

Theoretically and academically, this leads to many avenues for future research. The most obvious and basic approach would be a 2x2 factorial experimental design (3x3 with control groups). Using two songs, one each from artists with opposing political party affiliations (Democrat / Republican in the United States) and having subjects self-select as being from one of those two opposing parties, measurements of attitudes toward the ad and brand could be taken, then group mean differences could be statistically tested. A stronger research design would include degrees of political activism of artists, and a self-report degree of political sensitivity by subjects. While the artists would need to have a well-established political affiliation, the advertisements would have to be for fictional products to control for preconceived product or brand perceptions.

In the event that a researcher could identify contemporary advertisements that use music from politically charged artists, similar to those mentioned in an earlier section of this chapter, qualitative research could also be conducted. This would be beneficial because depth interviews or focus groups could get to a deeper level of perception among viewers of the commercials.

CONCLUSION

This chapter explored using sonic elements of advertising to appeal to a consumer segment based on homogeneous political beliefs. Support comes from prior research on a number of topics. Foundational knowledge relied upon is related to segmentation and targeting, how advertising elements are perceived, and the synergistic power of combining multiple elements of content through a strategic combination of IMC channels. A slightly higher level of knowledge through previous research was presented about how political views affect perception and behavior. The higher level, most recent research is related to fragmenting television viewing practices of audiences. A merging of Internet and linear television is developing a world where televisions are becoming only one of many screen types, and access is provided through non-traditional, a.k.a. streaming platforms.

The fairly recent decision for Netflix, one of the original streaming services, to offer an ad based option is a signal that advertising is not going away - it is morphing. This presents an opportunity for marketers to reinvent their approach to IMC strategy and especially content development. Taking a streaming first approach means thinking about how people watch television before developing content, as opposed to developing content and then finding a place to put it (Levin, 2021).

Embedded in this approach is recognition that fragmentation of the viewing market brings with it the opportunity for finding new ways of appealing to very specific market segments - segments that can be targeted with much greater precision than linear television. Therefore, it is important to identify as many ways as possible for creating effective content. Sonic elements of advertising that connect the political views of musical artists with those of a homogeneous market segment is one way of doing this.

REFERENCES

Allan, D. (2008). A Content Analysis of Music Placement in Prime-Time Television Advertising. *Journal of Advertising Research*, *48*(3), 404–417. doi:10.2501/S0021849908080434

Allan, D. (2010). They're Playing My Brand. *International Journal of Integrated Marketing Communications*, *2*(1), 40–46.

Anyiwo, N., Watkins, D. C., & Rowley, S. J. (2022). "They Can't Take Away the Light": Hip-Hop Culture and Black Youth's Racial Resistance. *Youth & Society*, *54*(4), 611–634. doi:10.1177/0044118X211001096

Baines, P. R., Worcester, R. M., Jarrett, D., & Mortimore, R. (2003). Market Segmentation and Product Differentiation in Political Campaigns: A Technical Feature Perspective. *Journal of Marketing Management*, *19*(1–2), 225–249. doi:10.1080/0267257X.2003.9728208

Barretta, P. G. (2017). Tracing the color line in the American music market and its effect on contemporary music marketing. *Arts and the Market*, *7*(2), 213–234. doi:10.1108/AAM-08-2016-0016

Batra, R., & Ray, M. L. (1986). Affective Responses Mediating Acceptance of Advertising. *Journal of Consumer Research*, *13*(2), 234–249. doi:10.1086/209063

Belch, G. E., & Belch, M. A. (2021). *Advertising and Promotion. An Integrated Marketing Communications Perspective* (12th ed.). McGraw-Hill.

Belcher, J. D., & Haridakis, P. (2011). From "Alternative" to "Trance": The Role of Music in Facilitating Political Group Activity and Activism. *Ohio Communication Journal*, *49*, 145–174.

Bilby, J., Koslow, S., & Sasser, S. L. (2023). Fear in Adland: How Client Risk Aversion and Agency Clientelism Limit the Development of Great Creative Campaigns. *Journal of Advertising*, *52*(1), 57–74. doi:10.1080/00913367.2021.1981497

Blair, M. E., & Shimp, T. A. (1992). Consequences of an Unpleasant Experience with Music: A Second-Order Negative Conditioning Perspective. *Journal of Advertising*, *21*(1), 35–43. doi:10.1080/00913367.1992.10673358

Blake, A. (2024, February 14). Analysis | Much of the GOP is on-board with the Taylor Swift conspiracy theories. *Washington Post*. https://www.washingtonpost.com/politics/2024/02/14/gop-swift-superbowl/

Broadwater, L. (2023, February 8). They, the Republicans, Recite the Constitution For an Edge in Patriotism. *The New York Times*. https://www.proquest.com/newspapers/they-republicans-recite-constitution-edge/docview/2774028201/se-2

Brodnax, N. M., & Sapiezynski, P. (2022). From Home Base to Swing States: The Evolution of Digital Advertising Strategies during the 2020 US Presidential Primary. *Political Research Quarterly*, *75*(2), 460–478. doi:10.1177/10659129221078046

Brooks, G. (2007). Whose territory? *New Media Age*, 25–25.

Carney, D. R., Jost, J. T., Gosling, S. D., & Potter, J. (2008). The Secret Lives of Liberals and Conservatives: Personality Profiles, Interaction Styles, and the Things They Leave Behind. *Political Psychology*, *29*(6), 807–840. doi:10.1111/j.1467-9221.2008.00668.x

Chang, C. (2009). "Being Hooked" By Editorial Content: The Implications for Processing Narrative Advertising. *Journal of Advertising*, *38*(1), 21–34. doi:10.2753/JOA0091-3367380102

Cher drops new 'Take Me Home' remix as featured in latest MAC commercial—RETROPOP - Fashionably Nostalgic | News, Interviews, Reviews, and more... (n.d.). Retrieved August 9, 2023, from https://retropopmagazine.com/cher-take-me-home-remix-mac-commercial/

Chevy Silverado 2014 TV Spot, "New Anthem: Born Free" Song by Kid Rock. (n.d.). Retrieved October 2, 2023, from https://www.ispot.tv/ad/7CRs/2014-chevy-silverado-truck-guys-song-by-kid-rock

da Silva Klehm, V., de Souza Braga, R., & de Lucena Jr, V. F. (2022). A Survey of Digital Television Interactivity Technologies. *Sensors*, *22*(17), 6542. doi:10.3390/s22176542 PMID:36080995

de Run, E. C., & Ting, H. (2014). Determining Attitudinal Beliefs About Controversial Advertising. *International Journal of Business & Society*, *15*(3), 465–476.

Dunaway, D. K. (1987). Music and Politics in the United States on JSTOR. *Folk Music Journal*, *5*(3), 268–294.

Fernandes, D., Ordabayeva, N., Han, K., Jung, J., & Mittal, V. (2022). How Political Identity Shapes Customer Satisfaction. *Journal of Marketing*, *86*(6), 116–134. doi:10.1177/00222429211057508

FirstBank's Off-Beat Advertising Generates Viewer Response—And Controversy. (2015). ABA Bank Marketing & Sales, 47(7), 3–4. https://ezproxy.wagner.edu/login?url=https://search.ebscohost.com/login.aspx?direct=true&db=buh&AN=109330318&site=ehost-live&scope=site

Flight, R. L., & Coker, K. (2022). Birds of a feather: Brand attachment through the lens of consumer political ideologies. *Journal of Product and Brand Management*, *31*(5), 731–743. doi:10.1108/JPBM-01-2020-2719

Flores, Y. (2021). Science, Context, and Gender Fluidity in Public Policy. *Public Integrity*, *23*(6), 595–609. doi:10.1080/10999922.2020.1825181

Gibbs, S. (2016, November 2). Mobile web browsing overtakes desktop for the first time. *The Guardian*. https://www.theguardian.com/technology/2016/nov/02/mobile-web-browsing-desktop-smartphones-tablets

Goenka, S., & van Osselaer, S. M. J. (2023). Why Is It Wrong to Sell Your Body? Understanding Liberals' Versus Conservatives' Moral Objections to Bodily Markets. *Journal of Marketing*, *87*(1), 64–80. doi:10.1177/00222429211046936

Gordon, B. R., Lovett, M. J., Luo, B., & Reeder, J. C. I. III. (2023). Disentangling the effects of ad tone on voter turnout and candidate choice in presidential elections. *Management Science*, *69*(1), 220–243. doi:10.1287/mnsc.2022.4347

Gorn, G. J. (1982). The Effects of Music In Advertising On Choice Behavior: A Classical Conditioning Approach. *Journal of Marketing*, *46*(1), 94–101. doi:10.1177/002224298204600109

Granato, J., & Wong, M. C. S. (2004). Political Campaign Advertising Dynamics. *Political Research Quarterly*, *57*(3), 349–361. doi:10.1177/106591290405700301

Greenberg, D. M., Matz, S. C., Schwartz, H. A., & Fricke, K. R. (2021). The self-congruity effect of music. *Journal of Personality and Social Psychology*, *121*(1), 137–150. doi:10.1037/pspp0000293 PMID:32614219

Halliday, J. (2002, August 14). *Ford signs "Angry American" Singer for TV Ads*. Ad Age. https://adage.com/article/news/ford-signs-angry-american-singer-tv-ads/35471

Harris, J. L., Salus, D., Rerecich, R., & Larsen, D. (1996). Distinguishing detection from identification in subliminal auditory perception: A review and critique of Merikle's study. *The Journal of General Psychology, 123*(1), 41–50. doi:10.1080/00221309.1996.9921258 PMID:8901209

Hill, J. C. (2022). Activist Musicians: A Framework for Leaders of Social Change. *Journal of Leadership Education, 21*(2), 164–180. doi:10.12806/V21/I2/T1

Huh, J., DeLorme, D. E., & Reid, L. N. (2013). Irritation and Ad Avoidance Behaviors: Influencing Factors in the Context of Otc Analgesic Advertising. American Academy of Advertising Conference Proceedings, 110–111.

Hung, K. (2000). Narrative Music in Congruent and Incongruent TV Advertising. *Journal of Advertising, 29*(1), 25–34. doi:10.1080/00913367.2000.10673601

Hung, K. (2001). Framing Meaning Perceptions with Music: The Case of Teaser Ads. *Journal of Advertising, 30*(3), 39–49. doi:10.1080/00913367.2001.10673644

Jaques, T. (2013). Ensnared in a gay health controversy: A comparative study in responding to issue activism. Journal of Public Affairs, 13(1), 53–60. doi:10.1002/pa.1442

Kamen, J. M. (1977). Controlling "just noticeable differences" in quality. *Harvard Business Review, 55*(6), 12–164. https://ezproxy.wagner.edu/login?url=https://search.ebscohost.com/login.aspx?direct=true&db=edb&AN=3867518&site=eds-live

Kaplan, N., Park, D. K., & Ridout, T. N. (2006). Dialogue in American Political Campaigns? An Examination of Issue Convergence in Candidate Television Advertising. *American Journal of Political Science, 50*(3), 724–736. doi:10.1111/j.1540-5907.2006.00212.x

Kaplan, R. L. (2013). The Economics and Politics of Nineteenth-Century Newspapers. *American Journalism, 10*(1–2), 84–101.

Kashmiri, S., Gala, P., & Nicol, C. D. (2019). Seeking pleasure or avoiding pain: Influence of CEO regulatory focus on firms' advertising, R&D, and marketing controversies. *Journal of Business Research, 105*, 227–242. doi:10.1016/j.jbusres.2019.08.022

Kellaris, J. J., & Cox, A. D. (1989). The Effects of Background Music in Advertising: A Reassessment. *The Journal of Consumer Research, 16*(1), 113–118. doi:10.1086/209199

Kew, J., & Bowker, J. (2020, September 8). Racist Advertising Controversy Hits South Africa's Biggest Pharmacy Chain. Bloomberg.Com; Bloomberg, L.P. https://ezproxy.wagner.edu/login?url=https://search.ebscohost.com/login.aspx?direct=true&db=buh&AN=145626797&site=ehost-live&scope=site

Khamis, S., & Keogh, B. (2021). Sonic branding and the aesthetic infrastructure of everyday consumption. *Popular Music*, *40*(2), 281–296. doi:10.1017/S0261143021000118

Lantos, G. P., & Craton, L. G. (2012). A model of consumer response to advertising music. *Journal of Consumer Marketing*, *29*(1), 22–42. doi:10.1108/07363761211193028

Lee, A. H.-Y. (2022). Social Trust in Polarized Times: How Perceptions of Political Polarization Affect Americans' Trust in Each Other. *Political Behavior*, *44*(3), 1533–1554. doi:10.1007/s11109-022-09787-1 PMID:35340916

Lee, J., & Kim, H. (2022). How to survive in advertisement flooding: The effects of schema–product congruity and attribute relevance on advertisement attitude. *Journal of Consumer Behaviour*, *21*(2), 214–230. doi:10.1002/cb.1991

Levin, A. (2021). Say Goodbye to the Traditional TV Upfronts: Media buying plans should start mirroring video viewing habits. *Broadcasting & Cable - Multichannel News, 151*(5), 41–41.

Lim, H. S., Moon, W.-K., & Ciszek, E. (2023). Advertising for Brands and Society: The Role of Perceived Authenticity in Corporate Transgender Advocacy Advertising Campaigns. *Journal of Homosexuality*, 1–29. doi:10.1080/00918369.2023.2245522 PMID:37555702

Lisjak, M., & Ordabayeva, N. (2023). How Political Ideology Shapes Preferences for Observably Inferior Products. *Journal of Consumer Research*, *49*(6), 1014–1031. doi:10.1093/jcr/ucac030

MacKenzie, S. B., Lutz, R. J., & Belch, G. E. (1986). The Role of Attitude Toward the Ad as a Mediator of Advertising Effectiveness: A Test of Competing Explanations. *Journal of Marketing Research*, *23*(2), 130–143. doi:10.1177/002224378602300205

Mangrum, B. (2021). Market Segmentation and Shirley Jackson's Domestic Humor. *American Literary History*, *33*(1), 50–74. doi:10.1093/alh/ajab001

McCleskey, J. A. (2021). The Inconvenient Truth about Sex Appeal in Advertising. *IABS Journal*, *1*(5), 43–67.

Merikle, P. M. (1988). Subliminal Auditory Messages: An Evaluation. *Psychology and Marketing*, *5*(4), 355–372. doi:10.1002/mar.4220050406

Mulhern, F. (2009). Integrated marketing communications: From media channels to digital connectivity. *Journal of Marketing Communications*, *15*(2/3), 85–101. doi:10.1080/13527260902757506

Murray, N. M., & Murray, S. B. (1996). Music and Lyrics in Commercials: A Cross-Cultural Comparison between Commercials Run in the Dominican Republic and in the United States. *Journal of Advertising*, *25*(2), 51–63. doi:10.1080/00913367 .1996.10673499

Peterson, R. A. (1997). *Creating Country Music: Fabricating Authenticity* (1st ed.). University Of Chicago Press. doi:10.7208/chicago/9780226111445.001.0001

Ramsøy, T. Z., & Skov, M. (2014). Brand preference affects the threshold for perceptual awareness. *Journal of Consumer Behaviour*, *13*(1), 1–8. doi:10.1002/cb.1451

Ramswell, P. Q. (2018). *Division, Derision and Decisions: The Domino Effect of Brexit and Populism's Intersection of Rights and Wrongs*. Nova Science Publishers, Inc. https://ezproxy.wagner.edu/login?url=https://search.ebscohost.com/login.aspx ?direct=true&db=nlebk&AN=1724465&site=eds-live

Rogers, S. (1992). How a Publicity Blitz Created The Myth of Subliminal Advertising. *Public Relations Quarterly*, *37*(4), 12–17.

Rose, T. (1991). "Fear of a Black Planet": Rap Music and Black Cultural Politics in the 1990s. *The Journal of Negro Education*, *60*(3), 276–290. doi:10.2307/2295482

Schenck-Hamlin, W. J., Procter, D. E., & Rumsey, D. J. (2000). The influence of Negative Advertising Frames on Political Cynicism and Politician Accountability. *Human Communication Research*, *26*(1), 53–74. doi:10.1111/j.1468-2958.2000. tb00749.x

Schmitt, B., Brakus, J. J., & Biraglia, A. (2022). Consumption Ideology. *The Journal of Consumer Research*, *49*(1), 74–95. doi:10.1093/jcr/ucab044

Scott, L. M. (1990). Understanding Jingles and Needledrop: A Rhetorical Approach to Music in Advertising. *The Journal of Consumer Research*, *17*(2), 223–236. doi:10.1086/208552

Smaldino, P. E. (2019). Social identity and cooperation in cultural evolution. *Behavioural Processes*, *161*, 108–116. doi:10.1016/j.beproc.2017.11.015 PMID:29223462

Smaldino, P. E., Flamson, T. J., & McElreath, R. (2018). The Evolution of Covert Signaling. *Scientific Reports*, *8*(1), 4905. doi:10.1038/s41598-018-22926-1 PMID:29559650

Stammerjohan, C., Wood, C. M., Chang, Y., & Thorson, E. (2005). An Empirical Investigation of the Interaction between Publicity, Advertising, and Previous Brand Attitudes and Knowledge. *Journal of Advertising*, *34*(4), 55–67. doi:10.1080/009 13367.2005.10639209

Steinberg, B. (2021, February 6). *How Bruce Springsteen Agreed To Do a Super Bowl Commercial for Jeep—Variety* [Magazine]. Variety. https://variety.com/2021/ tv/news/bruce-springsteen-super-bowl-commercials-jeep-1234902575/

Stewart, D. W., Farmer, K. M., & Stannard, C. I. (1990). Music As a Recognition Cue in Advertising-Tracking Studies. *Journal of Advertising Research*, *30*(4), 39–48.

Stewart, K., Kammer-Kerwick, M., Auchter, A., Koh, H. E., Dunn, M. E., & Cunningham, I. (2019). Examining digital video advertising (DVA) effectiveness: The role of product category, product involvement, and device. *European Journal of Marketing*, *53*(11), 2451–2479. doi:10.1108/EJM-11-2016-0619

Tekman, H. G., & Hortaçsu, N. (2002). Music and social identity: Stylistic identification as a response to musical style. *International Journal of Psychology*, *37*(5), 277–285. doi:10.1080/00207590244000043

TJ Maxx TV Spot, "Get Everything You Want" Song by Demi Lovato. (n.d.). Retrieved August 9, 2023, from https://www.ispot.tv/ad/bvhf/tj-maxx-get-everything-you-want-song-by-demi-lovato

Torrente, F., Low, D., & Yoris, A. (2022). Risk perception, but also political orientation, modulate behavioral response to COVID-19: A randomized survey experiment. *Frontiers in Psychology*, *13*, 1–17. doi:10.3389/fpsyg.2022.900684 PMID:36059740

Villagra, N., Clemente-Mediavilla, J., López-Aza, C., & Sánchez-Herrera, J. (2021). When polarization hits corporations: The moderating effect of political ideology on corporate activism. *El Profesional de la Información*, *30*(6), 1–20. doi:10.3145/ epi.2021.nov.02

Voght, K., & Parker, A. (2024, February 5). A Taylor Swift endorsement? It's delicate. *Washington Post*. https://www.washingtonpost.com/style/2024/02/04/ taylor-swift-joe-biden-2024-endorsement-question/

Wedel, M., & Pieters, R. (2000). Eye Fixations on Advertisements and Memory for Brands: A Model and Findings. *Marketing Science*, *19*(4), 297–312. doi:10.1287/mksc.19.4.297.11794

Wilcox, C. D. (2022). Dropkick Murphys vs. Scott Walker: Unpacking Populist Ideological Discourse in Digital Space. *Media and Communication*, *10*(4), 202–212. doi:10.17645/mac.v10i4.5747

Wilkins, L., & Christians, C. (2001). Philosophy Meets the Social Sciences: The Nature of Humanity in the Public Arena. *Journal of Mass Media Ethics*, *16*(2/3), 99–120. doi:10.1207/S15327728JMME1602&3_3

Witzling, L., & Shaw, B. R. (2019). Lifestyle segmentation and political ideology: Toward understanding beliefs and behavior about local food. *Appetite*, *132*, 106–113. doi:10.1016/j.appet.2018.10.003 PMID:30300669

Wolin, L. D. (2003). Gender Issues in Advertising—An Oversight Synthesis of Research: 1970-2002. *Journal of Advertising Research*, *43*(1), 111–129. doi:10.2501/JAR-43-1-111-130

Zhu, R., & Meyers-Levy, J. (2005). Distinguishing Between the Meanings of Music: When Background Music Affects Product Perceptions. *Journal of Marketing Research*, *42*(3), 333–345. doi:10.1509/jmkr.2005.42.3.333

Chapter 5
An Investigation Into Sound and Music in Branding:
Premises and Practices of Production

Cristiana Martins de Matos
University of the State of Rio de Janeiro, Brazil

ABSTRACT

This chapter presents the production perspective of the sound branding and music branding agencies, the core mission being to investigate the notions of those who produce the sound and musical identity of brands, what is thought about the public, their reactions, and how this influences the development of projects. Given the scarcity of contributions on the perception of professionals and scholars regarding sound and music in branding, an exploratory qualitative approach was implemented. Six individualized semi-structured interviews were conducted with professionals from agencies specializing in the development of sound and music products for brands, three Brazilians and three Portuguese, and one interview with a neuroscientist and neuromarketing specialist. Therefore, about consistent with practical implications, producers of branded sound and music experiences and brand audiences can benefit from the results of this research.

INTRODUCTION

The decline of traditional visual and auditory communication and the exponential growth of products, services, and organizations, coincides with the existence of an experience economy, a concept put forward by Pine and Gilmore in 1999. The experience economy, which was established from the end of the 20th century into

DOI: 10.4018/979-8-3693-0778-6.ch005

the 21ˢᵗ century, in a scenario of search for differentiation, occurred concomitantly with the emergence of markets such as sensorial branding and, more specifically for this study, sound and musical brand communication, such as sound branding and music branding.

This conjuncture is characterized as mediatized and increasingly crossed by technological innovations that affect the physical and emotional senses of individuals, making clear the importance of investigating the stimulation of sensorial experiences of brands. Therefore, the notion of experience economy is considered, in which, instead of assets and services, sensations are an economic activity, and affections occur through the senses (Pine & Gilmore, 1999, p. 12). As such, there is the sensorial branding, a differentiated strategy in terms of reducing the use of traditional visual and auditory media in communication between brands and their stakeholders.

Then, using stimuli to the five human senses to generate emotion, experience, and memory, and creating a sensory identity for brands, sensorial branding is a growing market based on the production of new forms of interaction through the body´s main sensations, which are visual, auditory, tactile, gustatory, and olfactory. The current demands of the market scenario have created, thus, a search for deeper experience and relevance of the brand with their consumer audiences through tools that affect the subject, on a neurological level, such as the cerebral impacts of the use of sound and music, constituting an auditory sensorial dimension of brands.

In view of this, it should be added that the study in question involves the perception of auditory sensory experiences of brands in view of the existence of a neurological concept of taste. This concept is understood as a construction of taste, and in more detail of taste for sounds and music attributed to brands, which is constituted through the individual´s ability to process information at a non-conscious level, without having immediate and complete perception. Gustafsson (2015, p. 31) presents that there are quantitative consumer studies – for example Oakes & North (2008), Crisinel et al. (2012), Vijaykumar et al. (2012) – proposing that sonic branding works mainly on a subconscious level, which can be utilized by marketers.

What is argued here is that what is constituted is a memory of the body, and not specifically a memory that originates from conscious attention. This definition is considered due to the significant increase in investment in multisensory communication in the last few years. In terms of multisensory communication, according to researcher Erthal (2018, p. 189), "[…] the Sound Branding agencies, which create audiologues, jingles, brandsong, brandvoice, brandsoundscapes etc. planning characteristic soundscapes" are part of new forms of business, being considered emerging markets that work with corporeal affectations, taste, and consciousness.

In short, the overview of this chapter includes the experience economy, concomitant with the emerging sensorial branding and sound and music branding markets, to the relationship between stimulus to differentiation and neuroscientific perspectives. Thus, the main objective of the study is to investigate the notions – on the production process and its effectiveness with the public – of those who produce the sound and musical identity of brands in agencies that work specifically with the elements sound and music to communicate brand identities. The contact was made with agencies in the emerging Brazilian and Portuguese markets in order to analyze what they think about the public, their reactions, and how this influences the development of sound branding and music branding projects.

The chapter is organized as follows: after presenting the most pertinent literature review, the results were discussed of a qualitative investigation that included 7 individualized semi-structured interviews with six professionals from sound branding and music branding agencies, three Brazilians and three Portuguese, and with one neuroscientist and neuromarketing specialist. Finally, then, were presented the conclusions, the implications, and the avenues for future research.

LITERATURE REVIEW

Contemporary Audible Experiences

In view of the focus on the production of audible experiences in contemporaneity, it is relevant to observe what, possibly, these experiences produce in individuals, in other words, the impact of sound and music on routine. The function of this discussion, here, is to demonstrate the impact of the appropriation of sound and music by advertising, since "[…] sounds and music are already important elements that impact individuals in their daily lives and transmit emotions, having the power of emotional regulation". As researcher Gustafsson (2015, p. 20) said: "Music affects consumers instantly – and it can be a powerful marketing tool – notably because of its ability to invoke nostalgic memories and strong feelings related to these".

For a better understanding, it is also necessary to give importance to sound and music studies, to the transition process of the music market at the beginning of the 21st century, and to the commercial possibilities of the digital market. Initially, it is known that the study fields of science, society, and arts relate the intensification of the soundscape – the result of the concentration of sound resulting from the formation of modern cultures, the process of social urbanization, and the concentration of individuals – with an idea of controlling individuals using sound. According to the researcher Iazzetta (2015, p. 155-157), this happens due to the emergence of both sound reproduction technologies and the increase in the number of technologies whose operation produces sounds, in a context of different historical, aesthetic, and cultural issues that have modified the acoustic perception of the world.

This scenario, then, remits to the politics of sound and music, and the concept of soundscape. The notion of soundscape was introduced in the 1970s by the composer Schafer (2001, p. 24). It consists of heard events, or the result of the sum of all the sounds in a given space, and considers, in addition to auditory perception, the notation and the photography of sounds. According to Obici (2008, p. 39), one of the initial objectives of the World Soundscape Project was to modify and improve the sound environment, since Schafer saw the soundscape as a great musical composition that should be perfected to generate well-being and health, with the "ideal" being silence and contact with the sounds of nature, and noise being articulated as sound pollution and power. It is possible to highlight that Obici questions Schafer´s proposal of sound ecology and sees these restrictive categorizations as simplistic.

Therefore, about everyday life, the social scientist Simone de Sá (2010, p. 92) presents the utopian and dystopian dimensions of sound experiences which demonstrate, precisely, two perspectives on experiences with sound and listening. While the utopian dimension deals with the social dimension of listening, especially the music, which enables the creation of affective connections, collective identities, and intimate, cozy, and aesthetically modulated environments, the dystopian dimension concerns the oppressive, excessive, deafening, and disciplinary perspective of noise. Then, the impact of sound and music on people´s routines can be pleasurable or repulsive.

Furthermore, as researcher De Nora (2004, p. 1) mentioned, music has a direct link with cognitive habits, modes of consciousness, and historical development, as well as training the unconscious of individuals. As a result, the conditions for the emergence of listening involve the notion of culture and the ideas and changes relating to hearing and audibility, even more contemporarily. In accordance with the thesis by researcher Matos (2023, p. 132), this leads to a reality, the generation of "anxious listening", in which individuals, mostly young people, do not have the patience to listen to songs longer than three minutes.

The beginning of the 21st century brought not only changes in the music market and commercial opportunities in the digital market, but also a logic that conceives algorithmic taste through groupings of digital data and is, in contemporaneity, inserted into digital platforms, interfering in human behavior. As Matos (2023, p. 133) points out, the support – physical or digital – on which are found the sounds and music consumed by individuals affect the body in different ways. In recent years, according to researcher Herschmann (2010, p. 11), streaming services have been redesigning the stages of production, circulation, and consumption of sound and music media, constituting an opportunity for the phonographic business.

After the eras of the long-playing record (LP), the cassette tape, the compact disc (CD), and few others, stand out the experiences with live music and digital music consumption. This way, it is notorious that the most noticeable audible experiences of the contemporaneity are face-to-face experiences with sounds and music, whether intentional or unintentional, and sound and music consumption on digital platforms. The operation of these digital platforms involves the intensive use of complex algorithms, such as music recommendation systems for users, which create a programmed randomness of songs and play a decisive role in solidifying the taste and mobilizing the emotions of users of these digital platforms. Then, this is artificial intelligence work, which is a current commercial possibility in the digital market.

According to De Marchi (2018, p. 220): "In the case of music recommendation systems, the algorithms of music platforms deliver digital content in a personalized way, building a chain of information [...]". This information chain includes the taste of each user; metadata entered by producers and/or content aggregators; the taste of other users; the taste of various other users, based on metadata provided by producers/aggregators; and an analysis of users´ emotional reactions to each song. The conjuncture created is one of taste bubbles, which can either facilitate or limit individuals´ access to new musical perceptions.

The Spotify streaming service can be used as an example, just as Netflix does with its film and series recommendations. The algorithm of these streaming services works in a similar way, capturing the preferences of their users based on what is searched, played, shared, and even "rejected" by them. As a result, users receive similar recommendations for songs, podcasts, movies, series, and more. This is the case with Spotify´s "Chosen for you" playlist and Netflix´s "Suggestions you will love" section. The question is that these suggestions, because they are automated, can become repetitive, and this limits the discovery of new musical genres or movie genres, for example.

Finally, there are many digital possibilities in contemporaneity, and it is not the intention of this study to present them all. But one thing seems noteworthy: agencies that work with managing the sound and music identity of brands keep up with consumer trends, the music market, and the digital market, and are always willing to use current mechanisms as strategies to be updated and aligned with people´s daily lives, and to achieve satisfactory results in producing connections between brands and individuals.

Audible Experiences and Brand Identity

More specifically, the impact of sound and music on people´s routines is also in the upward relationship between brand management and the use of sound and music to promote emotional connections. An example of this is the theme song for the Brazilian brand Metrô Rio, structured by the first sound branding agency in Latin America, Zanna Sound. Metrô Rio, located in the city of Rio de Janeiro, obtained a pleasant distraction for public transport users on their daily journeys by acquiring this personalized sound and music product.

The Metrô Rio brand song has become a kind of sound meme throughout the city of Rio de Janeiro, and is regularly used at parties, events, graduations, and artistic creations. Including, there is a Facebook page called "Random scenes to the sound of Metrô Rio´ music", in which any kind of scene appears with Metrô Rio´s theme song making up the soundtrack of the videos. Zanna, who is a singer, songwriter, and owner of the Zanna Sound agency, has been the official voice of Metrô Rio for over 10 years, and emphasizes that a significant closeness has been created with cariocas and visitors to the city of Rio de Janeiro.

In this way, the sound and music products structured by sound branding and music branding agencies are designed to sensorially and emotionally involve individuals in their routines, and to remain in their affective memories, making it possible to create an attachment and preference for a particular brand. In addition, the focus on delivering differentiation is an obvious reference to the Experience Economy (Pine & Gilmore, 1999), since these emerging markets are starting their trajectories during this economic scenario linked to the staging of sensations.

In the context of the late 20th century and early 21st century, according to Pine and Gilmore (1999, p. 16), the search for differentiation is the result, especially, of the relationship with the nature of economic value and its natural progression from commodities to assets and services and then, to sensations; of the technology that makes it possible to offer a variety of sensations; and of increased competition. At the same time, the differentiation strategies found in experience marketing, in accordance with Kotler and Keller (2006, p. 312), both add value to the brand and help to avoid commoditization. In short, everything seems to be connected: audible sensory experiences from brands as examples of authentic and differentiated experiences, in line with Pine and Gilmore´s (1999) notions of differentiation, and Kotler et al.´s (2021) notions of marketing, which point to sensoriality and personalized responses.

Danish author Lindstrom (2005, p. 73) emphasizes, also, the importance of presence at all possible contact points. For him, "[…] the more sensory contact points consumers can access when they are thinking about buying a brand, the greater the number of sensory memories activated" and, as a result, "[…] the stronger the connection between the brand and the consumer". As such, there are various sound and music products, for all possible points of contact with consumer audiences. Amid the stages, highlighted by Zanna (2015, p. 34-38), such as research, dynamics between those responsible for the project, production, data collection, and possible others, the products relating to sound branding and music branding are structured.

About the numerous tools used to manage the sound and musical identity of brands, Guerra (2013, p. 77) highlights sound logo, brand voice, sound design on brand products, jingles, exclusive songs and remixes, associations with musical artists, soundtracks, sound in physical locations, and virtual sound. However, other tools are increasingly being used, such as music programming in consumer spaces and events, promotional spots, vignettes and locutions, and recent tools such as playlists and curation on streaming platforms, music and content for social networks, and DJs for events. Lastly, special projects can also use more innovative tools, such as playlists with commentary and online and offline integrations via barcodes or QR codes.

Therefore, there are many sound and musical crossings in the daily lives of individuals, and there are many brands that demand recognition and connection from their target audiences. In this context, observing the thoughts of those who receive sensory bodily stimuli means observing what is expected of individuals who are affected unconsciously.

RESEARCH METHODOLOGICAL STRUCTURE

Study Design

The qualitative investigation, carried out between December 2021 and June 2022, included six individualized semi-structured interviews with professionals from sound branding and music branding agencies, three Brazilians and three Portuguese. The identification of these agencies can be seen in Table 1 below.

Table 1. Identification of Agencies

Identification	Localization	Collaborators	Clients	Foundation	Purpose
Zanna Sound	Rio de Janeiro, Brazil	7	50	10 current active	2008	Sound Branding, Music branding and Affection Marketing
Audiobranding	Lisboa, portugal	1	5	2021	Sound Identity
Digital Mix	Lisboa, Portugal	-	-	-	-
Gomus	Rio de Janeiro and São Paulo, Brazil	15	More than 100	2004	Especially, Music Branding
Índigo	Lisboa, Portugal	5	40	1996	Audio Branding and Sound Experiences
Rádio Ibiza	Rio de Janeiro, Brazil	-	-	-	-

Source: Developed by author

The interviews integrate questions about four categories – Market, Clients, Production, and Audience – with the intention of structuring an updated panel on the production of brand experiences with sound and music. The conversations began by identifying the interviewee and the agency, and were organized into two parts, "Part A – Production" and "Part B – Consumers". These categorizations were made following dialogues with the professionals in question and with the aim of summarizing and guiding the reader through the themes and empirical conceptions.

In the case of the individualized semi-structured interview with one neuroscientist and neuromarketing specialist, also carried out between December 2021 and June 2022, the main interest was to get an idea of the level at which neuroscience is thought of by sound and music branding companies. The interview began with the identification of the interviewee, and was organized into one part, "Brain and Brands", with the analyses extracted from the answers to the questions in this part. In addition, the main reference information will be presented in tables throughout the chapter. These are data obtained during the period of the interviews, and there may be changes after this time.

In general, the seven interviews lasted around forty-five minutes each, were audio-recorded and, finally, transcribed. The ethical principles of the empirical research include identifying the interviewees by number (Interviewees 1, 2, 3, 4, 5, 6 and 7), randomly, and providing information with their consent. Lastly, for this phase of the research, procedures were considered such as designating the agency producers and specialists to be interviewed, conducting individualized semi-structured interviews – pre-defined questions and adapted to the dialogue –, analyzing the empirical data obtained, and structuring evaluations. Therefore, in this study, the content analysis was guided by empirical data, which was then related to theoretical topics.

Sample Characteristics

Six professionals from sound and music branding agencies, three Brazilian and three Portuguese, and one Brazilian neuroscientist and neuromarketing specialist, were selected through research and contact with leading names/agencies in the development of sound and music experiences for brands, both in Brazil and Portugal. It is worth pointing out that the research and analyses comprise a small portion of these markets and do not represent the whole. Furthermore, as Matos (2023, p. 137) points out, "[…] the opportunity to make contact with companies from Portugal allows a look beyond Brazil, even of it is not very comprehensive".

The agencies where the professionals work are mostly concentrated in large cities with more than 500 thousand inhabitants, such as Rio de Janeiro and São Paulo in Brazil, and Lisbon in Portugal. Brazilian agencies have a greater number of employees and clients, having started their activities in the 21st century. Portugal, a country with a smaller area than Brazil, has one agency at the end of the 20th century and the other two in the 21st century.

Another point is the variation in how each agency identifies itself, both in Brazil and Portugal. The production of brand identity can cover sound constructions or musical programs, or both, and the denomination of the company´s purpose is not just between Sound Branding and Music Branding. Nomenclatures range from just sound identity to a range of designations, such as Affection Marketing, Audio Branding, Sound Experiences, among others.

Finally, the professionals were interviewed via the online meeting platforms Zoom and Google Meet. Arranged randomly, Interviewees 1, 2 and 3 are Brazilian, two women and one man, and Interviewees 4, 5 and 6 are Portuguese, all men. The Interviewee 7, who specializes in neuroscience and neuromarketing, is a Brazilian man. The main results that emerged from the individualized semi-structured interviews are presented in the next section.

INVESTIGATION RESULTS

As expected, considering that sounds and music are directly linked to emotions and memories, it is common for those interviewed to attribute a sense of affection to sound and musical stimuli. What is noticeable is that the opinions are based on the notion that there is the rational that works, but if the rational does not work, the first instinct will be emotional and, if there is action, the action will possibly be of an emotional nature.

According to Interviewee 1, the process of moving from a more traditional view of marketing to a more sophisticated view of branding helps to define what the central objective of production would be. In short, the aim is to devise strategies to attract attention of individuals for two purposes, "[…] to get them to the point of sale and sell products and services (this appears to be a capitalist bias aimed at inducing consumer behavior), and to create a brand persona, identifiable communication, and emotional spaces and relationships […]".

The hypothesis, based on Interviewee 6, is that information is obtained not only from the properties of products and services, but, fundamentally, from what the mind does with the information and what contributions it makes. It is understood that it is possible to know a specific object as it is, but it is the mind of each individual that will uniquely process the stimuli and how they are returned to the external world. In this sense, neuroscience helps to understand how the mind behaves when faced with different stimuli, bringing together scientific discoveries about the brain with what the nervous system gives back to individuals. In accordance with Interviewee 6,

[…] the auditory cortex is in the temporal lobe – one of the four lobes situated in the left and right hemispheres of the brain –, which is associated with memory, language

and emotions, with auditory stimuli being processed a thousand times faster than virtual stimuli (the visual cortex being in the occipital area) (INTERVIEWEE6, 2023).

Therefore, the next subheadings correspond to each of the categories already presented, namely, Market, Clients, Production, and Audience, and to the "Brain and Brands" part of the interview with the neuroscientist and neuromarketing expert.

Market: Brazil and Portugal

As far as the Brazilian market is concerned, there was a division between professional DJs and audio sound companies until, in the first decade of the year 2000, agencies specializing in sound and musical identity for brands began to emerge. This happened at the same time as the use of the same music – ambient music – by brands and establishments became noticeable. Today, during a scenario of expansion and consolidation in the Brazilian market, there are a considerable number of small companies in the sector, with less structure than the better-known agencies, and brands sending a greater number of requests.

On the other hand, the market in Portugal is significantly smaller and more recent. The conjuncture described is one of growth, but it is small, with around two main players and other smaller and less developed players working on sound and music communication for Portuguese companies. Even so, around 10 to 20 years ago there was a greater emphasis on the concept of the jingle, and today there is a more solidified culture of closeness and identification, capturing the potential audience by creating empathy, emotional relationships, sensory stimuli, and more. In any case, Interviewee 3 states that "[…] the greater understanding of brands and the better reception of new marketing professionals in companies to this growing service is the result of years of hard work".

Clients: Brands Interested in Communicating Identity with Sounds and Music

With Table 2 as a reference, looking at an agency´s main clients and their profiles shows which niches these companies most often work with and the types of brands that have most realized the need to innovate, going beyond traditional contact with the public. Then, what is noticeable is that brands are currently seeking deeper and more precise communication, through sensoriality and communication from the perspective of neuroscience. Also, brands have sought to convey affection to their audiences through communication that has artistic quality and without "auditory harassment". This shows that organizations are trying to be heard in a different way in the midst of so many traditional, standardized or excessive sound and musical stimuli.

Table 2. Clients

	Clients	
	Main clients	**Profile**
Interviewee 1	Havaianas; Hering	Retail
Interviewee 2	Farm; Reserva; Maria Filó; Copacabana Palace; Group Ancar Shopping Center; Stations Am Pm	Main: fashion I Other: hotels; gastronomy
Interviewee 3	Loccitane; Metro Rio; Metro São Paulo	Transmitting affection with artistic quality, without "auditory harassment"
Interviewee 4	Sonae (Continente and Worten); Millenium and Novo Banco banks; EDP; Galp	Banks; energy brands; image brands; drinks; radios
Interviewee 5	EDP; Sonae Group; Auchan Group; Insurances I Sound design of Escape Rooms	Energy; insurance I Escape rooms
Interviewee 6	Fox Portugal Studios; Pingo Doce	Film producers; agencies and direct clients

Source: Developed by author

In relation to Brazil, even though brand sound and music identity agencies are always willing to work with all kinds of client profiles, it seems that each of those who took part in the interviews has expertise in a specific niche. While Interviewee 1 mentioned the retail niche, with brands such as Havaianas and Hering, Interviewee 2 highlighted fashion and other segments such as hotels and gastronomy as the main segment, with brands such as Farm, Copacabana Palace, and Postos Am Pm, and Interviewee 3 mentioned the transport niche, with brands such as Metrô Rio and Metrô São Paulo.

On the other hand, Portugal has agencies that all seem to work with a greater variety of niches. As an example, the three Portuguese interviewees 4, 5 and 6, highlight supermarket chains as clients, with brands such as Continente, Auchan and Pingo Doce, respectively, as well as other segments, such as bank brands, energy brands, radio brands, insurance brands, escape room brands, film production companies, among others. In other words, the agencies present themselves as open to different types of client profiles, not so much with specific segments that occur more often. Furthermore, Interviewee 6 points out that there are companies that work both for production companies and agencies and for direct clients – brands.

Production: Driven by the Vision of Professionals

In the Production category, which can be explored with Table 3, it is possible to observe what the interviewees perceive about the issues related to the production process of their workspaces. This helps to better understand the perspective of sound and music identity companies and what is involved in developing structured services and experiences for brands, considering the vision of the professionals from the agencies studied in this research.

Table 3. Production

	Production				
	Services and experiences	**Installations**	**Strategies**	**Difficulties**	**Innovations**
Interviewee 1	Campaign tracks; point-of-sale programming; fashion show tracks; streaming channel curation; in-store events; consulting, production, and activation	Studio for production	Curation process; pleasant, congruent, and memorable brand	Noise pollution; pulverization of the service; loss of value of music with the advent of streaming and becoming a mass product	Technology; "disneynization" process
Interviewee 2	Curation for points of sale; curation for online (example: QR code for home delivery)	Work with existing songs; software and forwarding of the link to the client via subscription (installation on the client´s computer); recording vignettes, spots, and jingles in studio for personalized radio stations	Collection of the client´s main information for a musical study; research into the musical identity to be delivered to the client together with a defense; approval; development of the complete program in line with the client´s profile; construction together with the client in accordance with their demands	Lyrics – Avoid songs with bad language, and that convey the wrong message	Desire for constant improvement of the software; use of ios and android systems for those who don´t want to use a computer; curatorship seeking to bring artists together with the brand and insertion of brands in social media
Interviewee 3	-	-	Mapping/study; 2 workshops to define sound or musical attributes; collaborative work	Sound branding is still a trend; convincing partners that affection is a relevant investment; excessive repetition	Attention to sonorities; consistent investment by brands
Interviewee 4	Example: Continente stores – in-store playlist (70% Portuguese and 30% modern international music, not too fast); radio spots; sound for TV movies; complete audio branding or audio logo; digital signature; composition of original music; licensing of international and Portuguese music; sound for stores; sound for museums	-	Analysis of the brand; analysis of the competition; points of contact between the brand and its public; workshop with people related to the brand; briefing; composition; adaptation to the various points of contact; going live; testing; renewal; proposal of surprising experiences	Measurement, which leads to investment difficulties; difficulties with equipment and production	-
Interviewee 5	Audio logo; advertising music; sound products; music programming	-	Advertising agency (first contact with the brand) already sends information; definition of sound identity and sound elements; briefing; submission for consideration; production	Projecting yourself on the national market, since the work always goes to the same agencies and production companies, with greater resources and money	-

Continued on following page

Table 3. Continued

	Production				
	Services and experiences	**Installations**	**Strategies**	**Difficulties**	**Innovations**
Interviewee 6	Commercials; spots; sound and music production; audio production for television; feature films and short films; music consultancy for commercial spaces	2 studios: stereo mixing studio (day-to-day); multichannel studio, essentially aimed at cinema	Reach the audience emotionally, through sensory; create memories; concrete (reasoning, understandable) + perception (sensory, subjective)	Communication noise	Differentiated and complementary spaces, with specific playlists; valuing silence in the midst of too much noise

Source: Developed by author

Initially, the most sought-after services and experiences in Brazil are related to the music branding segmentation, as they involve music programming and playlists that have an affinity with the brand´s identity. Some of the music products mentioned were curation and programming for points of sale, soundtracks for fashion shows, curation for streaming or online channels, and others. With some similarity, Portuguese interviewees 4, 5 and 6 mentioned music consultancy and music playlists for commercial spaces. On this topic, as Gustafsson (2015, p. 21) emphasized, music is one of several parts of the shop´s "atmosphere"; it is part of a wider in store experience that also requires other parts (colours, textures, light, smell, taste) to be successful.

One Portuguese example is the Continente supermarket. Continente features around 70% Portuguese music and 30% modern international music. However, the greatest incidence in Portugal is for services and experiences relating to sound branding segmentation. The demands presented by the Portuguese agencies were for sound for shops and institutions, such as museums; radio spots; sound for television films; complete audio branding; audio logos; digital signage; advertising music; commercials; and audio production for television and feature and short films.

Regarding the installations in which the services and experiences are developed, in Brazil, Interviewee 1 mentioned a studio for production and Interviewee 2, who prepares software to be installed on the client´s computer and a link for sending music, mentioned the option of a radio-only studio with the ultimate aim of recording vignettes, spots and jingles. As for installations in Portugal, the clearest answer came from Interviewee 6, who mentioned two studios. In this case, there is "[…] a stereo mixing studio for day-to-day use, and a multichannel studio, essentially aimed at cinema". In short, it seems that in both Brazil and Portugal, when the agency does not have a studio for sound productions, it uses the help of an audio and music production company.

Corresponding to strategies for developing brand experiences with sounds and music, Brazil prioritizes the collection and study of key information about its clients. This information can contain brand data such as profile, target audience, values, brand history, essence and needs, which will summarize the brands´ identity and enable personalized sound and music branding work.

Agencies in Portugal, on the other hand, think about strategies in a way that is not entirely similar, but obtaining and analyzing data is always part of the main tactics. The Portuguese interviewees also mention attention to surprising experiences and how to emotionally reach the brands´ audience, adding the concrete (what is understandable and reasonable) and perception (what is subjective and sensorial). This understanding takes up the idea of thinking about communication through the lens of neuroscience. There are also agencies that have contact with data that comes from advertising agencies. In this case, the sound and musical elements are submitted for appraisal and then, the production stage takes place.

Another important topic for production is the difficulties. The Brazilian interviewees cited noise pollution, the pulverization of the service, the notion that music has lost its value as a mass product amid the rise of streaming, the loss of quality in terms of lyrics, excessive repetition and the obstacle of convincing potential partners that affection is a relevant investment for the brand. Sound and music branding is still a trend, and the market has taken a while to absorb this new tool.

In Portugal, with reference to the interviewees´ experiences with their agencies, the challenge lies mainly in the difficulty of measurement, which results in investment difficulties. As a result, there are difficulties with equipment and production; difficulties with projection in the national market, since with a small market the main work goes to the same agencies and production companies, with better resources and better end results; and difficulties with communicative noise. So, the Portuguese market has problems with a market that is still structured in small proportions and has little space for varied investments.

Finally, the topic of innovations brought the interviewees´ perceptions of the development of innovative products and how to innovate in this market. The conclusion is that the agencies´ focus is on differentiation, technological advances and possible solutions to reduce difficulties. In addition, the main products and the relevant cases of these agencies can be considered through the lens of the domains and dimensions of experiences defined by Pine and Gilmore (1999), since each product developed from sound branding and music branding promotes an unusual experience for individuals.

Audience: Professionals´ Perspectives

The essential category Audience seeks to delimit the understanding and expectations that the production side has of the audience of interest to its clients, which can help in the analysis of how the market for sound and musical affectations is constructed on the production side. It is known that there are differences in the view of the role of the consumer in relation to music. According to Gustafsson (2015, p. 28), these are the power of music in relation to consumers and the power of branded/commercialized music in relation to the consumer, which means that "[…] the conflicting perspectives are about how to act when music lends itself to being used by actors, such as companies, with the intent of affecting consumers to perceive of a brand in a certain way".

The perceptions that have of the public are the information obtained in this study about the public of interest, both for Brazil and Portugal. Part of this is in Table 4. The audience´s tastes are always considered, and the producers try to align the audience´s musical vocabulary with the brand´s identity.

Table 4. Public – Part 1

	Public – Part 1		
	Perception	**Interference**	**Expectation of feelings**
Interviewee 1	Focus on the type of musical vocabulary	Total interference, everything is done for consumers too, but mainly for them	-
Interviewee 2	Always think about the audience, and from there the production starts to the soundtrack; always be aligned with the client	There is interference	Feeling of being as comfortable as possible, since shopping is also an emotional act; get in the mood of the brand with the soundtrack; connection with the brand and the desire to remain in the environment
Interviewee 3	Think about style and habits	The consumer is considered, but the brand needs to have its own personality, because it won´t be able to speak to everyone, but with audiences that with who the brand is	-
Interviewee 4	Thinking of the public as upfated and think about taking risks with them	Yes. The audience profile, for example, guides ideas	-
Interviewee 5	Ideally, information about the public should already be included in the first brand identity survey	Example: involving the public through voting	Sometimes the music is in the background, sometimes the intensity keeps away
Interviewee 6	Inputs come from agencies	There is interference and influence. But the first step is the agency, with whom the client has the first contact	-

Source: Developed by author

Another important topic is that the way the public is perceived by production interferes with the development of structured products and services for brands. When it comes to Brazil, for example, interviewees 1 and 2 point out that experiences are made for the audience too (because they also think about the employees at the points of sale, for example), but mainly for them. Interviewee 3, on the other hand, points out that the audience is considered, but, knowing that it is not feasible to communicate with everyone, but rather with the individuals who are in tune with what they represent, brands need to have their personalities disseminated.

Next, the topic of whether what the public is expected to feel can lead to the production of the sound and musical identity of brands was contributed to by interviewees 2 and 5. Agencies expect to stimulate a feeling of closeness to brands and avoid as much as possible a feeling of distance. For Interviewee 2, it is important that the public is comfortable in the consumer space, that they get into the brand´s mood with the soundtrack, and they connect with the brand by wanting to stay in the environment. From another perspective, which concerns distancing, Interviewee 5 mentions that care should be taken with loud sounds and music, which can lead to people leaving the premises.

This Audience category also delimited themes such as measurement, objectives, behavior planning, and strategies, as shown in Table 5. The topic of measurement refers to whether or not there is a way of measuring how the public perceives and experiences what is developed by the production and, initially, all the interviewees, both Brazilian and Portuguese, confirmed that measurement takes place. However, each of them presented, or not, how this is done in each agency and the difficulty of carrying out this task in question. In general, measurement in this type of work is presented as complicated to carry out.

Table 5. Public – Part 2

	Public – Part 2			
	Measurement	**Objectives**	**Behavior planning**	**Strategies**
Interviewee 1	Monitoring with consumers asking whether they like the programming, whether or not they think it matches the brand (for clients who hire this service, because value); measuring this type of work is complicated	Draw attention of consumers, to bring them to points of sale and sell products and services; create relationship	-	Create ambience and communicate the brand
Interviewee 2	In general, brands do a survey; positioning/feedbacks can change the positioning and style music; constant contact with the customer	Involve the consumer to buy with the creation of interesting and well-being ambience	There are studies that prove that music can even influence the product customer chooses (example: in a wine store, with French music, the consumer is more likely to pick up wine from France); Listening to music that like and relate well-being with buying	Music as background that can´t disturb
Interviewee 3	-	-	This approach is not chosen by the agency in question, but this possibility does exist	Example: agitated music to accelerate the public
Interviewee 4	Every action tries to measure in some way, including through complaints	Create proximity with the brand and tend to search for the product, through consistency	Some professionals already thinking about directing public behavior	-
Interviewee 5	Measurement is carried out and this data collection directs and assists in more accurate work, including rebranding; data is obtained from advertising agencies, for tracking campaigns	Brand to be known and recognized by sound	When you think about the characteristics of sound, for example rhythm to define a soundtrack, you are influencing more or less directly listeners; the public ends up being molded into identities that are created	Think about the characteristics of sound and influencing more or less directly the listener
Interviewee 6	Carried out by market research companies; measure the results and adjust strategy according to the results; questionnaire (people can be exposed to the product or not)	Draw attentio of the audience; arouse their interest; arouse a desire to purchase	There is a thought of leaving the field of consumer perception open, so that if the client accepts, adherence will be natural; injection of dopamine in the brain; it is invasive, but people have freedom of choice (the ethical question is supervised)	Combining ambience with the structuring of strategy for connecting sound with consumption

Source: Developed by author

Interviewee 1 says that consumers are followed up with questions, such as whether or not they like the programming and whether or not they think it suits the brand, but this only happens for clients who hire this service, which adds an extra cost for the contracting brand. On the other hand, Interviewee 2 explains that it is usually the brands that carry out a measurement survey and offer it to the agencies to enable them to analyze whether the products and services are pleasing them and whether they need to change their positioning and musical style. The Portuguese interviewees explained that the agencies they work for do not carry out measurement but obtain this data through advertising agencies or market research companies.

The objectives for the public range from the desire to be involved with the brand and recognized by the sound to the more intuitive desire to buy the product or service sold by the brand. Regarding the Brazilian market, the interviewees present the objective of attracting the public´s attention, involving them with an interesting ambience that conveys well-being at points of sale, and selling products and services. The purposes cited by the interviewees in Portugal are like those in Brazil.

The Portuguese market shows that it is important to structure differentiated experiences in order to attract the public´s attention, to present them with memorable experiences and, effectively, to make a purchase. Interviewee 4 mentions creating proximity to the brand and encouraging the public to search for the product, always using consistency; Interviewee 5 mentions the goal of the brand always being know and recognized by sound; and Interviewee 6, in congruence with the majority of interviewees, mentions the importance of arousing the public´s interest and their desire to buy. Once the objectives have been set, it is then possible to see if there is a plan for the public´s behavior so that these objectives can be achieved, and if there are specific methods that benefit from knowing how individuals react.

What can be seen is that the interviewees do not clearly state that sound and musical stimuli and, consequently, bodily affections, direct behavior, but they do show that this happens indirectly. Interviewee 3 affirms that this possibility does exist, but points out that it is considered dangerous reasoning, since sending subliminal messages that lead to some action is considered auditory harassment. Interviewee 5 reinforces that in some way this is thought about and ends up molding the public to the identities that are created for the brands, which demonstrates an issue to be considered not only in Brazil.

In view of this, considering the competencies of sounds and music, Matos (2023, p. 158) states that "[…] what professionals who work with structuring the sound and musical identity of brands know is that sounds and music, to some degree, direct feelings and behaviors". An example cited by Interviewee 5 is when thinking about the characteristics of sound, for example the rhythm that will define a brand´s soundtrack, knowing that this tactic has a partially influence on the listener.

In addition, about Interviewee 6, he points out that this method is nonetheless invasive, but as long as it is not harmful, there is no question of ethics. It is also argued that people have freedom of choice and that there is a supervisory entity, the Regulatory Entity for the Social Communication (ERC), former High Authority for the Social Communication (AACS), in terms of Portugal.

Finally, the last theme brings together the strategies designed to achieve the objectives in question. Corresponding to Brazil, it mentions paying attention to the rhythm of the music according to the intended result (loud music speeds up the audience and quiet music slows down the audience) and music as a background that should not get in the way of the experience with the brand and the brand´s intention. Furthermore, based on the reflection of Interviewee 5, Portuguese, each demand will structure a specific strategic line. What can be seen is that most of the strategies combine the creation of ambience with the structuring of the connection between sound and consumption.

Brain and Brands: A Vision of Neuroscience

This section is dedicated to the main observations obtained from the interview with Interviewee 7, a specialist in neuroscience and neuromarketing. Summarized information is in the Table 6. The primary objective of this interview was to investigate the extent to which neuroscience is considered by sound branding and music branding companies. It is clear that the combination of neuroscience and marketing is a way of observing that brand actions have some level of neurological influence on the behavior of individuals, making it possible to structure more effective campaigns.

Table 6. Brain and Brands

Intended effects	Intention to affect the body, change brain waves, and provoke dopamine – brain chemical; intention to provoke the public to act
Intention	Studying the senses, capturing information, and seeing how this interferes with people´s behavior (positive and negative)
Experience from neuroscience	Agencies still don´t use, very few use neuromarketing, as an "attempt"; choose a pattern of music that works, and work on repetition and memorization (a lot of publicity, not necessarily efficiency); patterns are created, but very little is studied and is relatively recent (about 20 to 40 years)
Structuring experiences	Immersive experiences: events have the ability to move with people; gang behavior, biological: you lose the capacity for rationality when in a group; there´s also the individual, because our brains have different experiences, different memories; if the brain is inside people, they have free choice and they are the ones who buy, even if it´s by touch, smell, and others (the social sciences criticize it and biology sees it as the person´s brain, so "all together"
Impact	There is an impact, but what exists is the provocation of patterns; behaviors change as scenarios change, but biological patterns don´t change for a long time
Physical and mental reactions	All of them, since the world is perceived by the senses, receptors of information from the environment; sounds change our physics and chemistry; when a sound enters the ear, it passes through and becomes into brain waves and neurotransmitters, into chemistry, and provokes an action potential in the neuron that will action in the brain; physical actions on the brain; action on the body (example: moving feet with music), calming or causing euphoria
Production and consumption	These are indirect things: you hear the sound, it will excite or discourage you, but that doesn´t indicate that there will be consumption; discoveries: fast sound makes the body react faster and calm sounds make the body act more slowly – this means that the person can stay longer in the store, or get out faster; it generates a provocation, makes the person prone (a happier person may or may not buy) and not a structuring of behavior that affects on a neurological level and generate a movement/consumption; patterns are discovered and patterns are provoked
Brands, markets and brains	Brands "compete" in markets and in brains, so, in the supermarket, in the brands on the shelf and in your brain, in the brands in head; and depending on the situation at the time

Source: Developed by author

Interviewee 7´s main argument is that there seems to be an intention to discover and use and stimulate innate patterns, in other words, patterns that are not acquired or learnt. Some examples of these patterns would be gaining energy, saving energy, saving time, how a group moves away from another group, among other possible ones. In the case of the "gain energy" pattern, this can be stimulated by restaurant chain brands, just as the "save time" pattern can be stimulated by food delivery and market apps. The discovery of patterns is also associated with some innate paradigms, such as categorization; habits; gang behavior, and so on.

Another important argument from Interviewee 7 is that each individual receives stimuli in a particular way. According to this interviewee, "[…] the areas that are activated are the same between people because they are of the same species, however, there is the influence of culture, the environment, and more, since the brain does not operate in a vacuum". Therefore, patterns can serve to guide a brand´s communication and stimulate the consumption of products and services, and this, for the expert, without the intention of manipulation.

In view of this, when asked about the intended effects of brand experiences with sounds and music, especially by agencies that have a broader perception of this content in question, the expert, in summary, pointed to bodily effects and the desire for attachment and/or acquisition. These include affecting the audience´s body, changing brain waves and provoking dopamine and brain chemistry, and provoking individuals to act.

In addition, another significant theme is the intentions of brands and production companies in structuring experiences that affect individuals´ bodies without the presence of consciousness. In the opinion of Interviewee 7, since experiences are lived through the senses, the intention of studying the senses and capturing information is to understand how they affect the behavior (positive or negative) of the audience, which can be useful for carrying out effective actions, in this study, sound branding and music branding.

The expert also explains that brand sound and music identity agencies still do not use the practice of thinking about and structuring their sound and music products based on neuroscience, and a few use neuromarketing without being clear about this. What sometimes happens is that sounds and music are used that "stick", in other words, a pattern that works and that, together with repetition and memorization, can lead to the expected result. However, this can happen due to the volume of exposure, and not necessarily due to effectiveness. It is also worth pointing out that patterns can be created, but this is still a little-studied and relatively recent subject, around the last 20 to 40 years.

Regarding the structuring of experiences, three points of observation were presented. Firstly, attention to the organization of immersive experiences, since events tend to affect the audience. Then, attention to gang behavior, which is considered biological. The neuroscientist and neuromarketing specialist explain: "[…] Individuals lose some of their capacity for rationality when they are in a group and react in a similar way, but the individual cannot be excluded, as the brain stores distinct experiences and memories". Lastly, on behavioral orientation, the opinion that the brain is within the individual and each person has free will. Therefore, it is the individual who carries out the action of buying, and stimuli and free choose are jointly responsible.

Next, there is an impact of bodily affections and behavioral stimuli on the effectiveness of brand experiences with sound and music, but, according to Interviewee 7, what happens is a provocation of patterns. Biological patterns do not change for long, but behaviors can change as scenarios change. In other words, regarding the research in question, structuring an effective sound and music identity is related to creating stimuli attributed to innate patterns, as these are more consistent and more easily applicable in any context.

The reality is that physical – bodily – and mental reactions are expected from contact with the sound and musical stimuli designed to communicate brand identities. Another concrete point in this reflection is that production and consumption are related to the brain, the body and bodily affections. On this topic, Interviewee 7 considers that these are indirect things, since, for him, it is possible to listen to a sound or piece of music, feel excited or discouraged, but there is no indication that there will be buying behavior. What the expert indicates is that a provocation is reproduced that "[…] makes the person prone to (a happier person may or may not buy), and not a structuring of behavior that affects at a neurological level and generates a movement/consumption".

Finally, the connection between brand intentions and brains can drive results, just as brands compete both in markets and in individuals´ brains. Interviewee 7 affirms this, and exemplifies it by citing the supermarket conjuncture, in which brands compete for the public´s attention with the other brands on the shelves and with the brands that are in the individual´s head, without forgetting the possible interference of the situation at the time.

CONCLUSION

The conclusion of this chapter provides, firstly, a discussion of the overall coverage of the chapter. The central notion obtained in this chapter is that sound producers and music branding agencies use some tactics that touch on neuroscience, but mostly without them being clearly aware of it. In view of this, some observations can be presented. One is that, according to Sá (2010), sound branding and music branding experiences are in the order of the utopian dimension, as they relate to the creation of affective bonds and aesthetically modulated environments, but they can be in the order of the dystopian dimension when they give the impression of excess, of discipline through noise, and of the logic of "sound abuse".

What is also noticeable is that agencies are concerned with productions that create emotional relationships between brands and individuals, with the aim of focusing less on the qualities of products and services and placing more emphasis on values and emotional stimuli. This shows that producers realize that the processing of sound and musical stimuli and the resulting reactions are done by the mind of each person, with sounds and music having a direct link to emotions and memories. Moreover, in brief, the main objectives are to attract people´s attention, involve them emotionally through differentiated experiences, create memories and, finally, sell products and services as a result of their desire to buy.

Finally, there are some conclusions about how individuals are thought of by the producers of the agencies in question, and some observations based on the field of neuroscience and neuromarketing. It can be seen that the focus is on the sound and musical vocabulary listened to by the audience of interest rather than on their sound and musical tastes; it can be seen that there is a concern with the feeling of closeness to the brands, with the desire to remain in their physical and digital environments, and with the annulment of the desire to distance oneself; and it is understood that it is known that sounds and music – through the bodily and non-conscious involvement of individuals – to some degree direct feelings and behaviors.

Therefore, it can be seen that there is an intention to discover, use and stimulate individuals' innate patterns in the processes of structuring brand communications with sounds and music. In the same way, it can be identified that each individual perceives the stimuli in their own way because there is an influence from culture, the environment, and more, even though the brain areas activated are the same. Lastly, it is said that sounds and music have the power to generate excitement or discouragement, but there is no evidence of consumption due to these effects. There is a propensity to consume, which is used as an argument for the statement "individuals have free choice".

What cannot be denied is that the reactions of the human body originate from physical reactions in the brain, which are enhanced by the action of neurons when a sound or piece of music enters the individual's ear. And this is well known to anyone who works with sounds and music.

Future Research Directions

The view on the future of the research theme of structuring brands and engaging individuals through sound and music is that there are still many topics to be studied and the volume of literature needs to grow. With regard to Gustafsson (2015, p. 29), one line of research - Graakjaer and Jantzen (2009) – emphasizes that "[…] sonic branding has been a last minute finishing touch in most cases until very recently, meaning that in most cases it has not been used to its full potential yet". However, this researcher emphasizes that there is a tendency to elevate sound and music in branding as something that should be understood as a strategy.

This suggests opportunities for future research, such as delving deeper into the perception of individual consumers about brand experiences structured by sound branding and music branding tactics, as well as the relationship between brand communication with sounds and music, and, specifically, the events niche; immersive experiences; and the contemporary technological elements pointed out by Kotler et al. (2021) in reference to marketing 5.0.

REFERENCES

Crisinel, A., Cosser, S., King, S., Jones, R., James, P., & Spence, C. (2012). A bittersweet symphony: Systematically modulating the taste of food by changing the sonic properties of the soundtrack playing in the background. *Food Quality and Preference*, *1*(24), 201–204. doi:10.1016/j.foodqual.2011.08.009

De Marchi, L. (2018). *Cultural diversity in the communication and culture markets: an overview of discussions and research methods in the music industry*. Postgraduate Program in Social Sciences – UFJF, v. 13, n. 2, p. 210-223.

De Nora, T. (2004). *Music in everyday life*. Cambridge University Press.

Erthal, A. (2018). *Multisensory communication: understanding ways of feeling*. E-papers.

Graakjaer, N., & Jantzen, C. (2009). Producing corporate sounds: An interview with Karsten Kjems and Soren Holme on sonic branding. In C. N. Graakjaer (Ed.), *Music in Adverstising: Commercial Sounds in Media Communication and Other Settings* (pp. 259–274). Aalborg University Press.

Guerra, G. (2013). *Music Branding. What is your brand sound?* Elsevier.

Gustafsson, C. (2015). Sonic branding: A consumer-oriented literature review. *Journal of Brand Management*, *22*(1), 20–37. doi:10.1057/bm.2015.5

Herschmann, M. (2010). *Music industry in transition*. Letters and Colors Station & Faperj.

Iazzetta, F. (2015). *Sound studies: a field in gestation*. Research and Training Center, n. 1.

Kotler, P., & Keller, K. (2006). *Marketing administration* (12th ed.). Pearson.

Lindstrom, M. (2005). Brandsense: Sensorial secrets behind the things we buy. *The Bookman*.

Matos, C. (2023). *Perception and effectiveness of sound and music brand expressions: the neurological bias of sound branding and music branding practices*. Social Communication Faculty, University of the State of Rio de Janeiro.

Oakes, S., & North, A. C. (2008). Using music to influence cognitive and affective response in queues of low and high crowd density. *Journal of Marketing Management,* *24*(5-6), 589–602. doi:10.1362/026725708X326002

Obici, G. (2008). Condition of listening: Media and sound territories. *Letras.*

Pine, J., & Gilmore, J. (1999). *The spectacle of business: the experience economy.* Campus.

Sá, S. (2010). The soundtrack of a silent story: sound, music, audibilities and technologies from the perspective of Sound Studies. In Sá, S. (org.) Towards Music Culture – Business, Aesthetics, Languages and Audibility. Sulina.

Schafer, R. (2001). *Tuning the world.* Unesp.

Vijaykumar, K., Kellaris, J. J., & Aurand, T. W. (2012). Sonic logos: Can sound influence willingness to pay? *Journal of Product and Brand Management, 21*(4), 275–284. doi:10.1108/10610421211246685

Zanna. (2015). *Sound branding: the sound life of brands.* Matrix.

Chapter 6
Sonic Branding in the Telecom Sector:
A Case Study of Airtel's Jingle

Natasha Saqib
University of Kashmir, India

Hardik Dhull
Matu Ram Institute of Engineering and Management, India

Sanskriti Agrawal
Lakhmi Chand University, India

ABSTRACT

The purpose of this study is to explore the strategic utilization of sound and music in brand communication, known as sonic branding, with a particular emphasis on the telecom sector. This research aims to investigate the profound impact of Airtel's jingle on the development of brand identity and its influence on consumer engagement within the telecom industry. This research employs an exploratory case study approach. The jingle was found to evoke both emotional and cognitive associations with the brand, contributing significantly to consumer engagement. The findings emphasize the critical role of sonic branding in the telecom sector and its potential to create a distinctive sonic identity. This study contributes to the growing body of knowledge on the significance of sonic branding in contemporary marketing. It adds value by specifically examining the telecom sector and Airtel's jingle as a case study, offering insights that can be valuable to both academics and practitioners in the field.

DOI: 10.4018/979-8-3693-0778-6.ch006

INTRODUCTION

As a result of intense competition within the marketplace, an increasing number of brands are embracing the strategy of multisensory marketing to establish a distinct and unique brand identity and brand equity (Iglesias et al., 2019; Rodrigues et al., 2018). In contemporary times, numerous brands employ strategic sounds, called sonic branding, to establish a distinct identity (Jackson,2003; Minsky, 2017). Sonic branding, a specialized niche within branding, harnesses the power of sound to create a unique and memorable brand identity (Kemp et al., 2023a; Steiner, 2014). It extends beyond traditional visual branding elements to focus on auditory components. These include jingles, sound logos, brand music, and other sonic elements that evoke emotions, associations, and recognition. (Bronner, 2008; Nufer & Moser, 2018). The concept of sonic branding is deeply rooted in the psychology of sound. Humans have an innate connection to sound, which can trigger powerful emotions and memories (Perlovsky, 2010). The strategic use of sound allows brands to connect with their audience on a deeper level, forging emotional connections that are often long-lasting.

Moreover, sound travels across linguistic and cultural boundaries, making it a universally understood medium. A well-crafted sonic brand can transcend language barriers and resonate with diverse audiences, a phenomenon witnessed in the success of several global brands. Bonde and Hansen's (2013) research has demonstrated the effectiveness of sonic branding as a marketing tool for effectively communicating the appropriate brand identity (Techawachirakul et al., 2023). The number of brands using sonic branding has increased by 22% over the years (McCullough, 2021).

One example of a telecom company that has harnessed the power of sonic branding is Bharti Airtel, commonly referred to as Airtel. Airtel is a prominent telecommunications service provider in India with a substantial international footprint, catering to a vast customer base spanning multiple countries and regions. The trajectory of its progression is evidence of the influential capacity of branding, encompassing both visual and sonic elements, within the telecommunications industry. Airtel's narrative is distinguished by its innovative branding strategy, notably through the utilization of a memorable jingle to establish a unique brand identity. The aforementioned musical composition, crafted by the esteemed Indian composer A.R. Rahman, has been closely associated with the brand, surpassing cultural limitations and establishing an enduring emotional bond with consumers.

This case study examines the efficacy of Airtel's jingle as a prominent illustration of successful sonic branding within the telecommunications industry. This research paper aims to provide insights into the strategic utilization of sound to establish a compelling brand identity and foster an emotional connection with customers. This will be achieved by analyzing jingles' evolution, cultural significance, and impact on brand identity. The primary research inquiries that provide direction for this particular case study are as follows: RQ 1: To what extent has Airtel's jingle played a role in fostering customer engagement within the telecommunications industry? This case study explores the strategic and emotional aspects of branding in the telecommunications industry, specifically examining the impact of sonic branding through the example of Airtel's jingle.

The paper is structured as follows: In the next section, we comprehensively review the literature related to sonic branding. Section 3 provides an overview of the research methodology employed in this study. Section 4 offers an in-depth analysis of the case under examination. The fifth section of the paper analyses the findings from the case study. In the sixth section, we present the concluding remarks of our study. The implications of the research are presented in Section 7. Section 8 of the study discusses the limitations of the research findings and proposes potential directions for future research.

LITERATURE REVIEW

Sonic Branding

Brands are currently allocating unprecedented levels of investment towards the domain of sound. According to McCullough (2021), sonic branding has emerged as a widely recognized and established strategy in the field of branding (Techawachirakul et al., (2023). The inception of sonic branding encompasses a crucial concept extensively examined in academic literature, referred to as "Atmospherics." Kotler (1973) conceptualizes the contemporary concept known as 'marketing of the senses' (Hulten et al., 2008; Krishna, 2013), which involves exploring a marketing strategy incorporating music. The analysis of music as an element within the in-store environment, either as a component of the overall atmosphere or as a means of engaging the senses, serves to underscore the significance of music as an integral part of a comprehensive in-store experience, which necessitates the presence of other elements such as colours, textures, light, smell, and taste in order to achieve success (Gustafsson, 2015). Sonic branding encompasses a comprehensive and deliberate branding approach that intentionally incorporates auditory components, including jingles, sound logos, and brand music, within a brand's identity and communication strategy (Kemp et al., 2023b). The auditory components mentioned in the statement function as discernible and enduring sonic signals intentionally crafted to establish a distinct and enduring brand image, foster emotional bonds with consumers, and elicit specific associations and recognition among the intended recipients (Kellaris, 1997).

The concept of sonic branding extends beyond conventional visual branding methods, which primarily depend on elements such as logos, colours, and typography.

The primary emphasis is placed on the auditory aspect of the brand encounter. In a contemporary society characterized by abundant visual stimuli, sound presents a distinctive and frequently overlooked means of distinguishing one's brand. This technology enables brands to engage with their target audience in a more immersive and emotionally impactful manner. The significance of sound in branding extends beyond its functional purpose, as it operates on a more profound and emotive level. When sound is effectively coordinated, it can evoke profound emotions, stimulate recollections, and elicit instinctive reactions. Essentially, it captivates the audience by evoking sensory and emotional responses separate from the visual components of branding.

Sound exhibits an extraordinary ability to elicit emotions and establish enduring connections with consumers. The auditory stimuli associated with familiar experiences, such as the cheerful jingle of a beloved childhood snack or the soothing melody accompanying logging into a well-known application, can transport individuals to specific moments. Additionally, these sounds can evoke emotions of comfort, nostalgia, or excitement and establish emotional connections with a particular brand (North et al., 2003). The effectiveness of sonic branding is primarily centred around establishing an emotional connection. Brands that effectively establish a cohesive alignment between their brand identity and the auditory components they utilize have the potential to cultivate not only customers but also devoted advocates who develop a profound personal attachment to the brand's narrative and principles. Establishing emotional connections is pivotal in fostering enduring customer loyalty and advocacy.

Theoretical Foundations of Sonic Branding

The field of sonic branding is characterized by its multidimensional nature, as it incorporates diverse theoretical frameworks that include the psychology of sound, consumer behaviour, and the universal nature of auditory experiences. A substantial corpus of scholarly literature has significantly contributed to our comprehension of how auditory stimuli can alter our perception and establish a connection with various brands. The work by Beckerman (2014) highlights the significant influence of sound in moulding our cognitive interpretations and actions. This study explores the complex correlation between sound and brand engagement, positing that sound can foster emotional connections, shape consumer choices, and establish unique brand identities. The study by Minsky and Fahey in 2017 thoroughly examines various strategies employed in audio branding. This statement emphasizes the strategic utilization of sound to establish a compelling and cohesive brand identity. The authors emphasize the role of sound in effectively engaging consumers at both a sensory and emotional level.

The theoretical underpinnings of sonic branding revolve around sound's psychological and emotional aspects. Numerous psychology and consumer behaviour studies have consistently revealed sound's significant impact on human emotions and perceptions. Rossiter and Percy (1987) researched the relationship between sound and emotions, which has significantly impacted the development of sonic branding strategies. The auditory stimulus possesses the distinct capacity to elicit particular affective reactions. As an illustration, a mellow and melodious composition can evoke sentiments of nostalgia and a sense of comfort.

In contrast, a vibrant and rhythmic rhythm has the potential to elicit a state of exhilaration and vitality. Sonic branding effectively leverages emotional reactions by incorporating auditory components to establish brand encounters that deeply resonate with individuals. The impact of sound on consumer behaviour and sensory marketing has been extensively studied and documented. Research has consistently shown that the emotional potency of sound plays a significant role in shaping brand preference, purchase choices, and customer loyalty.

The universality of sound is a captivating element and serves as a fundamental foundation for sonic branding. The auditory modality can surpass linguistic and cultural boundaries, thereby establishing itself as a universally comprehensible and valued form of communication. The study conducted by Spence and Zampini (2011) investigated the cross-cultural interpretation of sound, emphasizing its capacity to communicate emotions, intentions, and information within various cultural settings. The widespread applicability of sound serves as a fundamental factor in its efficacy as a means of brand communication. A skillfully designed sonic brand can elicit emotions and establish universally relatable connections, transcending linguistic and cultural barriers. Appealing to a global audience is a valuable advantage for brands aiming to establish an internationally uniform and easily identifiable image.

Components of Sonic Branding

Sonic branding encompasses various essential elements, each fulfilling a distinct function in developing a brand's auditory identity. The components above operate synergistically to create a unified and memorable auditory representation of a brand.

- *Jingles:* Jingles refer to concise and memorable melodies or musical motifs frequently composed to represent a particular brand. Using jingles as mnemonic devices for brand recognition has been shared (Craig, 2011; Belch & Belch, 2015). Jingles are regarded as the preeminent and easily identifiable element of sonic branding. In a concise musical format, these compositions effectively capture the fundamental characteristics of a brand, establishing an immediate and enduring association with the brand within the consciousness of consumers. Jingles are renowned for their capacity to engender robust brand recognition and foster affective bonds. The Intel Inside jingle, comprising a concise sequence of five musical notes, is among the most renowned jingles in the technology sector. It can promptly elicit associations with Intel's brand image and its commitment to excellence.

- *Sound Logos:* Sound logos, alternatively referred to as sonic or audio logos or mnemonics, are identifiable auditory representations that are closely linked to a specific brand (Flaig, 2022; Krishnan et al., 2012). Typically, these auditory stimuli are brief and lack melodic qualities. They frequently use concise sound bites or musical motifs, serving as mnemonic devices that are readily identifiable and easily retained in memory. Sound logos function as auditory markers for a brand, akin to visual logos. These auditory cues offer a distinctive and exclusive auditory signal that can be employed across brand touchpoints, including advertisements, videos, and product launches. Sound logos enhance brand recognition and establish a cohesive brand identity (McCusker, 1997; Wazir & Wazir, 2015; Bonde Hansen, 2013). The sound logo known as the "Intel Bong" serves as an iconic auditory representation that strengthens the brand's connection with technology and innovation.

- *Brand Music:* Brand music distinguishes itself from other sound branding by utilizing traditional song structures, such as verse and chorus. This characteristic gives marketers greater adaptability when employing brand music in various contexts (Treasure, 2011). While audio logos and jingles are primarily used in advertising, brand music is a more versatile tool for broader promotional endeavours. Brand music offers a more immersive and emotionally resonant dimension to a brand's auditory identity. It conveys the brand's personality, values, and messaging through music that complements its identity. Brand music is often used in longer-form content, such as advertisements, brand videos, and events, to establish a deeper emotional connection with the audience. Example: The song "All You Need Is Love" by The Beatles in a Coca-Cola commercial is a prominent example of brand music that conveys the brand's message of unity, happiness, and positivity.

The various elements comprising sonic branding are not independent entities; instead, they synergistically combine to form a comprehensive auditory brand identity. Jingles, sound logos, and brand music synergistically reinforce the brand's identity across various contexts and diverse audiences. Jingles are crucial in establishing prompt brand recognition, serving as a conduit to the brand's realm. Sound logos strengthen brand recognition and are efficient auditory markers across different touchpoints. In contrast, brand music enhances the emotional bond between consumers and a brand by offering a cohesive and engaging auditory encounter. When these components are employed strategically and consistently, they generate an auditory environment that profoundly connects with consumers, elicits emotional responses, and cultivates enduring brand allegiance. Integrating these elements in establishing a comprehensive auditory brand identity guarantees that the brand's sound is not merely a singular aspect but a multifaceted and influential entity that effectively resonates with consumers, leaving an enduring impact.

Emotional Resonance and Cognitive Associations in Sonic Branding

Sound, a fundamental component of sonic branding, can elicit particular emotions and strengthen cognitive connections with a brand. Establishing solid and enduring connections with consumers is contingent upon considering the emotional and cognitive aspects of sonic branding. The utilization of sonic logos in advertising has the potential to facilitate the elicitation of favorable emotions in consumers within decision-making contexts that are characterized by a high level of effect. Sonic logos can elicit favorable emotions, foster active involvement, and enhance the overall brand encounter, particularly among individuals who exhibit a propensity for decision-making influenced by emotions. Kemp et al., 2023 and North et al., 2003 examined the impact of music on consumers' emotional and cognitive states. It offers valuable insights into the potential impact of music on emotional states and cognitive associations. The study's findings indicate that using familiar and highly favoured music can elicit positive emotional responses and strengthen brand loyalty.

The jingle associated with the Intel Inside campaign is a notable illustration of the capacity to evoke emotional responses and establish cognitive connections. The "Intel Bong," characterized by its unique five-note sequence, has become closely linked with innovation, dependability, and credibility. The utilization of this sonic brand has played a pivotal role in the establishment of Intel's brand identity and the reinforcement of its esteemed reputation for excellence and technological progress. The renowned jingle "I am Loving It" by Pharrell Williams, which has become synonymous with McDonald's, is a prime illustration of how auditory stimuli can effectively elicit favourable sentiments and strengthen connections with a brand. The melodic and memorable nature of the jingle, along with its underlying message, has established a strong association between McDonald's and the notions of pleasure, contentment, and convenience within fast food. The examples above prove the significant influence that skillfully designed sonic branding can exert on consumer behaviour and brand perception. The auditory stimuli generated by sound play a significant role in fostering heightened brand allegiance, favorable connotations, and, ultimately, a more profound bond with customers. Sonic branding can evoke emotional reactions that surpass linguistic and cultural boundaries, thereby establishing a universal brand identity that resonates with consumers profoundly and instinctively.

The auditory stimuli, encompassing various forms of sound, such as music and jingles, can elicit a diverse spectrum of emotional responses (Williams & Aaker, 2002). According to Scott et al. (2022), the utilization of lively and optimistic melodies and rhythms has the potential to evoke sensations of joy and happiness. A notable illustration of this phenomenon is the renowned Intel jingle, commonly linked to notions of innovation and favourable vitality. Nostalgia is evoked when melodies that resonate with familiar and sentimental tunes are encountered, thereby facilitating the transportation of listeners to cherished memories or moments. The utilization of fast-paced and rhythmic compositions can engender a feeling of excitement and eager expectation, as exemplified in the context of sports anthems and event music.

The utilization of sonic branding effectively strengthens brand associations through the establishment of consistent auditory signals that are in alignment with the intended brand image. For example, the attribute of trustworthiness can be effectively communicated through a gentle and calming jingle or sound logo. This can be incredibly impactful in sectors such as healthcare or finance, where establishing trust and reliability is paramount. Using sonic elements featuring futuristic or cutting-edge sounds effectively communicates a brand's dedication to innovation and proactive approach to maintaining a competitive edge.

Importance of Sonic Branding in Marketing

Sonic branding plays a significant role in marketing as it provides distinct advantages and opportunities for brands to establish a deeper connection with consumers. This strategy's multisensory approach to brand communication surpasses the reliance on visual elements, thus establishing itself as a valuable and strategic asset within a brand's marketing arsenal. Numerous empirical studies have provided compelling evidence suggesting that sonic branding possesses the capacity to impact consumer behaviour (Graakjaer, 2013). Extensive research has been conducted on the effects of extended musical compositions on individuals' perceptions and various outcomes associated with consumption. The outcomes discussed in the study by Roschk et al. (2017) include various factors such as product selection, sales performance, and customer flow within a retail establishment. Furthermore, it has been observed that extended compositions of music can significantly impact individuals' perceptions and attitudes toward various brands (Park & Young, 1986).

Positioning is a strategy of finding the desired consumer perception of a product/ brand and filling an empty slot/window in the minds of the target customers by creating and communicating an image that differentiates its unique position from competitors to gain a competitive advantage in the market. (Saqib, 2021; Saqib &

Shah 2022; Saqib & Satar, 2023). Sonic branding, through strategic use of music and sound, enhances brand positioning by creating memorable auditory cues that evoke emotional connections with consumers. Consistent sonic elements across touchpoints reinforce brand identity, differentiate from competitors, and convey brand values, fostering recognition and loyalty in a crowded marketplace.

Sonic branding, achieved through jingles and sound logos, establishes distinct auditory signatures with high memorability. These auditory cues serve as stimuli that elicit the recollection of a particular brand. According to Wazir and Wazir (2015), the immediate association between consumers and a brand's jingle or sound logo strengthens brand recognition and recall. In the current era of saturated advertising, achieving memorable brand recall is a significant competitive advantage. The auditory stimulus can elicit emotional responses and establish affective bonds. The implementation of sonic branding has the potential to elicit distinct emotional responses in consumers, including but not limited to feelings of joy, sentimentality, or enthusiasm. By strategically associating these emotions with the brand, marketers can cultivate a more profound and significant bond with their target audience. Emotionally invested consumers are more inclined to develop loyalty towards a brand and actively promote it. Using sonic branding is crucial in establishing a distinctive and easily identifiable brand identity (Jackson, 2003).

In conjunction with visual branding, integrating auditory elements is pivotal in shaping a comprehensive brand persona (Puligadda & VanBergen, 2023). Based on the findings of Müller and Kirchgeorg (2011), the effective integration of a brand's sound logo with other brand elements successfully communicates a cohesive brand personality, ultimately facilitating the establishment of a strong brand identity. Rodero et al. (2013) propose that incorporating musical patterns can serve as a strategic approach to augment brand attitudes and effectively communicate brand values, thereby transmitting brand personality traits. As an illustration, a brand that seeks to cultivate a perception of trustworthiness and dependability may employ soft, soothing melodies in its sonic branding endeavors, thereby strengthening these attributes. The establishment of a consistent brand identity has the potential to effectively distinguish the brand from its competitors and enhance its positioning within the market. In the contemporary era of technology, marketing endeavors encompass a diverse array of platforms and touchpoints, encompassing traditional mediums such as television and radio and digital platforms like websites, social media, and mobile applications. Using sonic branding provides the benefit of ensuring consistency across multiple platforms. A meticulously crafted jingle or sound logo can be seamlessly integrated across diverse marketing channels, guaranteeing a consistent and harmonious brand representation. Sound is a universally comprehensible means of communication that surpasses the limitations of language and cultural differences. Sonic branding that is skillfully crafted can evoke a positive response from audiences on a global scale, irrespective of their linguistic or cultural diversity. The concept of universality enables brands to effectively target a wide range of markets and audiences by utilizing a singular sonic identity. Sonic branding can significantly augment the ability to remember and the efficacy of advertisements.

According to Morris and Boone (1998), using a recognizable jingle or sound logo in an advertisement attracts the viewer's attention and strengthens the messaging associated with the brand. Research suggests that individuals are more inclined to retain and actively interact with advertisements that integrate sonic branding components. The utilization of music enables the formation of emotional connections, thereby enhancing the transmission of brand values (Mas et al. (2017). Even concise musical cues can elicit emotional resonance. Prior research has established that audio logos possess the ability to elicit emotional distress when individuals attempt to recall information (Nomura &Mitsukura, 2015). Sonic branding represents a unique approach to differentiating oneself within a highly competitive market. Key factors are differentiating a brand from its competitors and creating a memorable impact on consumers. Companies that allocate resources toward developing robust sonic branding strategies can achieve a competitive advantage by crafting distinctive and memorable brand encounters.

METHODOLOGY

Qualitative approaches facilitate understanding complex phenomena (Yin, 2009), such as sonic branding (Khamis & Keogh, 2021). An exploratory single case study was deemed essential given the relatively early research stage in connecting business model innovation with competitive advantage. This research design aligns with the definition of a case study as an empirical inquiry that investigates a contemporary phenomenon within its real-life context when the boundaries between the phenomenon and context are not evident and in which multiple sources of evidence are used (Yin, 1984).

There are specific reasons for opting for the single-case methodology. First, it offers the flexibility to explore relatively uncharted areas at various levels without being restricted by pre-established tools or data types (Eisenhardt, 1989). Second, it addresses the need to comprehensively investigate the sonic branding process, as highlighted by studies such as Techawachirakul et al. 2023. Third, there is a limited prior understanding of the sonic branding as a source of customer engagement

Consequently, an explorative historical case analysis was undertaken. This approach combines predetermined concepts from the sonic branding and cognitive literature with inductive theoretical propositions. It allows us to trace the entire longitudinal process, starting from a startup to achieving brand identity, customer engagement, and brand loyalty and ultimately becoming a profitable company. Unlike mainstream case studies, this historical approach circumvents many problems typical of contemporary materials and interviews. By relying on rich historical data, we can mitigate the issues associated with biased retrospective interviews and incomplete document information that may affect the quality of qualitative case studies.

Our choice to study Airtel serves as an illustrative example of a company whose jingle model has played a pivotal role in attaining customer engagement and brand loyalty, while the Airtel case lacks direct generalizability; it provides a conceptual representativeness suitable for exploring the sonic branding as a source of customer engagement in theoretical terms. Our data collection followed a structured process. We began with an in-depth historical analysis of Airtel and its market environment, seeking to understand Airtel's evolution within its context. We initially gathered academic publications focusing on Airtel's history as part of a broader research program. These publications were carefully reviewed to create a timeline of significant historical events in Airtel's development and to gain insight into how other researchers have approached Airtel's sonic branding. In addition to academic research reports, we collected newspaper articles, business magazine reports, and other publicly available materials. These sources were triangulated with the academic research reports, providing a more comprehensive and robust dataset for our analysis. This approach allowed us to study Airtel's historical development and sonic branding from multiple angles, enriching our understanding of how its business model contributed to its competitive advantage. Top of Form

AIRTEL'S JINGLE: A CASE STUDY

Overview of Airtel

Bharti Airtel Limited, widely recognized as Airtel, is an Indian multinational telecommunications service provider with its corporate headquarters in New Delhi, India. Airtel, a telecommunications company, was founded in 1985 and has emerged as a prominent player in the global market. As of the financial year 2021, Airtel operates in 18 countries spanning Asia and Africa, offering its services to a broad customer base. Additionally, it is noteworthy that this particular cellular network service provider holds second in India regarding its extensive subscriber base. As of December 2022, Bharti Airtel held a dominant market share of more than 34 percent in the rural telecommunications sector in India. It also maintains a substantial presence in urban areas of India. Airtel held a market share of approximately 32.2 percent in the wireless subscriber market, positioning it as the second-largest player after Reliance Jio. In the year 2023, Airtel disclosed a notable surge in revenue, amounting to more than 1.39 trillion Indian rupees, which represents a substantial growth when compared to the previous year (Figure 1).

Figure 1. Revenue of Bharti Airtel Limited from Financial Year 2013 to 2023 (in Billion Indian Rupees)
Source: Statista, 2023

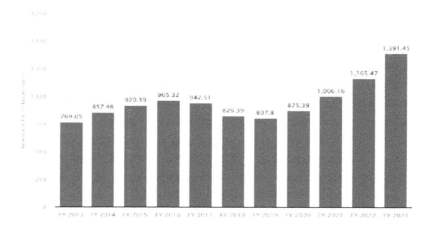

Bharti Airtel provides a range of services to its customers, including Telemedia and digital TV services, in addition to its highly sought-after mobile services. The number of subscribers for all of its services is steadily growing nationwide. As of fiscal year 2022, the subscriber base of Bharti Airtel digital TV services in India was approximately 15.9 million. The diverse range of services Airtel provides its customers and its continuously expanding subscriber base have positioned Bharti Airtel as one of the prominent brands in India. According to Figure 2, the brand value of Bharti Airtel in 2023 amounted to approximately 7.5 billion U.S. dollars. Airtel, a prominent player in the Indian market, has established a robust presence in various sectors, such as mobile data services, digital television, software, and cloud products, catering to the rapidly expanding market (Statista, 2023).

Figure 2. The Brand Value of Bharti Airtel from 2016 to 2023 (in Billion U.S. Dollars)
Source: Statista, 2023

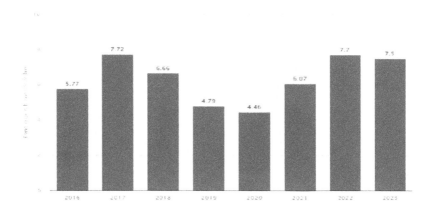

Airtel has consistently demonstrated a commitment to innovation by spearheading the introduction of novel technologies and services to enhance connectivity. The entity in question has significantly contributed to mobile telephony's expansion in India and Africa. Airtel's achievement can be partially attributed to its robust customer-centric approach. The organization has prioritized providing superior services and groundbreaking solutions to address the changing demands of its clientele. Airtel's foray into international markets, particularly in Africa, has positioned it as a prominent participant in the global telecommunications industry. The multinational nature of the company highlights its prominence within the global arena (Pandey & Hallur, 2023; Priya, 2016). Airtel underwent multiple alterations in its brand identity, yet it consistently maintained a steadfast dedication to innovation and customer-centric services. The dedication to this cause was evident in the company's branding strategy, encompassing its memorable jingle. The utilization of sonic branding by Airtel, which encompasses its distinctive jingle, has emerged as a prominent element in shaping the brand's identity. The composition, attributed to A.R. Rahman, enjoys widespread recognition and has significantly contributed to establishing a robust and enduring auditory brand identity (Kaur, 2022). The transformation of Airtel from a regional telecommunications provider to a prominent global player, coupled with its dedication to innovation, customer contentment, and the implementation of sonic branding, renders it a captivating topic for a case analysis. This examination sheds light on the dynamic nature of the telecommunications sector and underscores the significance of branding within this industry.

Evolution of Airtel's Sonic Branding

Airtel's sonic identity, characterized by its iconic jingle composed by A.R. Rahman (Figure 3), has undergone a fascinating evolution over the years (Adgully, 2019).

Figure 3. Airtel Jingle Advertisement
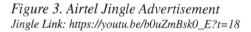
Jingle Link: https://youtu.be/b0uZmBsk0_E?t=18

- *Genesis of Airtel's Sonic Branding*: The genesis of Airtel's sonic branding can be traced back to the early 2000s when the company rapidly expanded and established itself as a prominent player in the Indian telecom sector. During this period, Airtel recognized the need to create a unique and memorable auditory brand identity to set itself apart from competitors.
- *Collaboration with A.R. Rahman:* One of the defining moments in the evolution of Airtel's sonic identity was the collaboration with renowned Indian composer A.R. Rahman. A.R. Rahman, known for his groundbreaking work in the music industry, was tasked with creating a jingle that would capture the essence of Airtel and resonate with consumers.
- *The Birth of the Iconic Jingle:* A.R. Rahman's composition for Airtel created an iconic and catchy jingle with a simple yet captivating melody. The tune of the jingle was designed to be easily recognizable and memorable, serving as a unique sonic identifier for Airtel (Kaur, 2022).

- *Consistency and Recognition*: Airtel's commitment to using its jingle consistently across various touchpoints and marketing channels was crucial to its success. The jingle became synonymous with the Airtel brand, reinforcing brand recognition and recall (Sharma & Shah, 2007).

- *Contemporary Reinterpretations:* Airtel has periodically revisited and refreshed its sonic identity over the years. New interpretations and variations of the jingle have been created to align with changing brand messaging and market dynamics. Jingles like " Har Ek friend Jaruri Hota hai" and "Jo Tera hai, Wo Mera hai" for Gen Z have worked brilliantly for them (Shastri, 2023). These adaptations have helped keep Airtel's sonic branding contemporary and relevant.

- *Emotional Resonance and Brand Trust:* The Airtel jingle has created a solid emotional connection with consumers. The uplifting and melodic nature of the jingle conveys messages of connectivity, reliability, and happiness, fostering trust and brand loyalty among customers.

- *Lasting Legacy:* Airtel's sonic branding, particularly its jingle, has left a lasting legacy in the telecom industry. It is a prime example of the power of sound in shaping brand identity and creating memorable brand experiences. Airtel's sonic branding has had a tangible impact on consumer behaviour and brand perception, contributing to its enduring success in the telecom sector.

The evolution of Airtel's sonic identity, from its inception to its global adaptations and contemporary reinterpretations, reflects the brand's commitment to innovation, customer-centricity, and the effective use of auditory branding as a powerful tool in the telecom industry. This journey serves as a compelling case study on the transformative role of sound in brand identity and customer engagement.

Brand Communication through Airtel's Jingle

The jingle created by A.R. Rahman for Airtel demonstrates its efficacy as a potent instrument for brand communication. The primary focus of Airtel's jingle revolves around connectivity and communication. The melodic and lyrical elements of the jingle elicit a perception of a harmonious and effective linkage and exchange. The statement suggests that Airtel functions as a telecommunications enterprise and a mediator of interpersonal connections, fostering proximity among individuals and facilitating seamless and dependable communication. The jingle emanates a tone that is optimistic and inspiring. The melody and lyrics of the composition effectively evoke feelings of happiness and joy. The positivity above conveys a compelling message regarding Airtel's affiliation with favorable encounters and contentment among its customers. The statement conveys the brand's dedication to improving the overall well-being of its clientele.

The jingle of Airtel establishes an emotional connection linked to the perception of dependability and credibility. The consistent utilization of the jingle across different brand touchpoints strengthens the perception that Airtel is a reliable and reputable telecommunications provider. It cultivates a perception of safety and confidence among clientele.

It possesses a universal appeal, demonstrating its ability to be customized to suit specific regional contexts. The adaptability of the jingle enables it to effectively connect with linguistically and culturally diverse audiences, effectively conveying Airtel's understanding and responsiveness to the distinct requirements of its global customer base. The adaptability demonstrated by Airtel shows the company's dedication to inclusivity and prioritization of customer needs.

The utilization of Airtel's jingle is a mechanism for fostering an emotional bond with its customer base. The melodic composition and emotionally evocative nature of the jingle, combined with its optimistic messaging, contribute to the establishment of a lasting impact on individuals, thereby cultivating a sense of allegiance towards the brand. This statement suggests that Airtel understands the emotional value of maintaining connections and appreciates the opportunities for meaningful experiences facilitated by such connectivity. The persistent utilization of Airtel's jingle across diverse brand touchpoints enhances brand recognition and establishes a distinct brand identity. The statement posits that Airtel is a perpetual symbol for customers, reinforcing that the company is a reliable ally in facilitating connectivity. Consistency maintenance plays a crucial role in Airtel's brand communication strategy. Airtel's inclination towards innovation and flexibility in modifying its jingle to cater to various markets and evolving circumstances effectively conveys the brand's dedication to remaining pertinent and receptive to customer demands. The evolution of the jingle demonstrates Airtel's ability to adapt and its commitment to innovation.

Airtel's Jingle and Brand Identity

According to Ghodeswar (2008), brand identity can be defined as a distinct combination of brand associations that effectively conveys a commitment to customers. Aaker (1996) posits that a differentiation can be made between a brand's fundamental and expanded identities. A brand's core identity is its fundamental and enduring essence, while the extended identity includes dynamic characteristics that may change in response to different contexts. Aaker (1996) posits that brand identity encompasses a unique assemblage of brand associations that brand strategists seek to establish or maintain. De Chernatony (2010) argues that brand identity consists of the distinctive or fundamental idea of a brand and how the brand successfully communicates this idea to different stakeholders. Similarly, Kapferer (2012) defines brand identity as the symbolic manifestation of a brand that the organization effectively co-organization and Joachimsthaler (2002) asserts that a well-defined brand identity is paramount in cultivating trust, differentiating an entity from its rivals, exhibiting dedication to customers, and offering insights into its forthcoming endeavors.

Moreover, it enhances the customers' ability to recognize a particular brand (Baumgarth & Schmidt, 2010) while also promoting the development of a relationship between the brand and the customer through the provision of a value proposition that encompasses functional, emotional, and self-expressive advantages (Aaker, 1996). The brand's intangible benefits play a crucial role in this endeavor, as relying solely on functional benefits for differentiation tends to have a limited lifespan. Hence, establishing brand identity plays a crucial role in cultivating an emotional bond and establishing a connection between the brand and its clientele (Urde, 2003; Muhonen et al., 2017).

The Airtel jingle, commonly known as the "Airtel tune," is highly recognizable in Indian advertising. The company has effectively established a robust emotional bond with consumers individually. The Airtel jingle, composed by renowned musician A.R. Rahman, has become an integral component of the cultural fabric in India for a period exceeding ten years. For many individuals, it serves as a sentimental representation of the 2000s era, during which mobile devices and connectivity rapidly evolved, fundamentally altering how individuals communicate. The melody possesses an inherent quality of nostalgia, eliciting recollections of bygone eras characterized by the luxury status of mobile phones and the Airtel network serving as the means of interpersonal connection. The jingle's lively and optimistic melody is crafted to elicit emotions of joy and optimism. The concept is linked to maintaining interpersonal connections with individuals who are held dear, a sentiment universally regarded as favorable.

The jingle, regardless of its medium, such as a television commercial or a ringtone, can promptly enhance an individual's emotional state. The Airtel jingle encompasses a melodious composition and embodies trust and dependability. Airtel has emerged as a dependable telecommunications network for numerous individuals, facilitating seamless connectivity with their acquaintances irrespective of geographical boundaries. The jingle strengthens the notion that Airtel is a reliable network that ensures seamless and uninterrupted communication. The jingle holds personal and cultural connotations for numerous individuals. The auditory perception of one's residence or the sound of an affectionate individual frequently elicits a profound emotional attachment. Within Indian culture, music holds a deep and meaningful significance, and the jingle above effectively taps into the cultural affinity and appreciation for music prevalent within this cultural milieu. The repetition of "Airtel" in the jingle enhances brand recall and recognition, thereby facilitating customers' ability to remember and establish a connection between the melody and the brand. The melodic structure of the jingle is intentionally crafted to facilitate ease of humming and enhance memorability, thereby fostering a lasting impression on the audience. This phenomenon contributes to the enhancement of brand retention and recall. The jingle possesses a high degree of versatility and adaptability, enabling Airtel to employ it across diverse contexts and for multiple campaigns, thereby ensuring the preservation of a cohesive brand identity. The jingle of Airtel frequently integrates components derived from Indian culture and music. The cultural significance of this phenomenon holds particular importance, particularly within the context of a diverse and culturally vibrant nation such as India. When the melodic composition coincides with cultural elements, it engenders a sense of affiliation among consumers, signifying that the brand is deeply ingrained within their cultural framework and personal identity. This enhances the brand's affiliation with its intended demographic.

The Airtel jingle is a strategic tool that significantly establishes the brand's identity, extending beyond its musical composition. The strategy above facilitates the establishment of a profound and practical bond with consumers while also ensuring congruence with cultural aspects, sustaining brand coherence, and embodying the brand's core principles. Implementing a multifaceted strategy has yielded a brand identity that possesses both recognizability and emotional resonance among its target audience.

Airtel's Jingle and Consumer Engagement

Engaging customers with brands or businesses and with each other is known as customer engagement. The emotional connection that a consumer experiences during regular and continuous contact is referred to as customer engagement. Engagement is boosted by brand excitement. Bowden (2009) states that "consumers go through a sequential psychological process called customer engagement before they become brand loyalists. Engagement serves as a means of enhancing consumer loyalty for both new and current clients. A.R. Rahman's jingle for Airtel has been crucial in establishing a strong emotional connection between the company and its patrons, encouraging brand loyalty, and engaging consumers emotionally.

The goal of Airtel's jingle is to evoke strong feelings in customers. The jingle's melody and upbeat tone evoke joy, community, and nostalgia. Customers feel more than merely users of a telecom service because of this emotional resonance; they feel a part of a community that recognizes maintaining relationships with loved ones. There is a direct correlation between brand loyalty and the emotional bond established by the jingle. Customers are more inclined to stick with Airtel if they have favorable emotional associations with the company. In addition to utiliziutilizing's services, this commitment includes promoting the company and, in essence, becoming brand ambassadors. The notion that Airtel is a reputable and dependable telecom provider is strengthened by the jingle's constant usage across various brand touchpoints. This feeling of trust significantly influences customer involvement. Customers are more inclined to interact with a business they feel confident in, and the jingle is essential to building this confidence.

The memorable tune and familiarity of the jingle help to improve brand memory. Customers instantly recognize it when they hear it in commercials, on-hold music, or mobile apps. In addition to keeping Airtel at the forefront of consumers' minds, this improved recall motivates users to interact with the brand through its offerings. The jingle enhances the general Airtel service user experience. While on hold or during customer contact, hearing the jingle produces a pleasant and positive experience. Higher levels of engagement and satisfaction follow from this. A consistent brand experience is ensured by Airtel's dedication to deploying its jingle regularly across a range of marketing channels and customer touchpoints. Customers hear the same sounds in mobile apps, radio and television commercials, and customer service conversations. By establishing a recognizable and consistent brand presence, this cross-channel consistency improves engagement.

Inclusivity is promoted by Airtel's readiness to modify its jingle to fit various linguistic and cultural circumstances. It increases consumer involvement by giving customers from various backgrounds the impression that the company respects and recognizes their cultural identity and understands their particular demands. Because it can be customized, jingle has a broad appeal. It strikes a chord with audiences worldwide, connecting the brand with customers in many nations. This worldwide reach increases customer engagement and grows Airtel's clientele.

As a result, Airtel's jingle serves as a potent instrument for customer interaction and a musical component of the brand. It guarantees constant cross-channel interaction, builds emotional ties, strengthens brand loyalty, and reaffirms dependability and trust. The jingle is a vital component of Airtel's successful marketing strategy because of its versatility and universal appeal, which enhance its capacity to engage consumers in various markets.

FINDINGS

The research commences by highlighting the significance of sonic branding within the telecommunications industry and the primary aim of examining Airtel's jingle as a specific instance for analysis. The research has revealed significant findings through an exploratory case study approach within the context of the Indian telecommunications industry. The study demonstrates that Airtel's jingle has elicited favorable consumer perceptions. The effectiveness of the jingle in establishing a unique brand identity for Airtel within the fiercely competitive telecommunications industry is apparent. This discovery highlights sound and music's influence on consumer perceptions and establishes an enduring impact. One of the most noteworthy discoveries is that Airtel's jingle elicits emotional and cognitive connections with the brand. The simultaneous effect of this phenomenon plays a crucial role in augmenting consumer involvement. The jingle fosters an emotional bond that engenders feelings of familiarity, trust, and warmth within consumers. Concurrently, cognitive associations, encompassing attributes such as reliability and innovation, significantly shape a comprehensive brand image. Combining emotions and rationality is potent in cultivating robust brand loyalty and fostering customer relationships.

Additionally, the jingle employed by Airtel demonstrates a notable influence on consumers' ability to remember and associate with the brand. The melodic composition of the tune contributes to the establishment of brand awareness and the ability to retrieve information from memory. The jingle associated with Airtel is readily identifiable by consumers, indicating the jingle's efficacy in augmenting brand saliency. Telecom companies strive to capture consumers' attention in a highly competitive market. Airtel's jingle functions as a unique auditory representation, enabling the brand to differentiate itself and maintain a prominent presence in consumers' consciousness. The research also sheds light on the potential impact of Airtel's jingle on consumer engagement in the telecommunications industry. The results suggest that individuals who connect with the jingle are more inclined to interact with Airtel's brand offerings. This engagement can be demonstrated through various activities, including subscribing to Airtel's services, actively participating in promotional campaigns, and advocating for the brand—the jingle, due to its ability to evoke emotional and cognitive responses. The favorable results underscore the significance of sonic branding in the telecommunications industry.

CONCLUSION

The immediate impact of music on customers, coupled with its potential as a potent marketing instrument, is a noteworthy phenomenon. This is mainly attributed to its capacity to elicit nostalgic recollections and intense emotions, as supported by the research of Fulberg (2003), Jackson (2003), and Kilian (2009). This case study has examined the significance of sound branding within the telecommunications industry, specifically highlighting the renowned jingle associated with Airtel. This paper examines Airtel's historical development and growth as a prominent telecommunications corporation. It delves into the concept of sonic branding, its constituent components, the emotional and cognitive responses it elicits, and its significance within the marketing realm. The analysis of Airtel's jingle has focused on its significance in establishing a distinct brand image, cultivating sentimental associations, and influencing consumer involvement. The results are succinctly described: Sonic branding, as seen by Airtel's jingle, is a highly influential instrument within the telecommunications industry. It facilitates the distinction of brands, fosters trust, establishes emotional bonds, and augments brand recollection. The jingle of Airtel is distinguished by its melodious and memorable composition, straightforward lyrics, unwavering uniformity, versatility, and the profound emotional impact it evokes. These components jointly contribute to the effectiveness of the subject. The jingle employed by Airtel effectively communicates several themes, such as connectedness, positivity, reliability, and emotional connection, cultivating trust and creating brand loyalty among its client base. Using a jingle facilitates increased customer engagement by establishing an emotional bond, fostering brand loyalty and trust, reinforcing brand recall, promoting good user experiences, ensuring consistency across many channels, promoting inclusion, demonstrating adaptability, and appealing to an international audience.

Implications

This study highlights the managerial implications of sonic branding as a strategic tool to attain customer engagement within the telecommunications sector. The significance of integrating a consistent and coherent sonic brand identity across multiple marketing channels is underscored, as it facilitates the creation of a unified and memorable brand experience for consumers. This study provides valuable insights for marketers in the telecommunications industry aiming to utilize branding strategies effectively. This emphasizes the importance of adopting a cohesive and deliberate brand communication strategy, encompassing visual and auditory components that effectively connect with consumers. This study provides insight into the increasing influence of sound and music in shaping consumer perceptions and cultivating brand loyalty within a broader societal framework. This statement highlights the significance of auditory components within the marketing industry and their ability to establish significant associations between brands and consumers.

Airtel's adept use of sound branding, especially with its catchy jingle, has several marketing strategy ramifications for the telecom industry and beyond. These ramifications highlight the importance of regularly using aural branding to improve brand communication and gain a competitive edge. In a crowded market, Sonic branding could be a potent differentiation. Telecom businesses can differentiate themselves from rivals by using audio branding to build a unique identity. A well-written jingle or sound logo in a competitive market can help the business stand out by becoming a distinctive and memorable auditory trademark. The popularity of Airtel's jingle shows how sonic branding may give businesses in the telecom industry a competitive edge. Building a solid brand identity requires consistent brand communication. Jingles and sound logos are sonic branding features that telecom firms could incorporate into their marketing channels and client touchpoints. A consistent auditory identity across all media platforms—including mobile apps, radio and television commercials, and customer service exchanges—guarantees that customers will see the brand as coherent and recognizable as essential principles are reaffirmed, and this integration improves brand recognition. The success of Airtel's jingle serves as a reminder of how important consistency is in brand messaging. Telecom firms should regularly use audio branding features to establish a distinctive brand identity. Customers feel more dependable and trustworthy when they hear the same auditory cues in many interactions and channels. Companies must keep sounds consistent to build a brand that connects with customers. Over time, market dynamics and consumer tastes change. Telecom firms must be flexible with their sonic branding aspects to accommodate evolving customer tastes and be relevant and engaging. The significance of adaptability and sensitivity to changing customer needs is demonstrated by Airtel's ability to modify its jingle for various markets and cultures. Reinterpreting sound branding can help firms remain relevant and keep customers interested. The success of Airtel's aural branding, incredibly recognizable, has important lessons and ramifications for marketing tactics used in the telecom industry and elsewhere. In the current branding landscape, an effective marketing plan must leverage sonic branding for competitive advantage, integrate it consistently across marketing channels, maintain brand communication consistency, and adjust to shifting consumer preferences.

Limitations And Future Research Directions

This case study offers valuable insights into Airtel's effective implementation of sonic branding. However, it is essential to acknowledge certain limitations associated with this study. The research primarily centers on Airtel and its jingle, potentially constraining its applicability to other telecommunications firms that employ other branding techniques. The case study relies on information that is publicly accessible and accurate as of the knowledge cutoff date in January 2022. Any subsequent developments occurring after that date should be addressed in this study. The research conducted does not use primary data from sources such as consumer surveys or in-depth interviews. Including such data could enhance the study's comprehensiveness in assessing the influence of Airtel's jingle on consumer behaviour and attitudes.

The case study presents avenues for further investigation into sound branding and its potential applications across diverse industries. Scholars can undertake comparative investigations to examine the efficacy of various acoustic branding methods within the telecommunications industry and their influence on consumer engagement.

Investigating the impact of cultural characteristics on the efficacy of sonic branding features and adjustments within various regions holds significant potential for global businesses to gain helpful information. Conducting a comprehensive examination of the enduring effects of sound branding on brand equity, consumer loyalty, and financial success has the potential to provide valuable insights into the enduring influence of auditory branding. The emergence of voice assistants and interactive audio platforms has opened avenues for scholarly inquiry into optimizing branding to augment user experiences.

REFERENCES

Aaker, D. A. (1996). Measuring brand equity across products and markets. *California Management Review*, *38*(3), 102–120. doi:10.2307/41165845

Aaker, D. A., & Joachimsthaler, E. (2002). *Brand Leadership*. Simon and Schuster.

Adgully Bureau. (2019, September 12). Advertising that has built the brand Airtel. Retrieved from https://www.adgully.com/advertising-that-has-built-brand-airtel-88237.html

Baumgarth, C. (2010). 'Living the brand': Brand orientation in the business-to-business sector. *European Journal of Marketing*, *44*(5), 653–671. doi:10.1108/03090561011032315

Belch, G. E., & Belch, M. S. (2015). *Introduction to Advertising and Promotion* (10th ed.). McGraw Hill.

Bonde, A., & Hansen, A. G. (2013). Audio logo recognition, reduced articulation, and coding orientation: Rudiments of quantitative research integrating branding theory, social semiotics, and music psychology. *Sound Effects – an Interdisciplinary Journal of Sound and Sound Experience, 3*(1/2), 112-135.

Bowden, J. (2009). A framework for assessing customer-brand relationships: The case of the restaurant industry. *Journal of Hospitality Marketing & Customer Engagement, pp.,* 37–41.

Bronner, K. (2008). Jingle all the way? Basics of audio branding. In P. Steiner (Ed.), *Audio Branding-Brands, Sound and Communication* (pp. 77–87). Nomos Edition.

Craig, S. (2011). A brief history of the American radio jingle. Conference: Popular culture association convention, San Antonio, TX.

De Chernatony, L. (2010). *From Brand Vision to Brand Evaluation* (3rd ed.). Butterworth-Heinemnn. doi:10.4324/9780080966649

Eisenhardt, K. M. (1989). Building theories from case study research. *Academy of Management Review*, *14*(4), 532–550. doi:10.2307/258557

Flaig, N. (2022). *Sound advice: Creating a sonic identity profile*. Sentient Decision Science.

Goldberg, P. (2003). Using sonic branding in the retail environment – An easy and effective way to create consumer brand loyalty while enhancing the in-store experience. *Journal of Consumer Behaviour*, *3*(2), 193–198. doi:10.1002/cb.132

Graakjær, N. J. (2013). Sounding out the logo shot. *Sound Effects - an Interdisciplinary Journal of Sound and Sound Experience, 3*(1/2), 78-95.

Gustafsson, C. (2015). Sonic branding: A consumer-oriented literature review. *Journal of Brand Management*, *22*(1), 20–37. doi:10.1057/bm.2015.5

Holbrook, M. B. (2008). Music meanings in movies: The case of the crime-plus-jazz genre. *Consumption Markets & Culture*, *11*(4), 307–327. doi:10.1080/10253860802391326

Iglesias, O., Markovic, S., & Rialp, J. (2019). How does sensory brand experience influence brand equity? Considering the roles of customer satisfaction, customer affective commitment, and employee empathy. *Journal of Business Research*, *96*, 343–354. doi:10.1016/j.jbusres.2018.05.043

Jackson, D. M. (2003). *Sonic Branding: An Introduction*. Palgrave Macmillan. doi:10.1057/9780230503267

Kapferer, J. N. (2012). *The New Strategic Brand Management: Creating and Sustaining Brand Equity Long Term* (5th ed.). Kogan Page.

Kastner, S. (2013). Heimatklänge: The conceptual design of branded spaces by means of sonic branding. In S. Sonnenburg & L. Baker (Eds.), *Branded Spaces: Experience Enactments and Entanglements*. doi:10.1007/978-3-658-01561-9_11

Kaur, C. (2022). AR Rahman's Airtel melody that Indians 'Live Every Moment.' *Brand Equity*. Retrieved from https://brandequity.economictimes.indiatimes.com/news/advertising/ar-rahmans-airtel-melody-that-indians-live-every-moment/92910971

Kemp, E., Cho, Y.-N., Bui, M., & Kintzer, A. (2023a). Music to the ears: The role of sonic branding in advertising. *International Journal of Advertising*, 1–21. Advance online publication. doi:10.1080/02650487.2023.2273645

Kemp, E., Kopp, S. W., & Bui, M. (2023b). Healthcare brands sound off: Evaluating the influence of sonic branding in shaping consumer perceptions. *International Journal of Pharmaceutical and Healthcare Marketing, 17*(3), 340–352. doi:10.1108/IJPHM-10-2022-0093

Khamis, S., & Keogh, B. (2021). Sonic branding and the aesthetic infrastructure of everyday consumption. *Popular Music, 40*(2), 281–296. doi:10.1017/S0261143021000118

Kilian, K. (2009). From brand identity to audio branding. In H. Bronner & H. Rainer (Eds.), *Audio Branding: Brands, Sound and Communication* (pp. 35–48). Nomos. doi:10.5771/9783845216935-36

Kotler, P. (1973). Atmospherics as a marketing tool. *Journal of Retailing, 49*(4), 48.

Krishna, A. (2013). *Customer Sense: How the 5 Senses Influence Buying Behavior.* Palgrave Macmillan. doi:10.1057/9781137346056

Krishnan, V., Kellaris, J. J., & Aurand, T. W. (2012). Sonic logos: Can sound influence willingness to pay? *Journal of Product and Brand Management, 21*(4), 275–284. doi:10.1108/10610421211246685

Mas, L., Collell, M. R., & Xifra, J. (2017). The sound of music or the history of Trump and Clinton family singers: Music branding as a communication strategy in 2016 presidential campaign. *The American Behavioral Scientist, 61*(6), 584–599. doi:10.1177/0002764217701214

McCusker, G. (1997). The audio logo: A case study of Radio Scotland's on-air identity. *Journal of Communication Management (London), 1*(4), 362–373. doi:10.1108/eb023439

Minsky, L., & Fahey, C. (2017). *Audio Branding: Using Sound to Build Your Brand.* Kogan Page.

Morris, J. D., & Boone, M. A. (1998). *The effects of music on emotional response, brand attitude, and purchase intent in an emotional advertising condition.* ACR North American Advances.

Muhonen, T., Hirvonen, S., & Laukkanen, T. (2017). SME brand identity: Its components and performance effects. *Journal of Product and Brand Management, 26*(1), 52–67. doi:10.1108/JPBM-01-2016-1083

Nomura, T., & Mitsukura, Y. (2015). EEG-based detection of TV commercials effects. *Procedia Computer Science, 60*, 131–140. doi:10.1016/j.procs.2015.08.112

Nufer, G., & Moser, H. (2018). The sound of brands. *Reutlingen Working Papers on Marketing & Management, 2019*(1). doi:10.15496/publikation-26654

Pandey, S., & Hallur, G. G. (2023). Study of the competition in the Indian telecom industry: 20 years with Airtel as the case company. AIP Conf. Proc., p., 2523, 030018.

Park, C. W., & Young, S. M. (1986). Consumer response to television commercials: The impact of involvement and background music on brand attitude formation. *JMR, Journal of Marketing Research, 23*(1), 11–24. doi:10.1177/002224378602300102

Perlovsky, L. (2010). Musical emotions: Functions, origins, evolution. *Physics of Life Reviews, 7*(1), 2–27. doi:10.1016/j.plrev.2009.11.001 PMID:20374916

Priya, P. (2016). Case Study: The study on consumer satisfaction of services provided by Airtel Telecommunication. *Advances in Management, 9*(10), 5–11.

Puligadda, S., & VanBergen, N. (2023). The influence of sound logo instruments on brand personality perceptions: An investigation of brand ruggedness and sophistication. *Journal of Business Research, 156*, 113531. doi:10.1016/j.jbusres.2022.113531

Rodero, E., Larrea, O., & Vazquez, M. (2013). Male and female voices in commercials. Analysis of effectiveness, adequacy for product, attention, and recall. *Sex Roles, 68*(5/6), 349–362. doi:10.1007/s11199-012-0247-y

Rodrigues, C., Rodrigues, P., Billore, S., & Tetsuhisa, O. (2018). The role of brand experience and authenticity in creating brand love: A cross-cultural comparative study. *Global Marketing Conference, Tokyo, pp.,* 1447-1447. 10.15444/GMC2018.12.03.03

Roschk, H., Loureiro, S. M. C., & Breitsohl, J. (2017). Calibrating 30 years of experimental research: A meta-analysis of the atmospheric effects of music, scent, and colour. *Journal of Retailing, 93*(2), 228–240. doi:10.1016/j.jretai.2016.10.001

Saqib, N. (2021). Positioning – a literature review. *PSU Research Review, 5*(2), 141–169. doi:10.1108/PRR-06-2019-0016

Saqib, N., & Satar, M. S. (2023). Development of empirically based customer-derived positioning taxonomy for consumer electronics sector in the Indian emerging market. *International Journal of Emerging Markets, 18*(10), 3868–3892. doi:10.1108/IJOEM-12-2020-1568

Saqib, N., & Shah, A. M. (2022). Development of empirically-based customer-derived positioning taxonomy for FMCG sector in the Indian emerging market. *Young Consumers, 23*(2), 233–254. doi:10.1108/YC-11-2020-1257

Scott, S. P., Sheinin, D., & Labrecque, L. I. (2022). Small sounds, significant impact: Sonic logos and their effect on consumer attitudes, emotions, brands, and advertising placement. *Journal of Product and Brand Management, 31*(7), 1091–1103. doi:10.1108/JPBM-06-2021-3507

Sharma, R., & Shah, G. (2007, November 25). The sound of music. *Livemint.* Retrieved from https://www.livemint.com/Consumer/IBkeN02j4lzXfCMt5scSnO/The-sound-of-music.html

Shastri, A. (2023). Airtel: Case Study on its Business Model and Marketing Strategy. Retrieved from https://iide.co/blog/airtel-marketing-strategy/

Steiner, P. (2014). *Sonic Branding*. Springer. doi:10.1007/978-3-8349-4015-5

Techawachirakul, M., Pathak, A., Motoki, K., & Calvert, G. A. (2023). Sonic branding of meat- and plant-based foods: The role of timbre. *Journal of Business Research, 165*, 114032. doi:10.1016/j.jbusres.2023.114032

Treasure, J. (2011). Sound Business (2nd ed.). Management Books 2000Lt.

Urde, M. (2003). Core value-based corporate brand building. *European Journal of Marketing, 37*(7/8), 1017–1040. doi:10.1108/03090560310477645

Wazir, M. I., & Wazir, O. (2015). Effects of sonic logo on brand recognition of the advertised brand. *City University Research Journal, 5*(2), 327–337.

Williams, P., & Aaker, J. L. (2002). Can mixed emotions peacefully coexist? *The Journal of Consumer Research, 28*(4), 636–649. doi:10.1086/338206

Yin, R. K. (1984). *Case Study Research: Design and Methods*. Sage Publications.

Yin, R. K. (2009). *Case Study Research: Design and Methods* (4th ed.). Sage Publications.

Chapter 7
Using Music to Assemble Dance and Exercise Class Experiencescapes

Anu Norrgrann
University of Vaasa, Finland

ABSTRACT

This chapter examines how service providers use music in assembling experiencescapes in the context of contemporary and street dance classes and group exercise services. Taking a socio-material approach, the role of music is explored in the interplay of practices, meaning making and entanglements between material/digital and social entities making up the service brand experience. The chapter discusses ways in which music is utilized, and draws attention to elements and interactions, and symbolic complementarities and tensions involved with its integration into the dance / exericise experiencescape. The rich empirical account draws on multiple forms of qualitative, ethnographic data, including in-depth interviews with dance and exercise class instructors.

After the warm up track, I feel ready and energized to get going. A musical jazz choreography begins to the tunes of an old Abba song. I like the easy flow of the movements, and in this moment, even this super worn-out song feels fun to move to. I hum the familiar lyrics in my mind as I go....Then it's time for the street styles parts of the workout. The participants change from barefoot to sneakers, I lace up my Vans, and a hip hop tune starts playing. In my mind, I transform from the

DOI: 10.4018/979-8-3693-0778-6.ch007

middle-aged ABBA-savvy woman to someone with 21th century street cred, bouncy moves and a cocky posture. That's not the usual me, but it's a version if me, that only surfaces in these dance classes and performances. I love how this part of the workout class really gets me pumped up and going. During the whole course of the workout, I shift identities a few more times as the music and dance genres change, and so do my feelings about how fun or tedious this hour of exercise feels.

INTRODUCTION

The autoethnographic note above, from participating in a group exercise class consisting of a mix of different dance styles, illustrates the role of music in shaping customer experience within a specific service context. It highlights the agentic role of music in influencing feelings, moods, motivation, and even the consumer's temporary identity, helping carry the consumer momentarily in and out of different, culturally constituted worlds, such as different subcultures, like hip hop, latin styles, or contemporary dance.

In this setting, music connects a multifaceted pool of symbolic resources of different stakeholders, from artists and choreographers to clothes brands and performances that serve as markers of different (sub)cultures of consumption, and functions as an element in an experiencescape (Mossberg 2007; Mody et al 2019; Kandampully et al 2022).

To conceptually grasp these interactions, this chapter draws on socio-culturally informed branding literature (e.g. Vallaster & von Wallpach 2013; Norrgrann & Saraniemi 2022), and specifically the idea of brand assemblage (Lucarelli et al, 2022; Hill et al 2014) based on assemblage thinking (Canniford & Bajde 2016). In doing so, we highlight the role of music in a service experience not only as a tactical marketing variable, but as a part of a broader set of interrelationships and dynamics that need to be understood in order to know when and how music has the ability to provide value in a service experience.

The empirical part of this chapter depicts a rich ethnographic study of dance and group exercise culture. It is based on multiple types of data from participant observation and author engagement in the community to qualitative, in-depth interviews with dance class instructors. In this chapter, the focus is foremost on the interview data, as these research participants can be seen as key actors in assembling the sonic experiencescape through their particular role in choosing music, and secondly, as the key connectors between service provision and co-created customer experience. Their front-line role is in other words crucial for assessing how the service experience unfolds in relation to the intended.

The interviewees represent both international exercise brand franchises and independent service providers who have established their own workout concepts. These two categories of informants illuminate the use of music in exercise from somewhat differing starting points, providing variation with regard to standardization/adaptation, and degree of autonomy in the sonic service design process. Secondary data such as company website material and social media content are used as a complement to the interviews.

To sum up, the purpose of this chapter is to examine **how service providers use music in assembling an experiencescape**. To this end, this chapter combines literature on assemblage thinking, and experiencescapes, and empirically explores the phenomenon in the context of dance and exercise class services. The empirical material illuminates symbolic complementarities and tensions involved with the attempts to use music to steer the design of the experiencescape; what it entails to attempt to bring consumers into differing cultural worlds through music.

Theoretical Underpinnings

This chapter participates in the discussion of sound in branding through applying a socio-material lens on brands and exploring it as assemblage. From this stance, brands are not only approached as objects, or images in the minds of individual consumers, but as dynamic representations formed through social processes in multi-stakeholder networks and communities where meaning-making takes place (Merz et al, 2009; Bode & Kjeldgaard 2017). In the empirical context of this chapter, this network comprises stakeholders such as service providers, instructors, music artists and service users.

The viewpoint taken is distinct from both the traditional firm-centric, and the purely consumer-centric view on brands, emphasizing instead the interactions between these spheres (Lucarelli et al 2022). Applying assemblage thinking, which is conceptually rooted in Actor-Network Theory and increasingly also used in studying various consumption phenomena (see Canniford & Bajde 2016) specifically on brands, implies framing brands as *"heterogeneous, co-creational and evolving configurations, involving multiple authors that not only includes firms and consumers, but also other heterogeneous and evolving sets of components with varying capacities"* (Lucarelli et al, 2022:70). This definition thus highlights distributed agency among a socio-material mesh of people, things and narratives, and the interrelationships between them.

As an analytical tool to help reveal these entities and interactions in empirical reality, practice theory (see Schatzki et al 2001) offers a way to identify habitual routine activities that shape everyday social life. Within this body of research, particularly Magaudda's (2011) work on digital music consumption offers useful analytical tools in approaching music utilization, proposing the notion of a *circuit of practice* to account for how meanings, activities and materiality are related. While practice theory usually focuses on tangible artifacts, Magaudda (2011) equates digital sound files with material objects, even though they are immaterial by nature. In this chapter, (digital) music is in a similar ontological vein regarded as an agentic object in the assemblage.

The empirical context that is depicted in this chapter is a service. In an ontologically similar way to the brand assemblage perspective, also service research highlights the complex network of intertwined actors, processes and artefacts that serve to co-create service experience (Chandler & Lusch 2015, Edvardsson et al., 2005). Music and sound has in prior service research been explicitly acknowledged as a factor in the servicescape (Bitner, 1992), i.e. a way to create ambience alongside the physical space and service performance. The closely related term experiencescape (see e.g. Mossberg, 2007; Mody et al 2019; Kandampully et al 2022) however explicitly considers how services are staged and consumed, and how customers interact with the environment to create their experiences. This broader term that stresses relationships and interactions instead of a provider perspective, aligns well with assemblage thinking. In this chapter, we therefore choose to regard the empirical setting as an experiencescape, drawing on the notion of service as providing value-in-experience, that is *"intra-and inter-subjective, both lived and imaginary, temporal in nature, and emerges from individually determined social contexts"* (Helkkula et al. 2012; Haanpää 2022).

Part of the experiencescape is what Jain & Bagdare (2011) refer to as musicscape, i.e. musical variables which emit audio signals and interact with auditory receptors. Such variables can, based on a review by Herrington and Capella (1994) be categorized into structural and affective types: observable characteristics such as rhythm, phrasing, pitch, harmony, orchestration, and experienced ones such as liking, familiarity, feeling, or mood.

In the empirical part of the chapter, we set out to investigate how the dance and exercise experiencescape is assembled and what role music plays in it. Before doing so, we first discuss the methodological choices.

METHODOLOGY

The empirical journey into the dance and exercise context draws on ethnographic research methodology. Ethnography can be characterized as an interpretive and explanatory social science practice of describing a group of people and their sociality, culture and behaviors. It focuses on studying and analyzing people and their interactions in typical, routine, or even ritualized situations (Madden, 2010: 16).

Participation can be considered as a cornerstone in ethnographic methodology (Madden, 2010: 93) and in the case of the present research, it implies a temporary membership and identity in what many consumer researchers regard as a consumer tribe (see for instance Goulding, Shankar, and Canniford, 2011). As presented in the vignette of this chapter, the author is a member of this specific culture of consumption, with a long background as a dance sport enthusiast, also at a competitive level in some of the dance disciplines discussed, and having at least some experience also of the other types of classes that are referred to in the interviews.

The researcher´s personal participation and engagement in the cultural context that is studied provides in addition to the *etic* (outsider), also an *emic* (insider) lens (Madden, 2010: 19-20), which helps the researcher understand the practices, meanings and values of a particular culture from the perspective of a person that participates in it. The dual role of the investigator as the researcher, and a participant also helped at a practical level to identify relevant research participants, discussion questions and themes, when the investigator possesses sufficient background knowledge of the research context.

In doing autoetnography, the role of corporality and senses is a central aspect in making observations. The researcher's bodily sensations function as a research instrument (Madden, 2010; Haanpää, 2022). In the case of this study, it implies an additional level at which to attain understanding of the researched phenomenon beyond the discursive and representational; *hearing* and *feeling* the experience, rather than only objectively observing it or verbally discussing it.

Ethnographic studies often rely on multiple types of data elicited through observation and immersion, but also through conversations and interviews. The author's autoethnographic role as a complete member in the social world that is studied (Anderson, 2006; Syrjälä & Norrgrann, 2018) has provided an opportunity to casual discussions on the research topic with multiple actors in the field, as a form of preliminary stage-setting for the study. This pre-understanding was used as a springboard to subsequent, in-depth, personal interviews with selected instructors, and provided direction for seeking online discussions (e.g. Reddit), websites and social media content related to dance and fitness, which were used to contextualize and corroborate the interview findings.

In this chapter, the spotlight is on the use of music in the assembling of a service. Therefore, the instructor perspectives were given particular emphasis, as they are the actors who select and make use of music in their classes and have a key role in service design, delivery and adaptation. With regard to music use, they are also the central actor connecting provider resources such as music brands or genres with the users, being able to sense the effects of the music as the experience unfolds, and assess its effectiveness and ability to serve its purpose.

The selected dance and fitness instructors under the pseudonyms "Nora", "Lisa" and "Sophie" were interviewed in the fall of 2023. The interviews were implemented in the form of recorded online meetings in Teams, and they provided transcripts comprising approximately 100 pages in total.

As the study is explorative by nature, seeking to provide an initial mapping of the phenomenon, which can be refined in more focused, in-depth subsequent research, the interviewees for this study were selected with variety and multidisciplinarity in mind. The participants represent different organizations from different geographical locations. Two of them are purely instructors/teachers, while one participant also has a co-founder/artistic leader role in their organization. While the participants are of varying age, all of them had at least 10 years of teaching experience in the field. However, the variety the interviewees represent, is most importantly reflected in the types of classes they teach. These range, firstly, from international concept classes that are licensed to fitness centers, to classes where the instructor has full control over the planning and execution of the class. Secondly, they teach different dance and workout disciplines, from high-energy workout-type of concepts such as indoor cycling and martial arts – inspired training, to street styles classes like hip hop, house or commercial, and performing arts classes such as show and contemporary dance. With this breadth regarding dance (sub)cultures and the corresponding typical music genres they are connected to, the aim is to illuminate the diversity in the roles that music can play in this type of service. Moreover, the different classes discussed in the material make use of music differently. Some classes, such as the licensed concept workouts, include a pre-determined, varied set of songs, which are connected to different activities throughout the duration of the class. At the other end of the spectrum, there are dance classes that are centered around one specific song that participants rehearse a choreography to (with the addition of other music for warm up, technique exercise or stretching phases) which means a specific piece of music has a more intertwined role with the core service of dancing, in contrast to the exercise classes where the core service is workout, and music functions more as an enabling or facilitating element of the service offering (Grönroos, 2015).

ASSEMBLING DANCE END EXERCISE CLASSES: EMPIRICAL ILLUSTRATIONS

To illuminate the assemblage of experiencescapes in the empirical setting, we structure the discussion by departing from a description of the practices and processes related to music in the service. Secondly, we delve into the characteristics and elements of the music that is used, and thirdly, zoom in on specific interactions.

Instructor Practices Related to Music

We begin the empirical journey by examining how dance and exercise class instructors' chose and integrate music into the practice of the class. Following the practice theoretical approach (Schatzki, et al, 2001; Magaudda, 2011) we focus analytically on activities, (digital) materialities, and meanings.

In designing the class, music, movement/choreography, and theme are highly intertwined elements. Music is, according to the interviewed instructors, often the first point of departure in the process. Nora exemplifies this: *"Music is always step one for me. I always choose the song before I choose the theme [for the choreography]. There can be times when I may have an idea of a certain style I'm looking for, but it's always the music that determines what I actually do"*. Sophie describes a similar process, where she may at first depart from an idea and seeks a song that would convey it, but *"you don't necessarily find that, so quite often it is a song or the music as the starting point"*. She depicts the inspirational role of music in choreography: *"Sometimes even when you have already started working to a song, you hear something different and realize that now* this *is it, you can envision it all straight away when you hear a song that is really inspiring"*

Nora continues on the interpretive and interactive effects that are set in motion: *"What I feel when I hear the music definitely affects how I choreograph. But I try not to tell [the participants] that when I teach, don't want my personal thoughts and feelings affect how they feel when they dance.* The service experience thus ultimately resides in the consumer sphere, in the individual interpretation and meaning-making of the participating consumers, even if the instructor has a certain mediator role.

The activity of finding music for the instructor's classes appears both systematic and purposeful, like keeping an eye on new releases from selected artists, and simultaneously open to, and seeking the unexpected and inspirational. To this end, the role of digital media such as Spotify's recommended, TikTok and Instagram stand out, but even following traditional media (radio) and entertainment phenomena (the ESC[1]) were mentioned among music seeking practices. Lisa sums up: *"I have a constant loop open. I scan things and save them to a Spotify list that has everything, accumulated over may years."* Also Sophie and Nora echo the role of Spotify lists for managing potentially useful songs as a reserves to draw upon. This is not only a personal depository, but collective practice of shared resource utilization, like Sophie illustrates*:*

"You can also explore other dance teachers' Spotify lists to find songs. We have also discussed among colleagues that we should have shared lists where we could collect songs together, because many feel it's difficult to come up with music to use. Even if everyone does their own routines for say warm-up, we could very well

share a list of potential music for that. It could save a lot of time. Because it's the searching that is time-consuming."

Different media and interactions that are a natural part of the everyday lives of the interviewees, intersect and can be drawn upon in integrating music into the dance class. Apart from Spotify also other technological tools and practices can intervene in mundane activities in channeling music into the practices of dance, as in this account by Sophie: *"sometimes when I'm in the car and something good is on the radio, I need to dig out my phone and shazam[2] it"*.

Nora in turn exemplifies the use of social media:

"Also TikTok provides a lot of recommendations and inspiration, especially if it's really new songs. They come out on TikTok before they start getting played elsewhere. And I follow many choreographers and dancers on social media. Sometimes, if they use songs that inspire me, that I haven't heard before, I save them on Spotify. Sometimes my friends send me song suggestions, that ´Maybe you could do something with this?´."

Sophie explains that her process starts with the desired style, which leads to music seeking among artists and songs within that genre, or on the other hand on a certain type of physical expression (slow, energetic etc) that the music should enable. She also emphasizes the lyrics – reflecting the narrative level of the practice - as something that is important to consider at an early stage in the process, particularly as she works with many children and teenagers. *"Does it fit with the message you want to convey, or are the lyrics maybe something you don't want the participants to embrace at all? It is easy to find songs where the beat is right, but then you have to diss them because of the lyrics."*

Digital media entities and practices of both instructors and participants, come into play both in the service design stage (seeking music), execution (playing in class), but also in the post-service encounter consumption stage (social media sharing). Within the dance community it is common to share videos of the performed choreography once it has been rehearsed, before the class moves on to a new one. This activity is done both by the instructors and/or the organization, and by individual participants as a consumption sharing and networking (tagging) practice. Music, connected to the choreography and the performance, becomes in a sense reintroduced in media as a reassembled entity, connected to new actants, meanings and practices, sometimes openly disseminated in social media, sometimes shared through more private, interpersonal communication tools like WhatsApp or other closed groups.

In the international concept classes, the music selection practice is more limited for the instructor. Les Mills provides a new release of workouts with a pre-selected tracklist of music every three months, but after a certain period of time, individual instructors are allowed to mix and replace some of the songs with favorites from older programs, thereby adapting to the preferences of the instructor and their specific clientele. Lisa illustrates this:

"Not all instructors remix, but personally, I couldn't put up with the same for too long, and I think it's customer service of me to listen to what the participants want, and make changes accordingly. A lot of our customers have been coming to the classes for years, so I know pretty well what they like. If I ask if they want something removed, they might say that 'That number 7 is horrible'."

Using Music Throughout the Service Process

Dance and exercise classes illustrate the process nature of services, where customer experiences emerge as responses and reactions to offering-related stimuli along a customer journey (Becker and Jaakkola, 2020; Voorhees et al. 2017; Grönroos 2015). While one, usually about an hour long lesson can be regarded as a service episode, it is typically a recurring hobby activity characterized by incremental learning, both of a specific routine or choreography, and of general skills development over an even longer time frame. The implication of this repetitive and incremental nature of the service is that instructors need to consider how to balance familiarity and variation in their approach to music in this experiencescape; providing enough repetition for participants to learn, while avoiding auditory fatigue. A dance choreography is typically rehearsed for 3-4 weeks, before moving on to a new one. The same music is thus consumed quite intensively for a short period, which may result in instructors (who have also consumed the song in the choreographing phase) growing tired of them, as mentioned earlier.

When examining dance classes from a process point of view, the single lesson can be divided into distinct stages that reflect a service journey (Følstad & Kvale 2018). In dance classes, these stages can comprise for instance warm-up, muscle group exercise, mobility training, technique exercises, the actual choreography practice, and stretching or relaxation as a cool-down. Music serves different purposes in each of these stages; ranging from a more thematic and expression-focused role in the main choreography, to somewhat more utilitarian in the sections before and after it. Nora exemplifies:

"I choose songs very deliberately match the tempo that is needed to e.g. be useful to train certain muscles or to be able to breathe out, and slow down your heart rate during stretching. When it comes to warm up, it's more flexible; I can take anything from my existing playlist. But I try to use something that matches the style of the

choreography that I teach, so there's a red thread throughout the whole lesson, for example if the theme is waacking, I could choose something like 70's-80's funk."

In a similar vein, Sophie emphasizes the ability of music choices to create an overarching theme for the whole lesson from beginning to end: *"If the main choreography is something fast and energetic, you can for instance have some pepping and energizing music as introduction and warm-up. That all parts really build up the atmosphere and maintain the level of energy"*. She also highlights the use of music as a mood-maker before the class begins: *"I think it's important to have some music on as the participants start coming in, to create a certain atmosphere and an indication of what is to come"*. Sophie also approaches the last cool-down track of the class as a kind of service design outro where music helps to condense the narrative: *"that helps people ´land´ after the lesson and kind of sum it up, so it's not an abrupt ending, but a specific feeling they take with them when they leave the class."*

Lisa, who teaches workout classes, emphasizes on the other hand, the role of variation to reflect different service stages. In the licensed concept classes, this heterogeneity is built in, but in her own classes she also aims for versatility between consecutive tracks and match with participant tastes. *"Somehow, what I think works well in indoor cycling, is metal sung by women; I could even do a whole class with just that. But that would become boring; the atmosphere needs to vary. I try to choose so that most participants would find their things. It's not only about me."*

She also illuminates the differences between songs used in different subsections of an exercise lesson: "Participants learn the structure of a class, and for instance in BodyPump™³ , they wait for their favorite track, that you, for instance, do squats to. And then it can be that there are other songs they don't like so much, and the atmosphere drops."

The entablement that is created between song and movement in the service, can sometimes be very memorable. Lisa explicates this:

"Sometimes, if there has been a really good combo, that the music matches the moves particularly well, they create a kind of memory trace. So even after some 10-15 years, when you hear a certain song, you feel like squatting or whatever the move was."

What's In The Music, And How Is It Used?

Next, we zoom in more closely on music as an element of the assemblage, and the ways it contributes to the experiencescape. In the light of the interviews, the use of music can be grouped under three types of aims; atmospheric, pedagogical and expressive, as illustrated in Figure 1. In the next, we discuss these more closely.

Figure 1. Ways of utilizing music

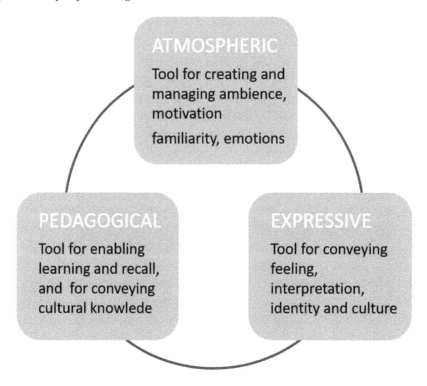

Music as an Atmospheric Tool

Good songs inspire and create enthusiasm, help build intensity and alignment between sound and movement. This applies to service customers but also the instructors. Not least is this evident in the case of concept classes, where songs come as given, and do hence mot always match with personal preferences, as Lisa describes: *"I find it hard to get the right feeling if it's a genre I'm not into. Then I just kind of wait for the song to end, so we can move on."*

In Nora's opinion, what characterizes appealing music is instrumental and rhythmical variation and the inclusion of *"interesting, odd sounds, like in Billie Eilish songs, that can contain sounds that have been recorded from the street, sounds of flickering lights etc"*. As a choreographer, also Sophie mentions *"particular beats and pounds that you can use to help participants learn the rhythmics and points of emphasis. That it's not plain and monotonous, but there are things that happen in it"*. Also textual elements such as specific words that stand out and can coupled to specific moves, were mentioned as ways to convey desired feeling in the choreography.

The instructors also highlight characteristics such as variation, modulation and intensity *(e.g. in terms of RPM[4] in cycling),* and above all the alignment with the planned movement. But music characteristics could also lineate with the instructor's own signature approach on a type of class, as Nora's comment exemplifies: *"I have a tendency to mostly choose songs with a fast tempo. It has to do with my personal style, which is easier to adapt to fast songs".*

At a more detailed level, Nora describes her approach, where she through the practices related to dance also offers a way to consume music, not only as a by-product of dance:

"I focus a lot on undertones and rhythms, things that aren't the first things you pay attention to in a song. We listen to sections of a song over and over to find those undertones. Maybe it simultaneously teaches [the participants] to listen to music in a different way?"

Depending on the instructors' target audiences, music familiarity and novelty were somewhat differently emphasized as means of creating a motivating atmosphere. While adult participants appreciate older hits and classics, Nora describes that *"New and popular songs usually hit home much better among teenagers. If they have recently heard the song, they are more hyped about the choreography.* She continues of the role of novelty: *"In the kids' classes, it's high tempo and new things all the time. They don't like repetition at all.*

Music as a Pedagogical Tool

Characteristics of the used music enables practicing for specific activities and learning objectives in like the examples Sophie provides:

"In contemporary dance, you may want something calm when we work on the alignments and technique. If you want sharp movements and a lot of dynamics, you need music that has those elements to draw on, or on the other hand, if you want to practice slow and viscous movements, you need something different. And in improvisation exercises preferably something instrumental so that the lyrics don't interfere too much"

In dance classes, the activities of learning and expression – mastering and remembering movements and channeling emotion - are interlinked. Music, and its sonic and lyrical elements intervene as factors assisting in both of these processes. Nora exemplifies this in the case of using K-Pop sung in Korean:

"Some people have explicitly told me that it's harder to recall the choreography when you don't understand what they're singing. These participants use the song lyrics, rather than the rhythm to learn the choreography. Whereas people who learn from the rhythm, can consider K-pop easier because it has such musical variation."

In a pedagogical sense, music can thus be used even in opposing ways by different learners. What is easier music to work with, depends on the way participants learn the choreographies.

The familiarity of the songs is another factor that was discussed to play a role, not only for the feeling and motivation in the class, but also in relation to learning. In Nora's words: *"Most people definitely pick up the choreography quicker if they know where the variations occur in the music. When you know the rhythm, you only need to learn the steps. But it everything is new, you need to learn the rhythm, the sound, the feeling, and on top of that, how to move to them."*

Sonically surprising elements not only makes music interesting to use, but in Nora's opinion, also links it with pedagogical objectives and helps the transition from recall to expression.

"They feel it's more interesting and exciting if it's not a typical track for the dance style, if it stands out somehow. That makes it easier to remember the choreography and enjoy the song instead of just thinking about your feet. At least I wish they can reach that point when they can enjoy the music while they dance, and not be stuck in their own thoughts about what comes next."

In dance, instruction usually makes use of 8-counts, i.e. counting the beat of the music in measures of 8 (in contrast to musicians' 4 beats). Music's ability to accommodate to this practice is something instructors consider. Sophie compares this for different pedagogical aims: *"For example for jazz exercises Ariana Grande usually has as a clear, straight rhythm that is easy to work with, while if we take Beyoncé, she has a lot of fun songs, but they are seldom 8 x 8, there is something irregular in between. They work for choreographies, but not so well for exercises."*

While counting is a dominant way to teach and learn dance, some learners tend to rely more on the sonic cues in the music. Instructors also often ask their classes whether they want to practice on count or with music. Nora explicates this: *"I have quite many people in my classes who don't count when they dance. We encourage to try to count, because then you will be more exact. But you don't necessarily need to. But if it's an unfamiliar song, so then you at least understand the rhythm, even if you don't know how the song goes.*

Music as an Expressive Tool

The instructor accounts highlight the use of music also as an expressive tool; both as creativity and engagement triggers for themselves, and for the participants. Nora illustrates:

"If I've choreographed in a very specific state of mind, there is often less technique and more emotion in it. And many actually tend to prefer those choreographies. A standard hip hop song for instance doesn't evoke that much emotion, music with more instrumental variation tends to affect me more".

Especially in choreographies that are rehearsed for public performance, the instructors engage in more analytical discussion with participants about what the attitude in the song is, and what they are supposed to express. The focus shifts more to analyzing what you hear and feel and channeling the music.

On the other hand, music is also used for more individual level expression and identity work (see Larsen, Lawson & Todd, 2010), which is illuminated particularly in classes or exercises that allow for more personal interpretations. In Nora's Commercial classes music can in these instances be approached by asking *"Can I use what the artist is expressing to enter a role and build my confidence? Does it help in finding myself, or the way I move?* In this context, Nora highlights acceptance and individuality, *"You can do these moves in different ways and they are all equally correct."*

Interactions in the Experiencescape

Next, we focus more specifically on the interplay between elements in the experiencescape. Not all these entanglements are, however, synergetic and co-creative by nature. To begin with, we start with interactions that are more challenging to integrate, and thereafter, discuss the role of different participating actors, technologies and symbols.

Explicit Lyrics: The Uneasy Component

A particular challenge that instructors raised, especially in street styles and when teaching minors, is the issue of explicit lyrics, particularly prevalent in hip hop music. Music that carries such meanings are integrated with some hesitation and unease into the assemblage. Nora pinpoints the general awareness of this phenomenon in today's world in contrast to earlier:

"In my own childhood, we happily sang along to everything, because we [as non-English-speakers] had no idea what the songs were about, and no one else cared either. Because I work for and represent this organization, I feel it's my professional responsibility to do it in a positive manner, and that's why try to choose appropriate songs or clean versions for kids' and teenagers' classes. You can usually find a clean version of almost anything."

Also Sophie acknowledges this phenomenon, as referred to in the discussion of music choices, when otherwise suitable songs are screened away because of their lyrics. *"Particularly within street styles, it can be difficult to find songs where they sing about anything reasonable. Sometimes if you find lyrics that are ok, they can again be a little lame, so it can be difficult to find something good in between"*

In the case of international, licensed classes, the issue is solved at the concept development end by a dedicated team of lyrics-checkers that recommend editing of e.g. violent and sexual lyrics, and even offer fully alternate versions for instructors to use if they prefer. In an article on company's own website (Les Mills Global Instructor team, 2019) suggestions from different instructors are offered on how others handle this issue. Of the interviewees for this study, Lisa sometimes considers timing shouting instructions or encouragement over the music to cover certain song sections, and Sophie has also used mixing practices to cut sections or add extra sounds as cover-up. Nora, in turn manages the dilemma by keeping a separate playlist of kid-friendly songs for children's classes. In practice, the lyrics are not necessarily recognized as an issue among class participants, particularly when they are in a non-native language. None of the interviewees had received feedback on the explicitness of the lyrics, even though they had sometimes used content that they were hesitant to use.

The instructors took a rigorous stance to this issue when the audiences were young, but Nora illuminates it in the case of classes with older participants: *"There, I don't have the same limitations. I can instead be more upfront, and say that these lyrics are going to be horrible, so you can totally ignore them and just focus on the music."*

Instead of attempting to erase or camouflage elements such as vulgar expressions, one mechanism that was mentioned to handle the lyrics challenges is to – in certain cases – embrace them and discuss them as a cultural characteristic. Nora explains this through the example of voguing; a style that originally emerged in African American and Latino LGBTQ communities, and where the performance of gender through dance is central[5].

"If I teach voguing, you can't escape it. There aren't any clean versions, if we put it like that. But it's also a cultural thing, related to how the style was born. We can't change it, and it is meaningful in itself. Then I'll rather explain where the music

comes from, and why they choose those words. That it's supposed to be those words. I'd rather have a discussion about the meanings and origin of the style, rather than ignore or hide it.

This exemplifies the symbolic, cultural knowledge that music carries as a way to bring a completely different knowledge layer into the dance class experience.

Actors at Social and Symbolic Levels

The social actors in the assemblage include on the one hand, class participants and their communities, and on the other hand, instructors with their own organizational and social connections. These personal level interactions are further enmeshed with material and symbolic entities, from media technologies and audio content to brands and their meanings. These layers of are visualized in Figure 2, and their interplay discussed in the next.

Figure 2. Actors in the assemblage

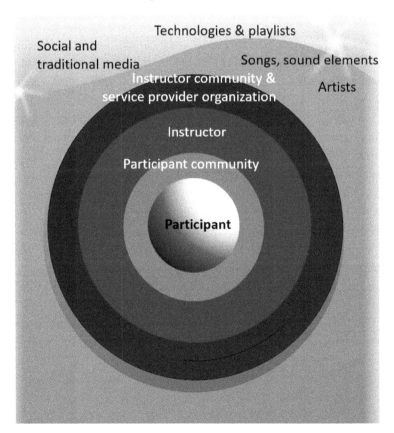

Rather than considering certain songs to have such intrinsic characteristics that would make them generally "work" as dance or workout music, the instructors highlighted the music's purposefulness for the type of class (tempo, genre, mood etc.) and its alignment with audience characteristics and the instructor's persona.

Lisa's customers are mostly in the age segment 30-60, reflecting music knowledge and taste that is less about current hits, and more towards nostalgia and pop/rock classics. Also Sophie recognizes how her adult participants enliven when nineties hits are used, while current list hits appeal to the youth and children, similarly as in Nora's accounts. From a branding perspective, the alignment between music brands, instructors and audiences can also manifest in music/artist brands that instructors make use of in their services creating symbolic imprints and contributing to branding the instructors as personal brands. To quote Lisa: *"I think if you played a set of songs to our regular customers and asked from which instructor's classes they are, that people would recognize them pretty quickly. Or at least rule out, that that one can't be that instructor's."*

In effect, this can even give rise to a more fine-tuned cultural segmentation and service differentiation, be it spontaneously emerging or consciously managed. Lisa continues:

*"I have a colleague who also instructs BodyPump and indoor cycling, and she is more [local schlager artist] whereas I am more Metallica. We have different styles, and I think we react differently to the songs we use. I don't think she would yell and be as demanding as I am. I think the customers are used to that kind of things coming from me, but not from her... And that I am one of those who sing along to the lyrics. Maybe it annoys someone, but I can't help it if there is a for instance a song about being strong and surviving towards the end of a workout. I think it elevates the atmosphere and energizes people. It makes people smile; hopefully with me, not at me". *laughter**

Sophie, on the other hand recognizes the similarities among her fellow instructors and interpersonal influence for the service. *"To some extent you can maybe see the instructor's own preferences and style, but it also shows that most instructors have been taking my or [co-founder]'s lessons before they have started teaching their own, so it's our concepts they know, and it kind of replicates."*

When discussing concrete examples of music brands that the other interviewed instructors considered particularly usable for their own purposes, Nora referred to female hip hop artists in general, but

"A go-to choice is Missy Elliott, she has a pretty versatile hip hop style, and Nicki Minaj (in clean versions). Beyoncé is of course a safe choice, although I don't use her songs that much, because it feels like everyone else does that.

Even if for instance K-pop was discussed, interestingly, the artists that interviewees spontaneously mentioned by name in the discussions, were almost exclusively female. For Nora, this focus has partly been a conscious choice.

"I use a lot of female artists, definitely. At some point I started choosing them, when there was the discussion about the difficulties of female artists to break through, girls listening to boy bands and boys not listening to female artists. So I deliberately wanted to promote those who don't get as much attention."

This example clearly pinpoints the agentic and influential role that dance instructors can take music dissemination.

Actors and Interaction Practices

While the degree of freedom for the instructor to choose music is more limited in the licensed concept classes compared to instructors who can act without the boundaries of predetermined material, in both types of cases, music selection has an interactive and co-creative nature. Feedback and requests from participants are received both face-to-face within service encounters, but also through other media, to which consumption of the core service is digitally extended before and after. Instructors may for instance post pre-class content, where they introduce the music in an upcoming lesson, or even ask their followers which song, for instance out of two alternatives, they would prefer.

Incorporating participants' wishes and requests can be a useful impulse in service design, but they are not always easily adopted as Lisa illustrates: *"When participants give feedback, it can be that someone says a certain song is super good, and another waits for it to be changed, so the preferences are not always aligned."*. And even if the inputs are welcome, the instructor's highlight their own vision in the process. As Nora puts it: *"I always encourage that, and I appreciate having a list [of requests] to draw on, but I also remind them that as a choreographer, I'm 90% vibes. It's all about what inspires me in the moment when I make the choreography."*

This draws attention to the function of music not only in motivating and engaging participants, but also for the service provider's ability to convey and maintain their own engagement during the time span of repeated service encounters. Nora furthermore continues: *"I always choose songs that I personally really like and think are interesting, so I don't get fed up with them by the last week. Because that can also reflect on how others feel the song and the choreography"* Also Lisa pinpoints the link from music through the instructor to the participant's experience: *"There's music that I just perform through, that don't evoke any particular emotions in me, and then there's something that feels good, a successful combination with the moves, and a good flow. I think that shows in how excitedly the instructor cheers and encourages the participants to do their workout."*

The inter-personal influence that music offsets can be co-creative, but possibly even co-destructive as Nora exemplifies.

"It helps to choose a song you don't mind listening to over and over again. And it helps seeing how happy everyone is and how they enjoy a song, even when I myself have already heard it too many times… But particularly children are really good in sensing your feelings; it's difficult to hide it from them if you are getting tired of a song."

As a mechanism to handle this, Nora describes a restrictive music consumption practice where individual and professionally utilitarian music consumption intersect.

"After hearing a new song a few times, I usually know whether it's something I will choreograph to. If it is, I'll try refrain from listening to it too much, to avoid wearing it out. And I avoid listening to a song outside class during the weeks I'm teaching it."

In Lisa's case, when she asks for feedback from the participants for remixing songs for the concept lessons, an interesting observation is that participants often don't refer to music they want to replace or bring in with their brand names, but through euphemisms. This illustrates music consumption in a form where knowledge of what is consumed may be rather limited, even when engagement is high. Rather, the focus may be more on the larger assemblage (situation, movement and sound) than on consuming the specific song or the artist. In fact, Lisa describes a change over time in the licensed workouts, from using content from established artists, towards an increased use of *"anonymous versions or non-originals that people have not necessarily heard before. Nowadays there is often a big contrast when you hear a radio version of song, say for instance Marilyn Manson's slow "Sweet dreams" compared to the up-tempo version we work out to. So this remix culture really makes the music very different."* In this example, music remains at a clearly more instrumental role for service execution, in contrast to instances where classes using original artists can work as music dissemination intermediaries, and even help participants discover new favorite artists or brands through their hobby.

CONCLUSIONS AND IMPLICATIONS
FOR BRAND MANAGEMENT

This exploratory study into the connections between music and its utilization in dance and exercise class experiencescapes highlights the relationships and interconnections between sonic material, physical performance and semiotic elements, and how these in combination can receive differing meanings than what they have as separate entities. Music brands become "translated" into new meanings by being assembled into a specific experiencescape.

For actors involved in music and artist branding and marketing, this research draws attention to the role of dance and exercise **service providers as intermediaries in music dissemination**. This kind of services embeds music into a consumptionscape, where music brands become entangled and re-assembled with other cultural symbols, practices, and consumption communities, thereby shifting the control of brand meanings at least partly out of the brand owner's sphere. The value the music brand provides for consumers can in this sense be situated in a specific, sometimes only temporary, experiencescape. Managerially, this challenges the traditional take on target groups for music brands, as persons appreciating and interested in a certain type of music content. Rather, when the music brand is part of a larger socio-material assemblage, the focus is on the fleeting situation, rather than the individual, and on value-in-use, rather than value in itself. The value of the music brand can thus reside in the momentary identity construction opportunities it provides for a consumer, functioning as a space where music enables the creation of a "possible self" (see Larsen et al, 2010) or in the music's ability to fill a motivational, pedagogical or other instrumental role in the broader service experience. Simultaneously, through the dance / exercise class experiencescape, participants become exposed to artist brands they may not otherwise become as aware of, and as the empirical accounts illustrated, the service that the music brand is a part of, may even augment the delivery of music by assisting participants to analyze and culturally contexualize it, as in the case of genres like voguing.

For the service providers, the brand assemblage approach depicted in this chapter draws attention to handling the connections between music and movement not only as a functional and pedagogical symbiosis, that enables on the one hand learning, and on the other hand expression and performance, but also from a commercial point of view as a matter of **brand co-creation – and possibly even brand co-destruction**. Carefully executed music choices can augment the service offering by elevating the service experience, and even enable service brand differentiation. Music can be used as a way to brand the service provider (organizational level), a specific class (the service offering level) and even to create and enhance distinct instructor profiles (personal brand level). However, the data also illuminated pitfalls where the brand assemblage contained more problematic entities, for instance songs that were incongruent with the tastes of some participants, or that had sonic or lyrical elements that made them more challenging to utilize for intended purposes and audiences. From the viewpoint of customer orientation, this is something service providers and particularly instructors are the service designers should pay attention to. Nonetheless, the empirical accounts also revealed mechanisms how such brand meaning discrepancies could be handled, including openness and dialogue with participants to facilitate feedback and member inputs regarding music preferences, and, in the case of music brand content (problematic lyrics), practices of neutralizing these elements by for instance "camouflaging" them away or explicitly contextualizing their meanings for the participants.

REFERENCES

Anderson, L. (2006). Analytic Autoethnography. *Journal of Contemporary Ethnography*, *35*(4), 373–395. doi:10.1177/0891241605280449

Becker, L., & Jaakkola, E. (2020). Customer experience: Fundamental premises and implications for research. *Journal of the Academy of Marketing Science*, *48*(4), 630–648. doi:10.1007/s11747-019-00718-x

Bitner, M. J. (1992). Servicescapes: The Impact of Physical Surroundings on Customers and Employees. *Journal of Marketing*, *56*(2), 57–71. doi:10.1177/002224299205600205

Bode, M. & Kjeldgaard, D. (2017). Brand doings in a performative perspective: an analysis of conceptual brand discourses. In: Sherry, J & Fisher, E. red. Contemporary consumer culture theory. Routledge.

Canniford, R., & Bajde, D. (Eds.). (2016). *Assembling consumption. Researching actors, networks and markets*. Routledge.

Chandler, J., & Lusch, R. (2015). Service Systems: A Broadened Framework and Research Agenda on Value Propositions, Engagement, and Service Experience. *Journal of Service Research*, *18*(1), 6–22. doi:10.1177/1094670514537709

Edvardsson, B., Enquist, B., & Johnston, B. (2005). Co-Creating Customer Value Through Hyperreality in the Pre-purchase Service Experience. *Journal of Service Research*, *8*(2), 149–161. doi:10.1177/1094670505279729

Følstad, A., & Kvale, K. (2018). Customer journeys: A systematic literature review. *Journal of Service Theory and Practice*, *28*(2), 196–227. doi:10.1108/JSTP-11-2014-0261

Goulding, C., Shankar, A., & Canniford, R. (2011). Learning to be tribal: Facilitating the formation of consumer tribes. *European Journal of Marketing*, *47*(5/6), 813–832. doi:10.1108/03090561311306886

Grönroos, C. (2015). *Service management and marketing: managing the service profit logic*. Wiley.

Haanpää, M. (2022). Co-creation as choreography. *Qualitative Market Research*, *25*(5), 614–624. doi:10.1108/QMR-01-2022-0018

Helkkula, A., Kelleher, C., & Pihlström, M. (2012). Characterizing Value as an Experience: Implications for Service Researchers and Managers. *Journal of Service Research*, *15*(1), 59–75. doi:10.1177/1094670511426897

Herrington, J. D., & Capella, L. M. (1996). Effects of music in service environments: A field study. *Journal of Services Marketing*, *10*(2), 26–41. doi:10.1108/08876049610114249

Hill, T., Canniford, R., & Mol, J. (2014). Non-representational marketing theory. *Marketing Theory*, *14*(4), 377–394. doi:10.1177/1470593114533232

Jain, R., & Bagdare, S. (2011). Music and consumption experience: A review. *International Journal of Retail & Distribution Management*, *39*(4), 289–302. doi:10.1108/09590551111117554

Kandampully, J., Bilgihan, A., & Amer, S. M. (2023). Linking servicescape and experiencescape: Creating a collective focus for the service industry. *Journal of Service Management*, *34*(2), 316–340. doi:10.1108/JOSM-08-2021-0301

Larsen, G., Lawson, R., & Todd, S. (2010). The symbolic consumption of music. *Journal of Marketing Management*, *26*(7-8), 7–8, 671–685. doi:10.1080/0267257X.2010.481865

Les Mills Global Instructor team. (2019) *Sooooo… What do you really think about the lyrics?* Article on company website] Published July 8th, 2019. Fetched 25.10.2023. Available at https://www.lesmills.com/us/instructors/instructor-news/lyric-debate/

Lucarelli, A., Cassigner, C., & Östberg, J. (2022). Reassessing brand co-creation: towards a critical performativity approach. In S. Markovic, R. Gyrd-Jones, S. von Wallpach, & A. Lindgreen (Eds.), *Research handbook on brand co-creation, Theory, practice, and ethical implications*. Edward Elgar Publishing. doi:10.4337/9781839105425.00012

Madden, R. (2010). *Being ethnographic, A Guide to the Theory and Practice of Ethnography*. Sage Publsihing.

Magaudda, P. (2011). When materiality 'bites back': Digital music consumption practices in the age of dematerialization. *Journal of Consumer Culture*, *11*(1), 15–36. doi:10.1177/1469540510390499

Merz, M. A., He, Y., & Vargo, S. L. (2009). The evolving brand logic: A service-dominant logic perspective. *Journal of the Academy of Marketing Science*, *37*(3), 328–344. doi:10.1007/s11747-009-0143-3

Mossberg, L. (2007). A Marketing Approach to the Tourist Experience. *Scandinavian Journal of Hospitality and Tourism*, *7*(1), 59–74. doi:10.1080/15022250701231915

Norrgrann, A., & Saraniemi, S. (2022). Dealing with discrepancies of a brand in change: recomposition of value and meanings in the network. In S. Markovic, R. Gyrd-Jones, S. von Wallpach, & A. Lindgreen (Eds.), *Research handbook on brand co-creation, Theory, practice, and ethical implications*. Edward Elgar Publishing. doi:10.4337/9781839105425.00016

Schatzki, T., Knorr-Cetina, K., & von Savigny, E. (Eds.). (2001). *The Practice Turn in Contemporary Theory*. Routledge.

Syrjälä, H., & Norrgrann, A. (Eds.). (2018). *Multifaceted Autoethnography Theoretical Advancements, Practical Considerations and Field Illustrations*. Nova Science Publishers.

Vallaster, S., & von Wallpach, C. (2013). An online discursive inquiry into the social dynamics of multi-stakeholder brand meaning co-creation. *Journal of Business Research*, *66*(9), 1505–1515. doi:10.1016/j.jbusres.2012.09.012

Voorhees, C. M., Fombelle, P. W., Gregoire, Y., Bone, S., Gustafsson, A., Sousa, R., & Walkowiak, T. (2017). Service encounters, experiences and the customer journey: Defining the field and a call to expand our lens. *Journal of Business Research*, *79*, 269–280. doi:10.1016/j.jbusres.2017.04.014

ENDNOTES

[1]   Eurovision Song Contest
[2]   Using the mobile application Shazam identify music based on recording a sample of it
[3]   https://www.lesmills.com/workouts/fitness-classes/bodypump/
[4]   revolutions per minute
[5]   "A Brief History of Voguing". *The National Museum of African American History & Culture*. Smithsonian Institution. Retrieved 5 November 2023.

Chapter 8

Harmonizing Brand Experience:
The Role of Sound in Shaping the Customer Brand Experience Journey

Mohamed Adel Abdelrazek

https://orcid.org/0000-0002-2993-0098
University of Sadat City, Egypt

Marwa Tourky

https://orcid.org/0000-0002-2074-0159
Cranfield University, UK

William S. Harvey

https://orcid.org/0000-0002-8771-4000
University of Melbourne, Australia

ABSTRACT

This chapter analyses the pivotal role of sound in shaping the customer journey and elevating brand experiences. We explain the profound influence of auditory elements, in particular sound, music, silence, or noise, on consumer perception and behavior. By demystifying sonic branding and its implications for brand experiences, we highlight the often-overlooked potency of sound in creating memorable customer experiences. Finally, we draw on a real-world case study of Intel to illustrate sound strategies that have been successful for businesses.

DOI: 10.4018/979-8-3693-0778-6.ch008

INTRODUCTION

As the marketing landscape of the modern age becomes more dynamic, the customer journey has become increasingly salient for brands and marketers around the world. There has been a shift in traditional marketing avenues from being dominated by isolated engagements and sporadic touchpoints to those that encompass a more holistic approach (Lemon & Verhoef, 2016). Modern brands place a high priority on understanding and guiding the entire arc of the customer's interaction with their products and services, from the infancy of awareness to the enduring advocacy behaviors of consumers' post-purchase (Følstad & Kvale, 2018; Meyer & Schwager, 2007; Tueanrat et al., 2021).

Until recently, marketing strategies have primarily been guided by visual elements. However, sound has increasingly become an important sensory component (Gustafsson, 2015). Sounds evoke feelings like evocative melodies or nostalgic tunes (Bruner, 1990). Auditory elements possess the intrinsic ability to shape and enhance consumer perceptions, establishing themselves deeply in the minds of consumers. In the UK, this impact can be seen through a number of examples, including the iconic McDonald's 'I'm Lovin' It' jingle, which resonates with consumers across generations, and the distinctive soundscapes experienced in British Airways' commercials and in-flight announcements. Whether these audio cues are melodious notes that make up a captivating jingle or ambient background music that sets the mood for a brand's retail environment, they play an important role in shaping the brand's identity and perception.

The purpose of this chapter is to explore the intricate interplay between sound and experiential marketing, illustrating the impact of sound on the customer journey and the subsequent impact on brand experiences. We aim to reveal the rarely recognized significance of sound by analyzing how it can enhance customers' experience into something more comprehensive and memorable.

Sensory Marketing and Customer Experience

In an increasingly competitive market, brands face the challenge of differentiating themselves and providing memorable experiences amidst a sea of similar products. Sensory marketing, which engages the full spectrum of human senses, is a potent method for achieving such differentiation (Krishna & Schwarz, 2014), leading to enriched brand experiences. Sensory marketing is becoming increasingly important to create immersive consumer experiences within the contemporary marketing paradigm. Defined as a comprehensive approach that integrates all five senses—sight, sound, taste, touch, and smell—into the consumer experience, this method transcends traditional visual and auditory cues (Hultén, 2011). Based on this perspective, consumers are engaged beyond product attributes, as multisensory interactions influence perception, emotion, and behavior (Krishna, 2012; Lindstrom, 2005).

The evolving perception of consumers, from purchasing to experiencing products, has driven sensory marketing to emphasize the holistic experience offered by a brand rather than the features it offers (Huang et al., 2009; Schlosser, 2003). The goal of sensory marketing is to elicit emotional responses through the stimulation of multiple senses, focusing on the affective and experiential elements of consumption beyond the product's utility aspects (Krishna, 2012; Krishna et al., 2016).

In a landscape transformed by digital innovation, it is important for brands to resonate effectively with their target audience (Araujo et al., 2020). The auditory aspect of brand experience has evolved beyond traditional roles, becoming a fundamental component of the holistic sensory branding approach (Moreira et al., 2017a). Engaging consumers through sound involves more than the mere volume or melody; it requires forging an emotional and memorable connection (Hwang & Oh, 2020). Hence, a brand's auditory experience includes a variety of elements that define its presence on the physical or digital environment. A National Geographic documentary, for example, provides a soothing experience that transports viewers all over the world through the soothing sounds of nature. A PlayStation console's distinctive startup sound creates a unique feeling of anticipation and excitement, uniquely characterizing the gaming experience. Such examples illustrate how distinct jingles and immersive soundscapes are integral in different ways for building a brand's unique auditory identity.

Sensory marketing offers consumers a rich palette of sensory experiences and is an essential element for any brand aiming to make a profound impact. By recognizing and applying a diverse array of sensory stimuli, brands can not only improve their competitive advantage but also enhance consumer engagement and foster loyalty (Bhatia et al., 2021; Hultén, 2011; Shahid et al., 2022).

Sensory Marketing Dimensions

The dimensions of sensory marketing represent the breadth and depth of sensory stimuli—sight, sound, taste, touch, and smell—each of which can be strategically manipulated to influence consumer behavior and perceptions.

Visual Dimension: The first sense to engage in a marketing context is sight. This encompasses product design, packaging, logos and colors, as well as the visual ambiance of retail environments. Displays with a visual appeal can captivate the attention of consumers, convey messages, and influence consumer judgment and emotions (Bloch, 1995; Zha et al., 2022). In terms of sight, Apple Inc. exemplifies excellence in visual marketing. Their sleek product design, minimalist packaging, and distinctive logo create a powerful visual identity that is instantly recognizable and appealing to consumers.

Audio Dimension: As previously described, sound is a powerful sensory tool. It encompasses music, jingles, brand anthems, ambient noises in retail environments, customer service voice tones, and sound logos. Using sound to evoke memories and emotions can influence atmospherics and consumer perceptions (Kemp et al., 2023; Melzner & Raghubir, 2023). For example, Spotify stands out with its personalized playlists and curated soundscapes. Their use of tailored music selections creates a unique auditory experience that resonates with users, enhancing brand perception and loyalty.

Olfactory Dimension: It is well known that scent is closely associated with memory, and can be emotive. Using scents, we can create a certain environment (like a car showroom that smells of leather), induce certain moods or feelings, and even signal product quality or freshness (Morrin & Ratneshwar, 2003). For instance, Lush Cosmetics demonstrates the impact of scent. Their stores are known for their distinct fragrances, which create an inviting atmosphere for some as they seek to reinforce the natural, handmade quality of their products.

Gustatory Dimension: This is essential for food and beverage marketing but can also be applied to experiential marketing for other products, such as toothpaste flavors or store samples. As the most direct form of sensory marketing (Hoegg & Alba, 2007), taste can directly influence product evaluations. To illustrate, Starbucks' seasonal flavors, like Pumpkin Spice Latte, offers a prime example. These flavors not only attract customers but also create a sensory experience that enhances the brand's appeal and distinctiveness.

Tactile Dimension: Touch is the physical sensations experienced when interacting with a product. It conveys quality, comfort, and other product characteristics when experienced. Especially for products that are touched and used physically, such as clothing and gadgets (Peck & Childers, 2003), tactile experiences can play a key role in decision-making processes. For example, Nike's focus on the tactile dimension is evident in their footwear and athletic wear. The materials used provide comfort, durability, and a sense of quality, influencing consumer decisions and enhancing the overall brand experience.

A holistic consumer experience can be created by operating each dimension individually and in concert. By tapping into consumers' affective and cognitive responses, sensory marketing creates a memorable brand experience, which can lead to an increase in consumer loyalty and satisfaction (Zarantonello & Schmitt, 2010). The emotional resonance generated by sensory experiences can have a lasting impact on consumers, even if they do not recall the specific details of a marketing campaign.

Using these sensory dimensions - visual, auditory, olfactory, gustatory, and tactile – Table 1 summarizes the complex ways in which sensory stimuli can be manipulated to create a memorable brand experience. A marketer wishing to strengthen an emotional connection with consumers, enhance their product appeal, and differentiate themselves in a competitive environment will benefit from an integrated approach summarised here. By strategically integrating sensory elements into the marketing mix, brands can craft experiences that resonate deeply with consumers, potentially resulting in increased loyalty and brand advocacy on the part of consumers.

Table 1 provides a structured summary of the sensory dimensions utilized in sensory marketing, highlighting how each sense is used to influence consumer behavior and perceptions. As the name implies, sensory marketing focuses on the premise that consumers perceive brands through a multi-faceted sensory experience, rather than through a single sense. In the table, each column describes a particular sensory dimension, describes its role in the marketing context, and cites key academic references that have contributed to a greater understanding of its impact.

Table 1. Dimensions of Sensory Marketing and Their Impact on Consumer Experience

Sensory Dimension	Description	Prominent Organisational Example	Key References
Visual	Focuses on the use of design elements like product aesthetics, packaging visuals, and store ambiance to capture consumer attention and communicate brand values.	Apple Inc's minimalist design and distinctive product packaging create a strong visual identity.	Bloch (1995); Stead et al. (2022); Kujur & Singh (2020)
Auditory	Includes elements such as music, jingles, brand anthems, ambient noises, customer service tones, and sound logos that influnces memory and emotions, impacting how consumers perceive the brand.	Spotify's personalized playlists and soundscapes offer an auditory brand experience tailored to individual user preferences.	Melzner & Raghubir (2023); Poushneh (2021); Spence & Shankar (2010)
Olfactory	Employs scents to create atmosphere, induce moods, and signal product quality, leveraging the strong link between emotions and memories.	Lush Cosmetics's use of distinctive store fragrances to create a memorable brand experience.	Morrin & Ratneshwar (2003); Roy & Singh (2023); Cowan et al. (2023)
Gustatory	Involves flavor as a direct influencer of product experience and evaluation, critical in food and beverage and experiential sectors.	Starbucks' seasonal flavors, like Pumpkin Spice Latte, which provide a taste experience associated with the brand.	Hoegg & Alba, (2007); Szocs et al. (2023)
Tactile	Relates to the sense of touch, conveying the product attributes such as quality and comfort and influenecing the decision-making process.	Nike's emphasis on the tactile feel of their sportswear and footwear to enhance consumer perception of high quality and performance.	Peck & Childers (2003); Pantoja et al. (2020)

Integrating Sensory Stimuli for a Holistic Brand Experience

Sensory marketing reaches its pinnacle of effectiveness when it engages consumers across cognitive, emotional, and physiological levels, creating a comprehensive and cohesive brand experience (Brakus et al., 2009; Schmitt, 1999). Each sensory input can play a specific role in this multi-faceted engagement.

Cognitive Engagement: At the cognitive level, sensory stimuli are processed and can influence awareness, perception, and memory. A recognizable brand logo and color scheme can enhance brand recognition and aid in recall, whereas a catchy jingle can aid in brand differentiation and recall. For example, the recognizable golden arches of McDonald's enhances brand recognition and aids in recall across various cultures and languages. This visual consistency contributes to a cognitive map in the mind of the consumer, associating those arches with a quick-service dining experience. Together, these elements contribute to the development of a cognitive map in the mind of the consumer, creating an association between sensory experiences and brand awareness (Krishna, 2012).

Emotional Engagement: Sensory marketing can evoke emotional reactions and affective states that influence consumer decisions and attitudes. There is a connection between the feel of a product, the ambiance created by the design of a store, and the emotional tone set by the background music playlist. Take, for instance, the warm and inviting atmosphere of Starbucks stores, with their comfortable seating and the aroma of coffee, combined with a carefully curated music playlist, which can create a sense of belonging and comfort, fostering an emotional bond with the brand. These can foster feelings such as trust, happiness, or comfort that establish an emotional bond with the brand (Kim et al., 2021; Shahid et al., 2022).

Physiological Engagement: Physiological responses can be induced by sensory stimuli, including salivation in response to food cues or relaxation in response to certain scents or sounds (Spence & Shankar, 2010). Physiological responses can also be induced by sensory stimuli, such as the mouth-watering induced by the sight and smell of a Cinnabon store in an airport. These sensory cues can trigger immediate physiological responses, embedding the brand within the consumer's physiological responses, often subconsciously (Spence et al., 2014).

The power of a holistic sensory brand experience lies in its ability to create a seamless and engaging narrative across all touch points. In today's crowded and competitive market, consumers are bombarded with a multitude of sensory stimuli that interact and resonate at multiple levels. They do not experience sensory stimuli in isolation when they interact with a brand.

A Coca-Cola campaign called "Taste the Feeling" incorporated a consistent melody and sound of a bottle being opened, along with images of people from various cultures enjoying a Coke, thus evoking a sense of connection across cultures.

A multi-sensory effect is achieved through the tactile feel of the iconic Coke bottle and the taste of the beverage, reinforcing cognitive associations, eliciting emotional reactions, and possibly stimulating physiological reactions (Krishna, 2012; Krishna & Schwarz, 2014).

The theoretical and practical implications of a holistic approach are extensive. Based on embodied cognition theory (Barsalou, 2008), sensory processing is fundamentally intertwined with cognitive functions. In addition to developing memorable experiences, marketers can use it to improve customer satisfaction and loyalty by developing experiences with greater impact (Kim et al., 2012).

Developing a holistic sensory brand experience requires careful consideration of how different sensory components work together to create a harmonious and engaging consumer environment (Moreira et al., 2017) An overwhelming amount or uncoordinated stimuli can lead to consumer confusion or negative associations as evidenced by Abercrombie & Fitch's strategy of combining a strong in-store fragrance with loud music and dim lighting. The overpowering scent was perceived as invasive and uncomfortable by customers, illustrating the importance of moderation in sensory marketing (Bruce & Daly, 2006; Hultén, 2011). This moderation is equally crucial in the auditory realm, where too loud, repetitive, or misaligned music can alienate rather than attract consumers. In light of this example, sensory stimuli that are calibrated and aligned with consumer preferences can be used to enhance the shopping experience rather than detract from it. Similarly, if not carefully calibrated, it can contribute to sensory overload (Douce & Adams, 2020) or dissonance. The design of these experiences therefore requires a strategic understanding of how sensory information is processed and integrated by consumers (Wiedmann et al., 2018).

Theoretical Foundations of Sensory Marketing

A thorough understanding of the theoretical frameworks supporting sensory marketing is necessary to appreciate the full extent and effectiveness of sensory marketing. Using sensory cues, consumers can influence their behavior and shape their perception of brands through a variety of mechanisms. The following table presents a synopsis of the key theories that have shaped sensory marketing as both a discipline and as a practical marketing methodology.

Table 2. Theoretical Frameworks Underpinning Sensory Marketing

Theoretical Concept	Description	Implications for Sensory Marketing
Experiential Marketing Theory	Proposes that consumers seek value in experiences, not just products (Holbrook & Hirschman, 1982; Schmitt, 1999).	Sensory marketing must create engaging experiences that offer emotional and cognitive stimulation, moving beyond the basic utility of products.
Multisensory Integration Theory	Explains how the human brain integrates sensory stimuli from various sources to create a unified perception of an object or experience (Stein & Meredith, 1993; Wörfel et al., 2022).	Sensory marketing strategies should ensure that all sensory stimuli are harmoniously integrated to form a consistent and compelling perception of the brand.
Sensory Cue Theory	Suggests that sensory cues can activate associative networks, enhancing consumer perception and experience (Krishna, 2012).	Marketers should design sensory cues that are meaningful and capable of evoking strong associative responses to enrich the brand narrative.
Cognitive Load Theory	Addresses the amount of information that the working memory can hold at one time (Sweller, 1988).	Sensory marketing should balance the complexity and number of sensory cues to avoid overwhelming consumers, ensuring the sensory experience remains cognitively manageable.
Consumer Experience Concept	Encompasses the affective, cognitive, social, and sensorial dimensions of consumer interactions with a brand (Meyer & Schwager, 2007).	Sensory marketing must address all dimensions of the consumer experience, recognizing the varied ways in which consumers engage with and respond to brand stimuli. This involves targeting emotions, thoughts, social contexts, and direct sensory experiences to create a holistic and memorable brand experience.

Table 2 presents a multidimensional understanding of how sensory experiences are integrated by consumers which contributes to the overall experience of a brand based on theories drawn from a wide body of academic literature. In experiential marketing, for example, consumers value brands primarily for their experiences, rather than their products or services. The goal of sensory marketing is to create immersive experiences that stir the emotions of the consumer (Shahid et al., 2022). Moreover, the theory of multisensory integration describes how the brain integrates sensory information from a variety of sources into coherent experiences (Stein & Meredith, 1993). As a result, multisensory marketing campaigns will have significant implications that deliver a unified brand message across multiple sensory touchpoints.

Table 2 also provides guidance on creating effective sensory stimuli without overloading a consumer's cognitive capacity, including sensory cue theory and cognitive load theory, as well as other theoretical constructs. A sensory marketing program is a method of creating memorable consumer experiences that foster emotional connections and brand loyalty among consumers because of these theories (Bhatia et al., 2021; Hultén, 2011; Krishna & Schwarz, 2014). A better understanding of the 'why' and 'how' behind the impact of sensory elements on consumer perception and behavior can be gained by examining these frameworks by marketers and brand strategists. In today's competitive marketplace, it is crucial to develop sensory marketing strategies that are both research based and practicably effective by taking into consideration this integrated approach suggested by these theories.

Engaging Consumers Across Multiple Dimensions with Sensory Elements

Sensory stimuli have a profound capacity to engage with consumers beyond the mere act of perception; they touch upon the cognitive, emotional, and physical aspects of our experiences. In his influential work, Spence (2012) highlighted how particular scents could change the way we perceive and interact with an environment. In a similar vein, auditory signals such as a distinctive brand melody have the power to evoke memories, thus strengthening emotional connections and fostering brand loyalty (Spence et al., 2021). Starbucks provides an excellent example of how sensory elements can be used to engage consumers on multiple levels. As coffee is brewed in the company's stores, there is a distinct aroma that creates a comfortable environment (olfactory), a sound of steaming milk and baristas calling out drink orders enhances the ambiance (auditory), and cozy furniture enhances the sense of comfort. The use of these sensory elements contributes to the creation of a unique environment that encourages customers to stay longer. The sensory experience is consistent over all Starbucks locations globally, reinforcing the brand's identity and enhancing customer loyalty. Combined with the sound of grounding coffee beans and the visual aesthetic of the store, Starbucks creates a distinctive Starbucks experience that engages customers cognitively (brand recognition), emotionally (pleasure and relaxation), and physically (consuming their beverages), strengthening brand loyalty and encouraging repeat visits (Hultén, 2011a; Michon et al., 2005).

The true essence of sensory marketing is its all-encompassing approach. It goes beyond immediate sensory effects to consider the full psychological impact, including the activation of memories, emotions, and subsequent behaviors (Ambler et al., 2000; Reed & Forehand, 2016). Sound, by virtue of its enveloping nature, commands a special role in this realm. The tempo of background music in a store, or the faint sound notifications from a device, can significantly impact consumer behavior. Spence (2012) uncovered that particular sound frequencies can prompt distinct emotional reactions, giving brands the opportunity to carefully craft their soundscapes to match their brand identity and goals (Peck & Wiggins, 2006).

The influence of sound also extends into the realm of implicit or background noises (Biswas et al., 2019). The fine-tuned playlists in trendy cafes or the designed silence in high-end showrooms emphasize the deliberate use of sound. These elements, though often subtle, are crucial in forging an atmospheric brand identity that guides consumer perception and action, thereby defining the overall brand experience. For example, in retail environments, the tempo of background music is a strategic element that influences customer behavior (Hwang & Oh, 2020). Research shows that a fast tempo can energize customers and encourage quicker decision-making, beneficial for fast fashion stores and quick service restaurants that aim to serve a high volume of customers (Loureiro et al., 2021). Zara, one of the world's largest fast fashion chains, exemplifies the use of sound by playing contemporary, upbeat music that aligns with its trendy image and fast-paced shopping environment. This energetic auditory setting supports Zara's business model by encouraging swift movement through the store, mirroring the quick turnover of its fashion items.

Conversely, a slower tempo can induce a more leisurely browsing experience, suitable for luxury goods stores where the intent is for customers to ponder their purchases (Rodgers et al., 2021; Loureiro et al., 2021). Luxury brands like Rolex use sound tactically throughout their boutiques and advertising to create a unique consumer experience. Rolex stores may create a sense of timelessness, precision, and exclusivity through the use of classical music or the subtle, sophisticated ticking of a watch as part of the soundscape. The auditory branding of Rolex watches has resulted in the perception that these watches are thoughtful and significant investments. In this calm and refined auditory environment invites customers to appreciate the craftsmanship and exclusivity of the brand, often leading to high-value purchases (Keh et al., 2021).

The collective experience of sound also has a significant impact on emotions. When a group shares a sound experience, like in a live music venue or a bustling square, it can create a collective emotional state—a shared sentiment that unites people in a communal moment (Brengman et al., 2022; Scott et al., 2022). Retailers can harness this by selecting music that not only represents their brand but also cultivates a communal emotional atmosphere, potentially enhancing the social experience of shopping (Melzner & Raghubir, 2023). Hence, brands must skillfully manage these dynamic emotional responses to sound, adapting their auditory strategies to stay attuned to consumer moods and contexts (Scott et al., 2022; Zha et al., 2022).

In summary, the interplay between sound and emotion is complex yet impactful, carrying significant weight in how brands engage with their customers. By embedding the appropriate auditory elements into a brand's narrative, marketers can discreetly influence emotions and perceptions, aligning them with their strategic vision. The integration of sound into the sensory marketing mix, when executed with care, can serve as a powerful catalyst for brand distinction and enduring customer loyalty.

Experiential Marketing: Beyond Traditional Brand Interactions

Experiential marketing, also known as 'experience marketing', represents a shift from the conventional strategies that merely serve to showcase a product or service to potential consumers (Schmitt, 1999). It is, in essence, a form of marketing that considers the consumer's interaction as a dynamic, multi-sensory experience, rather than treating people passively. Consequently, a discerning consumer today, surrounded by numerous options, particularly in oversaturated markets, demands more than just a product or service. They ardently seek an experience that is memorable and unique (Hultén, 2011b; Moreira et al., 2017).

The concept of experiential marketing cannot be seen as a separate strategy, but rather as an integral component of the overall brand experience, aiming to provide holistic engagement (Chevtchouk et al., 2018; Kharat et al., 2018). Using this method, each touchpoint, whether it be digital, tangible, in-store, or sensory, is carefully calibrated to reflect the brand's ethos and elicit the desired emotional response. Apple, as a quintessential example, transcends the confines of being a mere technological company. As a result of its experiential marketing activities, it offers a multi-faceted experience characterized by innovation, user-centric design, and aesthetic excellence. In Apple stores, for example, you will find more than simply retail space; they are designed to function as a modern-day town square where people can gather for entertainment, learning, and exploration. In Apple stores, products are displayed on tables for hands-on experimentation, encouraging customers to fully engage with their products. Embracing this immersive approach allows brands to not only establish a niche in an increasingly competitive market, but also build deeper emotional bonds with consumers, resulting in the conversion of casual consumers into loyal brand advocates (Brakus et al., 2009).

Navigating the Customer Journey with Auditory Enhancements

An integral aspect of experiential marketing is the orchestration of many touchpoints, designed to resonate profoundly with consumers across cognitive, emotional, and sensory dimensions. In particular, the auditory realm has emerged as a potent tool for changing consumer perceptions and emotions not only in the realm of physical products but also throughout the service journey. Just as ambient music in a hotel lobby can set the tone for a guest's stay, sound can guide the consumer through the service process, enhancing their experience at every step (Lee et al., 2019; Prahalad & Ramaswamy, 2004). It is similar to the profound impact of a poignant musical composition that well-curated sonic brand experiences can have on the consumer journey, making it memorable and unique for the consumer. For services, sound becomes a continuous narrative thread that accompanies the consumer, whether in the calming environment of a spa, the energetic atmosphere of a theme park, or the attentive ambiance of a fine dining restaurant (Hulten, 2011; Keh et al., 2021; Loureiro et al., 2021). This broadened scope highlights the managerial potential of sonic elements to craft not just moments, but sustained experiences in service settings.

A visual representation of a customer journey is analogous to a chart showing the course of a relationship. The process begins with awareness, progresses through to consideration and decision-making, and ultimately leads to loyalty and advocacy following the purchase (Lemon & Verhoef, 2016). Multiple touchpoints – moments of interaction and engagement between the brand and the consumer – punctuate this intricate progression. When considering services, these touchpoints include not just the immediate environment but also the entire sequence of service delivery, where sound can play a critical role in shaping the consumer's perception of the service quality and brand identity (Rodgers et al., 2021). The integration of these touchpoints with the right auditory cues can lead to powerful brand imprints, thus amplifying brand perception, affinity, and loyalty.

Awareness: The Symphony of Brand Introduction

In the customer journey, awareness serves as the first touch point between the brand and potential customers. This is true for both product and service brands. For instance, the welcoming chime when entering a store or the distinctive ringtone of a customer service line serves as auditory cues that begin the consumer's brand experience (Hwang et al., 2020). At this pivotal juncture, auditory touchpoints become essential in laying the foundation for brand identity (Parise et al., 2016). A distinct space is carved out in the consumer's auditory memory by sonic branding, whether it is through memorable jingles or unique sound logos. These sonic signatures act as mnemonic devices, enhancing the retention of brand identity in the mind of the consumer. Nokia's classic ringtone or McDonald's "I'm Lovin' It" jingle are two great examples of how sonic branding can bring a brand into the collective consciousness of consumers. As auditory anchors, these sonic elements facilitate faster and deeper brand recall (Roggeveen et al., 2020). As a result of this auditory insignia, brand recognition is enhanced, as well as the groundwork for subsequent brand-consumer interactions is laid. Brand recognition can be fleeting or it can be long-lasting when these auditory elements are strategically crafted and positioned (Lindstrom, 2005).

Consideration: Crafting A Resonant Brand Dialogue

In the "Consideration" stage, consumers actively evaluate the brand's offerings, moving from mere recognition to a deeper level of brand engagement. As a result, brands will need to strike a harmonious balance between emotive and intellectual engagement during this phase (Yakhlef & Nordin, 2021). In order to significantly increase the resonance of a brand with consumers, auditory cues, such as ambient soundscapes in product demos or voiceovers in narrations, can be strategically utilized. In addition to providing a richer context for understanding the brand's offerings, these auditory elements not only serve to fulfill the emotive dimension by evoking emotions and memories but also enhance the brand's emotional dimension. For example, at a bank or during an online service interaction, auditory cues can provide reassurance and clarity, aiding the decision-making process and enriching the overall customer experience. It is crucial to ensure that consumers' hearts and minds are aligned with the brand's ethos through these dual auditory engagements, resulting in a holistic brand experience (Krishna, 2012).

During the consideration stage, the brand encourages consumers to dig deeper through a blend of rational and emotional cues (Sultan, 2018). Sound not only conveys information, but also creates an emotional ambience (Brengman et al., 2022). A subtle hum in Tesla's showroom or the background score of a product explainer video serves as a subtle cue that encourages consumers to make purchasing decisions. Consumers find products more appealing when the auditory experience is in line with their expectations when they receive appropriate auditory stimuli (Biswas et al., 2019).

Purchase: The Auditory Seal of Approval

Contrary to popular perception, the "Purchase" stage is not just a transactional endpoint; it is an experiential crescendo. The auditory elements infused throughout this phase play a crucial role in enhancing the overall purchasing process. When an auditory detail is considered, such as the satisfying click sound of a luxury pen cap or the sonorous beep that confirms a digital transaction, it can amplify the sense of satisfaction derived from the purchase to a great extent. In spite of often being overlooked, these sounds serve as auditory endorsements, reinforcing the consumer's decision and choice (Spence & Shankar, 2010). For example, The Montblanc Meisterstück Classique pen, known for its high-quality craftsmanship, features a distinctive mechanism that is often enhanced by a subtle but satisfying sound produced by the smooth twist of its mechanism, reinforcing its high-quality nature. Likewise, the clear beep sound that accompanies a successful Apple Pay transaction on an iPhone not only confirms the action, but also contributes to Apple's reputation for providing a seamless and sophisticated user experience. In addition to enhancing the immediate purchase experience, auditory reinforcements serve as a solid foundation for long-term brand loyalty by providing a positive experience during the purchase process. Ultimately, in the world of branding, it is these subtle nuances that have the most lasting impact (Spence, 2012).

The act of purchasing, often viewed as a culmination, is in fact a crescendo in the consumer's journey. Sound serves as reassuring signals, validating the consumer's decisions. A crisp rustling of luxury shopping bags, a soft ding of a successful online payment, or a resonating chime after the luxury car door closes all serve as auditory validations. These sounds provide a tangible sense of quality, thereby reinforcing the purchase decision. Congruent auditory feedback can enhance the user experience, making transactions smoother and more satisfying (Lageat et al., 2003).

Retention: Crafting Sonic Bonds for Lasting Loyalty

A brand's "Retention" phase, or relationship maintenance phase, requires it to continually reinforce the value it offers to consumers (Mosley, 2007). Brands are shifting their focus from attracting to retaining at this juncture, and sound becomes an indispensable ally in this effort. A customized auditory interaction, such as a voice message of gratitude or an update, provides a direct and emotional connection between the brand and the consumer, expressing the brand's appreciation for their patronage (Jain et al., 2017). Additionally, loyalty programs are an integral part of retention strategies that can be enhanced by providing distinct auditory cues that stimulate immediate rewards. By integrating sonic elements into brand communication, such integrations create an auditory tapestry that fosters a sense of belonging and attachment to the brand, which promotes loyalty as well as advocacy (Reinoso-Carvalho et al., 2020).

On-hold music can also be strategically chosen to enhance the brand's identity, ensuring passive interactions remain consistent with the brand's narrative, despite often being overlooked touchpoints (Michon et al., 2005; Spence et al., 2014). However, the strategic selection of on-hold music underscores the broader necessity for a nuanced approach to sonic branding. In order to enhance the customer's perception of the brand even while waiting, a luxury brand might utilize smooth, classical music to convey a sense of sophistication and elegance. In contrast, there are instances where on-hold music can be detrimental (Ülkü et al., 2020). Being put on hold for a long time while listening to the British Airways theme tune, for example, is likely to erode customer perceptions of the brand. This is particularly significant when considering consumer diversity; for example, individuals with sensory defensiveness may find certain types of music or sound levels distressing rather than soothing. A listener may feel frustrated and uncomfortable when the music is poor quality, repetitive, or jarringly out of sync with the brand's identity (Milliman, 1986).

Moreover, varying taste preferences among consumers mean that what appeals to one segment may alienate another, underscoring the need for brands to carefully curate their sonic environment to cater to a broad audience (Ülkü et al., 2020). It is common to encounter tinny or distorted music in customer service lines, which is detrimental to the customer's experience with the brand This highlights a critical aspect of sonic branding: the potential for negative consumer reactions to auditory stimuli (Klein et al., 2021), which can vary widely among different consumer segments (Cha et al., 2020). The negative aspect underscores the importance of not only selecting the appropriate music but also ensuring that its delivery is of high quality. Thus, while the use of sound can significantly enhance or detract from customer experiences, its effective deployment requires careful consideration of consumer characteristics, such as sensory defensiveness or varying taste preferences. Therefore, customer experiences can be significantly enhanced or detracted from by ensuring that on-hold music is pleasant, reflects the brand, and is transmitted clearly (North & Hargreaves, 1998).

At the retention stage, sound becomes a conduit for continuous engagement as brands nurture and solidify their relationships with consumers (Park & Kim, 2003). These auditory touchpoints serve to remind, reassure, and reconnect consumers, whether it is the melodious voice of a virtual assistant helping them navigate a new gadget, or the jingle that plays at the end of a customer service call. Research has demonstrated that consistent and positive auditory interactions can bolster consumer loyalty, proving that sound indeed plays a pivotal role in retention strategies (Poushneh, 2021).

Advocacy: The Sonic Encore of Brand Evangelists

As a result of reaching the advocacy stage (de Regt et al., 2021), consumers transform from passive recipients to active promoters of a brand's narrative. As advocates, their advocacy is grounded in genuine appreciation and trust, which holds high potential for brand outreach. Brands can use sound to further enhance advocacy experiences (Nguyen et al., 2022). Advocacy can increase the engagement of their promotional efforts by creating bespoke soundscapes for events and campaigns. For these brand evangelists, exclusive audio content, such as podcasts, interviews, and behind-the-scenes insights, can serve as valuable tools, aiding in their storytelling. Endorsing user-generated sound narratives is also an effective way to empower consumers and enhance brand credibility. Through such auditory initiatives, the brand's narrative reverberates far and wide, strengthening its position and enhancing its positioning (Kumar et al., 2010; Schmitt, 1999).

The advocacy stage can be enhanced further by crafting unique sonic experiences for brand events, or by providing advocates with exclusive auditory content. Brands such as Spotify have often utilized user playlists as a method of advocacy, with users proudly sharing their curated collections. As well as validating the consumers' efforts, recognizing and amplifying such sound narratives enhances the brand's commitment to community. When given the appropriate tools and platforms, engaged consumers can significantly enhance brand reach and equity (Blasco-Arcas et al., 2016).

Figure 1. Customer's Journey with a Brand

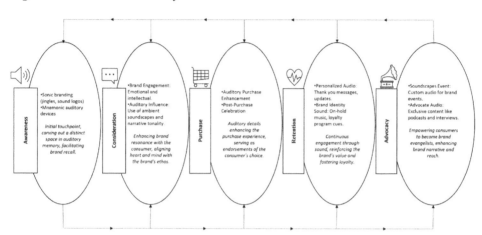

Figure 1 showcases a customer's journey with a brand, focusing on how sound shapes their experience. It starts with 'Awareness,' where catchy tunes or unique sounds help a brand stick in your mind. Moving to 'Consideration,' the brand uses sound to connect on an emotional level, making you think and feel more about their products. The 'Purchase' part is where the sounds at the checkout or the click of a product make buying feel good. 'Retention' is about keeping you hooked: a thank you message, or familiar hold music can make you feel valued and more likely to stick around. Lastly, 'Advocacy' is where happy customers talk up the brand, and unique audio content helps them spread the word. This diagram paints a picture of how the right sounds at the right time can turn a one-time buyer into a lifelong fan and even a brand champion. By holistically integrating these auditory cues into the customer journey, brands can craft a symphony of experiences, each note resonating with the consumer, creating a harmonious brand relationship that stands the test of time.

Case Intel: Intel's Sonic Logo - The "Intel Bong"

The Intel sonic signature, commonly known as the 'Bong,' has become an iconic example of effective auditory branding. In a case of how sound transcends auditory boundaries to become a symbol of technology reliability and innovation, the simple, yet unmistakable melody of five notes provides an excellent example of how sound can transcend auditory boundaries. Through the lens of experiential marketing and multisensory integration theories, this case study explores Intel's sonic logo's development and impact.

In the 1990s, the personal computing industry experienced rapid growth and an increase in competition. It was in this context that Intel emerged with a clear objective: to establish itself as the core of personal computers, as well as to create a relationship with consumers that transcended their hardware needs. Intel's products offer a high level of functional excellence, so it was necessary to create a brand identity that resonated at a personal level while being deeply grounded in functional excellence.

In the evolution of the Intel Bong, Intel sought to encapsulate the brand's essence through a short, memorable, and distinctive sound. In a distinctive five-note sequence, Intel's sonic logo concludes Intel's multi-media commercials across multiple media channels as an auditory bookmark. Television advertisements, radio advertisements, online videos, as well as event sponsorships have consistently incorporated this sonic signature. By integrating this sound into various media, from traditional broadcast channels to digital media and public events, Intel has strengthened its brand identity and made the sound as distinctive as their logo.

By syncing with the Intel Bong, consumers were not simply concluding an advertisement, but were also reliving it in their auditory memories. It was the choice of notes, their rhythm, and the accompanying visual logo that created a multisensory experience that has become a trademark of the brand. This marketing strategy aimed not only to differentiate the Intel brand, but also to associate it with technological prowess and trust, aiming for the Bong to become as iconic as the company's tagline, "Intel Inside."

Integrating theoretical frameworks

In accordance with experiential marketing theory, customers are seeking more than just products or services (Brakus et al., 2009; Schmitt, 1999). For Intel, the Bong became more than just a sound; it became an integral part of the technology purchase and usage experience. The Bong was consistently paired with cutting-edge technology featured in Intel's ads, creating a unique experience that enhanced Intel's association with technological innovation. Each note played reinforced that association.

In accordance with the Multisensory Integration Theory, consumer experiences can be enhanced by simultaneously stimulating multiple senses. An Intel sonic logo is a combination of an auditory stimulus (the Bong), visual (the commercials, the logo) and cognitive components, which involves processes of recognition, memory, and associative learning (e.g., associating the distinct sound with the brand's image of innovation and quality), resulting in a stronger, more memorable brand experience that is based on the integration of these elements. Through this integration, brands can reach both the conscious and subconscious levels of consumer engagement, enhancing their ability to be recognized and remembered by consumers.

Impact on Consumer Experience

A variety of dimensions can be used to analyze the effects of Intel Bong on the consumer experience.

- **Affective:** Intel Bong is a technological device that evokes an emotional response, instilling trust and confidence in its capabilities. In sensory marketing, emotional resonance plays a crucial role, which seeks to transcend functional benefits to touch consumers' emotional chords.
- **Cognitive:** As a result of its sound, the Bong stimulates recognition and promotes brand awareness. The sound serves as an auditory cue that Intel processors play an essential role in computing technology but are invisible. The impact of this is largely due to cognitive processes, especially those involving memory and recognition.
- **Behavioral:** Over time, repeated exposure to Intel Bongs may influence consumer behavior. Because sound is associated with quality and reliability, consumers are more likely to purchase products that have the "Intel Inside" than those that do not.
- **Sensory:** From a purely sensory perspective, the Bong stands out in the clutter of modern advertising noise. The distinctiveness of Intel's branding ensures that consumers will be engaged and provide a sensory break through the auditory aspect.

Implications for Practice

There are several practical implications for sensory marketing that can be derived from the deployment of the Intel Bong:

- **Consistency:** Using the Bong repeatedly has reinforced branding recognition and loyalty, demonstrating the importance of a consistent sensory marketing strategy over several platforms and decades.
- **Sensory Synergy:** Intel's approach demonstrates the benefits of combining auditory elements with other senses. The visual representation of the brand, in combination with the auditory logo, helps to create a stronger overall image of the company.

- **Emotional Branding:** Using sensory marketing in the Intel case illustrates how it is possible to build an emotional bond between a brand and its customers. The Bong is not just heard and felt by customers. It also conveys a message of innovation and reliability.

This case illustrates how well-executed sensory marketing strategies, based on robust theoretical frameworks, can significantly impact the consumer experience when well executed. This demonstration demonstrates how sound has the power to create an emotional and cognitive connection with customers, influence behavior, and leave an indelible sensory impression. The sonic branding strategy employed by Intel demonstrates the potential for sensory marketing to not only communicate, but also connect, resonate, and endure in the collective consciousness of consumers.

CONCLUSION

In our examination of the symbiotic relationship between sound and consumer journey dynamics, several salient insights have crystallized. We identify sound as an integral component of the customer journey as a key theme. Rather than simply contributing to background noise, carefully selected jingles, store ambient noise, or even distinctive alerts have a significant impact on consumer perceptions of brands. Sound elements enhance the entire customer journey-from the moment a brand captures the attention of the consumer to the point at which they become loyal advocates-by evoking emotions and memories that cement the brand's image in the mind of the consumer.

Sound has the ability to enhance brand recall by lingering in a consumer's memory. A memorable melody or signature sound can linger in their memory, making the brand more recognizable and accessible when they are ready to make a purchase. Auditory branding is more than simply creating an appealing sound; it is also about weaving a narrative that resonates emotionally, allowing the brand to stand out in crowded markets and establish an emotional connection that can lead to long-term customer loyalty. As a result, sound can serve as a powerful tool to enhance a brand's presence and deepen its relationship with customers when used correctly.

Sound plays a significant role in brand marketing, not just as an auxiliary element, but as a strategic pillar. Sound can transform ordinary brand experiences into extraordinary, memorable ones when integrated thoughtfully. Brands can create harmonious relationships over time by creating a symphony of experiences that resonate with consumers.

As a strategic component, sound cannot be overlooked and should be included. As the landscape of brand marketing evolves, where experiences matter more than ever, sound serves as a profound means of touching consumers' hearts, stirring their souls, and leaving an indelible impression. It is imperative that brands recognize and incorporate sound into their narratives so that they are not only seen and heard, but truly listened to.

REFERENCES

Ambler, T., Ioannides, A., & Rose, S. (2000). Brands on the brain: Neuro-images of advertising. *Business Strategy Review*, *11*(3), 17–30. doi:10.1111/1467-8616.00144

Araujo, T., Copulsky, J. R., Hayes, J. L., Kim, S. J., & Srivastava, J. (2020). From purchasing exposure to fostering engagement: Brand–consumer experiences in the emerging computational advertising landscape. *Journal of Advertising*, *49*(4), 428–445. doi:10.1080/00913367.2020.1795756

Barsalou, L. W. (2008). Grounded cognition. *Annual Review of Psychology*, *59*(1), 617–645. doi:10.1146/annurev.psych.59.103006.093639 PMID:17705682

Bhatia, R., Garg, R., Chhikara, R., Kataria, A., & Talwar, V. (2021). Sensory marketing–a review and research agenda. *Academy of Marketing Studies Journal*, *25*(4), 1–30.

Biswas, D., Lund, K., & Szocs, C. (2019). Sounds like a healthy retail atmospheric strategy: Effects of ambient music and background noise on food sales. *Journal of the Academy of Marketing Science*, *47*(1), 37–55. doi:10.1007/s11747-018-0583-8

Blasco-Arcas, L., Hernandez-Ortega, B. I., & Jimenez-Martinez, J. (2016). Engagement platforms: The role of emotions in fostering customer engagement and brand image in interactive media. *Journal of Service Theory and Practice*, *26*(5), 559–589. doi:10.1108/JSTP-12-2014-0286

Bloch, P. H. (1995). Seeking the Ideal Form: Product Design and Consumer Response. *Journal of Marketing*, *59*(3), 16–29. doi:10.1177/002224299505900302

Brakus, J. J., Schmitt, B. H., & Zarantonello, L. (2009). Brand Experience: What Is It? How Is It Measured? Does It Affect Loyalty? *Journal of Marketing*, *73*(3), 52–68. doi:10.1509/jmkg.73.3.052

Brengman, M., Willems, K., & De Gauquier, L. (2022). Customer engagement in multi-sensory virtual reality advertising: The effect of sound and scent congruence. *Frontiers in Psychology*, *13*, 747456. doi:10.3389/fpsyg.2022.747456 PMID:35386898

Bruce, M., & Daly, L. (2006). Buyer behaviour for fast fashion. *Journal of Fashion Marketing and Management*, *10*(3), 329–344. doi:10.1108/13612020610679303

Bruner, G. C. II. (1990). Music, mood, and marketing. *Journal of Marketing*, *54*(4), 94–104. doi:10.1177/002224299005400408

Cha, K. C., Suh, M., Kwon, G., Yang, S., & Lee, E. J. (2020). Young consumers' brain responses to pop music on Youtube. *Asia Pacific Journal of Marketing and Logistics*, *32*(5), 1132–1148. doi:10.1108/APJML-04-2019-0247

Chevtchouk, Y., Veloutsou, C., & Paton, R. (2018). The Process of Brand Experience: An Interdisciplinary Perspective: An Abstract. *Academy of Marketing Science Journal*, *499–500*, 499–500. Advance online publication. doi:10.1007/978-3-319-66023-3_168

Cowan, K., Ketron, S., Kostyk, A., & Kristofferson, K. (2023). Can you smell the (virtual) roses? The influence of olfactory cues in virtual reality on immersion and positive brand responses. *Journal of Retailing*, *99*(3), 385–399. doi:10.1016/j.jretai.2023.07.004

de Regt, A., Plangger, K., & Barnes, S. J. (2021). Virtual reality marketing and customer advocacy: Transforming experiences from story-telling to story-doing. *Journal of Business Research*, *136*, 513–522. doi:10.1016/j.jbusres.2021.08.004

Doucé, L., & Adams, C. (2020). Sensory overload in a shopping environment: Not every sensory modality leads to too much stimulation. *Journal of Retailing and Consumer Services*, *57*, 102154. doi:10.1016/j.jretconser.2020.102154

Følstad, A., & Kvale, K. (2018). Customer journeys: A systematic literature review. *Journal of Service Theory and Practice*, *28*(2), 196–227. doi:10.1108/JSTP-11-2014-0261

Gustafsson, C. (2015). Sonic branding: A consumer-oriented literature review. *Journal of Brand Management*, *22*(1), 20–37. doi:10.1057/bm.2015.5

Hoegg, J., & Alba, J. W. (2007). Taste perception: More than meets the tongue. *The Journal of Consumer Research*, *33*(4), 490–498. doi:10.1086/510222

Huang, P., Lurie, N. H., & Mitra, S. (2009). Searching for experience on the web: An empirical examination of consumer behavior for search and experience goods. *Journal of Marketing*, *73*(2), 55–69. doi:10.1509/jmkg.73.2.55

Hultén, B. (2011a). Sensory marketing: The multi-sensory brand-experience concept. *European Business Review*, *23*(3), 256–273. doi:10.1108/09555341111130245

Hultén, B. (2011b). Sensory marketing: The multi-sensory brand-experience concept. *European Business Review*, *23*(3), 256–273. doi:10.1108/09555341111130245

Hwang, A. H.-C., & Oh, J. (2020). Interacting with background music engages E-Customers more: The impact of interactive music on consumer perception and behavioral intention. *Journal of Retailing and Consumer Services*, *54*, 101928. doi:10.1016/j.jretconser.2019.101928

Hwang, A. H. C., Oh, J., & Scheinbaum, A. C. (2020). Interactive music for multisensory e-commerce: The moderating role of online consumer involvement in experiential value, cognitive value, and purchase intention. *Psychology and Marketing*, *37*(8), 1031–1056. doi:10.1002/mar.21338

Jain, R., Aagja, J., & Bagdare, S. (2017). Customer experience–a review and research agenda. *Journal of Service Theory and Practice*, *27*(3), 642–662. doi:10.1108/JSTP-03-2015-0064

Keh, H. T., Wang, D., & Yan, L. (2021). Gimmicky or effective? The effects of imaginative displays on customers' purchase behavior. *Journal of Marketing*, *85*(5), 109–127. doi:10.1177/0022242921997359

Kemp, E., Cho, Y.-N., Bui, M., & Kintzer, A. (2023). Music to the ears: The role of sonic branding in advertising. *International Journal of Advertising*, ●●●, 1–21. doi:10.1080/02650487.2023.2273645

Kharat, M. G. M. G., Jha, M. K., Chikhalkar, R. D., & Kharat, M. G. M. G. (2018). Brand experience: Development of the conceptual framework and critical research propositions. *International Journal of Management Concepts and Philosophy*, *11*(3), 340. doi:10.1504/IJMCP.2018.093495

Kim, J. H., Ritchie, J. R. B., & McCormick, B. (2012). Development of a scale to measure memorable tourism experiences. *Journal of Travel Research*, *51*(1), 12–25. doi:10.1177/0047287510385467

Kim, M., Kim, J.-H., Park, M., & Yoo, J. (2021). The roles of sensory perceptions and mental imagery in consumer decision-making. *Journal of Retailing and Consumer Services*, *61*, 102517. doi:10.1016/j.jretconser.2021.102517

Klein, K., Melnyk, V., & Voelckner, F. (2021). Effects of background music on evaluations of visual images. *Psychology and Marketing*, *38*(12), 2240–2246. doi:10.1002/mar.21588

Krishna, A. (2012). An integrative review of sensory marketing: Engaging the senses to affect perception, judgment and behavior. *Journal of Consumer Psychology*, *22*(3), 332–351. doi:10.1016/j.jcps.2011.08.003

Krishna, A., Cian, L., & Sokolova, T. (2016). The power of sensory marketing in advertising. *Current Opinion in Psychology*, *10*, 142–147. doi:10.1016/j.copsyc.2016.01.007

Krishna, A., & Schwarz, N. (2014). Sensory marketing, embodiment, and grounded cognition: A review and introduction. *Journal of Consumer Psychology*, *24*(2), 159–168. doi:10.1016/j.jcps.2013.12.006

Kujur, F., & Singh, S. (2020). Visual communication and consumer-brand relationship on social networking sites-uses & gratifications theory perspective. *Journal of Theoretical and Applied Electronic Commerce Research*, *15*(1), 30–47. doi:10.4067/S0718-18762020000100104

Kumar, V., Petersen, J. A., & Leone, R. P. (2010). Driving profitability by encouraging customer referrals: Who, when, and how. *Journal of Marketing*, *74*(5), 1–17. doi:10.1509/jmkg.74.5.001

Lageat, T., Czellar, S., & Laurent, G. (2003). Engineering hedonic attributes to generate perceptions of luxury: Consumer perception of an everyday sound. *Marketing Letters*, *14*(2), 97–109. doi:10.1023/A:1025462901401

Lee, M., Lee, S., & Koh, Y. (2019). Multisensory experience for enhancing hotel guest experience: Empirical evidence from big data analytics. *International Journal of Contemporary Hospitality Management*, *31*(11), 4313–4337. doi:10.1108/IJCHM-03-2018-0263

Lemon, K. N., & Verhoef, P. C. (2016). Understanding customer experience throughout the customer journey. *Journal of Marketing*, *80*(6), 69–96. doi:10.1509/jm.15.0420

Lindstrom, M. (2005). Broad sensory branding. *Journal of Product and Brand Management*, *14*(2), 84–87. doi:10.1108/10610420510592554

Loureiro, S. M. C., Guerreiro, J., & Japutra, A. (2021). How escapism leads to behavioral intention in a virtual reality store with background music? *Journal of Business Research*, *134*, 288–300. doi:10.1016/j.jbusres.2021.05.035

Melzner, J., & Raghubir, P. (2023). The sound of music: The effect of timbral sound quality in audio logos on brand personality perception. *JMR, Journal of Marketing Research*, *60*(5), 932–949. doi:10.1177/00222437221135188

Meyer, C., & Schwager, A. (2007). Understanding customer experience. *Harvard Business Review, 85*(2), 116. PMID:17345685

Michon, R., Chebat, J.-C., & Turley, L. W. (2005). Mall atmospherics: The interaction effects of the mall environment on shopping behavior. *Journal of Business Research, 58*(5), 576–583. doi:10.1016/j.jbusres.2003.07.004

Milliman, R. E. (1986). The influence of background music on the behavior of restaurant patrons. *The Journal of Consumer Research, 13*(2), 286–289. doi:10.1086/209068

Moreira, A. C., Fortes, N., & Santiago, R. (2017a). Influence of sensory stimuli on brand experience, brand equity and purchase intention. *Journal of Business Economics and Management, 18*(1), 68–83. doi:10.3846/16111699.2016.1252793

Moreira, A. C., Fortes, N., & Santiago, R. (2017b). Influence of sensory stimuli on brand experience, brand equity and purchase intention. *Journal of Business Economics and Management, 18*(1), 68–83. doi:10.3846/16111699.2016.1252793

Morrin, M., & Ratneshwar, S. (2003). Does it make sense to use scents to enhance brand memory? *JMR, Journal of Marketing Research, 40*(1), 10–25. doi:10.1509/jmkr.40.1.10.19128

Mosley, R. W. (2007). Customer experience, organisational culture and the employer brand. *Journal of Brand Management, 15*(2), 123–134. doi:10.1057/palgrave.bm.2550124

Nguyen, T., Quach, S., & Thaichon, P. (2022). The effect of AI quality on customer experience and brand relationship. *Journal of Consumer Behaviour, 21*(3), 481–493. doi:10.1002/cb.1974

North, A. C., & Hargreaves, D. J. (1998). The effect of music on atmosphere and purchase intentions in a cafeteria 1. *Journal of Applied Social Psychology, 28*(24), 2254–2273. doi:10.1111/j.1559-1816.1998.tb01370.x

Parise, S., Guinan, P. J., & Kafka, R. (2016). Solving the crisis of immediacy: How digital technology can transform the customer experience. *Business Horizons, 59*(4), 411–420. doi:10.1016/j.bushor.2016.03.004

Park, C., & Kim, Y. (2003). A framework of dynamic CRM: Linking marketing with information strategy. *Business Process Management Journal, 9*(5), 652–671. doi:10.1108/14637150310496749

Peck, J., & Childers, T. L. (2003). Individual differences in haptic information processing: The "need for touch" scale. *The Journal of Consumer Research*, *30*(3), 430–442. doi:10.1086/378619

Peck, J., & Wiggins, J. (2006). It just feels good: Customers' affective response to touch and its influence on persuasion. *Journal of Marketing*, *70*(4), 56–69.

Poushneh, A. (2021). Impact of auditory sense on trust and brand affect through auditory social interaction and control. *Journal of Retailing and Consumer Services*, *58*, 102281. doi:10.1016/j.jretconser.2020.102281

Prahalad, C. K., & Ramaswamy, V. (2004). Co-creation experiences: The next practice in value creation. *Journal of Interactive Marketing*, *18*(3), 5–14. doi:10.1002/dir.20015

Reed, I. I. A. II, & Forehand, M. R. (2016). The ebb and flow of consumer identities: The role of memory, emotions and threats. *Current Opinion in Psychology*, *10*, 94–100. doi:10.1016/j.copsyc.2015.12.015

Reinoso-Carvalho, F., Gunn, L., Molina, G., Narumi, T., Spence, C., Suzuki, Y., ter Horst, E., & Wagemans, J. (2020). A sprinkle of emotions vs a pinch of crossmodality: Towards globally meaningful sonic seasoning strategies for enhanced multisensory tasting experiences. *Journal of Business Research*, *117*, 389–399. doi:10.1016/j.jbusres.2020.04.055

Roggeveen, A. L., Grewal, D., & Schweiger, E. B. (2020). The DAST framework for retail atmospherics: The impact of in-and out-of-store retail journey touchpoints on the customer experience. *Journal of Retailing*, *96*(1), 128–137. doi:10.1016/j.jretai.2019.11.002

Roy, S., & Singh, P. (2023). The olfactory experience (in retail) scale: Construction, validation and generalization. *Journal of Service Management*, *34*(3), 403–432. doi:10.1108/JOSM-05-2021-0173

Schlosser, A. E. (2003). Experiencing products in the virtual world: The role of goal and imagery in influencing attitudes versus purchase intentions. *The Journal of Consumer Research*, *30*(2), 184–198. doi:10.1086/376807

Schmitt, B. (1999). Experiential Marketing. *Journal of Marketing Management*, *15*(1–3), 53–67. doi:10.1362/026725799784870496

Scott, S. P., Sheinin, D., & Labrecque, L. I. (2022). Small sounds, big impact: Sonic logos and their effect on consumer attitudes, emotions, brands and advertising placement. *Journal of Product and Brand Management*, *31*(7), 1091–1103. doi:10.1108/JPBM-06-2021-3507

Shahid, S., Paul, J., Gilal, F. G., & Ansari, S. (2022). The role of sensory marketing and brand experience in building emotional attachment and brand loyalty in luxury retail stores. *Psychology and Marketing*, *39*(7), 1398–1412. doi:10.1002/mar.21661

Spence, C. (2012). Managing sensory expectations concerning products and brands: Capitalizing on the potential of sound and shape symbolism. *Journal of Consumer Psychology*, *22*(1), 37–54. doi:10.1016/j.jcps.2011.09.004

Spence, C., Puccinelli, N. M., Grewal, D., & Roggeveen, A. L. (2014). Store atmospherics: A multisensory perspective. *Psychology and Marketing*, *31*(7), 472–488. doi:10.1002/mar.20709

Spence, C., & Shankar, M. U. (2010). The influence of auditory cues on the perception of, and responses to, food and drink. *Journal of Sensory Studies*, *25*(3), 406–430. doi:10.1111/j.1745-459X.2009.00267.x

Spence, C., Wang, Q. J., Reinoso-Carvalho, F., & Keller, S. (2021). Commercializing sonic seasoning in multisensory offline experiential events and online tasting experiences. *Frontiers in Psychology*, *12*, 740354. doi:10.3389/fpsyg.2021.740354 PMID:34659056

Stead, S., Wetzels, R., Wetzels, M., Odekerken-Schröder, G., & Mahr, D. (2022). Toward multisensory customer experiences: A cross-disciplinary bibliometric review and future research directions. *Journal of Service Research*, *25*(3), 440–459. doi:10.1177/10946705221079941

Stein, B. E., & Meredith, M. A. (1993). *The merging of the senses*. MIT press.

Sultan, A. J. (2018). Orchestrating service brand touchpoints and the effects on relational outcomes. *Journal of Services Marketing*, *32*(6), 777–788. doi:10.1108/JSM-12-2016-0413

Sweller, J. (1988). Cognitive load during problem solving: Effects on learning. *Cognitive Science*, *12*(2), 257–285. doi:10.1207/s15516709cog1202_4

Szocs, C., Kim, Y., Lim, M., Mera, C. A., & Biswas, D. (2023). The store of the future: Engaging customers through sensory elements, personalized atmospherics, and interpersonal interaction. *Journal of Retailing*, *99*(4), 605–620. doi:10.1016/j.jretai.2023.11.005

Tueanrat, Y., Papagiannidis, S., & Alamanos, E. (2021). Going on a journey: A review of the customer journey literature. *Journal of Business Research*, *125*, 336–353. doi:10.1016/j.jbusres.2020.12.028

Ülkü, S., Hydock, C., & Cui, S. (2020). Making the wait worthwhile: Experiments on the effect of queueing on consumption. *Management Science*, *66*(3), 1149–1171. doi:10.1287/mnsc.2018.3277

Wiedmann, K.-P., Labenz, F., Haase, J., & Hennigs, N. (2018). The power of experiential marketing: Exploring the causal relationships among multisensory marketing, brand experience, customer perceived value and brand strength. *Journal of Brand Management*, *25*(2), 101–118. doi:10.1057/s41262-017-0061-5

Wörfel, P., Frentz, F., & Tautu, C. (2022). Marketing comes to its senses: A bibliometric review and integrated framework of sensory experience in marketing. *European Journal of Marketing*, *56*(3), 704–737. doi:10.1108/EJM-07-2020-0510

Yakhlef, A., & Nordin, F. (2021). Effects of firm presence in customer-owned touch points: A self-determination perspective. *Journal of Business Research*, *130*, 473–481. doi:10.1016/j.jbusres.2019.12.044

Zarantonello, L., & Schmitt, B. H. (2010). Using the brand experience scale to profile consumers and predict consumer behaviour. *Journal of Brand Management*, *17*(7), 532–540. doi:10.1057/bm.2010.4

Zha, D., Foroudi, P., Jin, Z., & Melewar, T. C. (2022). Making sense of sensory brand experience: Constructing an integrative framework for future research. *International Journal of Management Reviews*, *24*(1), 130–167. doi:10.1111/ijmr.12270

Compilation of References

Aaker, D. A. (1996). Measuring brand equity across products and markets. *California Management Review*, *38*(3), 102–120. doi:10.2307/41165845

Aaker, D. A., & Joachimsthaler, E. (2002). *Brand Leadership*. Simon and Schuster.

Adgully Bureau. (2019, September 12). Advertising that has built the brand Airtel. Retrieved from https://www.adgully.com/advertising-that-has-built-brand-airtel-88237.html

Akaka, M. A., Vargo, S. L., & Schau, H. J. (2015). The context of experience. *Journal of Service Management*, *26*(2), 206–223. doi:10.1108/JOSM-10-2014-0270

Ali, S., Mishra, M., & Javed, H. M. U. (2021). The impact of mall personality and shopping value on shoppers' well-being: Moderating role of compulsive shopping. *International Journal of Retail & Distribution Management*, *49*(8), 1178–1197. doi:10.1108/IJRDM-07-2020-0272

Allan, D. (2008). A Content Analysis of Music Placement in Prime-Time Television Advertising. *Journal of Advertising Research*, *48*(3), 404–417. doi:10.2501/S0021849908080434

Allan, D. (2010). They're Playing My Brand. *International Journal of Integrated Marketing Communications*, *2*(1), 40–46.

Alnuman, N., & Altaweel, M. Z. (2020). Investigation of the Acoustical Environment in A Shopping Mall and Its Correlation to the Acoustic Comfort of the Workers. *Applied Sciences (Basel, Switzerland)*, *10*(3), 1170. doi:10.3390/app10031170

Alvarsson, J. J., Wiens, S., & Nilsson, M. E. (2010). Stress recovery during exposure to nature sound and environmental noise. *International Journal of Environmental Research and Public Health*, *7*(3), 1036–1046. doi:10.3390/ijerph7031036 PMID:20617017

Ambler, T., Ioannides, A., & Rose, S. (2000). Brands on the brain: Neuro-images of advertising. *Business Strategy Review*, *11*(3), 17–30. doi:10.1111/1467-8616.00144

Anderson, L. (2006). Analytic Autoethnography. *Journal of Contemporary Ethnography*, *35*(4), 373–395. doi:10.1177/0891241605280449

Andersson, P. K., Kristensson, P., Wästlund, E., & Gustafsson, A. (2012). Let the music play or not: The influence of background music on consumer behavior. *Journal of Retailing and Consumer Services*, *19*(6), 553–560. doi:10.1016/j.jretconser.2012.06.010

Anyiwo, N., Watkins, D. C., & Rowley, S. J. (2022). "They Can't Take Away the Light": Hip-Hop Culture and Black Youth's Racial Resistance. *Youth & Society*, *54*(4), 611–634. doi:10.1177/0044118X211001096

Araujo, T., Copulsky, J. R., Hayes, J. L., Kim, S. J., & Srivastava, J. (2020). From purchasing exposure to fostering engagement: Brand–consumer experiences in the emerging computational advertising landscape. *Journal of Advertising*, *49*(4), 428–445. doi:10.1080/00913367.2020.1 795756

Areni, C. S., & Kim, D. (1993). The influence of background music on shopping behaviour: Classical versus top-forty music in a wine store. *Advances in Consumer Research. Association for Consumer Research (U. S.)*, *20*, 336–340.

Aucouturier, J. J., & Pachet, F. (2003). Representing musical genre: A state of the art. *Journal of New Music Research*, *32*(1), 83–93. doi:10.1076/jnmr.32.1.83.16801

Augé, M. (1995). *Non-Places: An Introduction to Anthropology of Supermodernity* (J. Howe, Trans.). Verso. (Original work published 1992)

Axelsson, Ö., Nilsson, M. E., & Berglund, B. (2010). A principal components model of soundscape perception. *The Journal of the Acoustical Society of America*, *128*(5), 2836–2846. doi:10.1121/1.3493436 PMID:21110579

Baines, P. R., Worcester, R. M., Jarrett, D., & Mortimore, R. (2003). Market Segmentation and Product Differentiation in Political Campaigns: A Technical Feature Perspective. *Journal of Marketing Management*, *19*(1–2), 225–249. doi:10.1080/0267257X.2003.9728208

Bakker, D. R., & Martin, F. H. (2015). Musical chords and emotion: Major and minor triads are processed for emotion. *Cognitive, Affective & Behavioral Neuroscience*, *15*(1), 15–31. doi:10.3758/s13415-014-0309-4 PMID:24957406

Barretta, P. G. (2017). Tracing the color line in the American music market and its effect on contemporary music marketing. *Arts and the Market*, *7*(2), 213–234. doi:10.1108/AAM-08-2016-0016

Barsalou, L. W. (2008). Grounded cognition. *Annual Review of Psychology*, *59*(1), 617–645. doi:10.1146/annurev.psych.59.103006.093639 PMID:17705682

Batra, R., & Ray, M. L. (1986). Affective Responses Mediating Acceptance of Advertising. *Journal of Consumer Research*, *13*(2), 234–249. doi:10.1086/209063

Baumgarth, C. (2010). 'Living the brand': Brand orientation in the business-to-business sector. *European Journal of Marketing*, *44*(5), 653–671. doi:10.1108/03090561011032315

Becker, L., & Jaakkola, E. (2020). Customer experience: Fundamental premises and implications for research. *Journal of the Academy of Marketing Science*, *48*(4), 630–648. doi:10.1007/s11747-019-00718-x

Belcher, J. D., & Haridakis, P. (2011). From "Alternative" to "Trance": The Role of Music in Facilitating Political Group Activity and Activism. *Ohio Communication Journal*, *49*, 145–174.

Belch, G. E., & Belch, M. A. (2021). *Advertising and Promotion. An Integrated Marketing Communications Perspective* (12th ed.). McGraw-Hill.

Belch, G. E., & Belch, M. S. (2015). *Introduction to Advertising and Promotion* (10th ed.). McGraw Hill.

Beverland, M., Lim, E. A., Morrison, M., & Terziovski, M. (2006). In-store music and consumer-brand relationships: Relational transformation following experiences of (mis)fit. *Journal of Business Research*, *59*(9), 982–989. doi:10.1016/j.jbusres.2006.07.001

Bhatia, R., Garg, R., Chhikara, R., Kataria, A., & Talwar, V. (2021). Sensory marketing–a review and research agenda. *Academy of Marketing Studies Journal*, *25*(4), 1–30.

Bilby, J., Koslow, S., & Sasser, S. L. (2023). Fear in Adland: How Client Risk Aversion and Agency Clientelism Limit the Development of Great Creative Campaigns. *Journal of Advertising*, *52*(1), 57–74. doi:10.1080/00913367.2021.1981497

Biswas, D., Lund, K., & Szocs, C. (2019). Sounds like a healthy retail atmospheric strategy: Effects of ambient music and background noise on food sales. *Journal of the Academy of Marketing Science*, *47*(1), 37–55. doi:10.1007/s11747-018-0583-8

Bitner, M. J. (1992). Servicescapes: The impact of physical surroundings on customers and employers. *Journal of Marketing*, *56*(2), 57–71. doi:10.1177/002224299205600205

Blair, M. E., & Shimp, T. A. (1992). Consequences of an Unpleasant Experience with Music: A Second-Order Negative Conditioning Perspective. *Journal of Advertising*, *21*(1), 35–43. doi: 10.1080/00913367.1992.10673358

Blake, A. (2024, February 14). Analysis | Much of the GOP is on-board with the Taylor Swift conspiracy theories. *Washington Post*. https://www.washingtonpost.com/politics/2024/02/14/gop-swift-superbowl/

Blasco-Arcas, L., Hernandez-Ortega, B. I., & Jimenez-Martinez, J. (2016). Engagement platforms: The role of emotions in fostering customer engagement and brand image in interactive media. *Journal of Service Theory and Practice*, *26*(5), 559–589. doi:10.1108/JSTP-12-2014-0286

Bloch, P. H. (1995). Seeking the Ideal Form: Product Design and Consumer Response. *Journal of Marketing*, *59*(3), 16–29. doi:10.1177/002224299505900302

Bode, M. & Kjeldgaard, D. (2017). Brand doings in a performative perspective: an analysis of conceptual brand discourses. In: Sherry, J & Fisher, E. red. Contemporary consumer culture theory. Routledge.

Bonde, A., & Hansen, A. G. (2013). Audio logo recognition, reduced articulation, and coding orientation: Rudiments of quantitative research integrating branding theory, social semiotics, and music psychology. *Sound Effects – an Interdisciplinary Journal of Sound and Sound Experience, 3*(1/2), 112-135.

Booms, B. H., & Bitner, M. J. (1982). Marketing services by managing the environment. *The Cornell Hotel and Restaurant Administration Quarterly, 23*(1), 35–40. doi:10.1177/001088048202300107

Bowden, J. (2009). A framework for assessing customer-brand relationships: The case of the restaurant industry. *Journal of Hospitality Marketing & Customer Engagement, pp.,* 37–41.

Brakus, J. J., Schmitt, B. H., & Zarantonello, L. (2009). Brand Experience: What Is It? How Is It Measured? Does It Affect Loyalty? *Journal of Marketing, 73*(3), 52–68. doi:10.1509/jmkg.73.3.052

Brengman, M., Willems, K., & De Gauquier, L. (2022). Customer engagement in multi-sensory virtual reality advertising: The effect of sound and scent congruence. *Frontiers in Psychology, 13*, 747456. doi:10.3389/fpsyg.2022.747456 PMID:35386898

Broadwater, L. (2023, February 8). They, the Republicans, Recite the Constitution For an Edge in Patriotism. *The New York Times*. https://www.proquest.com/newspapers/they-republicans-recite-constitution-edge/docview/2774028201/se-2

Brodnax, N. M., & Sapiezynski, P. (2022). From Home Base to Swing States: The Evolution of Digital Advertising Strategies during the 2020 US Presidential Primary. *Political Research Quarterly, 75*(2), 460–478. doi:10.1177/10659129221078046

Broekemier, G., Marquardt, R., & Gentry, J. W. (2008). An exploration of happy/sad and liked/disliked music effects on shopping intentions in a women's clothing store service setting. *Journal of Services Marketing, 22*(1), 59–67. doi:10.1108/08876040810851969

Bronner, K. (2008). Jingle all the way? Basics of audio branding. In P. Steiner (Ed.), *Audio Branding-Brands, Sound and Communication* (pp. 77–87). Nomos Edition.

Brooks, G. (2007). Whose territory? *New Media Age*, 25–25.

Brown, A. L. (2012). A review of progress in soundscapes and an approach to soundscape planning. *International Journal of Acoustics and Vibration, 17*(2), 73–81. doi:10.20855/ijav.2012.17.2302

Brown, S., Stevens, L., & Maclaran, P. (2018). Epic aspects of retail encounters: The Iliad of Hollister. *Journal of Retailing, 94*(1), 58–72. doi:10.1016/j.jretai.2017.09.006

Bruce, M., & Daly, L. (2006). Buyer behaviour for fast fashion. *Journal of Fashion Marketing and Management, 10*(3), 329–344. doi:10.1108/13612020610679303

Bruner, G. C. II. (1990). Music, Mood, and Marketing. *Journal of Marketing, 54*(4), 94–104. doi:10.1177/002224299005400408

Bull, M. (2000). *Sound Moves: iPod culture and urban experience*. Taylor and Francis.

Bull, M. (2012). IPod Culture: The Toxic Pleasures of Audiotopia. In T. Pinch & K. Bijsterveld (Eds.), *The Oxford Handbook of Sound Studies* (pp. 526–543).

Canniford, R., & Bajde, D. (Eds.). (2016). *Assembling consumption. Researching actors, networks and markets*. Routledge.

Carney, D. R., Jost, J. T., Gosling, S. D., & Potter, J. (2008). The Secret Lives of Liberals and Conservatives: Personality Profiles, Interaction Styles, and the Things They Leave Behind. *Political Psychology*, *29*(6), 807–840. doi:10.1111/j.1467-9221.2008.00668.x

Cha, K. C., Suh, M., Kwon, G., Yang, S., & Lee, E. J. (2020). Young consumers' brain responses to pop music on Youtube. *Asia Pacific Journal of Marketing and Logistics*, *32*(5), 1132–1148. doi:10.1108/APJML-04-2019-0247

Chandler, J., & Lusch, R. (2015). Service Systems: A Broadened Framework and Research Agenda on Value Propositions, Engagement, and Service Experience. *Journal of Service Research*, *18*(1), 6–22. doi:10.1177/1094670514537709

Chang, C. (2009). "Being Hooked" By Editorial Content: The Implications for Processing Narrative Advertising. *Journal of Advertising*, *38*(1), 21–34. doi:10.2753/JOA0091-3367380102

Chebat, J.-C., Chebat, C. G., & Vaillant, D. (2001). Environmental background music and in-store selling. *Journal of Business Research*, *54*(2), 115–123. doi:10.1016/S0148-2963(99)00089-2

Cher drops new 'Take Me Home' remix as featured in latest MAC commercial—RETROPOP - Fashionably Nostalgic | News, Interviews, Reviews, and more ... (n.d.). Retrieved August 9, 2023, from https://retropopmagazine.com/cher-take-me-home-remix-mac-commercial/

Chevtchouk, Y., Veloutsou, C., & Paton, R. (2018). The Process of Brand Experience: An Interdisciplinary Perspective: An Abstract. *Academy of Marketing Science Journal*, *499–500*, 499–500. Advance online publication. doi:10.1007/978-3-319-66023-3_168

Chevy Silverado 2014 TV Spot, "New Anthem: Born Free" Song by Kid Rock. (n.d.). Retrieved October 2, 2023, from https://www.ispot.tv/ad/7CRs/2014-chevy-silverado-truck-guys-song-by-kid-rock

Ciaburro, G. (2021). Deep Learning Methods for Audio Events Detection. Machine Learning for Intelligent Multimedia Analytics: Techniques and Applications, 147-166.

Ciaburro, G. (2021, July). Recycled materials for sound absorbing applications. [). Trans Tech Publications Ltd.]. *Materials Science Forum*, *1034*, 169–175. doi:10.4028/www.scientific.net/MSF.1034.169

Ciaburro, G., & Iannace, G. (2021). Acoustic characterization of rooms using reverberation time estimation based on supervised learning algorithm. *Applied Sciences (Basel, Switzerland)*, *11*(4), 1661. doi:10.3390/app11041661

Cowan, K., Ketron, S., Kostyk, A., & Kristofferson, K. (2023). Can you smell the (virtual) roses? The influence of olfactory cues in virtual reality on immersion and positive brand responses. *Journal of Retailing*, *99*(3), 385–399. doi:10.1016/j.jretai.2023.07.004

Craig, S. (2011). A brief history of the American radio jingle. Conference: Popular culture association convention, San Antonio, TX.

Crisinel, A., Cosser, S., King, S., Jones, R., James, P., & Spence, C. (2012). A bittersweet symphony: Systematically modulating the taste of food by changing the sonic properties of the soundtrack playing in the background. *Food Quality and Preference*, *1*(24), 201–204. doi:10.1016/j.foodqual.2011.08.009

Cristini, H., Kauppinen-Räisänen, H., Barthod-Prothade, M., & Woodside, A. (2017). Toward a general theory of luxury: Advancing from workbench definitions and theoretical transformations. *Journal of Business Research*, *70*, 101–107. doi:10.1016/j.jbusres.2016.07.001

da Silva Klehm, V., de Souza Braga, R., & de Lucena Jr, V. F. (2022). A Survey of Digital Television Interactivity Technologies. *Sensors*, *22*(17), 6542. doi:10.3390/s22176542 PMID:36080995

Dall'Ara, E., Dubois, D., & Fortin, D. (2018). The Effects of Music on Shopping Behavior: A Literature Review and Agenda for Future Research. In *Transformative Consumer Research for Personal and Collective Well-being* (pp. 101–115). Springer.

De Chernatony, L. (2010). *From Brand Vision to Brand Evaluation* (3rd ed.). Butterworth-Heinemnn. doi:10.4324/9780080966649

De Marchi, L. (2018). *Cultural diversity in the communication and culture markets: an overview of discussions and research methods in the music industry*. Postgraduate Program in Social Sciences – UFJF, v. 13, n. 2, p. 210-223.

De Nora, T. (2004). *Music in everyday life*. Cambridge University Press.

de Regt, A., Plangger, K., & Barnes, S. J. (2021). Virtual reality marketing and customer advocacy: Transforming experiences from story-telling to story-doing. *Journal of Business Research*, *136*, 513–522. doi:10.1016/j.jbusres.2021.08.004

de Run, E. C., & Ting, H. (2014). Determining Attitudinal Beliefs About Controversial Advertising. *International Journal of Business & Society*, *15*(3), 465–476.

DeNora, T. (2000). *Music in Everyday Life*. Cambridge University Press. doi:10.1017/CBO9780511489433

Ding, C. G., & Lind, C.-H. (2012). How does background music tempo work for online shopping? *Electronic Commerce Research and Applications*, *11*(3), 299–307. doi:10.1016/j.elerap.2011.10.002

Dion, D., & Borraz, S. (2017). Managing status: How luxury brands shape class subjectivities in the service encounter. *Journal of Marketing*, *81*(5), 67–85. doi:10.1509/jm.15.0291

Doucé, L., & Adams, C. (2020). Sensory overload in a shopping environment: Not every sensory modality leads to too much stimulation. *Journal of Retailing and Consumer Services*, *57*, 102154. doi:10.1016/j.jretconser.2020.102154

Du Gay, P., S. Hall, L. Janes, H. Mackay, and K. Negus (1997). *Doing cultural studies: the story of the Sony Walkman*. Sage in association with the Open University.

Dubois, D., & Gallet, P. (2011). The effects of background music on consumer behavior: A field experiment in a supermarket. *International Journal of Management and Marketing Research*, *4*(1), 61–72.

Dumyahn, S. L., & Pijanowski, B. C. (2011). Soundscape conservation. *Landscape Ecology*, *26*(9), 1327–1344. doi:10.1007/s10980-011-9635-x

Dunaway, D. K. (1987). Music and Politics in the United States on JSTOR. *Folk Music Journal*, *5*(3), 268–294.

Edvardsson, B., Enquist, B., & Johnston, B. (2005). Co-Creating Customer Value Through Hyperreality in the Pre-purchase Service Experience. *Journal of Service Research*, *8*(2), 149–161. doi:10.1177/1094670505279729

Eisenhardt, K. M. (1989). Building theories from case study research. *Academy of Management Review*, *14*(4), 532–550. doi:10.2307/258557

El Hedhli, K., Chebat, J. C., & Sirgy, M. J. (2013). Shopping well-being at the mall: Construct, antecedents, and consequences. *Journal of Business Research*, *66*(7), 856–863. doi:10.1016/j.jbusres.2011.06.011

Elmashhara, M. G., & Soares, A. M. (2020). The influence of atmospherics general interior variables on shoppers' emotions and behavior. *International Review of Retail, Distribution and Consumer Research*, *30*(4), 437–459. doi:10.1080/09593969.2020.1724556

Erthal, A. (2018). *Multisensory communication: understanding ways of feeling*. E-papers.

Fernandes, D., Ordabayeva, N., Han, K., Jung, J., & Mittal, V. (2022). How Political Identity Shapes Customer Satisfaction. *Journal of Marketing*, *86*(6), 116–134. doi:10.1177/00222429211057508

Finnair (2023, October 30). Finnair Brand Book. https://brand.finnair.com/en

FirstBank's Off-Beat Advertising Generates Viewer Response—And Controversy. (2015). ABA Bank Marketing & Sales, 47(7), 3–4. https://ezproxy.wagner.edu/login?url=https://search.ebscohost.com/login.aspx?direct=true&db=buh&AN=109330318&site=ehost-live&scope=site

Flaig, N. (2022). *Sound advice: Creating a sonic identity profile*. Sentient Decision Science.

Flight, R. L., & Coker, K. (2022). Birds of a feather: Brand attachment through the lens of consumer political ideologies. *Journal of Product and Brand Management*, *31*(5), 731–743. doi:10.1108/JPBM-01-2020-2719

Flores, Y. (2021). Science, Context, and Gender Fluidity in Public Policy. *Public Integrity, 23*(6), 595–609. doi:10.1080/10999922.2020.1825181

Følstad, A., & Kvale, K. (2018). Customer journeys: A systematic literature review. *Journal of Service Theory and Practice, 28*(2), 196–227. doi:10.1108/JSTP-11-2014-0261

Garaus, M. (2017). Atmospheric harmony in the retail environment: Its influence on store satisfaction and re-patronage intention. *Journal of Consumer Behaviour, 16*(3), 265–278. doi:10.1002/cb.1626

Garlin, F. V., & Owen, K. (2007). Setting the tone with the tune: A meta-analytic review of the effects of background music in retail setting. *Journal of Business Research, 59*(6), 755–764. doi:10.1016/j.jbusres.2006.01.013

Gibbs, S. (2016, November 2). Mobile web browsing overtakes desktop for the first time. *The Guardian.* https://www.theguardian.com/technology/2016/nov/02/mobile-web-browsing-desktop-smartphones-tablets

Gilstrap, C., Teggart, A., Cabodi, K., Hills, J., & Price, S. (2021). Social music festival brandscapes: A lexical analysis of music festival social conversations. *Journal of Destination Marketing & Management, 20*, 100567. doi:10.1016/j.jdmm.2021.100567

Goenka, S., & van Osselaer, S. M. J. (2023). Why Is It Wrong to Sell Your Body? Understanding Liberals' Versus Conservatives' Moral Objections to Bodily Markets. *Journal of Marketing, 87*(1), 64–80. doi:10.1177/00222429211046936

Goldberg, P. (2003). Using sonic branding in the retail environment – An easy and effective way to create consumer brand loyalty while enhancing the in-store experience. *Journal of Consumer Behaviour, 3*(2), 193–198. doi:10.1002/cb.132

Gordon, B. R., Lovett, M. J., Luo, B., & Reeder, J. C. I. III. (2023). Disentangling the effects of ad tone on voter turnout and candidate choice in presidential elections. *Management Science, 69*(1), 220–243. doi:10.1287/mnsc.2022.4347

Gorn, G. J. (1982). The Effects of Music In Advertising On Choice Behavior: A Classical Conditioning Approach. *Journal of Marketing, 46*(1), 94–101. doi:10.1177/002224298204600109

Goulding, C., Shankar, A., & Canniford, R. (2011). Learning to be tribal: Facilitating the formation of consumer tribes. *European Journal of Marketing, 47*(5/6), 813–832. doi:10.1108/03090561311306886

Graakjær, N. J. (2013). Sounding out the logo shot. *Sound Effects - an Interdisciplinary Journal of Sound and Sound Experience, 3*(1/2), 78-95.

Graakjaer, N., & Jantzen, C. (2009). Producing corporate sounds: An interview with Karsten Kjems and Soren Holme on sonic branding. In C. N. Graakjaer (Ed.), *Music in Adverstising: Commercial Sounds in Media Communication and Other Settings* (pp. 259–274). Aalborg University Press.

Granato, J., & Wong, M. C. S. (2004). Political Campaign Advertising Dynamics. *Political Research Quarterly, 57*(3), 349–361. doi:10.1177/106591290405700301

Greenberg, D. M., Matz, S. C., Schwartz, H. A., & Fricke, K. R. (2021). The self-congruity effect of music. *Journal of Personality and Social Psychology*, *121*(1), 137–150. doi:10.1037/pspp0000293 PMID:32614219

Greenberg, D. M., Wride, S. J., Snowden, D. A., Spathis, D., Potter, J., & Rentfrow, P. J. (2022). Universals and variations in musical preferences: A study of preferential reactions to Western music in 53 countries. *Journal of Personality and Social Psychology*, *122*(2), 286–309. doi:10.1037/pspp0000397 PMID:35130023

Grewal, D., Baker, J., Levy, M., & Voss, G. B. (2003). The effects of wait expectations and store atmosphere evaluations on patronage intentions in service-intensive retail stores. *Journal of Retailing*, *79*(4), 259–268. doi:10.1016/j.jretai.2003.09.006

Grönroos, C. (2015). *Service management and marketing: managing the service profit logic*. Wiley.

Guéguen, N., Jacob, C., & Le Guellec, H. (2004). Sound level of environmental music and drinking behavior: A field experiment with beer drinkers. *Alcohol, Clinical and Experimental Research*, *28*(3), 349–351.

Guerra, G. (2013). *Music Branding. What is your brand sound?* Elsevier.

Gummerus, J., Von Koskull, C., Kauppinen-Räisänen, H., & Medberg, G. (2023). Who creates luxury? Unveiling the essence of luxury creation through three perspectives: A scoping review. *Qualitative Market Research*. 10.1108/QMR-02-2023-0025

Gustafsson, C. (2019). Sonic Branding. The Oxford Handbook of Sound and Imagination, 1, 359.

Gustafsson, C. (2015). Sonic branding: A consumer-oriented literature review. *Journal of Brand Management*, *22*(1), 20–37. doi:10.1057/bm.2015.5

Haanpää, M. (2022). Co-creation as choreography. *Qualitative Market Research*, *25*(5), 614–624. doi:10.1108/QMR-01-2022-0018

Hailstone, J. C., Omar, R., Henley, S. M., Frost, C., Kenward, M. G., & Warren, J. D. (2009). It's not what you play, it's how you play it: Timbre affects perception of emotion in music. *Quarterly Journal of Experimental Psychology*, *62*(11), 2141–2155. doi:10.1080/17470210902765957 PMID:19391047

Halliday, J. (2002, August 14). *Ford signs "Angry American" Singer for TV Ads*. Ad Age. https://adage.com/article/news/ford-signs-angry-american-singer-tv-ads/35471

Harris, J. L., Salus, D., Rerecich, R., & Larsen, D. (1996). Distinguishing detection from identification in subliminal auditory perception: A review and critique of Merikle's study. *The Journal of General Psychology*, *123*(1), 41–50. doi:10.1080/00221309.1996.9921258 PMID:8901209

Helkkula, A., Kelleher, C., & Pihlström, M. (2012). Characterizing Value as an Experience: Implications for Service Researchers and Managers. *Journal of Service Research*, *15*(1), 59–75. doi:10.1177/1094670511426897

Hellström, B., Sjösten, P., Hultqvist, A., Dyrssen, C., & Mossenmark, S. (2011). Modelling the shopping soundscape. *Journal of Sonic Studies*, *1*(1).

Herrington, J. D., & Capella, L. M. (1996). Effects of music in service environments: A field study. *Journal of Services Marketing*, *10*(2), 26–41. doi:10.1108/08876049610114249

Herschmann, M. (2010). *Music industry in transition*. Letters and Colors Station & Faperj.

Hill, J. C. (2022). Activist Musicians: A Framework for Leaders of Social Change. *Journal of Leadership Education*, *21*(2), 164–180. doi:10.12806/V21/I2/T1

Hill, T., Canniford, R., & Mol, J. (2014). Non-representational marketing theory. *Marketing Theory*, *14*(4), 377–394. doi:10.1177/1470593114533232

Hoegg, J., & Alba, J. W. (2007). Taste perception: More than meets the tongue. *The Journal of Consumer Research*, *33*(4), 490–498. doi:10.1086/510222

Holbrook, M. B. (2008). Music meanings in movies: The case of the crime-plus-jazz genre. *Consumption Markets & Culture*, *11*(4), 307–327. doi:10.1080/10253860802391326

Huang, P., Lurie, N. H., & Mitra, S. (2009). Searching for experience on the web: An empirical examination of consumer behavior for search and experience goods. *Journal of Marketing*, *73*(2), 55–69. doi:10.1509/jmkg.73.2.55

Huh, J., DeLorme, D. E., & Reid, L. N. (2013). Irritation and Ad Avoidance Behaviors: Influencing Factors in the Context of Otc Analgesic Advertising. American Academy of Advertising Conference Proceedings, 110–111.

Hultén, B. (2011). Sensory marketing: The multi-sensory brand-experience concept. *European Business Review*, *23*(3), 256–273. doi:10.1108/09555341111130245

Hung, K. (2000). Narrative Music in Congruent and Incongruent TV Advertising. *Journal of Advertising*, *29*(1), 25–34. doi:10.1080/00913367.2000.10673601

Hung, K. (2001). Framing Meaning Perceptions with Music: The Case of Teaser Ads. *Journal of Advertising*, *30*(3), 39–49. doi:10.1080/00913367.2001.10673644

Hwang, A. H. C., & Oh, J. (2020). Interacting with background music engages E-Customers more: The impact of interactive music on consumer perception and behavioral intention. *Journal of Retailing and Consumer Services*, *54*, 101928. doi:10.1016/j.jretconser.2019.101928

Hwang, A. H. C., Oh, J., & Scheinbaum, A. C. (2020). Interactive music for multisensory e-commerce: The moderating role of online consumer involvement in experiential value, cognitive value, and purchase intention. *Psychology and Marketing*, *37*(8), 1031–1056. doi:10.1002/mar.21338

Hynes, N., & Manson, S. (2016). The Sound of Silence: Why music in supermarkets is just a distraction. *Journal of Retailing and Consumer Services*, *28*(1), 171–178. doi:10.1016/j.jretconser.2015.10.001

Iannace, G., & Ciaburro, G. (2021). Modelling sound absorption properties for recycled polyethylene terephthalate-based material using Gaussian regression. *Building Acoustics*, *28*(2), 185–196. doi:10.1177/1351010X20933132

Iannace, G., Ianniello, C., & Ianniello, E. (2015). Music in an Atrium of a Shopping Center. *Acoustics Australia*, *43*(2), 191–198. doi:10.1007/s40857-015-0017-4

Iazzetta, F. (2015). *Sound studies: a field in gestation.* Research and Training Center, n. 1.

Iglesias, O., Markovic, S., & Rialp, J. (2019). How does sensory brand experience influence brand equity? Considering the roles of customer satisfaction, customer affective commitment, and employee empathy. *Journal of Business Research*, *96*, 343–354. doi:10.1016/j.jbusres.2018.05.043

International Organization for Standardization. (2014). *ISO 12913-1: 2014 acoustics—Soundscape—part 1: definition and conceptual framework.* ISO.

Jackson, D. M. (2003). *Sonic Branding: An Introduction.* Palgrave Macmillan. doi:10.1057/9780230503267

Jacob, C. (2006). Styles of background music and consumption in a bar: An empirical evaluation. *International Journal of Hospitality Management*, *25*(4), 716–720. doi:10.1016/j.ijhm.2006.01.002

Jacob, C., Guéguen, N., Boulbry, G., & Sami, S. (2009). 'Love is in the air': Congruence between background music and goods in a florist. *International Review of Retail, Distribution and Consumer Research*, *19*(1), 75–79. doi:10.1080/09593960902781334

Jain, R., Aagja, J., & Bagdare, S. (2017). Customer experience–a review and research agenda. *Journal of Service Theory and Practice*, *27*(3), 642–662. doi:10.1108/JSTP-03-2015-0064

Jain, R., & Bagdare, S. (2011). Music and consumption experience: A review. *International Journal of Retail & Distribution Management*, *39*(4), 289–302. doi:10.1108/09590551111117554

Jaques, T. (2013). Ensnared in a gay health controversy: A comparative study in responding to issue activism. Journal of Public Affairs, 13(1), 53–60. doi:10.1002/pa.1442

Joy, A., Wang, J. J., Orazi, D. C., Yoon, S., LaTour, K., & Peña, C. (2023). Co-creating affective atmospheres in retail experience. *Journal of Retailing*, *99*(2), 297–317. doi:10.1016/j.jretai.2023.05.002

Kamen, J. M. (1977). Controlling "just noticeable differences" in quality. *Harvard Business Review*, *55*(6), 12–164. https://ezproxy.wagner.edu/login?url=https://search.ebscohost.com/login.aspx?direct=true&db=edb&AN=3867518&site=eds-live

Kandampully, J., Bilgihan, A., & Amer, S. M. (2023). Linking servicescape and experiencescape: Creating a collective focus for the service industry. *Journal of Service Management*, *34*(2), 316–340. doi:10.1108/JOSM-08-2021-0301

Kapferer, J. N. (2012). *The New Strategic Brand Management: Creating and Sustaining Brand Equity Long Term* (5th ed.). Kogan Page.

Kaplan, N., Park, D. K., & Ridout, T. N. (2006). Dialogue in American Political Campaigns? An Examination of Issue Convergence in Candidate Television Advertising. *American Journal of Political Science, 50*(3), 724–736. doi:10.1111/j.1540-5907.2006.00212.x

Kaplan, R. L. (2013). The Economics and Politics of Nineteenth-Century Newspapers. *American Journalism, 10*(1–2), 84–101.

Kashmiri, S., Gala, P., & Nicol, C. D. (2019). Seeking pleasure or avoiding pain: Influence of CEO regulatory focus on firms' advertising, R&D, and marketing controversies. *Journal of Business Research, 105*, 227–242. doi:10.1016/j.jbusres.2019.08.022

Kastner, S. (2013). Heimatklänge: The conceptual design of branded spaces by means of sonic branding. In S. Sonnenburg & L. Baker (Eds.), *Branded Spaces: Experience Enactments and Entanglements.* doi:10.1007/978-3-658-01561-9_11

Kauppinen-Räisänen, H., Koskull, C., Gummerus, J., & Cristini, H. (2019). The new wave of luxury: The meaning and value of luxury to the contemporary consumer. *Qualitative Market Research, 22*(3), 229–249. doi:10.1108/QMR-03-2016-0025

Kauppinen-Räisänen, H., Mühlbacher, H., & Taishoff, M. (2020). Exploring the luxurious shopping experiences. *Journal of Retailing and Consumer Services, 57.* 10.1016/j.jretconser.2020.102251

Kaur, C. (2022). AR Rahman's Airtel melody that Indians 'Live Every Moment.' *Brand Equity.* Retrieved from https://brandequity.economictimes.indiatimes.com/news/advertising/ar-rahmans-airtel-melody-that-indians-live-every-moment/92910971

Keh, H. T., Wang, D., & Yan, L. (2021). Gimmicky or effective? The effects of imaginative displays on customers' purchase behavior. *Journal of Marketing, 85*(5), 109–127. doi:10.1177/0022242921997359

Kellaris, J. J. (2008). Music and consumers. Handbook of Consumer Psychology, 828-847.

Kellaris, J. J., & Altsech, M. B. (1992). The experience of time as a function of musical loudness and gender of listener. *Advances in Consumer Research. Association for Consumer Research (U. S.), 19*, 725–729.

Kellaris, J. J., & Cox, A. D. (1989). The Effects of Background Music in Advertising: A Reassessment. *The Journal of Consumer Research, 16*(1), 113–118. doi:10.1086/209199

Kellaris, J. J., Cox, A. D., & Cox, D. (1993). The effect of background music on ad processing: A contingency explanation. *Journal of Marketing, 57*(4), 114–125. doi:10.1177/002224299305700409

Kellaris, J. J., & Kent, R. J. (1991). Exploring tempo and modality effects on consumer responses to music. *Advances in Consumer Research. Association for Consumer Research (U. S.), 18*, 243–248.

Kellaris, J. J., & Kent, R. J. (1992). The influence of music on consumers' temporal perceptions: Does time fly when you're having fun. *Journal of Consumer Psychology, 1*(4), 365–376. doi:10.1016/S1057-7408(08)80060-5

Kellaris, J. J., & Rice, R. C. (1993). The influence of tempo, loudness, and gender of listener on responses to music. *Psychology and Marketing*, *10*(1), 15–29. doi:10.1002/mar.4220100103

Kemp, E., Cho, Y.-N., Bui, M., & Kintzer, A. (2023a). Music to the ears: The role of sonic branding in advertising. *International Journal of Advertising*, 1–21. Advance online publication. doi:10.1080/02650487.2023.2273645

Kemp, E., Kopp, S. W., & Bui, M. (2023b). Healthcare brands sound off: Evaluating the influence of sonic branding in shaping consumer perceptions. *International Journal of Pharmaceutical and Healthcare Marketing*, *17*(3), 340–352. doi:10.1108/IJPHM-10-2022-0093

Kent, T. (2003). 2D23D: Management and design perspectives on retail branding. *International Journal of Retail & Distribution Management*, *31*(3), 131–142. doi:10.1108/09590550310465503

Kesari, B., & Atulkar, S. (2016). Satisfaction of mall shoppers: A study on perceived utilitarian and hedonic shopping values. *Journal of Retailing and Consumer Services*, *31*(4), 22–31. doi:10.1016/j.jretconser.2016.03.005

Kew, J., & Bowker, J. (2020, September 8). Racist Advertising Controversy Hits South Africa's Biggest Pharmacy Chain. Bloomberg.Com; Bloomberg, L.P. https://ezproxy.wagner.edu/login?url=https://search.ebscohost.com/login.aspx?direct=true&db=buh&AN=145626797&site=ehost-live&scope=site

Khamis, S., & Keogh, B. (2021). Sonic branding and the aesthetic infrastructure of everyday consumption. *Popular Music*, *40*(2), 281–296. doi:10.1017/S0261143021000118

Kharat, M. G. M. G., Jha, M. K., Chikhalkar, R. D., & Kharat, M. G. M. G. (2018). Brand experience: Development of the conceptual framework and critical research propositions. *International Journal of Management Concepts and Philosophy*, *11*(3), 340. doi:10.1504/IJMCP.2018.093495

Kilian, K. (2009). From brand identity to audio branding. In H. Bronner & H. Rainer (Eds.), *Audio Branding: Brands, Sound and Communication* (pp. 35–48). Nomos. doi:10.5771/9783845216935-36

Kim, J. H., Ritchie, J. R. B., & McCormick, B. (2012). Development of a scale to measure memorable tourism experiences. *Journal of Travel Research*, *51*(1), 12–25. doi:10.1177/0047287510385467

Kim, M., Kim, J.-H., Park, M., & Yoo, J. (2021). The roles of sensory perceptions and mental imagery in consumer decision-making. *Journal of Retailing and Consumer Services*, *61*, 102517. doi:10.1016/j.jretconser.2021.102517

Klein, K., Melnyk, V., & Voelckner, F. (2021). Effects of background music on evaluations of visual images. *Psychology and Marketing*, *38*(12), 2240–2246. doi:10.1002/mar.21588

Klingmann, A. (2010). *Brandscapes: Architecture in the experience economy*. Mit Press.

Knakkergaard, M. (2014). The Music That's Not There. In *M. Grimshaw-Aagaard, The Oxford Handbook of Virtuality* (pp. 392–404). Oxford University Press.

Konecni, V. J. (2008). Does music induce emotion? A theoretical and methodological analysis. *Psychology of Aesthetics, Creativity, and the Arts*, *2*(2), 115–129. doi:10.1037/1931-3896.2.2.115

Kontukoski, M., Luomala, H., Mesz, B., Sigman, M., Trevisan, M., Rotola-Pukkila, M., & Hopia, A. I. (2015). Sweet and sour: Music and taste associations. *Nutrition & Food Science*, *45*(3), 357–376. doi:10.1108/NFS-01-2015-0005

Korsmeyer, C., & Sutton, D. (2011). The sensory experience of food. *Food, Culture, & Society*, *14*(4), 461–475. doi:10.2752/175174411X13046092851316

Kotler, P. (1973). Atmospherics as a marketing tool. *Journal of Retailing*, *49*(4), 48–64.

Kotler, P., & Keller, K. (2006). *Marketing administration* (12th ed.). Pearson.

Krishna, A. (2012). An integrative review of sensory marketing: Engaging the senses to affect perception, judgment and behavior. *Journal of Consumer Psychology*, *22*(3), 332–351. doi:10.1016/j.jcps.2011.08.003

Krishna, A. (2013). *Customer Sense: How the 5 Senses Influence Buying Behavior*. Palgrave Macmillan. doi:10.1057/9781137346056

Krishna, A., Cian, L., & Sokolova, T. (2016). The power of sensory marketing in advertising. *Current Opinion in Psychology*, *10*, 142–147. doi:10.1016/j.copsyc.2016.01.007

Krishna, A., & Schwarz, N. (2014). Sensory marketing, embodiment, and grounded cognition: A review and introduction. *Journal of Consumer Psychology*, *24*(2), 159–168. doi:10.1016/j.jcps.2013.12.006

Kujur, F., & Singh, S. (2020). Visual communication and consumer-brand relationship on social networking sites-uses & gratifications theory perspective. *Journal of Theoretical and Applied Electronic Commerce Research*, *15*(1), 30–47. doi:10.4067/S0718-18762020000100104

Kumar, A., & Kim, Y. K. (2014). The store-as-a-brand strategy: The effect of store environment on customer responses. *Journal of Retailing and Consumer Services*, *21*(5), 685–695. doi:10.1016/j.jretconser.2014.04.008

Kumar, V., Petersen, J. A., & Leone, R. P. (2010). Driving profitability by encouraging customer referrals: Who, when, and how. *Journal of Marketing*, *74*(5), 1–17. doi:10.1509/jmkg.74.5.001

Lageat, T., Czellar, S., & Laurent, G. (2003). Engineering hedonic attributes to generate perceptions of luxury: Consumer perception of an everyday sound. *Marketing Letters*, *14*(2), 97–109. doi:10.1023/A:1025462901401

Laitala, K., & Klepp, I. G. (2016). Musical shopping lists: Effects of songs with prosocial lyrics on shopping behavior. *Journal of Environmental Psychology*, *46*, 24–30.

Lantos, G. P., & Craton, L. G. (2012). A model of consumer response to advertising music. *Journal of Consumer Marketing*, *29*(1), 22–42. doi:10.1108/07363761211193028

Larsen, G., Lawson, R., & Todd, S. (2010). The symbolic consumption of music. *Journal of Marketing Management*, *26*(7-8), 7–8, 671–685. doi:10.1080/0267257X.2010.481865

Lee, C. (2019). *Co-creating the brand modelling the perceived authenticity in a branded environment through co-creation* (Order No. 27737542). Available from ProQuest Dissertations & Theses Global. (2382062162). Retrieved from https://www.proquest.com/dissertations-theses/co-creating-brand-modelling-perceived/docview/2382062162/se-2

Lee, H.-K., & Ahn, S. (2014, February 28). A Study on the Characteristics of Branded Environments in Hotel Spaces. Korean Institute of Interior Design Journal. Korean Institute of Interior Design. . doi:10.14774/JKIID.2014.23.1.143

Lee, A. H.-Y. (2022). Social Trust in Polarized Times: How Perceptions of Political Polarization Affect Americans' Trust in Each Other. *Political Behavior*, *44*(3), 1533–1554. doi:10.1007/s11109-022-09787-1 PMID:35340916

Lee, D. J., Sirgy, M. J., Larsen, V., & Wright, N. D. (2002). Developing a subjective measure of consumer well-being. *Journal of Macromarketing*, *22*(2), 158–169. doi:10.1177/0276146702238219

Lee, J., & Kim, H. (2022). How to survive in advertisement flooding: The effects of schema–product congruity and attribute relevance on advertisement attitude. *Journal of Consumer Behaviour*, *21*(2), 214–230. doi:10.1002/cb.1991

Lee, M., Lee, S., & Koh, Y. (2019). Multisensory experience for enhancing hotel guest experience: Empirical evidence from big data analytics. *International Journal of Contemporary Hospitality Management*, *31*(11), 4313–4337. doi:10.1108/IJCHM-03-2018-0263

Lefebvre, H. (1991). The production of space. D. Nicholson-Smith, Trans. Blackwell.

Lemon, K. N., & Verhoef, P. C. (2016). Understanding customer experience throughout the customer journey. *Journal of Marketing*, *80*(6), 69–96. doi:10.1509/jm.15.0420

Les Mills Global Instructor team. (2019) *Sooooo… What do you really think about the lyrics?* Article on company website] Published July 8th, 2019. Fetched 25.10.2023. Available at https://www.lesmills.com/us/instructors/instructor-news/lyric-debate/

Levin, A. (2021). Say Goodbye to the Traditional TV Upfronts: Media buying plans should start mirroring video viewing habits. *Broadcasting & Cable - Multichannel News, 151*(5), 41–41.

Lim, H. S., Moon, W.-K., & Ciszek, E. (2023). Advertising for Brands and Society: The Role of Perceived Authenticity in Corporate Transgender Advocacy Advertising Campaigns. *Journal of Homosexuality*, 1–29. doi:10.1080/00918369.2023.2245522 PMID:37555702

Lindstrom, M. (1999). *Brand Sense: Sensory Secrets Behind the Stuff We Buy*. Simon & Schuster.

Lindstrom, M. (2005). Brandsense: Sensorial secrets behind the things we buy. *The Bookman*.

Lindstrom, M. (2005). Broad sensory branding. *Journal of Product and Brand Management*, *14*(2), 84–87. doi:10.1108/10610420510592554

Line, N. D., & Hanks, L. (2020). A holistic model of the servicescape in fast casual dining. *International Journal of Contemporary Hospitality Management*, *32*(1), 288–306. doi:10.1108/IJCHM-04-2019-0360

Lisjak, M., & Ordabayeva, N. (2023). How Political Ideology Shapes Preferences for Observably Inferior Products. *Journal of Consumer Research*, *49*(6), 1014–1031. doi:10.1093/jcr/ucac030

Liu, X., Burns, A. C., & Hou, Y. (2013). Comparing online and in-store shopping behavior towards luxury goods. *International Journal of Retail & Distribution Management*, *41*(11/12), 885–900. doi:10.1108/IJRDM-01-2013-0018

Loureiro, S. M. C., Guerreiro, J., & Japutra, A. (2021). How escapism leads to behavioral intention in a virtual reality store with background music? *Journal of Business Research*, *134*, 288–300. doi:10.1016/j.jbusres.2021.05.035

Lucarelli, A., Cassigner, C., & Östberg, J. (2022). Reassessing brand co-creation: towards a critical performativity approach. In S. Markovic, R. Gyrd-Jones, S. von Wallpach, & A. Lindgreen (Eds.), *Research handbook on brand co-creation, Theory, practice, and ethical implications*. Edward Elgar Publishing. doi:10.4337/9781839105425.00012

Lucas, M. R., Ayres, S., Santos, N., & Dionisio, A. (2021). Consumer experiences and values in Brazilian Northeast shopping centers. *Innovative Marketing*, *17*(3), 1–16. doi:10.21511/im.17(3).2021.01

MacInnis, D. J., & Price, L. L. (1987). The role of imagery in information processing: Review and extensions. *The Journal of Consumer Research*, *13*(4), 473–491. doi:10.1086/209082

MacKenzie, S. B., Lutz, R. J., & Belch, G. E. (1986). The Role of Attitude Toward the Ad as a Mediator of Advertising Effectiveness: A Test of Competing Explanations. *Journal of Marketing Research*, *23*(2), 130–143. doi:10.1177/002224378602300205

Madden, R. (2010). *Being ethnographic, A Guide to the Theory and Practice of Ethnography*. Sage Publsihing.

Magaudda, P. (2011). When materiality 'bites back': Digital music consumption practices in the age of dematerialization. *Journal of Consumer Culture*, *11*(1), 15–36. doi:10.1177/1469540510390499

Mangrum, B. (2021). Market Segmentation and Shirley Jackson's Domestic Humor. *American Literary History*, *33*(1), 50–74. doi:10.1093/alh/ajab001

Marques, S. H., Trindade, G., & Santos, M. (2016). The importance of atmospherics in the choice of hypermarkets and supermarkets. *International Review of Retail, Distribution and Consumer Research*, *26*(1), 17–34. doi:10.1080/09593969.2015.1042495

Mas, L., Collell, M. R., & Xifra, J. (2017). The sound of music or the history of Trump and Clinton family singers: Music branding as a communication strategy in 2016 presidential campaign. *The American Behavioral Scientist*, *61*(6), 584–599. doi:10.1177/0002764217701214

Matos, C. (2023). *Perception and effectiveness of sound and music brand expressions: the neurological bias of sound branding and music branding practices.* Social Communication Faculty, University of the State of Rio de Janeiro.

McCleskey, J. A. (2021). The Inconvenient Truth about Sex Appeal in Advertising. *IABS Journal*, *1*(5), 43–67.

McCusker, G. (1997). The audio logo: A case study of Radio Scotland's on-air identity. *Journal of Communication Management (London)*, *1*(4), 362–373. doi:10.1108/eb023439

Melzner, J., & Raghubir, P. (2023). The sound of music: The effect of timbral sound quality in audio logos on brand personality perception. *JMR, Journal of Marketing Research*, *60*(5), 932–949. doi:10.1177/00222437221135188

Merikle, P. M. (1988). Subliminal Auditory Messages: An Evaluation. *Psychology and Marketing*, *5*(4), 355–372. doi:10.1002/mar.4220050406

Merrilees, B., Miller, D., & Shao, W. (2016). Mall brand meaning: An experiential branding perspective. *Journal of Product and Brand Management*, *25*(3), 262–273. doi:10.1108/JPBM-05-2015-0889

Merz, M. A., He, Y., & Vargo, S. L. (2009). The evolving brand logic: A service-dominant logic perspective. *Journal of the Academy of Marketing Science*, *37*(3), 328–344. doi:10.1007/s11747-009-0143-3

Meyer, C., & Schwager, A. (2007). Understanding customer experience. *Harvard Business Review*, *85*(2), 116. PMID:17345685

Michel, A., Baumann, C., & Gayer, L. (2017). Thank you for the music–or not? The effects of in-store music in service settings. *Journal of Retailing and Consumer Services*, *36*, 21–32. doi:10.1016/j.jretconser.2016.12.008

Michon, R., Chebat, J.-C., & Turley, L. W. (2005). Mall atmospherics: The interaction effects of the mall environment on shopping behavior. *Journal of Business Research*, *58*(5), 576–583. doi:10.1016/j.jbusres.2003.07.004

Milliman, R. E. (1982). Using background music to affect the behavior of supermarket shoppers. *Journal of Marketing*, *46*(3), 86–91. doi:10.1177/002224298204600313

Milliman, R. E. (1986). The influence of background music on the behavior of restaurant patrons. *The Journal of Consumer Research*, *13*(2), 286–289. doi:10.1086/209068

Milliman, R. E., & Fugate, D. L. (1993). Atmospherics as an emerging influence in the design of exchange environments. *Journal of Marketing Management*, *3*(1), 66–74.

Minsky, L., & Fahey, C. (2017). *Audio Branding: Using Sound to Build Your Brand.* Kogan Page.

Mohammad Shafiee, M., & Es-Haghi, S. M. S. (2017). Mall image, shopping well-being and mall loyalty. *International Journal of Retail & Distribution Management*, *45*(10), 1114–1134. doi:10.1108/IJRDM-10-2016-0193

Moreira, A. C., Fortes, N., & Santiago, R. (2017a). Influence of sensory stimuli on brand experience, brand equity and purchase intention. *Journal of Business Economics and Management*, *18*(1), 68–83. doi:10.3846/16111699.2016.1252793

Moreno-Lobato, A., Di-Clemente, E., Hernández-Mogollón, J. M., & Campón-Cerro, A. M. (2023). How emotions sound. A literature review of music as an emotional tool in tourism marketing. *Tourism Management Perspectives*, *48*, 101154. doi:10.1016/j.tmp.2023.101154

Morin, S., Dubé, L., & Chebat, J. C. (2007). The role of pleasant music in servicescapes: A test of the dual model of environmental perception. *Journal of Retailing*, *83*(1), 115–130. doi:10.1016/j.jretai.2006.10.006

Morrin, M., & Ratneshwar, S. (2003). Does it make sense to use scents to enhance brand memory? *JMR, Journal of Marketing Research*, *40*(1), 10–25. doi:10.1509/jmkr.40.1.10.19128

Morris, J. D., & Boone, M. A. (1998). *The effects of music on emotional response, brand attitude, and purchase intent in an emotional advertising condition.* ACR North American Advances.

Mosley, R. W. (2007). Customer experience, organisational culture and the employer brand. *Journal of Brand Management*, *15*(2), 123–134. doi:10.1057/palgrave.bm.2550124

Mossberg, L. (2007). A Marketing Approach to the Tourist Experience. *Scandinavian Journal of Hospitality and Tourism*, *7*(1), 59–74. doi:10.1080/15022250701231915

Muhonen, T., Hirvonen, S., & Laukkanen, T. (2017). SME brand identity: Its components and performance effects. *Journal of Product and Brand Management*, *26*(1), 52–67. doi:10.1108/JPBM-01-2016-1083

Mulhern, F. (2009). Integrated marketing communications: From media channels to digital connectivity. *Journal of Marketing Communications*, *15*(2/3), 85–101. doi:10.1080/13527260902757506

Murray, N. M., & Murray, S. B. (1996). Music and Lyrics in Commercials: A Cross-Cultural Comparison between Commercials Run in the Dominican Republic and in the United States. *Journal of Advertising*, *25*(2), 51–63. doi:10.1080/00913367.1996.10673499

Ng, C. F. (2003). Satisfying shoppers' psychological needs: From public market to cyber-mall. *Journal of Environmental Psychology*, *23*(4), 439–455. doi:10.1016/S0272-4944(02)00102-0

Nguyen, T., Quach, S., & Thaichon, P. (2022). The effect of AI quality on customer experience and brand relationship. *Journal of Consumer Behaviour*, *21*(3), 481–493. doi:10.1002/cb.1974

Nomura, T., & Mitsukura, Y. (2015). EEG-based detection of TV commercials effects. *Procedia Computer Science*, *60*, 131–140. doi:10.1016/j.procs.2015.08.112

Norrgrann, A., & Saraniemi, S. (2022). Dealing with discrepancies of a brand in change: recomposition of value and meanings in the network. In S. Markovic, R. Gyrd-Jones, S. von Wallpach, & A. Lindgreen (Eds.), *Research handbook on brand co-creation, Theory, practice, and ethical implications*. Edward Elgar Publishing. doi:10.4337/9781839105425.00016

North, A. C. (2012). The effect of background music on the taste of wine. *British Journal of Psychology*, *103*(3), 293–301. doi:10.1111/j.2044-8295.2011.02072.x PMID:22804697

North, A. C., & Hargreaves, D. J. (1996). Situational influences on reported musical preference. *Psychomusicology: Music, Mind, and Brain*, *15*(1-2), 30–45. doi:10.1037/h0094081

North, A. C., & Hargreaves, D. J. (1998). The effect of music on atmosphere and purchase intentions in a cafeteria 1. *Journal of Applied Social Psychology*, *28*(24), 2254–2273. doi:10.1111/j.1559-1816.1998.tb01370.x

North, A. C., Hargreaves, D. J., & McKendrick, J. (1999). Instore music affects product choice. *Nature*, *400*(6740), 269.

North, A. C., Hargreaves, D. J., & McKendrick, J. (1999). The influence of in-store music on wine selections. *The Journal of Applied Psychology*, *84*(2), 271–276. doi:10.1037/0021-9010.84.2.271

North, A. C., Hargreaves, D. J., & McKendrick, J. (2000). The Effects of Music on Atmosphere in a Bank and a Bar 1. *Journal of Applied Social Psychology*, *30*(7), 1504–1522. doi:10.1111/j.1559-1816.2000.tb02533.x

North, A. C., Sherdian, L. P., & Areni, C. S. (2016). Music congruity effects on product memory, perc and choice. *Journal of Retailing*, *92*(1), 83–95. doi:10.1016/j.jretai.2015.06.001

Nufer, G., & Moser, H. (2018). The sound of brands. *Reutlingen Working Papers on Marketing & Management, 2019*(1). doi:10.15496/publikation-26654

Oakes, S. (2000). The influence of the musicscape within service environments. *Journal of Services Marketing*, *14*(7), 539–556. doi:10.1108/08876040010352673

Oakes, S., & North, A. C. (2008). Using music to influence cognitive and affective response in queues of low and high crowd density. *Journal of Marketing Management*, *24*(5-6), 589–602. doi:10.1362/026725708X326002

Obici, G. (2008). Condition of listening: Media and sound territories. *Letras*.

Octaviani, R., Rizkiyani, D., Sudarsono, A. S., & Sarwono, S. J. (2021, August). Soundscape evaluation to identify audio visual aspects in café for student's activities. In *INTER-NOISE and NOISE-CON Congress and Conference Proceedings* (Vol. 263, No. 3, pp. 3845-3853). Institute of Noise Control Engineering. 10.3397/IN-2021-2539

Ozcevik, A., & Yuksel Can, Z. (2008). A study on the adaptation of soundscape to covered spaces: Part 2. *The Journal of the Acoustical Society of America*, *123*(5), 3812. doi:10.1121/1.2935537

Pachet, F., & Cazaly, D. (2000, April). A taxonomy of musical genres. In RIAO (pp. 1238-1245).

Pandey, S., & Hallur, G. G. (2023). Study of the competition in the Indian telecom industry: 20 years with Airtel as the case company. AIP Conf. Proc., p., 2523, 030018.

Parise, S., Guinan, P. J., & Kafka, R. (2016). Solving the crisis of immediacy: How digital technology can transform the customer experience. *Business Horizons*, *59*(4), 411–420. doi:10.1016/j.bushor.2016.03.004

Park, C. W., & Young, S. M. (1986). Consumer response to television commercials: The impact of involvement and background music on brand attitude formation. *JMR, Journal of Marketing Research*, *23*(1), 11–24. doi:10.1177/002224378602300102

Park, C., & Kim, Y. (2003). A framework of dynamic CRM: Linking marketing with information strategy. *Business Process Management Journal*, *9*(5), 652–671. doi:10.1108/14637150310496749

Parkes, D. N., & Thrift, N. J. (1980). *Time, Spaces, and Places: A Chronographic Perspective*. John Wiley & Sons.

Peck, J., & Childers, T. L. (2003). Individual differences in haptic information processing: The "need for touch" scale. *The Journal of Consumer Research*, *30*(3), 430–442. doi:10.1086/378619

Peck, J., & Wiggins, J. (2006). It just feels good: Customers' affective response to touch and its influence on persuasion. *Journal of Marketing*, *70*(4), 56–69.

Perlovsky, L. (2010). Musical emotions: Functions, origins, evolution. *Physics of Life Reviews*, *7*(1), 2–27. doi:10.1016/j.plrev.2009.11.001 PMID:20374916

Peterson, R. A. (1997). *Creating Country Music: Fabricating Authenticity* (1st ed.). University Of Chicago Press. doi:10.7208/chicago/9780226111445.001.0001

Pine, J., & Gilmore, J. (1999). *The Experience Economy*. Harvard Business School Press.

Pine, J., & Gilmore, J. (1999). *The spectacle of business: the experience economy*. Campus.

Polfuß, J. (2022). Hip-hop: A marketplace icon. *Consumption Markets & Culture*, *25*(3), 272–286. doi:10.1080/10253866.2021.1990050

Poushneh, A. (2021). Impact of auditory sense on trust and brand affect through auditory social interaction and control. *Journal of Retailing and Consumer Services*, *58*, 102281. doi:10.1016/j.jretconser.2020.102281

Prahalad, C. K., & Ramaswamy, V. (2004). Co-creation experiences: The next practice in value creation. *Journal of Interactive Marketing*, *18*(3), 5–14. doi:10.1002/dir.20015

Pridmore and Lyon. (2011). Marketing as Surveillance: Assembling Consumers as Brands. In *Zwick and J. Cayla, Inside Marketing: Practices, ideologies, devices* (500th ed., pp. 115–136). Oxford University Press.

Priya, P. (2016). Case Study: The study on consumer satisfaction of services provided by Airtel Telecommunication. *Advances in Management*, *9*(10), 5–11.

Puccinelli, N. M., Goodstein, R. C., Grewal, D., Price, R., Raghubir, P., & Stewart, D. (2009). Customer experience management in retailing: Understanding the buying process. *Journal of Retailing*, *85*(1), 15–30. doi:10.1016/j.jretai.2008.11.003

Puligadda, S., & VanBergen, N. (2023). The influence of sound logo instruments on brand personality perceptions: An investigation of brand ruggedness and sophistication. *Journal of Business Research*, *156*, 113531. doi:10.1016/j.jbusres.2022.113531

Puyana Romero, V., Maffei, L., Brambilla, G., & Ciaburro, G. (2016). Acoustic, visual and spatial indicators for the description of the soundscape of waterfront areas with and without road traffic flow. *International Journal of Environmental Research and Public Health*, *13*(9), 934. doi:10.3390/ijerph13090934 PMID:27657105

Puyana-Romero, V. P., Maffei, L., Brambilla, G., & Ciaburro, G. (2016). Modelling the soundscape quality of urban waterfronts by artificial neural networks. *Applied Acoustics*, *111*, 121–128. doi:10.1016/j.apacoust.2016.04.019

Puyana-Romero, V., Ciaburro, G., Brambilla, G., Garzón, C., & Maffei, L. (2019). Representation of the soundscape quality in urban areas through colours. *Noise Mapping*, *6*(1), 8–21. doi:10.1515/noise-2019-0002

Ramsøy, T. Z., & Skov, M. (2014). Brand preference affects the threshold for perceptual awareness. *Journal of Consumer Behaviour*, *13*(1), 1–8. doi:10.1002/cb.1451

Ramswell, P. Q. (2018). *Division, Derision and Decisions: The Domino Effect of Brexit and Populism's Intersection of Rights and Wrongs*. Nova Science Publishers, Inc. https://ezproxy.wagner.edu/login?url=https://search.ebscohost.com/login.aspx?direct=true&db=nlebk&AN=1724465&site=eds-live

Reed, I. I. A. II, & Forehand, M. R. (2016). The ebb and flow of consumer identities: The role of memory, emotions and threats. *Current Opinion in Psychology*, *10*, 94–100. doi:10.1016/j.copsyc.2015.12.015

Reinoso-Carvalho, F., Gunn, L., Molina, G., Narumi, T., Spence, C., Suzuki, Y., ter Horst, E., & Wagemans, J. (2020). A sprinkle of emotions vs a pinch of crossmodality: Towards globally meaningful sonic seasoning strategies for enhanced multisensory tasting experiences. *Journal of Business Research*, *117*, 389–399. doi:10.1016/j.jbusres.2020.04.055

Rentfrow, P. J., & Gosling, S. D. (2003). The do re mi's of everyday life: The structure and personality correlates of music preferences. *Journal of Personality and Social Psychology*, *84*(6), 12–36. doi:10.1037/0022-3514.84.6.1236 PMID:12793587

Rodero, E., Larrea, O., & Vazquez, M. (2013). Male and female voices in commercials. Analysis of effectiveness, adequacy for product, attention, and recall. *Sex Roles*, *68*(5/6), 349–362. doi:10.1007/s11199-012-0247-y

Rodrigues, C., Rodrigues, P., Billore, S., & Tetsuhisa, O. (2018). The role of brand experience and authenticity in creating brand love: A cross-cultural comparative study. *Global Marketing Conference, Tokyo, pp.,* 1447-1447. 10.15444/GMC2018.12.03.03

Rogers, S. (1992). How a Publicity Blitz Created The Myth of Subliminal Advertising. *Public Relations Quarterly, 37*(4), 12–17.

Roggeveen, A. L., Grewal, D., & Schweiger, E. B. (2020). The DAST framework for retail atmospherics: The impact of in-and out-of-store retail journey touchpoints on the customer experience. *Journal of Retailing, 96*(1), 128–137. doi:10.1016/j.jretai.2019.11.002

Roschk, H., Loureiro, S. M. C., & Breitsohl, J. (2017). Calibrating 30 years of experimental research: A meta-analysis of the atmospheric effects of music, scent, and colour. *Journal of Retailing, 93*(2), 228–240. doi:10.1016/j.jretai.2016.10.001

Rosenbaum, M. S., & Massiah, C. (2011). An expanded servicescape perspective. *Journal of Service Management, 22*(4), 471–490. doi:10.1108/09564231111155088

Rose, T. (1991). "Fear of a Black Planet": Rap Music and Black Cultural Politics in the 1990s. *The Journal of Negro Education, 60*(3), 276–290. doi:10.2307/2295482

Roy, S., & Singh, P. (2023). The olfactory experience (in retail) scale: Construction, validation and generalization. *Journal of Service Management, 34*(3), 403–432. doi:10.1108/JOSM-05-2021-0173

Sá, S. (2010). The soundtrack of a silent story: sound, music, audibilities and technologies from the perspective of Sound Studies. In Sá, S. (org.) Towards Music Culture – Business, Aesthetics, Languages and Audibility. Sulina.

Sadeghian, M., Hanzaee, K. H., Mansourian, Y., & Khonsiavash, M. (2020). Investigation the effective factors on malls patronage: A qualitative research approach. *Revista Conrado, 16*(72), 204–209.

Saqib, N. (2021). Positioning – a literature review. *PSU Research Review, 5*(2), 141–169. doi:10.1108/PRR-06-2019-0016

Saqib, N., & Satar, M. S. (2023). Development of empirically based customer-derived positioning taxonomy for consumer electronics sector in the Indian emerging market. *International Journal of Emerging Markets, 18*(10), 3868–3892. doi:10.1108/IJOEM-12-2020-1568

Saqib, N., & Shah, A. M. (2022). Development of empirically-based customer-derived positioning taxonomy for FMCG sector in the Indian emerging market. *Young Consumers, 23*(2), 233–254. doi:10.1108/YC-11-2020-1257

Schafer, R. Murray (1977). The soundscape: our sonic environment and the tuning of the world. [United States]: Distributed to the book trade in the United States by American International Distribution.

Schafer, M. (1993). *The soundscape: our sonic environment and the tuning of the world.* Destiny Books.

Compilation of References

Schafer, R. (2001). *Tuning the world*. Unesp.

Schafer, R. M. (1993). *The soundscape: Our sonic environment and the tuning of the world*. Simon and Schuster.

Schatzki, T., Knorr-Cetina, K., & von Savigny, E. (Eds.). (2001). *The Practice Turn in Contemporary Theory*. Routledge.

Schenck-Hamlin, W. J., Procter, D. E., & Rumsey, D. J. (2000). The influence of Negative Advertising Frames on Political Cynicism and Politician Accountability. *Human Communication Research*, *26*(1), 53–74. doi:10.1111/j.1468-2958.2000.tb00749.x

Schlosser, A. E. (2003). Experiencing products in the virtual world: The role of goal and imagery in influencing attitudes versus purchase intentions. *The Journal of Consumer Research*, *30*(2), 184–198. doi:10.1086/376807

Schmitt, B. (1999). Experiential Marketing. *Journal of Marketing Management*, *15*(1–3), 53–67. doi:10.1362/026725799784870496

Schmitt, B., Brakus, J. J., & Biraglia, A. (2022). Consumption Ideology. *The Journal of Consumer Research*, *49*(1), 74–95. doi:10.1093/jcr/ucab044

Schwartz, B. L., & Krantz, J. H. (2017). *Sensation and perception*. Sage Publications.

Scott, L. M. (1990). Understanding Jingles and Needledrop: A Rhetorical Approach to Music in Advertising. *The Journal of Consumer Research*, *17*(2), 223–236. doi:10.1086/208552

Scott, S. P., Sheinin, D., & Labrecque, L. I. (2022). Small sounds, significant impact: Sonic logos and their effect on consumer attitudes, emotions, brands, and advertising placement. *Journal of Product and Brand Management*, *31*(7), 1091–1103. doi:10.1108/JPBM-06-2021-3507

Seo, Y., & Maffioli, F. (2016). The impact of background music on adult consumers' shopping behavior: A meta-analysis. *Service Industries Journal*, *36*(1-2), 65–87.

Shahid, S., Paul, J., Gilal, F. G., & Ansari, S. (2022). The role of sensory marketing and brand experience in building emotional attachment and brand loyalty in luxury retail stores. *Psychology and Marketing*, *39*(7), 1398–1412. doi:10.1002/mar.21661

Sharma, R., & Shah, G. (2007, November 25). The sound of music. *Livemint*. Retrieved from https://www.livemint.com/Consumer/IBkeN02j4lzXfCMt5scSnO/The-sound-of-music.html

Shastri, A. (2023). Airtel: Case Study on its Business Model and Marketing Strategy. Retrieved from https://iide.co/blog/airtel-marketing-strategy/

Simmel, G. (1972). *On individuality and social forms*. University of Chicago Press.

Singh, H., & Prashar, S. (2014). Anatomy of shopping experience for malls in Mumbai: A confirmatory factor analysis approach. *Journal of Retailing and Consumer Services*, *21*(2), 220–228. doi:10.1016/j.jretconser.2013.08.002

Smaldino, P. E. (2019). Social identity and cooperation in cultural evolution. *Behavioural Processes*, *161*, 108–116. doi:10.1016/j.beproc.2017.11.015 PMID:29223462

Smaldino, P. E., Flamson, T. J., & McElreath, R. (2018). The Evolution of Covert Signaling. *Scientific Reports*, *8*(1), 4905. doi:10.1038/s41598-018-22926-1 PMID:29559650

Smith, P. C., & Curnow, R. (1966). Arousal hypothesis and the effects of music on purchasing behavior. *The Journal of Applied Psychology*, *50*(3), 255–256. doi:10.1037/h0023326 PMID:5936035

Smith, P. J., & Curnow, R. (1966). Effects of background music on concentration of workers. *The Journal of Applied Psychology*, *50*(6), 493–496. PMID:5978043

Southworth, M. (2011). Sonic environment and spatial behavior. In *The Sonic Environment of Cities* (pp. 147–158). Routledge.

Spence, C. (2011, April). Sound design: Using brain science to enhance auditory & multisensory product & brand development. In (((ABA))) [Nomos Verlagsgesellschaft mbH & Co. KG.]. *Audio Branding Academy Yearbook, 2010/2011*, 33–51.

Spence, C. (2012). Managing sensory expectations concerning products and brands: Capitalizing on the potential of sound and shape symbolism. *Journal of Consumer Psychology*, *22*(1), 37–54. doi:10.1016/j.jcps.2011.09.004

Spence, C., Puccinelli, N. M., Grewal, D., & Roggeveen, A. L. (2014). Store atmospherics: A multisensory perspective. *Psychology and Marketing*, *31*(7), 472–488. doi:10.1002/mar.20709

Spence, C., & Shankar, M. U. (2010). The influence of auditory cues on the perception of, and responses to, food and drink. *Journal of Sensory Studies*, *25*(3), 406–430. doi:10.1111/j.1745-459X.2009.00267.x

Spence, C., Wang, Q. J., Reinoso-Carvalho, F., & Keller, S. (2021). Commercializing sonic seasoning in multisensory offline experiential events and online tasting experiences. *Frontiers in Psychology*, *12*, 740354. doi:10.3389/fpsyg.2021.740354 PMID:34659056

Stammerjohan, C., Wood, C. M., Chang, Y., & Thorson, E. (2005). An Empirical Investigation of the Interaction between Publicity, Advertising, and Previous Brand Attitudes and Knowledge. *Journal of Advertising*, *34*(4), 55–67. doi:10.1080/00913367.2005.10639209

Stead, S., Wetzels, R., Wetzels, M., Odekerken-Schröder, G., & Mahr, D. (2022). Toward multisensory customer experiences: A cross-disciplinary bibliometric review and future research directions. *Journal of Service Research*, *25*(3), 440–459. doi:10.1177/10946705221079941

Stein, B. E., & Meredith, M. A. (1993). *The merging of the senses*. MIT press.

Steinberg, B. (2021, February 6). *How Bruce Springsteen Agreed To Do a Super Bowl Commercial for Jeep—Variety* [Magazine]. Variety. https://variety.com/2021/tv/news/bruce-springsteen-super-bowl-commercials-jeep-1234902575/

Steiner, P. (2014). *Sonic Branding*. Springer. doi:10.1007/978-3-8349-4015-5

Stevens, L., Maclaran, P., & Brown, S. (2019). An embodied approach to consumer experiences: The Hollister brandscape. *European Journal of Marketing*, *53*(4), 806–828. doi:10.1108/EJM-09-2017-0558

Stewart, D. W., Farmer, K. M., & Stannard, C. I. (1990). Music As a Recognition Cue in Advertising-Tracking Studies. *Journal of Advertising Research*, *30*(4), 39–48.

Stewart, K., Kammer-Kerwick, M., Auchter, A., Koh, H. E., Dunn, M. E., & Cunningham, I. (2019). Examining digital video advertising (DVA) effectiveness: The role of product category, product involvement, and device. *European Journal of Marketing*, *53*(11), 2451–2479. doi:10.1108/EJM-11-2016-0619

Strang, V. (2005). Common senses: Water, sensory experience and the generation of meaning. *Journal of Material Culture*, *10*(1), 92–120. doi:10.1177/1359183505050096

Sultan, A. J. (2018). Orchestrating service brand touchpoints and the effects on relational outcomes. *Journal of Services Marketing*, *32*(6), 777–788. doi:10.1108/JSM-12-2016-0413

Sweeney, J. C., & Wyber, F. (2002). The role of cognitions and emotions in the music-approach-avoidance behavior relationship. *Journal of Services Marketing*, *16*(1), 51–69. doi:10.1108/08876040210419415

Sweller, J. (1988). Cognitive load during problem solving: Effects on learning. *Cognitive Science*, *12*(2), 257–285. doi:10.1207/s15516709cog1202_4

Syrjälä, H., & Norrgrann, A. (Eds.). (2018). *Multifaceted Autoethnography Theoretical Advancements, Practical Considerations and Field Illustrations*. Nova Science Publishers.

Szocs, C., Kim, Y., Lim, M., Mera, C. A., & Biswas, D. (2023). The store of the future: Engaging customers through sensory elements, personalized atmospherics, and interpersonal interaction. *Journal of Retailing*, *99*(4), 605–620. doi:10.1016/j.jretai.2023.11.005

Techawachirakul, M., Pathak, A., Motoki, K., & Calvert, G. A. (2023). Sonic branding of meat- and plant-based foods: The role of timbre. *Journal of Business Research*, *165*, 114032. doi:10.1016/j.jbusres.2023.114032

Tekman, H. G., & Hortaçsu, N. (2002). Music and social identity: Stylistic identification as a response to musical style. *International Journal of Psychology*, *37*(5), 277–285. doi:10.1080/00207590244000043

Terblanche, N. S. (2018). Revisiting the supermarket in-store customer shopping experience. *Journal of Retailing and Consumer Services*, *40*(Jan), 48–59. doi:10.1016/j.jretconser.2017.09.004

Thompson, E. (2002). The soundscape of modernity. Architectural acoustics and the culture of.

Thompson, C. J., & Arsel, Z. (2004). The Starbucks brandscape and consumers'(anticorporate) experiences of glocalization. *The Journal of Consumer Research*, *31*(3), 631–642. doi:10.1086/425098

TJ Maxx TV Spot, "Get Everything You Want" Song by Demi Lovato. (n.d.). Retrieved August 9, 2023, from https://www.ispot.tv/ad/bvhf/tj-maxx-get-everything-you-want-song-by-demi-lovato

Torrente, F., Low, D., & Yoris, A. (2022). Risk perception, but also political orientation, modulate behavioral response to COVID-19: A randomized survey experiment. *Frontiers in Psychology*, *13*, 1–17. doi:10.3389/fpsyg.2022.900684 PMID:36059740

Treasure, J. (2011). Sound Business (2nd ed.). Management Books 2000Lt.

Trotta, F. (2020). *Annoying music in everyday life*. Bloomsbury Publishing USA. doi:10.5040/9781501360664

Tueanrat, Y., Papagiannidis, S., & Alamanos, E. (2021). Going on a journey: A review of the customer journey literature. *Journal of Business Research*, *125*, 336–353. doi:10.1016/j.jbusres.2020.12.028

Turley, L. W., & Milliman, R. E. (2000). Atmospheric Effects on Shopping Behavior: A Review of the Experimental Evidence. *Journal of Business Research*, *49*(2), 193–211. doi:10.1016/S0148-2963(99)00010-7

Ülkü, S., Hydock, C., & Cui, S. (2020). Making the wait worthwhile: Experiments on the effect of queueing on consumption. *Management Science*, *66*(3), 1149–1171. doi:10.1287/mnsc.2018.3277

Urde, M. (2003). Core value-based corporate brand building. *European Journal of Marketing*, *37*(7/8), 1017–1040. doi:10.1108/03090560310477645

Vallaster, S., & von Wallpach, C. (2013). An online discursive inquiry into the social dynamics of multi-stakeholder brand meaning co-creation. *Journal of Business Research*, *66*(9), 1505–1515. doi:10.1016/j.jbusres.2012.09.012

Vida, L., Obadia, C., & Kuntz, M. (2007). The effects of background music on consumer responses in a high-end supermarket. *International Review of Retail, Distribution and Consumer Research*, *17*(5), 469–482. doi:10.1080/09593960701631532

Vidler, A. (1999). *Warped Space: Art, Architechture, and Anxiety in Modern Culture*. The MIT Press.

Vijaykumar, K., Kellaris, J. J., & Aurand, T. W. (2012). Sonic logos: Can sound influence willingness to pay? *Journal of Product and Brand Management*, *21*(4), 275–284. doi:10.1108/10610421211246685

Villagra, N., Clemente-Mediavilla, J., López-Aza, C., & Sánchez-Herrera, J. (2021). When polarization hits corporations: The moderating effect of political ideology on corporate activism. *El Profesional de la Información*, *30*(6), 1–20. doi:10.3145/epi.2021.nov.02

Voght, K., & Parker, A. (2024, February 5). A Taylor Swift endorsement? It's delicate. *Washington Post*. https://www.washingtonpost.com/style/2024/02/04/taylor-swift-joe-biden-2024-endorsement-question/

Voorhees, C. M., Fombelle, P. W., Gregoire, Y., Bone, St., Gustafsson, A., Sousa, R., & Walkowiak, T. (2017). Service encounters, experiences and the customer journey: Defining the field and a call to expand our lens. *Journal of Business Research*, *79*, 269–280. doi:10.1016/j.jbusres.2017.04.014

Wargnier, P., & Dubois, D. (2010). The impact of music on consumer behaviour: A literature review and preliminary findings. *International Journal of Management Reviews*, *12*(2), 207–230.

Wazir, M. I., & Wazir, O. (2015). Effects of sonic logo on brand recognition of the advertised brand. *City University Research Journal*, *5*(2), 327–337.

Wedel, M., & Pieters, R. (2000). Eye Fixations on Advertisements and Memory for Brands: A Model and Findings. *Marketing Science*, *19*(4), 297–312. doi:10.1287/mksc.19.4.297.11794

Wiedmann, K. P., Labenz, F., Haase, J., & Hennigs, N. (2018). The power of experiential marketing: Exploring the causal relationships among multisensory marketing, brand experience, customer perceived value and brand strength. *Journal of Brand Management*, *25*(2), 101–118. doi:10.1057/s41262-017-0061-5

Wilcox, C. D. (2022). Dropkick Murphys vs. Scott Walker: Unpacking Populist Ideological Discourse in Digital Space. *Media and Communication*, *10*(4), 202–212. doi:10.17645/mac.v10i4.5747

Wilkins, L., & Christians, C. (2001). Philosophy Meets the Social Sciences: The Nature of Humanity in the Public Arena. *Journal of Mass Media Ethics*, *16*(2/3), 99–120. doi:10.1207/S15327728JMME1602&3_3

Williams, P., & Aaker, J. L. (2002). Can mixed emotions peacefully coexist? *The Journal of Consumer Research*, *28*(4), 636–649. doi:10.1086/338206

Wilson, S. (2003). The effect of music on perceived atmosphere and purchase intentions in a restaurant. *Psychology of Music*, *31*(1), 93–112. doi:10.1177/0305735603031001327

Witzling, L., & Shaw, B. R. (2019). Lifestyle segmentation and political ideology: Toward understanding beliefs and behavior about local food. *Appetite*, *132*, 106–113. doi:10.1016/j.appet.2018.10.003 PMID:30300669

Wolin, L. D. (2003). Gender Issues in Advertising—An Oversight Synthesis of Research: 1970-2002. *Journal of Advertising Research*, *43*(1), 111–129. doi:10.2501/JAR-43-1-111-130

Wörfel, P., Frentz, F., & Tautu, C. (2022). Marketing comes to its senses: A bibliometric review and integrated framework of sensory experience in marketing. *European Journal of Marketing*, *56*(3), 704–737. doi:10.1108/EJM-07-2020-0510

Wu, M.-Y., Wall, G., & Pearce, P. L. (2014). Shopping experiences: International tourists in Beijing's Silk Market. *Tourism Management*, *41*, 96–106. doi:10.1016/j.tourman.2013.09.010

Yakhlef, A., & Nordin, F. (2021). Effects of firm presence in customer-owned touch points: A self-determination perspective. *Journal of Business Research*, *130*, 473–481. doi:10.1016/j.jbusres.2019.12.044

Yalch, R. F., & Spangenberg, E. R. (1990). Effects of store music on shopping behavior. *Journal of Consumer Marketing*, *7*(2), 55–63. doi:10.1108/EUM0000000002577

Yalch, R., & Spangenberg, E. (1993). Using store music for retail zoning: A field experiment. *Advances in Consumer Research. Association for Consumer Research (U. S.)*, *20*, 632–636.

Yeoh, J. P. S., Han, M. G., & Spence, C. (2022). The impact of musical fit and sound design on consumers' perception of a luxury car ad. *Luxury*, *9*(2-3), 165–184. doi:10.1080/20511817.2022.2224496

Yeoh, J. P., & North, A. C. (2010). The effect of musical fit on consumers' memory. *Psychology of Music*, *38*(3), 368–378. doi:10.1177/0305735609360262

Yin, R. K. (1984). *Case Study Research: Design and Methods*. Sage Publications.

Yu, B., Kang, J., & Ma, H. (2016). Development of indicators for the soundscape in urban shopping streets. *Acta Acustica united with Acustica*, *102*(3), 462–473. doi:10.3813/AAA.918965

Zanna. (2015). *Sound branding: the sound life of brands*. Matrix.

Zarantonello, L., & Schmitt, B. H. (2010). Using the brand experience scale to profile consumers and predict consumer behaviour. *Journal of Brand Management*, *17*(7), 532–540. doi:10.1057/bm.2010.4

Zha, D., Foroudi, P., Jin, Z., & Melewar, T. C. (2022). Making sense of sensory brand experience: Constructing an integrative framework for future research. *International Journal of Management Reviews*, *24*(1), 130–167. doi:10.1111/ijmr.12270

Zhang, S., Guo, D., & Li, X. (2023). The rhythm of shopping: How background music placement in live streaming commerce affects consumer purchase intention. *Journal of Retailing and Consumer Services*, *75*, 103487. Advance online publication. doi:10.1016/j.jretconser.2023.103487

Zhu, R., & Meyers-Levy, J. (2005). Distinguishing Between the Meanings of Music: When Background Music Affects Product Perceptions. *Journal of Marketing Research*, *42*(3), 333–345. doi:10.1509/jmkr.2005.42.3.333

Zomerdijk, L. G., & Voss, C. A. (2010). Service design for experience-centric services. *Journal of Service Research*, *13*(1), 67–82. doi:10.1177/1094670509351960

Related References

To continue our tradition of advancing information science and technology research, we have compiled a list of recommended IGI Global readings. These references will provide additional information and guidance to further enrich your knowledge and assist you with your own research and future publications.

Abdul Razak, R., & Mansor, N. A. (2021). Instagram Influencers in Social Media-Induced Tourism: Rethinking Tourist Trust Towards Tourism Destination. In M. Dinis, L. Bonixe, S. Lamy, & Z. Breda (Eds.), *Impact of New Media in Tourism* (pp. 135-144). IGI Global. https://doi.org/10.4018/978-1-7998-7095-1.ch009

Abir, T., & Khan, M. Y. (2022). Importance of ICT Advancement and Culture of Adaptation in the Tourism and Hospitality Industry for Developing Countries. In C. Ramos, S. Quinteiro, & A. Gonçalves (Eds.), *ICT as Innovator Between Tourism and Culture* (pp. 30–41). IGI Global. https://doi.org/10.4018/978-1-7998-8165-0.ch003

Abtahi, M. S., Behboudi, L., & Hasanabad, H. M. (2017). Factors Affecting Internet Advertising Adoption in Ad Agencies. *International Journal of Innovation in the Digital Economy*, 8(4), 18–29. doi:10.4018/IJIDE.2017100102

Afenyo-Agbe, E., & Mensah, I. (2022). Principles, Benefits, and Barriers to Community-Based Tourism: Implications for Management. In I. Mensah & E. Afenyo-Agbe (Eds.), *Prospects and Challenges of Community-Based Tourism and Changing Demographics* (pp. 1–29). IGI Global. doi:10.4018/978-1-7998-7335-8.ch001

Agbo, V. M. (2022). Distributive Justice Issues in Community-Based Tourism. In I. Mensah & E. Afenyo-Agbe (Eds.), *Prospects and Challenges of Community-Based Tourism and Changing Demographics* (pp. 107–129). IGI Global. https://doi.org/10.4018/978-1-7998-7335-8.ch005

Agrawal, S. (2017). The Impact of Emerging Technologies and Social Media on Different Business(es): Marketing and Management. In O. Rishi & A. Sharma (Eds.), *Maximizing Business Performance and Efficiency Through Intelligent Systems* (pp. 37–49). Hershey, PA: IGI Global. doi:10.4018/978-1-5225-2234-8.ch002

Ahmad, A., & Johari, S. (2022). Georgetown as a Gastronomy Tourism Destination: Visitor Awareness Towards Revisit Intention of Nasi Kandar Restaurant. In M. Valeri (Ed.), *New Governance and Management in Touristic Destinations* (pp. 71–83). IGI Global. https://doi.org/10.4018/978-1-6684-3889-3.ch005

Alkhatib, G., & Bayouq, S. T. (2021). A TAM-Based Model of Technological Factors Affecting Use of E-Tourism. *International Journal of Tourism and Hospitality Management in the Digital Age*, 5(2), 50–67. https://doi.org/10.4018/IJTHMDA.20210701.oa1

Altinay Ozdemir, M. (2021). Virtual Reality (VR) and Augmented Reality (AR) Technologies for Accessibility and Marketing in the Tourism Industry. In C. Eusébio, L. Teixeira, & M. Carneiro (Eds.), *ICT Tools and Applications for Accessible Tourism* (pp. 277-301). IGI Global. https://doi.org/10.4018/978-1-7998-6428-8.ch013

Anantharaman, R. N., Rajeswari, K. S., Angusamy, A., & Kuppusamy, J. (2017). Role of Self-Efficacy and Collective Efficacy as Moderators of Occupational Stress Among Software Development Professionals. *International Journal of Human Capital and Information Technology Professionals*, 8(2), 45–58. doi:10.4018/IJHCITP.2017040103

Aninze, F., El-Gohary, H., & Hussain, J. (2018). The Role of Microfinance to Empower Women: The Case of Developing Countries. *International Journal of Customer Relationship Marketing and Management*, 9(1), 54–78. doi:10.4018/IJCRMM.2018010104

Antosova, G., Sabogal-Salamanca, M., & Krizova, E. (2021). Human Capital in Tourism: A Practical Model of Endogenous and Exogenous Territorial Tourism Planning in Bahía Solano, Colombia. In V. Costa, A. Moura, & M. Mira (Eds.), *Handbook of Research on Human Capital and People Management in the Tourism Industry* (pp. 282–302). IGI Global. https://doi.org/10.4018/978-1-7998-4318-4.ch014

Arsenijević, O. M., Orčić, D., & Kastratović, E. (2017). Development of an Optimization Tool for Intangibles in SMEs: A Case Study from Serbia with a Pilot Research in the Prestige by Milka Company. In M. Vemić (Ed.), *Optimal Management Strategies in Small and Medium Enterprises* (pp. 320–347). Hershey, PA: IGI Global. doi:10.4018/978-1-5225-1949-2.ch015

Aryanto, V. D., Wismantoro, Y., & Widyatmoko, K. (2018). Implementing Eco-Innovation by Utilizing the Internet to Enhance Firm's Marketing Performance: Study of Green Batik Small and Medium Enterprises in Indonesia. *International Journal of E-Business Research*, 14(1), 21–36. doi:10.4018/IJEBR.2018010102

Asero, V., & Billi, S. (2022). New Perspective of Networking in the DMO Model. In M. Valeri (Ed.), *New Governance and Management in Touristic Destinations* (pp. 105–118). IGI Global. https://doi.org/10.4018/978-1-6684-3889-3.ch007

Atiku, S. O., & Fields, Z. (2017). Multicultural Orientations for 21st Century Global Leadership. In N. Baporikar (Ed.), *Management Education for Global Leadership* (pp. 28–51). Hershey, PA: IGI Global. doi:10.4018/978-1-5225-1013-0.ch002

Atiku, S. O., & Fields, Z. (2018). Organisational Learning Dimensions and Talent Retention Strategies for the Service Industries. In N. Baporikar (Ed.), *Global Practices in Knowledge Management for Societal and Organizational Development* (pp. 358–381). Hershey, PA: IGI Global. doi:10.4018/978-1-5225-3009-1.ch017

Atsa'am, D. D., & Kuset Bodur, E. (2021). Pattern Mining on How Organizational Tenure Affects the Psychological Capital of Employees Within the Hospitality and Tourism Industry: Linking Employees' Organizational Tenure With PsyCap. *International Journal of Tourism and Hospitality Management in the Digital Age*, 5(2), 17–28. https://doi.org/10.4018/IJTHMDA.2021070102

Ávila, L., & Teixeira, L. (2018). The Main Concepts Behind the Dematerialization of Business Processes. In M. Khosrow-Pour, D.B.A. (Ed.), Encyclopedia of Information Science and Technology, Fourth Edition (pp. 888-898). Hershey, PA: IGI Global. https://doi.org/ doi:10.4018/978-1-5225-2255-3.ch076

Ayorekire, J., Mugizi, F., Obua, J., & Ampaire, G. (2022). Community-Based Tourism and Local People's Perceptions Towards Conservation: The Case of Queen Elizabeth Conservation Area, Uganda. In I. Mensah & E. Afenyo-Agbe (Eds.), *Prospects and Challenges of Community-Based Tourism and Changing Demographics* (pp. 56–82). IGI Global. https://doi.org/10.4018/978-1-7998-7335-8.ch003

Baleiro, R. (2022). Tourist Literature and the Architecture of Travel in Olga Tokarczuk and Patti Smith. In R. Baleiro & R. Pereira (Eds.), *Global Perspectives on Literary Tourism and Film-Induced Tourism* (pp. 202-216). IGI Global. https://doi.org/10.4018/978-1-7998-8262-6.ch011

Barat, S. (2021). Looking at the Future of Medical Tourism in Asia. *International Journal of Tourism and Hospitality Management in the Digital Age*, 5(1), 19–33. https://doi.org/10.4018/IJTHMDA.2021010102

Barbosa, C. A., Magalhães, M., & Nunes, M. R. (2021). Travel Instagramability: A Way of Choosing a Destination? In M. Dinis, L. Bonixe, S. Lamy, & Z. Breda (Eds.), *Impact of New Media in Tourism* (pp. 173-190). IGI Global. https://doi.org/10.4018/978-1-7998-7095-1.ch011

Bari, M. W., & Khan, Q. (2021). Pakistan as a Destination of Religious Tourism. In E. Alaverdov & M. Bari (Eds.), *Global Development of Religious Tourism* (pp. 1-10). IGI Global. https://doi.org/10.4018/978-1-7998-5792-1.ch001

Bartens, Y., Chunpir, H. I., Schulte, F., & Voß, S. (2017). Business/IT Alignment in Two-Sided Markets: A COBIT 5 Analysis for Media Streaming Business Models. In S. De Haes & W. Van Grembergen (Eds.), *Strategic IT Governance and Alignment in Business Settings* (pp. 82–111). Hershey, PA: IGI Global. doi:10.4018/978-1-5225-0861-8.ch004

Bashayreh, A. M. (2018). Organizational Culture and Organizational Performance. In W. Lee & F. Sabetzadeh (Eds.), *Contemporary Knowledge and Systems Science* (pp. 50–69). Hershey, PA: IGI Global. doi:10.4018/978-1-5225-5655-8.ch003

Bechthold, L., Lude, M., & Prügl, R. (2021). Crisis Favors the Prepared Firm: How Organizational Ambidexterity Relates to Perceptions of Organizational Resilience. In A. Zehrer, G. Glowka, K. Schwaiger, & V. Ranacher-Lackner (Eds.), *Resiliency Models and Addressing Future Risks for Family Firms in the Tourism Industry* (pp. 178–205). IGI Global. https://doi.org/10.4018/978-1-7998-7352-5.ch008

Bedford, D. A. (2018). Sustainable Knowledge Management Strategies: Aligning Business Capabilities and Knowledge Management Goals. In N. Baporikar (Ed.), *Global Practices in Knowledge Management for Societal and Organizational Development* (pp. 46–73). Hershey, PA: IGI Global. doi:10.4018/978-1-5225-3009-1.ch003

Bekjanov, D., & Matyusupov, B. (2021). Influence of Innovative Processes in the Competitiveness of Tourist Destination. In J. Soares (Ed.), *Innovation and Entrepreneurial Opportunities in Community Tourism* (pp. 243–263). IGI Global. https://doi.org/10.4018/978-1-7998-4855-4.ch014

Bharwani, S., & Musunuri, D. (2018). Reflection as a Process From Theory to Practice. In M. Khosrow-Pour, D.B.A. (Ed.), Encyclopedia of Information Science and Technology, Fourth Edition (pp. 1529-1539). Hershey, PA: IGI Global. doi:10.4018/978-1-5225-2255-3.ch132

Bhatt, G. D., Wang, Z., & Rodger, J. A. (2017). Information Systems Capabilities and Their Effects on Competitive Advantages: A Study of Chinese Companies. *Information Resources Management Journal*, *30*(3), 41–57. doi:10.4018/IRMJ.2017070103

Bhushan, M., & Yadav, A. (2017). Concept of Cloud Computing in ESB. In R. Bhadoria, N. Chaudhari, G. Tomar, & S. Singh (Eds.), *Exploring Enterprise Service Bus in the Service-Oriented Architecture Paradigm* (pp. 116–127). Hershey, PA: IGI Global. doi:10.4018/978-1-5225-2157-0.ch008

Bhushan, S. (2017). System Dynamics Base-Model of Humanitarian Supply Chain (HSCM) in Disaster Prone Eco-Communities of India: A Discussion on Simulation and Scenario Results. *International Journal of System Dynamics Applications*, 6(3), 20–37. doi:10.4018/IJSDA.2017070102

Binder, D., & Miller, J. W. (2021). A Generations' Perspective on Employer Branding in Tourism. In V. Costa, A. Moura, & M. Mira (Eds.), *Handbook of Research on Human Capital and People Management in the Tourism Industry* (pp. 152–174). IGI Global. https://doi.org/10.4018/978-1-7998-4318-4.ch008

Birch Freeman, A. A., Mensah, I., & Antwi, K. B. (2022). Smiling vs. Frowning Faces: Community Participation for Sustainable Tourism in Ghanaian Communities. In I. Mensah & E. Afenyo-Agbe (Eds.), *Prospects and Challenges of Community-Based Tourism and Changing Demographics* (pp. 83–106). IGI Global. https://doi.org/10.4018/978-1-7998-7335-8.ch004

Biswas, A., & De, A. K. (2017). On Development of a Fuzzy Stochastic Programming Model with Its Application to Business Management. In S. Trivedi, S. Dey, A. Kumar, & T. Panda (Eds.), *Handbook of Research on Advanced Data Mining Techniques and Applications for Business Intelligence* (pp. 353–378). Hershey, PA: IGI Global. doi:10.4018/978-1-5225-2031-3.ch021

Boragnio, A., & Faracce Macia, C. (2021). "Taking Care of Yourself at Home": Use of E-Commerce About Food and Care During the COVID-19 Pandemic in the City of Buenos Aires. In M. Korstanje (Ed.), *Socio-Economic Effects and Recovery Efforts for the Rental Industry: Post-COVID-19 Strategies* (pp. 45–71). IGI Global. https://doi.org/10.4018/978-1-7998-7287-0.ch003

Borges, V. D. (2021). Happiness: The Basis for Public Policy in Tourism. In A. Perinotto, V. Mayer, & J. Soares (Eds.), *Rebuilding and Restructuring the Tourism Industry: Infusion of Happiness and Quality of Life* (pp. 1–25). IGI Global. https://doi.org/10.4018/978-1-7998-7239-9.ch001

Bücker, J., & Ernste, K. (2018). Use of Brand Heroes in Strategic Reputation Management: The Case of Bacardi, Adidas, and Daimler. In A. Erdemir (Ed.), *Reputation Management Techniques in Public Relations* (pp. 126–150). Hershey, PA: IGI Global. doi:10.4018/978-1-5225-3619-2.ch007

Buluk Eşitti, B. (2021). COVID-19 and Alternative Tourism: New Destinations and New Tourism Products. In M. Demir, A. Dalgıç, & F. Ergen (Eds.), *Handbook of Research on the Impacts and Implications of COVID-19 on the Tourism Industry* (pp. 786–805). IGI Global. https://doi.org/10.4018/978-1-7998-8231-2.ch038

Bureš, V. (2018). Industry 4.0 From the Systems Engineering Perspective: Alternative Holistic Framework Development. In R. Brunet-Thornton & F. Martinez (Eds.), *Analyzing the Impacts of Industry 4.0 in Modern Business Environments* (pp. 199–223). Hershey, PA: IGI Global. doi:10.4018/978-1-5225-3468-6.ch011

Buzady, Z. (2017). Resolving the Magic Cube of Effective Case Teaching: Benchmarking Case Teaching Practices in Emerging Markets – Insights from the Central European University Business School, Hungary. In D. Latusek (Ed.), *Case Studies as a Teaching Tool in Management Education* (pp. 79–103). Hershey, PA: IGI Global. doi:10.4018/978-1-5225-0770-3.ch005

Camillo, A. (2021). *Legal Matters, Risk Management, and Risk Prevention: From Forming a Business to Legal Representation*. IGI Global. doi:10.4018/978-1-7998-4342-9.ch004

Căpusneanu, S., & Topor, D. I. (2018). Business Ethics and Cost Management in SMEs: Theories of Business Ethics and Cost Management Ethos. In I. Oncioiu (Ed.), *Ethics and Decision-Making for Sustainable Business Practices* (pp. 109–127). Hershey, PA: IGI Global. doi:10.4018/978-1-5225-3773-1.ch007

Chan, R. L., Mo, P. L., & Moon, K. K. (2018). Strategic and Tactical Measures in Managing Enterprise Risks: A Study of the Textile and Apparel Industry. In K. Strang, M. Korstanje, & N. Vajjhala (Eds.), *Research, Practices, and Innovations in Global Risk and Contingency Management* (pp. 1–19). Hershey, PA: IGI Global. doi:10.4018/978-1-5225-4754-9.ch001

Charlier, S. D., Burke-Smalley, L. A., & Fisher, S. L. (2018). Undergraduate Programs in the U.S: A Contextual and Content-Based Analysis. In J. Mendy (Ed.), *Teaching Human Resources and Organizational Behavior at the College Level* (pp. 26–57). Hershey, PA: IGI Global. doi:10.4018/978-1-5225-2820-3.ch002

Chumillas, J., Güell, M., & Quer, P. (2022). The Use of ICT in Tourist and Educational Literary Routes: The Role of the Guide. In C. Ramos, S. Quinteiro, & A. Gonçalves (Eds.), *ICT as Innovator Between Tourism and Culture* (pp. 15–29). IGI Global. https://doi.org/10.4018/978-1-7998-8165-0.ch002

Dahlberg, T., Kivijärvi, H., & Saarinen, T. (2017). IT Investment Consistency and Other Factors Influencing the Success of IT Performance. In S. De Haes & W. Van Grembergen (Eds.), *Strategic IT Governance and Alignment in Business Settings* (pp. 176–208). Hershey, PA: IGI Global. doi:10.4018/978-1-5225-0861-8.ch007

Damnjanović, A. M. (2017). Knowledge Management Optimization through IT and E-Business Utilization: A Qualitative Study on Serbian SMEs. In M. Vemić (Ed.), *Optimal Management Strategies in Small and Medium Enterprises* (pp. 249–267). Hershey, PA: IGI Global. doi:10.4018/978-1-5225-1949-2.ch012

Daneshpour, H. (2017). Integrating Sustainable Development into Project Portfolio Management through Application of Open Innovation. In M. Vemić (Ed.), *Optimal Management Strategies in Small and Medium Enterprises* (pp. 370–387). Hershey, PA: IGI Global. doi:10.4018/978-1-5225-1949-2.ch017

Daniel, A. D., & Reis de Castro, V. (2018). Entrepreneurship Education: How to Measure the Impact on Nascent Entrepreneurs. In A. Carrizo Moreira, J. Guilherme Leitão Dantas, & F. Manuel Valente (Eds.), *Nascent Entrepreneurship and Successful New Venture Creation* (pp. 85–110). Hershey, PA: IGI Global. doi:10.4018/978-1-5225-2936-1.ch004

David, R., Swami, B. N., & Tangirala, S. (2018). Ethics Impact on Knowledge Management in Organizational Development: A Case Study. In N. Baporikar (Ed.), *Global Practices in Knowledge Management for Societal and Organizational Development* (pp. 19–45). Hershey, PA: IGI Global. doi:10.4018/978-1-5225-3009-1.ch002

De Uña-Álvarez, E., & Villarino-Pérez, M. (2022). Fostering Ecocultural Resources, Identity, and Tourism in Inland Territories (Galicia, NW Spain). In G. Fernandes (Ed.), *Challenges and New Opportunities for Tourism in Inland Territories: Ecocultural Resources and Sustainable Initiatives* (pp. 1-16). IGI Global. https://doi.org/10.4018/978-1-7998-7339-6.ch001

Delias, P., & Lakiotaki, K. (2018). Discovering Process Horizontal Boundaries to Facilitate Process Comprehension. *International Journal of Operations Research and Information Systems*, *9*(2), 1–31. doi:10.4018/IJORIS.2018040101

Denholm, J., & Lee-Davies, L. (2018). Success Factors for Games in Business and Project Management. In *Enhancing Education and Training Initiatives Through Serious Games* (pp. 34–68). Hershey, PA: IGI Global. doi:10.4018/978-1-5225-3689-5.ch002

Deshpande, M. (2017). Best Practices in Management Institutions for Global Leadership: Policy Aspects. In N. Baporikar (Ed.), *Management Education for Global Leadership* (pp. 1–27). Hershey, PA: IGI Global. doi:10.4018/978-1-5225-1013-0.ch001

Deshpande, M. (2018). Policy Perspectives for SMEs Knowledge Management. In N. Baporikar (Ed.), *Knowledge Integration Strategies for Entrepreneurship and Sustainability* (pp. 23–46). Hershey, PA: IGI Global. doi:10.4018/978-1-5225-5115-7.ch002

Dezdar, S. (2017). ERP Implementation Projects in Asian Countries: A Comparative Study on Iran and China. *International Journal of Information Technology Project Management*, *8*(3), 52–68. doi:10.4018/IJITPM.2017070104

Domingos, D., Respício, A., & Martinho, R. (2017). Reliability of IoT-Aware BPMN Healthcare Processes. In C. Reis & M. Maximiano (Eds.), *Internet of Things and Advanced Application in Healthcare* (pp. 214–248). Hershey, PA: IGI Global. doi:10.4018/978-1-5225-1820-4.ch008

Dosumu, O., Hussain, J., & El-Gohary, H. (2017). An Exploratory Study of the Impact of Government Policies on the Development of Small and Medium Enterprises in Developing Countries: The Case of Nigeria. *International Journal of Customer Relationship Marketing and Management*, *8*(4), 51–62. doi:10.4018/IJCRMM.2017100104

Durst, S., Bruns, G., & Edvardsson, I. R. (2017). Retaining Knowledge in Smaller Building and Construction Firms. *International Journal of Knowledge and Systems Science*, *8*(3), 1–12. doi:10.4018/IJKSS.2017070101

Edvardsson, I. R., & Durst, S. (2017). Outsourcing, Knowledge, and Learning: A Critical Review. *International Journal of Knowledge-Based Organizations*, *7*(2), 13–26. doi:10.4018/IJKBO.2017040102

Edwards, J. S. (2018). Integrating Knowledge Management and Business Processes. In M. Khosrow-Pour, D.B.A. (Ed.), Encyclopedia of Information Science and Technology, Fourth Edition (pp. 5046-5055). Hershey, PA: IGI Global. doi:10.4018/978-1-5225-2255-3.ch437

Eichelberger, S., & Peters, M. (2021). Family Firm Management in Turbulent Times: Opportunities for Responsible Tourism. In A. Zehrer, G. Glowka, K. Schwaiger, & V. Ranacher-Lackner (Eds.), *Resiliency Models and Addressing Future Risks for Family Firms in the Tourism Industry* (pp. 103–124). IGI Global. https://doi.org/10.4018/978-1-7998-7352-5.ch005

Eide, D., Hjalager, A., & Hansen, M. (2022). Innovative Certifications in Adventure Tourism: Attributes and Diffusion. In R. Augusto Costa, F. Brandão, Z. Breda, & C. Costa (Eds.), *Planning and Managing the Experience Economy in Tourism* (pp. 161-175). IGI Global. https://doi.org/10.4018/978-1-7998-8775-1.ch009

Ejiogu, A. O. (2018). Economics of Farm Management. In *Agricultural Finance and Opportunities for Investment and Expansion* (pp. 56–72). Hershey, PA: IGI Global. doi:10.4018/978-1-5225-3059-6.ch003

Ekanem, I., & Abiade, G. E. (2018). Factors Influencing the Use of E-Commerce by Small Enterprises in Nigeria. *International Journal of ICT Research in Africa and the Middle East*, *7*(1), 37–53. doi:10.4018/IJICTRAME.2018010103

Ekanem, I., & Alrossais, L. A. (2017). Succession Challenges Facing Family Businesses in Saudi Arabia. In P. Zgheib (Ed.), *Entrepreneurship and Business Innovation in the Middle East* (pp. 122–146). Hershey, PA: IGI Global. doi:10.4018/978-1-5225-2066-5.ch007

El Faquih, L., & Fredj, M. (2017). Ontology-Based Framework for Quality in Configurable Process Models. *Journal of Electronic Commerce in Organizations*, *15*(2), 48–60. doi:10.4018/JECO.2017040104

Faisal, M. N., & Talib, F. (2017). Building Ambidextrous Supply Chains in SMEs: How to Tackle the Barriers? *International Journal of Information Systems and Supply Chain Management*, *10*(4), 80–100. doi:10.4018/IJISSCM.2017100105

Fernandes, T. M., Gomes, J., & Romão, M. (2017). Investments in E-Government: A Benefit Management Case Study. *International Journal of Electronic Government Research*, *13*(3), 1–17. doi:10.4018/IJEGR.2017070101

Figueira, L. M., Honrado, G. R., & Dionísio, M. S. (2021). Human Capital Management in the Tourism Industry in Portugal. In V. Costa, A. Moura, & M. Mira (Eds.), *Handbook of Research on Human Capital and People Management in the Tourism Industry* (pp. 1–19). IGI Global. doi:10.4018/978-1-7998-4318-4.ch001

Gao, S. S., Oreal, S., & Zhang, J. (2018). Contemporary Financial Risk Management Perceptions and Practices of Small-Sized Chinese Businesses. In I. Management Association (Ed.), Global Business Expansion: Concepts, Methodologies, Tools, and Applications (pp. 917-931). Hershey, PA: IGI Global. doi:10.4018/978-1-5225-5481-3.ch041

Garg, R., & Berning, S. C. (2017). Indigenous Chinese Management Philosophies: Key Concepts and Relevance for Modern Chinese Firms. In B. Christiansen & G. Koc (Eds.), *Transcontinental Strategies for Industrial Development and Economic Growth* (pp. 43–57). Hershey, PA: IGI Global. doi:10.4018/978-1-5225-2160-0.ch003

Gencer, Y. G. (2017). Supply Chain Management in Retailing Business. In U. Akkucuk (Ed.), *Ethics and Sustainability in Global Supply Chain Management* (pp. 197–210). Hershey, PA: IGI Global. doi:10.4018/978-1-5225-2036-8.ch011

Gera, R., Arora, S., & Malik, S. (2021). Emotional Labor in the Tourism Industry: Strategies, Antecedents, and Outcomes. In V. Costa, A. Moura, & M. Mira (Eds.), *Handbook of Research on Human Capital and People Management in the Tourism Industry* (pp. 73–91). IGI Global. https://doi.org/10.4018/978-1-7998-4318-4.ch004

Giacosa, E. (2018). The Increasing of the Regional Development Thanks to the Luxury Business Innovation. In L. Carvalho (Ed.), *Handbook of Research on Entrepreneurial Ecosystems and Social Dynamics in a Globalized World* (pp. 260–273). Hershey, PA: IGI Global. doi:10.4018/978-1-5225-3525-6.ch011

Glowka, G., Tusch, M., & Zehrer, A. (2021). The Risk Perception of Family Business Owner-Manager in the Tourism Industry: A Qualitative Comparison of the Intra-Firm Senior and Junior Generation. In A. Zehrer, G. Glowka, K. Schwaiger, & V. Ranacher-Lackner (Eds.), *Resiliency Models and Addressing Future Risks for Family Firms in the Tourism Industry* (pp. 126–153). IGI Global. https://doi.org/10.4018/978-1-7998-7352-5.ch006

Glykas, M., & George, J. (2017). Quality and Process Management Systems in the UAE Maritime Industry. *International Journal of Productivity Management and Assessment Technologies*, 5(1), 20–39. doi:10.4018/IJPMAT.2017010102

Glykas, M., Valiris, G., Kokkinaki, A., & Koutsoukou, Z. (2018). Banking Business Process Management Implementation. *International Journal of Productivity Management and Assessment Technologies*, 6(1), 50–69. doi:10.4018/IJPMAT.2018010104

Gomes, J., & Romão, M. (2017). The Balanced Scorecard: Keeping Updated and Aligned with Today's Business Trends. *International Journal of Productivity Management and Assessment Technologies*, 5(2), 1–15. doi:10.4018/IJPMAT.2017070101

Gomes, J., & Romão, M. (2017). Aligning Information Systems and Technology with Benefit Management and Balanced Scorecard. In S. De Haes & W. Van Grembergen (Eds.), *Strategic IT Governance and Alignment in Business Settings* (pp. 112–131). Hershey, PA: IGI Global. doi:10.4018/978-1-5225-0861-8.ch005

Goyal, A. (2021). Communicating and Building Destination Brands With New Media. In M. Dinis, L. Bonixe, S. Lamy, & Z. Breda (Eds.), *Impact of New Media in Tourism* (pp. 1-20). IGI Global. https://doi.org/10.4018/978-1-7998-7095-1.ch001

Grefen, P., & Turetken, O. (2017). Advanced Business Process Management in Networked E-Business Scenarios. *International Journal of E-Business Research*, *13*(4), 70–104. doi:10.4018/IJEBR.2017100105

Guasca, M., Van Broeck, A. M., & Vanneste, D. (2021). Tourism and the Social Reintegration of Colombian Ex-Combatants. In J. da Silva, Z. Breda, & F. Carbone (Eds.), *Role and Impact of Tourism in Peacebuilding and Conflict Transformation* (pp. 66-86). IGI Global. https://doi.org/10.4018/978-1-7998-5053-3.ch005

Haider, A., & Saetang, S. (2017). Strategic IT Alignment in Service Sector. In S. Rozenes & Y. Cohen (Eds.), *Handbook of Research on Strategic Alliances and Value Co-Creation in the Service Industry* (pp. 231–258). Hershey, PA: IGI Global. doi:10.4018/978-1-5225-2084-9.ch012

Hajilari, A. B., Ghadaksaz, M., & Fasghandis, G. S. (2017). Assessing Organizational Readiness for Implementing ERP System Using Fuzzy Expert System Approach. *International Journal of Enterprise Information Systems*, *13*(1), 67–85. doi:10.4018/IJEIS.2017010105

Haldorai, A., Ramu, A., & Murugan, S. (2018). Social Aware Cognitive Radio Networks: Effectiveness of Social Networks as a Strategic Tool for Organizational Business Management. In H. Bansal, G. Shrivastava, G. Nguyen, & L. Stanciu (Eds.), *Social Network Analytics for Contemporary Business Organizations* (pp. 188–202). Hershey, PA: IGI Global. doi:10.4018/978-1-5225-5097-6.ch010

Hall, O. P. Jr. (2017). Social Media Driven Management Education. *International Journal of Knowledge-Based Organizations*, *7*(2), 43–59. doi:10.4018/IJKBO.2017040104

Hanifah, H., Halim, H. A., Ahmad, N. H., & Vafaei-Zadeh, A. (2017). Innovation Culture as a Mediator Between Specific Human Capital and Innovation Performance Among Bumiputera SMEs in Malaysia. In N. Ahmad, T. Ramayah, H. Halim, & S. Rahman (Eds.), *Handbook of Research on Small and Medium Enterprises in Developing Countries* (pp. 261–279). Hershey, PA: IGI Global. doi:10.4018/978-1-5225-2165-5.ch012

Hartlieb, S., & Silvius, G. (2017). Handling Uncertainty in Project Management and Business Development: Similarities and Differences. In Y. Raydugin (Ed.), *Handbook of Research on Leveraging Risk and Uncertainties for Effective Project Management* (pp. 337–362). Hershey, PA: IGI Global. doi:10.4018/978-1-5225-1790-0.ch016

Hass, K. B. (2017). Living on the Edge: Managing Project Complexity. In Y. Raydugin (Ed.), *Handbook of Research on Leveraging Risk and Uncertainties for Effective Project Management* (pp. 177–201). Hershey, PA: IGI Global. doi:10.4018/978-1-5225-1790-0.ch009

Hawking, P., & Carmine Sellitto, C. (2017). Developing an Effective Strategy for Organizational Business Intelligence. In M. Tavana (Ed.), *Enterprise Information Systems and the Digitalization of Business Functions* (pp. 222–237). Hershey, PA: IGI Global. doi:10.4018/978-1-5225-2382-6.ch010

Hawking, P., & Sellitto, C. (2017). A Fast-Moving Consumer Goods Company and Business Intelligence Strategy Development. *International Journal of Enterprise Information Systems*, *13*(2), 22–33. doi:10.4018/IJEIS.2017040102

Hawking, P., & Sellitto, C. (2017). Business Intelligence Strategy: Two Case Studies. *International Journal of Business Intelligence Research*, *8*(2), 17–30. doi:10.4018/IJBIR.2017070102

Hee, W. J., Jalleh, G., Lai, H., & Lin, C. (2017). E-Commerce and IT Projects: Evaluation and Management Issues in Australian and Taiwanese Hospitals. *International Journal of Public Health Management and Ethics*, *2*(1), 69–90. doi:10.4018/IJPHME.2017010104

Hernandez, A. A. (2018). Exploring the Factors to Green IT Adoption of SMEs in the Philippines. *Journal of Cases on Information Technology*, *20*(2), 49–66. doi:10.4018/JCIT.2018040104

Hollman, A., Bickford, S., & Hollman, T. (2017). Cyber InSecurity: A Post-Mortem Attempt to Assess Cyber Problems from IT and Business Management Perspectives. *Journal of Cases on Information Technology*, *19*(3), 42–70. doi:10.4018/JCIT.2017070104

Ibrahim, F., & Zainin, N. M. (2021). Exploring the Technological Impacts: The Case of Museums in Brunei Darussalam. *International Journal of Tourism and Hospitality Management in the Digital Age*, *5*(1), 1–18. https://doi.org/10.4018/IJTHMDA.2021010101

Igbinakhase, I. (2017). Responsible and Sustainable Management Practices in Developing and Developed Business Environments. In Z. Fields (Ed.), *Collective Creativity for Responsible and Sustainable Business Practice* (pp. 180–207). Hershey, PA: IGI Global. doi:10.4018/978-1-5225-1823-5.ch010

Iwata, J. J., & Hoskins, R. G. (2017). Managing Indigenous Knowledge in Tanzania: A Business Perspective. In P. Jain & N. Mnjama (Eds.), *Managing Knowledge Resources and Records in Modern Organizations* (pp. 198–214). Hershey, PA: IGI Global. doi:10.4018/978-1-5225-1965-2.ch012

Jain, P. (2017). Ethical and Legal Issues in Knowledge Management Life-Cycle in Business. In P. Jain & N. Mnjama (Eds.), *Managing Knowledge Resources and Records in Modern Organizations* (pp. 82–101). Hershey, PA: IGI Global. doi:10.4018/978-1-5225-1965-2.ch006

James, S., & Hauli, E. (2017). Holistic Management Education at Tanzanian Rural Development Planning Institute. In N. Baporikar (Ed.), *Management Education for Global Leadership* (pp. 112–136). Hershey, PA: IGI Global. doi:10.4018/978-1-5225-1013-0.ch006

Janošková, M., Csikósová, A., & Čulková, K. (2018). Measurement of Company Performance as Part of Its Strategic Management. In R. Leon (Ed.), *Managerial Strategies for Business Sustainability During Turbulent Times* (pp. 309–335). Hershey, PA: IGI Global. doi:10.4018/978-1-5225-2716-9.ch017

Jean-Vasile, A., & Alecu, A. (2017). Theoretical and Practical Approaches in Understanding the Influences of Cost-Productivity-Profit Trinomial in Contemporary Enterprises. In A. Jean Vasile & D. Nicolò (Eds.), *Sustainable Entrepreneurship and Investments in the Green Economy* (pp. 28–62). Hershey, PA: IGI Global. doi:10.4018/978-1-5225-2075-7.ch002

Joia, L. A., & Correia, J. C. (2018). CIO Competencies From the IT Professional Perspective: Insights From Brazil. *Journal of Global Information Management*, *26*(2), 74–103. doi:10.4018/JGIM.2018040104

Juma, A., & Mzera, N. (2017). Knowledge Management and Records Management and Competitive Advantage in Business. In P. Jain & N. Mnjama (Eds.), *Managing Knowledge Resources and Records in Modern Organizations* (pp. 15–28). Hershey, PA: IGI Global. doi:10.4018/978-1-5225-1965-2.ch002

K., I., & A, V. (2018). Monitoring and Auditing in the Cloud. In K. Munir (Ed.), *Cloud Computing Technologies for Green Enterprises* (pp. 318-350). Hershey, PA: IGI Global. https://doi.org/ doi:10.4018/978-1-5225-3038-1.ch013

Kabra, G., Ghosh, V., & Ramesh, A. (2018). Enterprise Integrated Business Process Management and Business Intelligence Framework for Business Process Sustainability. In A. Paul, D. Bhattacharyya, & S. Anand (Eds.), *Green Initiatives for Business Sustainability and Value Creation* (pp. 228–238). Hershey, PA: IGI Global. doi:10.4018/978-1-5225-2662-9.ch010

Kaoud, M. (2017). Investigation of Customer Knowledge Management: A Case Study Research. *International Journal of Service Science, Management, Engineering, and Technology*, 8(2), 12–22. doi:10.4018/IJSSMET.2017040102

Katuu, S. (2018). A Comparative Assessment of Enterprise Content Management Maturity Models. In N. Gwangwava & M. Mutingi (Eds.), *E-Manufacturing and E-Service Strategies in Contemporary Organizations* (pp. 93–118). Hershey, PA: IGI Global. doi:10.4018/978-1-5225-3628-4.ch005

Khan, M. Y., & Abir, T. (2022). The Role of Social Media Marketing in the Tourism and Hospitality Industry: A Conceptual Study on Bangladesh. In C. Ramos, S. Quinteiro, & A. Gonçalves (Eds.), *ICT as Innovator Between Tourism and Culture* (pp. 213–229). IGI Global. https://doi.org/10.4018/978-1-7998-8165-0.ch013

Kinnunen, S., Ylä-Kujala, A., Marttonen-Arola, S., Kärri, T., & Baglee, D. (2018). Internet of Things in Asset Management: Insights from Industrial Professionals and Academia. *International Journal of Service Science, Management, Engineering, and Technology*, 9(2), 104–119. doi:10.4018/IJSSMET.2018040105

Klein, A. Z., Sabino de Freitas, A., Machado, L., Freitas, J. C. Jr, Graziola, P. G. Jr, & Schlemmer, E. (2017). Virtual Worlds Applications for Management Education. In L. Tomei (Ed.), *Exploring the New Era of Technology-Infused Education* (pp. 279–299). Hershey, PA: IGI Global. doi:10.4018/978-1-5225-1709-2.ch017

Kővári, E., Saleh, M., & Steinbachné Hajmásy, G. (2022). The Impact of Corporate Digital Responsibility (CDR) on Internal Stakeholders' Satisfaction in Hungarian Upscale Hotels. In M. Valeri (Ed.), *New Governance and Management in Touristic Destinations* (pp. 35–51). IGI Global. https://doi.org/10.4018/978-1-6684-3889-3.ch003

Kożuch, B., & Jabłoński, A. (2017). Adopting the Concept of Business Models in Public Management. In M. Lewandowski & B. Kożuch (Eds.), *Public Sector Entrepreneurship and the Integration of Innovative Business Models* (pp. 10–46). Hershey, PA: IGI Global. doi:10.4018/978-1-5225-2215-7.ch002

Kumar, J., Adhikary, A., & Jha, A. (2017). Small Active Investors' Perceptions and Preferences Towards Tax Saving Mutual Fund Schemes in Eastern India: An Empirical Note. *International Journal of Asian Business and Information Management*, 8(2), 35–45. doi:10.4018/IJABIM.2017040103

Related References

Latusi, S., & Fissore, M. (2021). Pilgrimage Routes to Happiness: Comparing the Camino de Santiago and Via Francigena. In A. Perinotto, V. Mayer, & J. Soares (Eds.), *Rebuilding and Restructuring the Tourism Industry: Infusion of Happiness and Quality of Life* (pp. 157–182). IGI Global. https://doi.org/10.4018/978-1-7998-7239-9.ch008

Lavassani, K. M., & Movahedi, B. (2017). Applications Driven Information Systems: Beyond Networks toward Business Ecosystems. *International Journal of Innovation in the Digital Economy*, *8*(1), 61–75. doi:10.4018/IJIDE.2017010104

Lazzareschi, V. H., & Brito, M. S. (2017). Strategic Information Management: Proposal of Business Project Model. In G. Jamil, A. Soares, & C. Pessoa (Eds.), *Handbook of Research on Information Management for Effective Logistics and Supply Chains* (pp. 59–88). Hershey, PA: IGI Global. doi:10.4018/978-1-5225-0973-8.ch004

Lechuga Sancho, M. P., & Martín Navarro, A. (2022). Evolution of the Literature on Social Responsibility in the Tourism Sector: A Systematic Literature Review. In G. Fernandes (Ed.), *Challenges and New Opportunities for Tourism in Inland Territories: Ecocultural Resources and Sustainable Initiatives* (pp. 169–186). IGI Global. https://doi.org/10.4018/978-1-7998-7339-6.ch010

Lederer, M., Kurz, M., & Lazarov, P. (2017). Usage and Suitability of Methods for Strategic Business Process Initiatives: A Multi Case Study Research. *International Journal of Productivity Management and Assessment Technologies*, *5*(1), 40–51. doi:10.4018/IJPMAT.2017010103

Lee, I. (2017). A Social Enterprise Business Model and a Case Study of Pacific Community Ventures (PCV). In V. Potocan, M. Üngan, & Z. Nedelko (Eds.), *Handbook of Research on Managerial Solutions in Non-Profit Organizations* (pp. 182–204). Hershey, PA: IGI Global. doi:10.4018/978-1-5225-0731-4.ch009

Leon, L. A., Seal, K. C., Przasnyski, Z. H., & Wiedenman, I. (2017). Skills and Competencies Required for Jobs in Business Analytics: A Content Analysis of Job Advertisements Using Text Mining. *International Journal of Business Intelligence Research*, *8*(1), 1–25. doi:10.4018/IJBIR.2017010101

Levy, C. L., & Elias, N. I. (2017). SOHO Users' Perceptions of Reliability and Continuity of Cloud-Based Services. In M. Moore (Ed.), *Cybersecurity Breaches and Issues Surrounding Online Threat Protection* (pp. 248–287). Hershey, PA: IGI Global. doi:10.4018/978-1-5225-1941-6.ch011

Levy, M. (2018). Change Management Serving Knowledge Management and Organizational Development: Reflections and Review. In N. Baporikar (Ed.), *Global Practices in Knowledge Management for Societal and Organizational Development* (pp. 256–270). Hershey, PA: IGI Global. doi:10.4018/978-1-5225-3009-1.ch012

Lewandowski, M. (2017). Public Organizations and Business Model Innovation: The Role of Public Service Design. In M. Lewandowski & B. Kożuch (Eds.), *Public Sector Entrepreneurship and the Integration of Innovative Business Models* (pp. 47–72). Hershey, PA: IGI Global. doi:10.4018/978-1-5225-2215-7.ch003

Lhannaoui, H., Kabbaj, M. I., & Bakkoury, Z. (2017). A Survey of Risk-Aware Business Process Modelling. *International Journal of Risk and Contingency Management*, 6(3), 14–26. doi:10.4018/IJRCM.2017070102

Li, J., Sun, W., Jiang, W., Yang, H., & Zhang, L. (2017). How the Nature of Exogenous Shocks and Crises Impact Company Performance?: The Effects of Industry Characteristics. *International Journal of Risk and Contingency Management*, 6(4), 40–55. doi:10.4018/IJRCM.2017100103

Lopez-Fernandez, M., Perez-Perez, M., Serrano-Bedia, A., & Cobo-Gonzalez, A. (2021). Small and Medium Tourism Enterprise Survival in Times of Crisis: "El Capricho de Gaudí. In D. Toubes & N. Araújo-Vila (Eds.), *Risk, Crisis, and Disaster Management in Small and Medium-Sized Tourism Enterprises* (pp. 103–129). IGI Global. doi:10.4018/978-1-7998-6996-2.ch005

Mahajan, A., Maidullah, S., & Hossain, M. R. (2022). Experience Toward Smart Tour Guide Apps in Travelling: An Analysis of Users' Reviews on Audio Odigos and Trip My Way. In R. Augusto Costa, F. Brandão, Z. Breda, & C. Costa (Eds.), *Planning and Managing the Experience Economy in Tourism* (pp. 255-273). IGI Global. https://doi.org/10.4018/978-1-7998-8775-1.ch014

Malega, P. (2017). Small and Medium Enterprises in the Slovak Republic: Status and Competitiveness of SMEs in the Global Markets and Possibilities of Optimization. In M. Vemić (Ed.), *Optimal Management Strategies in Small and Medium Enterprises* (pp. 102–124). Hershey, PA: IGI Global. doi:10.4018/978-1-5225-1949-2.ch006

Malewska, K. M. (2017). Intuition in Decision-Making on the Example of a Non-Profit Organization. In V. Potocan, M. Ünğan, & Z. Nedelko (Eds.), *Handbook of Research on Managerial Solutions in Non-Profit Organizations* (pp. 378–399). Hershey, PA: IGI Global. doi:10.4018/978-1-5225-0731-4.ch018

Maroofi, F. (2017). Entrepreneurial Orientation and Organizational Learning Ability Analysis for Innovation and Firm Performance. In N. Baporikar (Ed.), *Innovation and Shifting Perspectives in Management Education* (pp. 144–165). Hershey, PA: IGI Global. doi:10.4018/978-1-5225-1019-2.ch007

Marques, M., Moleiro, D., Brito, T. M., & Marques, T. (2021). Customer Relationship Management as an Important Relationship Marketing Tool: The Case of the Hospitality Industry in Estoril Coast. In M. Dinis, L. Bonixe, S. Lamy, & Z. Breda (Eds.), Impact of New Media in Tourism (pp. 39-56). IGI Global. https://doi.org/doi:10.4018/978-1-7998-7095-1.ch003

Martins, P. V., & Zacarias, M. (2017). A Web-based Tool for Business Process Improvement. *International Journal of Web Portals*, 9(2), 68–84. doi:10.4018/IJWP.2017070104

Matthies, B., & Coners, A. (2017). Exploring the Conceptual Nature of e-Business Projects. *Journal of Electronic Commerce in Organizations*, 15(3), 33–63. doi:10.4018/JECO.2017070103

Mayer, V. F., Fraga, C. C., & Silva, L. C. (2021). Contributions of Neurosciences to Studies of Well-Being in Tourism. In A. Perinotto, V. Mayer, & J. Soares (Eds.), *Rebuilding and Restructuring the Tourism Industry: Infusion of Happiness and Quality of Life* (pp. 108–128). IGI Global. https://doi.org/10.4018/978-1-7998-7239-9.ch006

McKee, J. (2018). Architecture as a Tool to Solve Business Planning Problems. In M. Khosrow-Pour, D.B.A. (Ed.), Encyclopedia of Information Science and Technology, Fourth Edition (pp. 573-586). Hershey, PA: IGI Global. doi:10.4018/978-1-5225-2255-3.ch050

McMurray, A. J., Cross, J., & Caponecchia, C. (2018). The Risk Management Profession in Australia: Business Continuity Plan Practices. In N. Bajgoric (Ed.), *Always-On Enterprise Information Systems for Modern Organizations* (pp. 112–129). Hershey, PA: IGI Global. doi:10.4018/978-1-5225-3704-5.ch006

Meddah, I. H., & Belkadi, K. (2018). Mining Patterns Using Business Process Management. In R. Hamou (Ed.), *Handbook of Research on Biomimicry in Information Retrieval and Knowledge Management* (pp. 78–89). Hershey, PA: IGI Global. doi:10.4018/978-1-5225-3004-6.ch005

Melian, A. G., & Camprubí, R. (2021). The Accessibility of Museum Websites: The Case of Barcelona. In C. Eusébio, L. Teixeira, & M. Carneiro (Eds.), *ICT Tools and Applications for Accessible Tourism* (pp. 234–255). IGI Global. https://doi.org/10.4018/978-1-7998-6428-8.ch011

Mendes, L. (2017). TQM and Knowledge Management: An Integrated Approach Towards Tacit Knowledge Management. In D. Jaziri-Bouagina & G. Jamil (Eds.), *Handbook of Research on Tacit Knowledge Management for Organizational Success* (pp. 236–263). Hershey, PA: IGI Global. doi:10.4018/978-1-5225-2394-9.ch009

Menezes, V. D., & Cavagnaro, E. (2021). Communicating Sustainable Initiatives in the Hotel Industry: The Case of the Hotel Jakarta Amsterdam. In F. Brandão, Z. Breda, R. Costa, & C. Costa (Eds.), *Handbook of Research on the Role of Tourism in Achieving Sustainable Development Goals* (pp. 224-234). IGI Global. https://doi.org/10.4018/978-1-7998-5691-7.ch013

Menezes, V. D., & Cavagnaro, E. (2021). Communicating Sustainable Initiatives in the Hotel Industry: The Case of the Hotel Jakarta Amsterdam. In F. Brandão, Z. Breda, R. Costa, & C. Costa (Eds.), *Handbook of Research on the Role of Tourism in Achieving Sustainable Development Goals* (pp. 224-234). IGI Global. https://doi.org/10.4018/978-1-7998-5691-7.ch013

Mitas, O., Bastiaansen, M., & Boode, W. (2022). If You're Happy, I'm Happy: Emotion Contagion at a Tourist Information Center. In R. Augusto Costa, F. Brandão, Z. Breda, & C. Costa (Eds.), *Planning and Managing the Experience Economy in Tourism* (pp. 122-140). IGI Global. https://doi.org/10.4018/978-1-7998-8775-1.ch007

Mnjama, N. M. (2017). Preservation of Recorded Information in Public and Private Sector Organizations. In P. Jain & N. Mnjama (Eds.), *Managing Knowledge Resources and Records in Modern Organizations* (pp. 149–167). Hershey, PA: IGI Global. doi:10.4018/978-1-5225-1965-2.ch009

Mokoqama, M., & Fields, Z. (2017). Principles of Responsible Management Education (PRME): Call for Responsible Management Education. In Z. Fields (Ed.), *Collective Creativity for Responsible and Sustainable Business Practice* (pp. 229–241). Hershey, PA: IGI Global. doi:10.4018/978-1-5225-1823-5.ch012

Monteiro, A., Lopes, S., & Carbone, F. (2021). Academic Mobility: Bridging Tourism and Peace Education. In J. da Silva, Z. Breda, & F. Carbone (Eds.), *Role and Impact of Tourism in Peacebuilding and Conflict Transformation* (pp. 275-301). IGI Global. https://doi.org/10.4018/978-1-7998-5053-3.ch016

Muniapan, B. (2017). Philosophy and Management: The Relevance of Vedanta in Management. In P. Ordóñez de Pablos (Ed.), *Managerial Strategies and Solutions for Business Success in Asia* (pp. 124–139). Hershey, PA: IGI Global. doi:10.4018/978-1-5225-1886-0.ch007

Murad, S. E., & Dowaji, S. (2017). Using Value-Based Approach for Managing Cloud-Based Services. In A. Turuk, B. Sahoo, & S. Addya (Eds.), *Resource Management and Efficiency in Cloud Computing Environments* (pp. 33–60). Hershey, PA: IGI Global. doi:10.4018/978-1-5225-1721-4.ch002

Mutahar, A. M., Daud, N. M., Thurasamy, R., Isaac, O., & Abdulsalam, R. (2018). The Mediating of Perceived Usefulness and Perceived Ease of Use: The Case of Mobile Banking in Yemen. *International Journal of Technology Diffusion*, *9*(2), 21–40. doi:10.4018/IJTD.2018040102

Naidoo, V. (2017). E-Learning and Management Education at African Universities. In N. Baporikar (Ed.), *Management Education for Global Leadership* (pp. 181–201). Hershey, PA: IGI Global. doi:10.4018/978-1-5225-1013-0.ch009

Naidoo, V., & Igbinakhase, I. (2018). Opportunities and Challenges of Knowledge Retention in SMEs. In N. Baporikar (Ed.), *Knowledge Integration Strategies for Entrepreneurship and Sustainability* (pp. 70–94). Hershey, PA: IGI Global. doi:10.4018/978-1-5225-5115-7.ch004

Naumov, N., & Costandachi, G. (2021). Creativity and Entrepreneurship: Gastronomic Tourism in Mexico. In J. Soares (Ed.), *Innovation and Entrepreneurial Opportunities in Community Tourism* (pp. 90–108). IGI Global. https://doi.org/10.4018/978-1-7998-4855-4.ch006

Nayak, S., & Prabhu, N. (2017). Paradigm Shift in Management Education: Need for a Cross Functional Perspective. In N. Baporikar (Ed.), *Management Education for Global Leadership* (pp. 241–255). Hershey, PA: IGI Global. doi:10.4018/978-1-5225-1013-0.ch012

Nedelko, Z., & Potocan, V. (2017). Management Solutions in Non-Profit Organizations: Case of Slovenia. In V. Potocan, M. Üngan, & Z. Nedelko (Eds.), *Handbook of Research on Managerial Solutions in Non-Profit Organizations* (pp. 1–22). Hershey, PA: IGI Global. doi:10.4018/978-1-5225-0731-4.ch001

Nedelko, Z., & Potocan, V. (2017). Priority of Management Tools Utilization among Managers: International Comparison. In V. Wang (Ed.), *Encyclopedia of Strategic Leadership and Management* (pp. 1083–1094). Hershey, PA: IGI Global. doi:10.4018/978-1-5225-1049-9.ch075

Nedelko, Z., Raudeliūnienė, J., & Črešnar, R. (2018). Knowledge Dynamics in Supply Chain Management. In N. Baporikar (Ed.), *Knowledge Integration Strategies for Entrepreneurship and Sustainability* (pp. 150–166). Hershey, PA: IGI Global. doi:10.4018/978-1-5225-5115-7.ch008

Nguyen, H. T., & Hipsher, S. A. (2018). Innovation and Creativity Used by Private Sector Firms in a Resources-Constrained Environment. In S. Hipsher (Ed.), *Examining the Private Sector's Role in Wealth Creation and Poverty Reduction* (pp. 219–238). Hershey, PA: IGI Global. doi:10.4018/978-1-5225-3117-3.ch010

Obicci, P. A. (2017). Risk Sharing in a Partnership. In *Risk Management Strategies in Public-Private Partnerships* (pp. 115–152). Hershey, PA: IGI Global. doi:10.4018/978-1-5225-2503-5.ch004

Obidallah, W. J., & Raahemi, B. (2017). Managing Changes in Service Oriented Virtual Organizations: A Structural and Procedural Framework to Facilitate the Process of Change. *Journal of Electronic Commerce in Organizations*, *15*(1), 59–83. doi:10.4018/JECO.2017010104

Ojo, O. (2017). Impact of Innovation on the Entrepreneurial Success in Selected Business Enterprises in South-West Nigeria. *International Journal of Innovation in the Digital Economy*, *8*(2), 29–38. doi:10.4018/IJIDE.2017040103

Okdinawati, L., Simatupang, T. M., & Sunitiyoso, Y. (2017). Multi-Agent Reinforcement Learning for Value Co-Creation of Collaborative Transportation Management (CTM). *International Journal of Information Systems and Supply Chain Management*, *10*(3), 84–95. doi:10.4018/IJISSCM.2017070105

Olivera, V. A., & Carrillo, I. M. (2021). Organizational Culture: A Key Element for the Development of Mexican Micro and Small Tourist Companies. In J. Soares (Ed.), *Innovation and Entrepreneurial Opportunities in Community Tourism* (pp. 227–242). IGI Global. doi:10.4018/978-1-7998-4855-4.ch013

Ossorio, M. (2022). Corporate Museum Experiences in Enogastronomic Tourism. In R. Augusto Costa, F. Brandão, Z. Breda, & C. Costa (Eds.), Planning and Managing the Experience Economy in Tourism (pp. 107-121). IGI Global. https://doi.org/doi:10.4018/978-1-7998-8775-1.ch006

Ossorio, M. (2022). Enogastronomic Tourism in Times of Pandemic. In G. Fernandes (Ed.), *Challenges and New Opportunities for Tourism in Inland Territories: Ecocultural Resources and Sustainable Initiatives* (pp. 241–255). IGI Global. https://doi.org/10.4018/978-1-7998-7339-6.ch014

Özekici, Y. K. (2022). ICT as an Acculturative Agent and Its Role in the Tourism Context: Introduction, Acculturation Theory, Progress of the Acculturation Theory in Extant Literature. In C. Ramos, S. Quinteiro, & A. Gonçalves (Eds.), *ICT as Innovator Between Tourism and Culture* (pp. 42–66). IGI Global. https://doi.org/10.4018/978-1-7998-8165-0.ch004

Pal, K. (2018). Building High Quality Big Data-Based Applications in Supply Chains. In A. Kumar & S. Saurav (Eds.), *Supply Chain Management Strategies and Risk Assessment in Retail Environments* (pp. 1–24). Hershey, PA: IGI Global. doi:10.4018/978-1-5225-3056-5.ch001

Palos-Sanchez, P. R., & Correia, M. B. (2018). Perspectives of the Adoption of Cloud Computing in the Tourism Sector. In J. Rodrigues, C. Ramos, P. Cardoso, & C. Henriques (Eds.), *Handbook of Research on Technological Developments for Cultural Heritage and eTourism Applications* (pp. 377–400). Hershey, PA: IGI Global. doi:10.4018/978-1-5225-2927-9.ch018

Papadopoulou, G. (2021). Promoting Gender Equality and Women Empowerment in the Tourism Sector. In F. Brandão, Z. Breda, R. Costa, & C. Costa (Eds.), Handbook of Research on the Role of Tourism in Achieving Sustainable Development Goals (pp. 152-174). IGI Global. https://doi.org/ doi:10.4018/978-1-7998-5691-7.ch009

Papp-Váry, Á. F., & Tóth, T. Z. (2022). Analysis of Budapest as a Film Tourism Destination. In R. Baleiro & R. Pereira (Eds.), *Global Perspectives on Literary Tourism and Film-Induced Tourism* (pp. 257-279). IGI Global. https://doi.org/10.4018/978-1-7998-8262-6.ch014

Patiño, B. E. (2017). New Generation Management by Convergence and Individual Identity: A Systemic and Human-Oriented Approach. In N. Baporikar (Ed.), *Innovation and Shifting Perspectives in Management Education* (pp. 119–143). Hershey, PA: IGI Global. doi:10.4018/978-1-5225-1019-2.ch006

Patro, C. S. (2021). Digital Tourism: Influence of E-Marketing Technology. In M. Dinis, L. Bonixe, S. Lamy, & Z. Breda (Eds.), *Impact of New Media in Tourism* (pp. 234-254). IGI Global. https://doi.org/10.4018/978-1-7998-7095-1.ch014

Pawliczek, A., & Rössler, M. (2017). Knowledge of Management Tools and Systems in SMEs: Knowledge Transfer in Management. In A. Bencsik (Ed.), *Knowledge Management Initiatives and Strategies in Small and Medium Enterprises* (pp. 180–203). Hershey, PA: IGI Global. doi:10.4018/978-1-5225-1642-2.ch009

Pejic-Bach, M., Omazic, M. A., Aleksic, A., & Zoroja, J. (2018). Knowledge-Based Decision Making: A Multi-Case Analysis. In R. Leon (Ed.), *Managerial Strategies for Business Sustainability During Turbulent Times* (pp. 160–184). Hershey, PA: IGI Global. doi:10.4018/978-1-5225-2716-9.ch009

Perano, M., Hysa, X., & Calabrese, M. (2018). Strategic Planning, Cultural Context, and Business Continuity Management: Business Cases in the City of Shkoder. In A. Presenza & L. Sheehan (Eds.), *Geopolitics and Strategic Management in the Global Economy* (pp. 57–77). Hershey, PA: IGI Global. doi:10.4018/978-1-5225-2673-5.ch004

Pereira, R., Mira da Silva, M., & Lapão, L. V. (2017). IT Governance Maturity Patterns in Portuguese Healthcare. In S. De Haes & W. Van Grembergen (Eds.), *Strategic IT Governance and Alignment in Business Settings* (pp. 24–52). Hershey, PA: IGI Global. doi:10.4018/978-1-5225-0861-8.ch002

Pérez-Uribe, R. I., Torres, D. A., Jurado, S. P., & Prada, D. M. (2018). Cloud Tools for the Development of Project Management in SMEs. In R. Perez-Uribe, C. Salcedo-Perez, & D. Ocampo-Guzman (Eds.), *Handbook of Research on Intrapreneurship and Organizational Sustainability in SMEs* (pp. 95–120). Hershey, PA: IGI Global. doi:10.4018/978-1-5225-3543-0.ch005

Petrisor, I., & Cozmiuc, D. (2017). Global Supply Chain Management Organization at Siemens in the Advent of Industry 4.0. In L. Saglietto & C. Cezanne (Eds.), *Global Intermediation and Logistics Service Providers* (pp. 123–142). Hershey, PA: IGI Global. doi:10.4018/978-1-5225-2133-4.ch007

Pierce, J. M., Velliaris, D. M., & Edwards, J. (2017). A Living Case Study: A Journey Not a Destination. In N. Silton (Ed.), *Exploring the Benefits of Creativity in Education, Media, and the Arts* (pp. 158–178). Hershey, PA: IGI Global. doi:10.4018/978-1-5225-0504-4.ch008

Pipia, S., & Pipia, S. (2021). Challenges of Religious Tourism in the Conflict Region: An Example of Jerusalem. In E. Alaverdov & M. Bari (Eds.), *Global Development of Religious Tourism* (pp. 135-148). IGI Global. https://doi.org/10.4018/978-1-7998-5792-1.ch009

Poulaki, P., Kritikos, A., Vasilakis, N., & Valeri, M. (2022). The Contribution of Female Creativity to the Development of Gastronomic Tourism in Greece: The Case of the Island of Naxos in the South Aegean Region. In M. Valeri (Ed.), *New Governance and Management in Touristic Destinations* (pp. 246–258). IGI Global. https://doi.org/10.4018/978-1-6684-3889-3.ch015

Radosavljevic, M., & Andjelkovic, A. (2017). Multi-Criteria Decision Making Approach for Choosing Business Process for the Improvement: Upgrading of the Six Sigma Methodology. In J. Stanković, P. Delias, S. Marinković, & S. Rochhia (Eds.), *Tools and Techniques for Economic Decision Analysis* (pp. 225–247). Hershey, PA: IGI Global. doi:10.4018/978-1-5225-0959-2.ch011

Radovic, V. M. (2017). Corporate Sustainability and Responsibility and Disaster Risk Reduction: A Serbian Overview. In M. Camilleri (Ed.), *CSR 2.0 and the New Era of Corporate Citizenship* (pp. 147–164). Hershey, PA: IGI Global. doi:10.4018/978-1-5225-1842-6.ch008

Raghunath, K. M., Devi, S. L., & Patro, C. S. (2018). Impact of Risk Assessment Models on Risk Factors: A Holistic Outlook. In K. Strang, M. Korstanje, & N. Vajjhala (Eds.), *Research, Practices, and Innovations in Global Risk and Contingency Management* (pp. 134–153). Hershey, PA: IGI Global. doi:10.4018/978-1-5225-4754-9.ch008

Raman, A., & Goyal, D. P. (2017). Extending IMPLEMENT Framework for Enterprise Information Systems Implementation to Information System Innovation. In M. Tavana (Ed.), *Enterprise Information Systems and the Digitalization of Business Functions* (pp. 137–177). Hershey, PA: IGI Global. doi:10.4018/978-1-5225-2382-6.ch007

Rao, Y., & Zhang, Y. (2017). The Construction and Development of Academic Library Digital Special Subject Databases. In L. Ruan, Q. Zhu, & Y. Ye (Eds.), *Academic Library Development and Administration in China* (pp. 163–183). Hershey, PA: IGI Global. doi:10.4018/978-1-5225-0550-1.ch010

Ravasan, A. Z., Mohammadi, M. M., & Hamidi, H. (2018). An Investigation Into the Critical Success Factors of Implementing Information Technology Service Management Frameworks. In K. Jakobs (Ed.), *Corporate and Global Standardization Initiatives in Contemporary Society* (pp. 200–218). Hershey, PA: IGI Global. doi:10.4018/978-1-5225-5320-5.ch009

Rezaie, S., Mirabedini, S. J., & Abtahi, A. (2018). Designing a Model for Implementation of Business Intelligence in the Banking Industry. *International Journal of Enterprise Information Systems*, 14(1), 77–103. doi:10.4018/IJEIS.2018010105

Richards, V., Matthews, N., Williams, O. J., & Khan, Z. (2021). The Challenges of Accessible Tourism Information Systems for Tourists With Vision Impairment: Sensory Communications Beyond the Screen. In C. Eusébio, L. Teixeira, & M. Carneiro (Eds.), *ICT Tools and Applications for Accessible Tourism* (pp. 26–54). IGI Global. https://doi.org/10.4018/978-1-7998-6428-8.ch002

Rodrigues de Souza Neto, V., & Marques, O. (2021). Rural Tourism Fostering Welfare Through Sustainable Development: A Conceptual Approach. In A. Perinotto, V. Mayer, & J. Soares (Eds.), *Rebuilding and Restructuring the Tourism Industry: Infusion of Happiness and Quality of Life* (pp. 38–57). IGI Global. https://doi.org/10.4018/978-1-7998-7239-9.ch003

Romano, L., Grimaldi, R., & Colasuonno, F. S. (2017). Demand Management as a Success Factor in Project Portfolio Management. In L. Romano (Ed.), *Project Portfolio Management Strategies for Effective Organizational Operations* (pp. 202–219). Hershey, PA: IGI Global. doi:10.4018/978-1-5225-2151-8.ch008

Rubio-Escuderos, L., & García-Andreu, H. (2021). Competitiveness Factors of Accessible Tourism E-Travel Agencies. In C. Eusébio, L. Teixeira, & M. Carneiro (Eds.), *ICT Tools and Applications for Accessible Tourism* (pp. 196–217). IGI Global. https://doi.org/10.4018/978-1-7998-6428-8.ch009

Rucci, A. C., Porto, N., Darcy, S., & Becka, L. (2021). Smart and Accessible Cities?: Not Always – The Case for Accessible Tourism Initiatives in Buenos Aries and Sydney. In C. Eusébio, L. Teixeira, & M. Carneiro (Eds.), *ICT Tools and Applications for Accessible Tourism* (pp. 115–145). IGI Global. https://doi.org/10.4018/978-1-7998-6428-8.ch006

Ruhi, U. (2018). Towards an Interdisciplinary Socio-Technical Definition of Virtual Communities. In M. Khosrow-Pour, D.B.A. (Ed.), Encyclopedia of Information Science and Technology, Fourth Edition (pp. 4278-4295). Hershey, PA: IGI Global. doi:10.4018/978-1-5225-2255-3.ch371

Ryan, L., Catena, M., Ros, P., & Stephens, S. (2021). Designing Entrepreneurial Ecosystems to Support Resource Management in the Tourism Industry. In V. Costa, A. Moura, & M. Mira (Eds.), *Handbook of Research on Human Capital and People Management in the Tourism Industry* (pp. 265–281). IGI Global. https://doi.org/10.4018/978-1-7998-4318-4.ch013

Sabuncu, I. (2021). Understanding Tourist Perceptions and Expectations During Pandemic Through Social Media Big Data. In M. Demir, A. Dalgıç, & F. Ergen (Eds.), *Handbook of Research on the Impacts and Implications of COVID-19 on the Tourism Industry* (pp. 330–350). IGI Global. https://doi.org/10.4018/978-1-7998-8231-2.ch016

Safari, M. R., & Jiang, Q. (2018). The Theory and Practice of IT Governance Maturity and Strategies Alignment: Evidence From Banking Industry. *Journal of Global Information Management*, 26(2), 127–146. doi:10.4018/JGIM.2018040106

Sahoo, J., Pati, B., & Mohanty, B. (2017). Knowledge Management as an Academic Discipline: An Assessment. In B. Gunjal (Ed.), *Managing Knowledge and Scholarly Assets in Academic Libraries* (pp. 99–126). Hershey, PA: IGI Global. doi:10.4018/978-1-5225-1741-2.ch005

Related References

Saini, D. (2017). Relevance of Teaching Values and Ethics in Management Education. In N. Baporikar (Ed.), *Management Education for Global Leadership* (pp. 90–111). Hershey, PA: IGI Global. doi:10.4018/978-1-5225-1013-0.ch005

Sambhanthan, A. (2017). Assessing and Benchmarking Sustainability in Organisations: An Integrated Conceptual Model. *International Journal of Systems and Service-Oriented Engineering*, *7*(4), 22–43. doi:10.4018/IJSSOE.2017100102

Sambhanthan, A., & Potdar, V. (2017). A Study of the Parameters Impacting Sustainability in Information Technology Organizations. *International Journal of Knowledge-Based Organizations*, *7*(3), 27–39. doi:10.4018/IJKBO.2017070103

Sánchez-Fernández, M. D., & Manríquez, M. R. (2018). The Entrepreneurial Spirit Based on Social Values: The Digital Generation. In P. Isaias & L. Carvalho (Eds.), *User Innovation and the Entrepreneurship Phenomenon in the Digital Economy* (pp. 173–193). Hershey, PA: IGI Global. doi:10.4018/978-1-5225-2826-5.ch009

Sanchez-Ruiz, L., & Blanco, B. (2017). Process Management for SMEs: Barriers, Enablers, and Benefits. In M. Vemić (Ed.), *Optimal Management Strategies in Small and Medium Enterprises* (pp. 293–319). Hershey, PA: IGI Global. doi:10.4018/978-1-5225-1949-2.ch014

Sanz, L. F., Gómez-Pérez, J., & Castillo-Martinez, A. (2018). Analysis of the European ICT Competence Frameworks. In V. Ahuja & S. Rathore (Eds.), *Multidisciplinary Perspectives on Human Capital and Information Technology Professionals* (pp. 225–245). Hershey, PA: IGI Global. doi:10.4018/978-1-5225-5297-0.ch012

Sarvepalli, A., & Godin, J. (2017). Business Process Management in the Classroom. *Journal of Cases on Information Technology*, *19*(2), 17–28. doi:10.4018/JCIT.2017040102

Saxena, G. G., & Saxena, A. (2021). Host Community Role in Medical Tourism Development. In M. Singh & S. Kumaran (Eds.), *Growth of the Medical Tourism Industry and Its Impact on Society: Emerging Research and Opportunities* (pp. 105–127). IGI Global. https://doi.org/10.4018/978-1-7998-3427-4.ch006

Saygili, E. E., Ozturkoglu, Y., & Kocakulah, M. C. (2017). End Users' Perceptions of Critical Success Factors in ERP Applications. *International Journal of Enterprise Information Systems*, *13*(4), 58–75. doi:10.4018/IJEIS.2017100104

Saygili, E. E., & Saygili, A. T. (2017). Contemporary Issues in Enterprise Information Systems: A Critical Review of CSFs in ERP Implementations. In M. Tavana (Ed.), *Enterprise Information Systems and the Digitalization of Business Functions* (pp. 120–136). Hershey, PA: IGI Global. doi:10.4018/978-1-5225-2382-6.ch006

Schwaiger, K. M., & Zehrer, A. (2021). The COVID-19 Pandemic and Organizational Resilience in Hospitality Family Firms: A Qualitative Approach. In A. Zehrer, G. Glowka, K. Schwaiger, & V. Ranacher-Lackner (Eds.), *Resiliency Models and Addressing Future Risks for Family Firms in the Tourism Industry* (pp. 32–49). IGI Global. https://doi.org/10.4018/978-1-7998-7352-5.ch002

Scott, N., & Campos, A. C. (2022). Cognitive Science of Tourism Experiences. In R. Augusto Costa, F. Brandão, Z. Breda, & C. Costa (Eds.), Planning and Managing the Experience Economy in Tourism (pp. 1-21). IGI Global. https://doi.org/ doi:10.4018/978-1-7998-8775-1.ch001

Seidenstricker, S., & Antonino, A. (2018). Business Model Innovation-Oriented Technology Management for Emergent Technologies. In M. Khosrow-Pour, D.B.A. (Ed.), Encyclopedia of Information Science and Technology, Fourth Edition (pp. 4560-4569). Hershey, PA: IGI Global. doi:10.4018/978-1-5225-2255-3.ch396

Selvi, M. S. (2021). Changes in Tourism Sales and Marketing Post COVID-19. In M. Demir, A. Dalgıç, & F. Ergen (Eds.), *Handbook of Research on the Impacts and Implications of COVID-19 on the Tourism Industry* (pp. 437–460). IGI Global. doi:10.4018/978-1-7998-8231-2.ch021

Senaratne, S., & Gunarathne, A. D. (2017). Excellence Perspective for Management Education from a Global Accountants' Hub in Asia. In N. Baporikar (Ed.), *Management Education for Global Leadership* (pp. 158–180). Hershey, PA: IGI Global. doi:10.4018/978-1-5225-1013-0.ch008

Sensuse, D. I., & Cahyaningsih, E. (2018). Knowledge Management Models: A Summative Review. *International Journal of Information Systems in the Service Sector, 10*(1), 71–100. doi:10.4018/IJISSS.2018010105

Seth, M., Goyal, D., & Kiran, R. (2017). Diminution of Impediments in Implementation of Supply Chain Management Information System for Enhancing its Effectiveness in Indian Automobile Industry. *Journal of Global Information Management, 25*(3), 1–20. doi:10.4018/JGIM.2017070101

Seyal, A. H., & Rahman, M. N. (2017). Investigating Impact of Inter-Organizational Factors in Measuring ERP Systems Success: Bruneian Perspectives. In M. Tavana (Ed.), *Enterprise Information Systems and the Digitalization of Business Functions* (pp. 178–204). Hershey, PA: IGI Global. doi:10.4018/978-1-5225-2382-6.ch008

Shaqrah, A. A. (2018). Analyzing Business Intelligence Systems Based on 7s Model of McKinsey. *International Journal of Business Intelligence Research, 9*(1), 53–63. doi:10.4018/IJBIR.2018010104

Sharma, A. J. (2017). Enhancing Sustainability through Experiential Learning in Management Education. In N. Baporikar (Ed.), *Management Education for Global Leadership* (pp. 256–274). Hershey, PA: IGI Global. doi:10.4018/978-1-5225-1013-0.ch013

Shetty, K. P. (2017). Responsible Global Leadership: Ethical Challenges in Management Education. In N. Baporikar (Ed.), *Innovation and Shifting Perspectives in Management Education* (pp. 194–223). Hershey, PA: IGI Global. doi:10.4018/978-1-5225-1019-2.ch009

Sinthupundaja, J., & Kohda, Y. (2017). Effects of Corporate Social Responsibility and Creating Shared Value on Sustainability. *International Journal of Sustainable Entrepreneurship and Corporate Social Responsibility*, 2(1), 27–38. doi:10.4018/IJSECSR.2017010103

Škarica, I., & Hrgović, A. V. (2018). Implementation of Total Quality Management Principles in Public Health Institutes in the Republic of Croatia. *International Journal of Productivity Management and Assessment Technologies*, 6(1), 1–16. doi:10.4018/IJPMAT.2018010101

Skokic, V. (2021). How Small Hotel Owners Practice Resilience: Longitudinal Study Among Small Family Hotels in Croatia. In A. Zehrer, G. Glowka, K. Schwaiger, & V. Ranacher-Lackner (Eds.), *Resiliency Models and Addressing Future Risks for Family Firms in the Tourism Industry* (pp. 50–73). IGI Global. doi:10.4018/978-1-7998-7352-5.ch003

Smuts, H., Kotzé, P., Van der Merwe, A., & Loock, M. (2017). Framework for Managing Shared Knowledge in an Information Systems Outsourcing Context. *International Journal of Knowledge Management*, 13(4), 1–30. doi:10.4018/IJKM.2017100101

Sousa, M. J., Cruz, R., Dias, I., & Caracol, C. (2017). Information Management Systems in the Supply Chain. In G. Jamil, A. Soares, & C. Pessoa (Eds.), *Handbook of Research on Information Management for Effective Logistics and Supply Chains* (pp. 469–485). Hershey, PA: IGI Global. doi:10.4018/978-1-5225-0973-8.ch025

Spremic, M., Turulja, L., & Bajgoric, N. (2018). Two Approaches in Assessing Business Continuity Management Attitudes in the Organizational Context. In N. Bajgoric (Ed.), *Always-On Enterprise Information Systems for Modern Organizations* (pp. 159–183). Hershey, PA: IGI Global. doi:10.4018/978-1-5225-3704-5.ch008

Steenkamp, A. L. (2018). Some Insights in Computer Science and Information Technology. In *Examining the Changing Role of Supervision in Doctoral Research Projects: Emerging Research and Opportunities* (pp. 113–133). Hershey, PA: IGI Global. doi:10.4018/978-1-5225-2610-0.ch005

Stipanović, C., Rudan, E., & Zubović, V. (2022). Reaching the New Tourist Through Creativity: Sustainable Development Challenges in Croatian Coastal Towns. In M. Valeri (Ed.), *New Governance and Management in Touristic Destinations* (pp. 231–245). IGI Global. https://doi.org/10.4018/978-1-6684-3889-3.ch014

Tabach, A., & Croteau, A. (2017). Configurations of Information Technology Governance Practices and Business Unit Performance. *International Journal of IT/Business Alignment and Governance, 8*(2), 1–27. doi:10.4018/IJITBAG.2017070101

Talaue, G. M., & Iqbal, T. (2017). Assessment of e-Business Mode of Selected Private Universities in the Philippines and Pakistan. *International Journal of Online Marketing, 7*(4), 63–77. doi:10.4018/IJOM.2017100105

Tam, G. C. (2017). Project Manager Sustainability Competence. In *Managerial Strategies and Green Solutions for Project Sustainability* (pp. 178–207). Hershey, PA: IGI Global. doi:10.4018/978-1-5225-2371-0.ch008

Tambo, T. (2018). Fashion Retail Innovation: About Context, Antecedents, and Outcome in Technological Change Projects. In I. Management Association (Ed.), Fashion and Textiles: Breakthroughs in Research and Practice (pp. 233-260). Hershey, PA: IGI Global. https://doi.org/ doi:10.4018/978-1-5225-3432-7.ch010

Tantau, A. D., & Frățilă, L. C. (2018). Information and Management System for Renewable Energy Business. In *Entrepreneurship and Business Development in the Renewable Energy Sector* (pp. 200–244). Hershey, PA: IGI Global. doi:10.4018/978-1-5225-3625-3.ch006

Teixeira, N., Pardal, P. N., & Rafael, B. G. (2018). Internationalization, Financial Performance, and Organizational Challenges: A Success Case in Portugal. In L. Carvalho (Ed.), *Handbook of Research on Entrepreneurial Ecosystems and Social Dynamics in a Globalized World* (pp. 379–423). Hershey, PA: IGI Global. doi:10.4018/978-1-5225-3525-6.ch017

Teixeira, P., Teixeira, L., Eusébio, C., Silva, S., & Teixeira, A. (2021). The Impact of ICTs on Accessible Tourism: Evidence Based on a Systematic Literature Review. In C. Eusébio, L. Teixeira, & M. Carneiro (Eds.), *ICT Tools and Applications for Accessible Tourism* (pp. 1–25). IGI Global. doi:10.4018/978-1-7998-6428-8.ch001

Trad, A., & Kalpić, D. (2018). The Business Transformation Framework, Agile Project and Change Management. In M. Khosrow-Pour, D.B.A. (Ed.), Encyclopedia of Information Science and Technology, Fourth Edition (pp. 620-635). Hershey, PA: IGI Global. https://doi.org/ doi:10.4018/978-1-5225-2255-3.ch054

Trad, A., & Kalpić, D. (2018). The Business Transformation and Enterprise Architecture Framework: The Financial Engineering E-Risk Management and E-Law Integration. In B. Sergi, F. Fidanoski, M. Ziolo, & V. Naumovski (Eds.), *Regaining Global Stability After the Financial Crisis* (pp. 46–65). Hershey, PA: IGI Global. doi:10.4018/978-1-5225-4026-7.ch003

Trengereid, V. (2022). Conditions of Network Engagement: The Quest for a Common Good. In R. Augusto Costa, F. Brandão, Z. Breda, & C. Costa (Eds.), *Planning and Managing the Experience Economy in Tourism* (pp. 69-84). IGI Global. https://doi.org/10.4018/978-1-7998-8775-1.ch004

Turulja, L., & Bajgoric, N. (2018). Business Continuity and Information Systems: A Systematic Literature Review. In N. Bajgoric (Ed.), *Always-On Enterprise Information Systems for Modern Organizations* (pp. 60–87). Hershey, PA: IGI Global. doi:10.4018/978-1-5225-3704-5.ch004

Vargas-Hernández, J. G. (2017). Professional Integrity in Business Management Education. In N. Baporikar (Ed.), *Management Education for Global Leadership* (pp. 70–89). Hershey, PA: IGI Global. doi:10.4018/978-1-5225-1013-0.ch004

Varnacı Uzun, F. (2021). The Destination Preferences of Foreign Tourists During the COVID-19 Pandemic and Attitudes Towards: Marmaris, Turkey. In M. Demir, A. Dalgıç, & F. Ergen (Eds.), *Handbook of Research on the Impacts and Implications of COVID-19 on the Tourism Industry* (pp. 285–306). IGI Global. https://doi.org/10.4018/978-1-7998-8231-2.ch014

Vasista, T. G., & AlAbdullatif, A. M. (2017). Role of Electronic Customer Relationship Management in Demand Chain Management: A Predictive Analytic Approach. *International Journal of Information Systems and Supply Chain Management*, 10(1), 53–67. doi:10.4018/IJISSCM.2017010104

Vieru, D., & Bourdeau, S. (2017). Survival in the Digital Era: A Digital Competence-Based Multi-Case Study in the Canadian SME Clothing Industry. *International Journal of Social and Organizational Dynamics in IT*, 6(1), 17–34. doi:10.4018/IJSODIT.2017010102

Vijayan, G., & Kamarulzaman, N. H. (2017). An Introduction to Sustainable Supply Chain Management and Business Implications. In M. Khan, M. Hussain, & M. Ajmal (Eds.), *Green Supply Chain Management for Sustainable Business Practice* (pp. 27–50). Hershey, PA: IGI Global. doi:10.4018/978-1-5225-0635-5.ch002

Vlachvei, A., & Notta, O. (2017). Firm Competitiveness: Theories, Evidence, and Measurement. In A. Vlachvei, O. Notta, K. Karantininis, & N. Tsounis (Eds.), *Factors Affecting Firm Competitiveness and Performance in the Modern Business World* (pp. 1–42). Hershey, PA: IGI Global. doi:10.4018/978-1-5225-0843-4.ch001

Wang, C., Schofield, M., Li, X., & Ou, X. (2017). Do Chinese Students in Public and Private Higher Education Institutes Perform at Different Level in One of the Leadership Skills: Critical Thinking?: An Exploratory Comparison. In V. Wang (Ed.), *Encyclopedia of Strategic Leadership and Management* (pp. 160–181). Hershey, PA: IGI Global. doi:10.4018/978-1-5225-1049-9.ch013

Wang, J. (2017). Multi-Agent based Production Management Decision System Modelling for the Textile Enterprise. *Journal of Global Information Management*, 25(4), 1–15. doi:10.4018/JGIM.2017100101

Wiedemann, A., & Gewald, H. (2017). Examining Cross-Domain Alignment: The Correlation of Business Strategy, IT Management, and IT Business Value. *International Journal of IT/Business Alignment and Governance*, 8(1), 17–31. doi:10.4018/IJITBAG.2017010102

Wolf, R., & Thiel, M. (2018). Advancing Global Business Ethics in China: Reducing Poverty Through Human and Social Welfare. In S. Hipsher (Ed.), *Examining the Private Sector's Role in Wealth Creation and Poverty Reduction* (pp. 67–84). Hershey, PA: IGI Global. doi:10.4018/978-1-5225-3117-3.ch004

Yablonsky, S. (2018). Innovation Platforms: Data and Analytics Platforms. In *Multi-Sided Platforms (MSPs) and Sharing Strategies in the Digital Economy: Emerging Research and Opportunities* (pp. 72–95). Hershey, PA: IGI Global. doi:10.4018/978-1-5225-5457-8.ch003

Yaşar, B. (2021). The Impact of COVID-19 on Volatility of Tourism Stocks: Evidence From BIST Tourism Index. In M. Demir, A. Dalgıç, & F. Ergen (Eds.), *Handbook of Research on the Impacts and Implications of COVID-19 on the Tourism Industry* (pp. 23–44). IGI Global. https://doi.org/10.4018/978-1-7998-8231-2.ch002

Related References

Yusoff, A., Ahmad, N. H., & Halim, H. A. (2017). Agropreneurship among Gen Y in Malaysia: The Role of Academic Institutions. In N. Ahmad, T. Ramayah, H. Halim, & S. Rahman (Eds.), *Handbook of Research on Small and Medium Enterprises in Developing Countries* (pp. 23–47). Hershey, PA: IGI Global. doi:10.4018/978-1-5225-2165-5.ch002

Zacher, D., & Pechlaner, H. (2021). Resilience as an Opportunity Approach: Challenges and Perspectives for Private Sector Participation on a Community Level. In A. Zehrer, G. Glowka, K. Schwaiger, & V. Ranacher-Lackner (Eds.), *Resiliency Models and Addressing Future Risks for Family Firms in the Tourism Industry* (pp. 75–102). IGI Global. https://doi.org/10.4018/978-1-7998-7352-5.ch004

Zanin, F., Comuzzi, E., & Costantini, A. (2018). The Effect of Business Strategy and Stock Market Listing on the Use of Risk Assessment Tools. In *Management Control Systems in Complex Settings: Emerging Research and Opportunities* (pp. 145–168). Hershey, PA: IGI Global. doi:10.4018/978-1-5225-3987-2.ch007

Zgheib, P. W. (2017). Corporate Innovation and Intrapreneurship in the Middle East. In P. Zgheib (Ed.), *Entrepreneurship and Business Innovation in the Middle East* (pp. 37–56). Hershey, PA: IGI Global. doi:10.4018/978-1-5225-2066-5.ch003

About the Contributors

Minna-Maarit Jaskari (PhD) is a University Lecturer and Program manager in Marketing at the School of Marketing and Communication, University of Vaasa, Finland. Her current research interests include sounds in branding, consumer experiences in tourism, virtual brand communities, temporality and spatiality of market spaces, consumer understanding in innovation, and experiential pedagogies in higher marketing education. She has published in academic journals such as Qualitative Market Research, Journal of Marketing Education, and Nordic Journal of Business. She is an editorial board member for the Journal of Marketing Education.

***

Mohamed A. Abdelrazek is currently an Associate Professor in the Department of Business Administration at the Faculty of Commerce, University of Sadat City; holds a PhD in Marketing and Management from the University of Exeter, acclaimed for research on Eco-Certificates and Sales using a quasi-experimental approach. My research interests primarily lie in the marketing discipline and data analysis, with a special focus on experimental methodologies in marketing research. I have enriched postgraduate students at the University of Exeter with guest lectures on research methodology.

Paul G. Barretta received his Ph.D. in 2013 from University of Texas – Pan American (now UTRGV) with a specialization in Marketing. Prior to entering academia he spent 25 years in industry, primarily in the Music/Media/Entertainment Industry after having gained his BBA in Finance & Investements ('87), and MBA in International Business ('90) from Baruch College, City University of New York. He was a full-time faculty member at St. Bonaventure University for six years, five of which he was Marketing Department Chair. He moved to Wagner College, Nicolais School of Business in fall 2019 as Associate Professor of Marketing. His research interests are primarily in consumer behavior, cultural industry products including music and sport marketing, integrated marketing communications, and green marketing.

Hardik Dhull is an Assistant Professor at Matu Ram Institute of Engineering and Management in Rohtak. With dual Master's degrees in Technology and Business Administration, he is renowned for his engaging lectures and prolific research contributions. He actively participates in national and international academic events and has published extensively in esteemed journals. He is dedicated to fostering academic excellence and mentoring the next generation of scholars.

Clara Gustafsson is Senior Lecturer in Marketing at The Department of Business Administration, Lund University School of Management and Economics, Lund University, Sweden. Her main research area is Sonic Branding. She also specializes in Branding, Consumer Culture, Sound of Democracy, and Resourcification (i.e. how things become seen and used as resources through social processes).

William S. Harvey is the inaugural Director of the Social Purpose Centre and Professor of Leadership at Melbourne Business School. He is an International Research Fellow at the Oxford Centre for Corporate Reputation. William has published Reputations at Stake with Oxford University Press and is currently co-editing The Oxford Handbook of Social Purpose.

Marie-Nathalie Jauffret is a professor at the International University of Monaco. Her research focuses on innovation in invisible contexts such as subliminal and non verbal communication, biodigital characters, synesthesia and artificial intelligence in multicultural contexts. She has authored articles published in journals like Journal of Business Research and Qualitative Market Research.

Hannele Kauppinen-Räisänen is a Senior University Lecturer at the University of Helsinki, Finland, where she also holds the title of Docent in consumer research. She has a PhD (Econ.) from Hanken School of Economics and is associated with the International University of Monaco. She is involved in research addressing a variety of business issues. She has authored numerous articles published in journals like Tourism Management, Journal of Business Research, International Journal of Contemporary Hospitality Management, and Journal of Service Management.

Cristiana Matos Graduated in Social Communication, with a major in Advertising, from Fluminense Federal University (2011-2014). Master's in Communication from the Postgraduate Programme in Communication at University of the State of Rio de Janeiro (PPGCom/UERJ) (2016-2018), in the line of research Communication Technologies and Culture, with a scholarship granted by CAPES. PhD in Communication from the Postgraduate Programme in Communication at University of the State of Rio de Janeiro (PPGCom/UERJ) (2019-2023), in the line of research Communication Technologies and Culture, with a grant from CAPES. Her studies focus on topics such as the experience economy, sensory branding, sound branding and music branding, and neuroscience in conjunction with music, marketing and branding.

Anu Norrgrann (PhD) currently works a university teacher and program manager in Marketing at the School of Marketing and Communication, University of Vaasa, Finland. Her research interests range from socio-material consumption practices, consumer roles and agency, to co-creation of brands and other symbolic resources in supply networks and service ecosystems. She has also done research on interactive learning in online marketing education, and has a particular methodological interest in qualitative research methodologies such as netnography and autoethnography.

Natasha Saqib is currently working as Sr. Assistant Professor at the Department of Management Studies, University of Kashmir, India. She received her B.Sc. (Hon.) Industrial Chemistry from University of Kashmir, MBA from Islamic university of Science and Technology and Ph.D. from University of Kashmir, India. With over 14 years of experience in academia, Dr. Natasha has established herself as an experienced professional. Her academic journey includes significant contributions, evident in numerous research publications in esteemed journals such as the International Journal of Emerging Markets, Online Information Review, Journal of Entrepreneurship in Emerging Economies, Young Consumers, Journal of Tourism Analysis, International Journal of Innovation Science, Asia Pacific Journal of Innovation and Entrepreneurship, Management and Labour Studies, and PSU Research Review, among others.

Marwa Tourky is Associate Professor of Marketing and Brand Management at Cranfield University, School of Management. Her research primarily focuses on corporate marketing, encompassing brand identity, communications, and reputation management. She is the co-author of Integrated Marketing Communications: A Global Brand-Driven Approach, by Palgrave Macmillan. Dr. Tourky serves as Deputy Editor for the Journal of Marketing Communications and has published her research in leading scientific journals.

Index

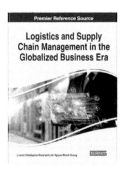

  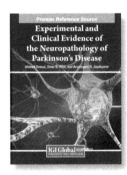 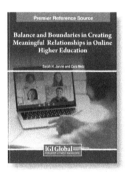

9 798369 307786